Motivating Students on a Time Budget:

Pedagogical Frames and Lesson Plans for In-Person and Online Information Literacy Instruction

edited by
Sarah Steiner and Miriam Rigby

Association of College and Research Libraries
A division of the American Library Association
Chicago, Illinois 2019

The paper used in this publication meets the minimum requirements of American National Standard for Information Sciences–Permanence of Paper for Printed Library Materials, ANSI Z39.48-1992. ∞

Cataloging-in-Publication data is on file with the Library of Congress.

Printed in the United States of America.

23 22 21 20 19 5 4 3 2 1

Table of Contents

Acknowledgments

We extend sincere gratitude to the inspiration for this work and author of its foreword, Trudi Jacobson. Erin Nevius was an inspiration and help throughout the process. Thanks to our colleagues and immediate families for their support and patience throughout this process, including special thanks to our toddlers, Ava and Fritz.

This work could not have been done without the skilled peer-review and editorial work of Eli Arnold, Melissa Bowles-Terry, Kaijsa Calkins, Celia Emmelhainz, Zoe Fisher, Emily Ford, Crystal Goldman, Amy Harris Houk, Carolina Hernandez, Beth McDonough, Hailey Mooney, Amanda Nichols Hess, Jason Puckett, Tammy Sugarman, Nicole Pagowsky, Erin Pappas, Krista Schmidt, Ryan Sittler, Maura Smale, Stephen Wagner, Annie Zeidman-Karpinski, and Jessica Zellers.

Foreword

"The learning process is something you can incite, literally incite, like a riot."

~ Audre Lorde[1]

Librarians enter classrooms or online teaching spaces excited about connecting with students on topics near and dear to their hearts. The hearts of the librarians, that is, not necessarily those of the students. Unfortunately, the enthusiasm we bring to teaching is not always mirrored by the students about their learning. As Johnson and Duguay write at the start of their chapter in this volume, "To librarians, an hour may seem like a paltry amount of time to cover everything they believe students should know. But to an unengaged student, an hour may seem endless." So, like all dedicated teachers, we are heavily invested in how best to structure learning experiences so that students become excited about the value of what we would like to share.

There are many educational and psychological theories, frameworks, and models that address motivation, and you will be introduced to some of them in this volume, including extrinsic and intrinsic motivation, Keller's ARCS model, feminist pedagogy, self-determination theory, and more. Understanding a variety of these is decidedly beneficial when designing learning experiences to meet students' needs, but at times it can feel a bit overwhelming.

I've recently been reading *Small Teaching: Everyday Lessons from the Science of Learning* by James M. Lang,[2] after having attended two inspirational workshops by the author at my university's teaching and learning center. Lang's pedagogical recommendations for college instructors are supported by a wealth of research studies. I appreciate having key studies and findings identified, but even more, I love his extension of the findings into practical suggestions for small but effective activities that enhance student understanding. I may not use all of them exactly as he does, but his suggestions kick start very productive brainstorming.

This rich compendium of resources that you are holding (or perhaps reading online) will provide inspiration and guidance, whether you are new to teaching or have more experience. The chapters acknowledge the limitations we too often face but push past the barriers and celebrate what we can do while providing ideas about how to excite and engage students. As with *Small Teaching*, this book's chapters provide windows into important models and research but are grounded in pedagogical practice. They foster understanding of what motivates the learners that we encounter in our information literacy sessions, and some provide actual lessons plans to engage these students— lesson plans that you can adapt for your students.

The scope of the chapters is broad: there are ideas relevant to undergraduates and graduate students, in-person and online courses, and first-year and more advanced students. The pedagogical foundations and teaching strategies are diverse. I found techniques I've used with great success in classes over the years and expect you will find ones you have used, too. Kristen Lemay, in her chapter "You're Batman's Only Hope" describes a use of BreakoutEDU that ties neatly into the Framework. I used this immersive platform for the first time this past semester in sections of a first-year course, Writing and Critical Inquiry. The six sections were spread over two different instructors, and the two scenarios we developed show the potential of this unusual teaching method. In one case, the goal was to introduce students to library services and resources. The course theme had to do with zombies, which allowed for the development of some rather intriguing clues along the way. The earlier set of classes had a different purpose. The goal was to enhance teamwork, emphasize inquiry, and promote a growth mindset. While a small amount of the material was connected to library services, inquiry of various types—while writing, researching, and working with others—was highlighted. The "a-ha!" moments students had about critical course themes that day were referred to many times during the rest of the semester.

Creative and outside-the-box session development can strengthen the collaboration between librarian and instructor. In my BreakoutEDU example, the course instructor, a colleague who co-developed and co-taught the sessions, and I jointly authored an article for *C&RL News*[3] about the learning experience for students. Indeed, the writing instructor was so excited about the teaching method, she asked the second teacher if she might attend her class sessions and then helped to co-facilitate the BreakoutEDU experience, emphasizing direct links to the course they both teach. These substantive interactions in pursuit of engaged student learning go far to overcome the limitations of a one-class-period information literacy session.

Librarians teaching course-related instruction sessions, of course, rarely have the opportunity to get to know the students they are teaching in the way that a course instructor does. This is a hurdle when designing learning outcomes and appropriate activities, but one that is, hopefully, mitigated through conversations with the instructor. A second, higher hurdle is the limited amount of time librarians have to help students understand the importance of information literacy, its scope, and its core components, which extend far beyond academic research. Disciplinary faculty often conceive of information literacy in a limited, research-related sense. *The Framework for Information Literacy for Higher Education*[4] puts an end to that conception, raising the bar high. Ideally, librarians have the opportunity to work with faculty members individually and with departments collectively to infuse information literacy throughout courses and curriculums. Yet for every such victory, there are many other instances where one class period is all that is available. The chapters in this book provide ideas that are designed to be effective in shorter teaching and learning situations, a great strength for librarians who have no other option.

I wish that I had this book years ago when I first started out in academic libraries. My first full-time professional position was as an interlibrary loan librarian with reference desk responsibilities. What I didn't know until after I took the position was that teaching was also required. Since I had no experience teaching, this was something of a shock, but I was assured I would be shown how to do it before being thrown into the classroom on my own. The "training" consisted of watching a long-time librarian hold up volume after volume from a book cart as he explained why each book was pertinent to the upcoming course assignment. During that very class period, I decided there had to be a better way because I was dying of boredom, and the students were in even worse shape. This may have been an extreme case of my new colleague needing to learn more about pedagogy and motivational theory, but the indelible impression this experience had on me shaped my entire career.

The process of learning should be exciting and, preferably, fun, for the students' sake as well as for the teacher's. That frisson of excitement, of the desire to incite learning, runs through the chapters in this book. I look forward to using these ideas and lesson plans in the classes that I teach.

Please, jump into this book and find those ideas that excite and motivate you.

Trudi E. Jacobson
Distinguished Librarian
Head, Information Literacy Department, University at Albany

Endnotes

1. Audre Lorde, *Sister Outsider: Essays and Speeches*, Crossing Press Feminist Series (Trumansberg, NY: Crossing Press, 1984), 98.
2. James M. Lang, *Small Teaching: Everyday Lessons from the Science of Learning* (John Wiley & Sons, 2016).
3. Susan Detwiler, Trudi Jacobson, and Kelsey O'Brien, "BreakoutEDU: Helping Students Break Out of Their Comfort Zones," *College & Research Libraries News* 79, no. 2 (February 2018): 62–66.

4. ACRL Board, "Framework for Information Literacy for Higher Education | Association of College and Research Libraries (ACRL)," 2015, http://www.ala.org/acrl/standards/ilframework.

Bibliography

ACRL Board. "Framework for Information Literacy for Higher Education | Association of College and Research Libraries (ACRL)." 2015. http://www.ala.org/acrl/standards/ilframework.

Detwiler, Susan, Trudi Jacobson, and Kelsey O'Brien. "BreakoutEDU: Helping Students Break Out of Their Comfort Zones." *College & Research Libraries News* 79, no. 2 (February 2018): 62–66.

Lang, James M. *Small Teaching: Everyday Lessons from the Science of Learning.* John Wiley & Sons, 2016.

Lorde, Audre. *Sister Outsider: Essays and Speeches.* Crossing Press Feminist Series. Trumansberg, NY: Crossing Press, 1984.

INTRODUCTION

Motivating Students on a Time Budget:

Pedagogical Frames and Lesson Plans for In-Person and Online Information Literacy Instruction

A desire to make good grades, the dream of graduation, anxiety about future job prospects: these motivators sit at the foundation of today's education system in many countries, including the United States. But where does that motivation structure leave educators who, by choice or by necessity, do not assign grades or control student matriculation? What about those of us who have only short periods of time with students? As librarians, we often find ourselves outside the traditional structure of our education system. Time limits add another layer of complexity; how can we motivate students to learn when we only see them for an hour or two?

All through primary school, I (Sarah) struggled mightily with math classes. I loathed feeling like I was not smart enough to keep up, so I disengaged, mentally and emotionally. I intermittently tried, but my sense of commitment was low and I carried a sense of internal shame. Then, as I entered twelfth grade, I finally met a math teacher who managed to motivate me, and she did it over the course of just a couple of class sessions. Her style of instruction helped me to embrace algebra with confidence, and it ultimately motivated me to pursue a career in education. She showed me that while long-term courses may offer more time in which to energize learners, motivation can also be built quickly, even with disengaged students. She created a supportive yet challenging learning environment where mistakes were accepted

1

and where my struggles were a part of the experience, rather than a point of shame. As information literacy leaders, we have an opportunity to do the same.

The editors were inspired to propose and edit this book because, although we found a robust body of literature focused on motivating students to cross information literacy thresholds over the course of a semester or school year, we found little on motivating them in the short-term. While librarians have made great strides in integrating information literacy into long-term curricula, many of us have only one class session to make a difference. Librarians have published extensively on motivation-related instruction topics (active learning being one of the most popular), yet we consider the motivation theory underpinnings of those activities less often. Consideration of human motivational strategies can have a profound effect on our attitude toward and approach to learners and, ultimately, on their levels of engagement, satisfaction, and success. Through the techniques outlined in this volume, we hope you will feel empowered to use motivation research to meet your students where they are, intellectually and emotionally, and empower and inspire them to cross conceptual thresholds critical to information interpretation and use.

Librarians' positions as guests or outsiders in our country's grade-based education system are often lamented, and not unfairly. In this volume, we will highlight the ways in which we can build true intrinsic motivation and honor intersectionality. Arnone, Reynolds, and Marshall note the library "is one of the few locations in schools where informal, self-determined, intrinsically motivated inquiry and learning can occur (and is in fact encouraged)."[1] The intrinsically motivated student pays sustained attention to argument analysis and is able to judge and evaluate information and solve problems—these concepts form the heart of information literacy.[2] While information literacy instructors often face tight time limitations, librarians are free to inspire student imaginations without the limitations of grades or judgment, and if we make a strong connection, students will seek us out with additional queries and ideas. Our goal, broadly, is to inspire students' curiosity and desire to seek information and diverse considerations on topics of interest and ensure they have the confidence and knowledge necessary to locate, analyze, and apply that information to their needs. Studies that consider the efficacy of ranking student effort/success with grades offer competing conclusions, but many argue that environments that privilege grades can undermine intrinsic motivation,[3] while environments that highlight learning goals, evaluative feedback, and autonomy over grades can have a positive effect on long-term intrinsic motivation levels.[4] These studies empower us to reframe our "constraints" as a gift: because we have only a short period of time with our students, we can exist outside the world of performance, tests, grades, and other extrinsic motivators and position ourselves as fellow curious explorers.

Many of the works in this volume embrace the power in shifting control to the students and in accounting for students' situated position both inside and outside of the classroom. Motivation theory meshes well with intersectional approaches to overcoming barriers to learning. Briefly put, the concept of intersectionality stems from the work of critical race theorist Kimberlé Williams Crenshaw[5] and sociologist Patricia Hill Collins[6] in the late 1980s and early 1990s and has become more widely adopted throughout and beyond the social sciences in recent decades. This theory points to the many intersecting aspects of a person's life that affect their relations with others and situate how they encounter the world. Race, class, and gender are the classic aspects, but myriad other influences can be taken into account. Some of these influences fall on a spectrum of changeability, including education level (somewhat able to change) and health and physical abilities (relatively outside of personal control). In shifting control of the classroom to students and working as a fellow explorer, librarians provide students with the opportunity to honor their own needs and life experiences as they develop their information literacy.

This volume begins with a section of research-based, broad-level considerations of student motivation as it relates to short-term information literacy instruction in person and online. The second section comprises activities and lesson plans which highlight specific motivational strategies and pedagogies. Each encourages the spirit of play, autonomy, and active learning in a grade-free environment. As you read, you may find many of the activities and approaches you embed for intuitive reasons have a grounding in motivational theory. We hope you find the chapters useful for your own teaching and learning.

~Sarah Steiner and Miriam Rigby

Endnotes

1. Marilyn P. Arnone, Rebecca Reynolds, and Todd Marshall, "The Effect of Early Adolescents' Psychological Needs Satisfaction upon Their Perceived Competence in Information Skills and Intrinsic Motivation for Research," *School Libraries Worldwide* 15, no. 2 (2009): 118.
2. Robert H. Ennis, "A Logical Basis for Measuring Critical Thinking Skills," *Educational Leadership* 43, no. 2 (1985): 44–48; Peter A. Facione, *Critical Thinking: A Statement of Expert Consensus for Purposes of Educational Assessment and Instruction, Research Findings and Recommendations* (American Philosophical Association, Newark, DE., 1990), https://eric.ed.gov/?id=ED315423; Diane F. Halpern, "Teaching Critical Thinking for Transfer Across Domains: Dispositions, Skills, Structure Training, and Metacognitive Monitoring," *American Psychologist* 53, no.4 (1998): 449–55; Richard Paul, "Critical Thinking: What, Why, and How," *New Directions for Community Colleges* 1992, no. 77 (1992): 3–24; Matthew Lipman,

"Critical Thinking—What Can It Be?," *Educational Leadership* 46, no.1, (1988):38–43; Gerald Tindal and Victor Nolet, "Curriculum-Based Measurement in Middle and High Schools: Critical Thinking Skills in Content Areas," *Focus on Exceptional Children* 27, no. 7 (1995): 1–22; Daniel T. Willingham, "Critical Thinking," *American Educator* 31, no. 3 (2007): 8–19.

3.   Edward L. Deci, Richard Koestner, and Richard M. Ryan, "A Meta-Analytic Review of Experiments Examining the Effects of Extrinsic Rewards on Intrinsic Motivation," *Psychological Bulletin* 125, no. 6 (1999): 627–68; Alfie Kohn, *Punished by Rewards: The Trouble with Gold Stars, Incentive Plans, A's, Praise, and Other Bribes* (Houghton Mifflin Harcourt, 1999).

4.   John T. Guthrie, Allan Wigfield, and Clare VonSecker, "Effects of Integrated Instruction on Motivation and Strategy Use in Reading," *Journal of Educational Psychology* 92, no. 2 (2000): 331–41; Sarah Gillard, Sharlett Gillard, and David Pratt, "A Pedagogical [*sic*] Study of Intrinsic Motivation in the Classroom through Autonomy, Mastery, and Purpose," *Contemporary Issues in Education Research (Online)* 8, no. 1 (2015): 1–6; and Chris McMorran, Kiruthika Ragupathi, and Simei Luo, "Assessment and Learning Without Grades? Motivations and Concerns with Implementing Gradeless Learning in Higher Education," *Assessment & Evaluation in Higher Education* 42, no. 3 (2017): 361–77.

5.   Sumi Cho, Kimberlé Williams Crenshaw, and Leslie McCall, "Toward a Field of Intersectionality Studies: Theory, Applications, and Praxis," *Signs* 38, no. 4 (2013): 785–810, doi:10.1086/669608.

6.   Patricia Hill Collins, *Black Feminist Thought: Knowledge, Consciousness, and the Politics of Empowerment*, Rev. 10th Anniversary ed., Perspectives on Gender, (New York: Routledge, 2000).

Bibliography

Arnone, Marilyn P., Rebecca Reynolds, and Todd Marshall. "The Effect of Early Adolescents' Psychological Needs Satisfaction upon Their Perceived Competence in Information Skills and Intrinsic Motivation for Research." *School Libraries Worldwide* 15, no. 2 (2009): 115–34.

Cho, Sumi, Kimberlé Williams Crenshaw, and Leslie McCall. "Toward a Field of Intersectionality Studies: Theory, Applications, and Praxis." *Signs* 38, no. 4 (2013): 785–810. doi:10.1086/669608.

Deci, Edward L., Richard Koestner, and Richard M. Ryan. "A Meta-Analytic Review of Experiments Examining the Effects of Extrinsic Rewards on Intrinsic Motivation." *Psychological Bulletin* 125, no. 6 (1999): 627–68.

Ennis, Robert H. "A Logical Basis for Measuring Critical Thinking Skills." *Educational Leadership* 43, no. 2 (1985): 44–48.

Facione, Peter A. *Critical Thinking: A Statement of Expert Consensus for Purposes of Educational Assessment and Instruction. Research Findings and Recommendations.* American Philosophical Association, Newark, DE., 1990. https://eric.ed.gov/?id=ED315423.

Gillard, Sarah, Sharlett Gillard, and David Pratt. "A Pedagogical [*sic*] Study of Intrinsic Motivation in the Classroom through Autonomy, Mastery, and Purpose." *Contemporary Issues in Education Research (Online)* 8, no. 1 (2015): 1–6.

Guthrie, John T., Allan Wigfield, and Clare VonSecker. "Effects of Integrated Instruction on Motivation and Strategy Use in Reading." *Journal of Educational Psychology* 92, no. 2 (2000): 331–41.

Halpern, Diane F. "Teaching Critical Thinking for Transfer Across Domains: Dispositions, Skills, Structure Training, and Metacognitive Monitoring." *American Psychologist* 53, no.4 (1998): 449–55.

Hill Collins, Patricia. *Black Feminist Thought: Knowledge, Consciousness, and the Politics of Empowerment.* Rev. 10th Anniversary ed. Perspectives on Gender. New York: Routledge, 2000.

Kohn, Alfie. *Punished by Rewards: The Trouble with Gold Stars, Incentive Plans, A's, Praise, and Other Bribes.* Houghton Mifflin Harcourt, 1999.

Lipman, Matthew. "Critical Thinking—What Can It Be?" *Educational Leadership* 46, no.1, (1988): 38–43.

McMorran, Chris, Kiruthika Ragupathi, and Simei Luo. "Assessment and Learning Without Grades? Motivations and Concerns with Implementing Gradeless Learning in Higher Education." *Assessment & Evaluation in Higher Education* 42, no. 3 (2017): 361–77.

Paul, Richard. "Critical Thinking: What, Why, and How." *New Directions for Community Colleges* 1992, no. 77 (1992): 3–24.

Tindal, Gerald, and Victor Nolet. "Curriculum-Based Measurement in Middle and High Schools: Critical Thinking Skills in Content Areas." *Focus on Exceptional Children* 27, no. 7 (1995): 1–22.

Willingham, Daniel T. "Critical Thinking." *American Educator* 31, no. 3 (2007): 8–19.

CHAPTER 1

The ARCS Model and Audience Analysis:
Learning About Student Motivations and Instructional Preferences

Krista Reynolds

Introduction

The energy level in the room is high. Students work together diligently, examining their computer screens and sharing ideas to try to solve a problem. When the instructor asks them to share their findings, several students raise their hands and offer insightful observations. After the session is over, a couple of students take the time to tell the instructor the value of what they learned in class and how helpful it will be to them. This scenario is what we instructors strive for—that our students will be engaged in our sessions and leave feeling their time was well-spent.

I began reflecting on and studying the role of motivation in library instruction after several years of teaching one-shot information literacy (IL) sessions and experiencing classes where some students were interested in learning and some students were reluctant to participate. Librarians who teach one-shots face unique challenges. Librarians Latham and Gross, in their paper on instructional preferences of first-year college students, stated, "In the case of the standalone workshop, students often fail to see the relevance of instruction to their academic work or their personal lives, and the resulting lack of interest and low motivation create obstacles to learning."[1]

Moreover, librarians often meet students in a one-shot session on the day of instruction. We lack the advantage of being able to develop relationships with students over time and determine what motivates them and what instructional strategies might work best with the group. Students are often unclear about what librarians do and how they can help. Students who have grown up using computers and search engines daily also often assume they have the requisite skills to perform academic research.[2] All of these factors might impact students' motivation and desire to actively participate in library instruction, and I endeavored to explore and address these potential impediments through my own study of undergraduates' motivations to learn research skills. A literature review revealed that Keller's[3] ARCS motivation model, originally developed and described in the 1980s, has been applied most frequently in a library instruction context. ARCS stands for attention, relevance, confidence, and satisfaction, and these four variables were derived from well-established motivational theories, such as Wigfield and Eccles' expectancy-value model.[4] Keller, an educational psychologist, asserted that these categories encompass the major aspects of learning motivation, and he emphasized the need to address all four categories in instructional design. More recently, Keller created a second model to account for people's intentions and commitment to achieving goals and their self-regulation strategies—"behaviors and attitudes that are related to persistent effort to accomplish a goal."[5] Keller's *Motivational Design for Learning and Performance* offers a full description of the ARCS model and the newer MVP model.

In this chapter, I build on librarians' previous work using ARCS in library instruction and share how I gained a greater understanding of student characteristics at my institution to design motivational instruction using the ARCS model. I wanted to learn whether students were motivated to learn research skills and why, and to determine whether they preferred the pedagogies that other researchers have identified as motivating. My ultimate goal was to use this information to create more relevant sessions—regarding content and pedagogy—and increase intrinsic motivation. I provide information on my research as a guide for other librarians who might wish to undertake similar studies at their institutions. I offer instructional content that aligns with each ARCS component (attention, relevance, confidence, and satisfaction) so information literacy instruction can be more relevant to students.

Literature Review

Current educational systems in the US stress extrinsic motivational strategies. Student achievement is often focused on grades, scores on standardized exams, pleasing the teacher, and attaining external rewards and honors.

Students internalize extrinsic motivators, and these become a part of their self-regulation process.[6] They become motivated to achieve rather than to learn.[7] Thus, it is no surprise that students' intrinsic motivation declines as they progress through school and that a high number of students have low intrinsic motivation.[8] However, many students view instructional relevance through the lens of utility value, such as learning's applicability to future academic and career goals. Instructors, then, must demonstrate how its value relates to these extrinsic motivators. But students will be more deeply engaged in instruction if they can also see how it connects to their existing skills and knowledge and how they are valued as learners.[9] In his discussion of making instruction more personally relevant, rather than relying solely on extrinsic motivators, Keller stated, "To stimulate the motivation to learn, it is best to build relevance by connecting instruction to the learners' backgrounds, interests, and goals."[10] Even though students' expectancy for success in a specific academic setting is derived from many factors, including factors out of an instructor's control, librarians must communicate an expectancy that students will succeed in completing research tasks. Students missing the basic facets of a positive expectancy for success and perceived value of instruction may not attempt learning tasks or otherwise engage with instruction.

The ARCS model is applicable to one-shot library instruction because it is customizable to any learning scenario and flexible for motivational analysis and design. An instructor uses what he or she knows about his or her audience to select "motivational strategies that are compatible with the learners, instructors, and learning environment."[11] Keller asserted that even a general knowledge of audience characteristics is helpful, which is often the only information librarians have about students in a particular session. Because librarians often meet a group of students for the first time on the day a one-shot session takes place, they know they must build rapport with students quickly to create a welcoming classroom environment where students are comfortable sharing and participating. Many ARCS instructional strategies center on instructor behaviors that meet that need. Because students may have trouble understanding how library instruction can be applied beyond the classroom, the relevance piece of ARCS is useful for addressing that issue. Kuhlthau's groundbreaking work on the information search process (ISP)[12] and Head's[13] more recent study on freshmen attitudes about research highlight the affective side of research; students exhibit various emotional states including confusion, anxiety, and a lack of confidence as they plan for and conduct research. The ARCS model incorporates strategies that address the affective side of learning, particularly confidence and satisfaction. Moreover, these affective pieces correlate with the dispositional outcomes of the Framework for Information Literacy[14]—those outcomes that include students' values, motivations, and attitudes about research. Librarians want students to develop positive feelings and beliefs about research, so the model may help librarians accomplish goals outlined in the framework as well.

Librarians can intentionally design their sessions using instructional techniques based on the four ARCS components to increase student interest and engagement. Ruth Small, librarian-researcher at Syracuse University, brought attention to the ARCS model in the 1990s[15] and early 2000s[16] and published several studies related to librarians' use of motivational strategies. In their book *Motivating Students in Information Literacy Classes,* Jacobson and Xu[17] also used the ARCS model extensively to recommend pedagogies for term-length and one-shot library instruction.

Keller stressed that instructors need to know the motivational attributes of their audience, such as attitudes, probable attention level, perceptions of relevance, and confidence levels to select the most effective motivational strategies[18] and to make instruction most relevant to students. Citing Keller's ARCS model, Muddiman and Frymier questioned whether college students believe the relevance tactics instructors intentionally use are actually motivating since previous research on relevance-designed instruction had yielded mixed results.[19] When surveyed about content relevance tactics that their faculty used, students discussed many of the same relevance-increasing strategies Keller promoted, such as connecting with students' interests, future lives, and popular culture, and using discussions and participatory activities.[20] Students' proclivity for these tactics reinforces their potential effectiveness. However, in contrast with Keller, Muddiman and Frymier suggested that "perceived relevance is an *outcome* of effective teaching rather than a *component* of effective teaching."[21] Regardless, their research draws attention to the importance of relevance in instruction. For librarians who teach one-shot sessions, determining audience attributes and appealing content is particularly challenging because often our first experience with a group is on the day instruction takes place. However, Keller suggested that even a general sense of audience characteristics would be helpful,[22] and Muddiman and Frymier's work as well as the research cited below provides useful insights about college students' instructional preferences. In the spring of 2015, I undertook a study to discover what generally compelled Concordia University undergraduate students to learn research skills. My goals were to gain greater understanding of their motivations and to learn which instructional methods might appeal to them.

Undergraduate Student Survey

The goals of this survey were to gather information from CU undergraduate students to describe and better understand their motivation to learn research skills, their confidence and anxiety levels related to completing a research assignment, and their attitudes about various classroom instruction methods that have been shown to motivate students. Further, I wanted to understand student perceptions of the utility or value of learning research skills. With this information, I could use the ARCS model more effectively to plan and customize my one-shot sessions to meet students' pedagogical needs and preferences. As Keller suggested, knowing a group's goals, attitudes, and motivational attributes allows the instructor to choose appropriate ARCS instructional strategies and to determine which of the four components might require more (or less) emphasis. For example, if students generally believe learning research skills is relevant to them upon arriving at a session, an instructor need not spend as much time helping students come to that conclusion. Ideally, one would obtain this information from every group of students; since this is not practical for one-shot sessions, having a general idea of student characteristics is more realistic. While my survey questions were not selected based on the Framework for Information Literacy, the information I gleaned relates particularly to the dispositional outcomes of the framework—those that include students' values, motivations, and attitudes about various aspects of research.

I sought a validated instrument related to college students and library instruction, motivation, or attitudes through a literature review but was not able to locate an instrument that matched my precise needs. Thus, I developed survey questions based on Latham and Gross's[23] study on instructional preferences of college students, Christophel's[24] work on student motivation and teacher immediacy behaviors, Jacobson and Xu's[25] recommendations for motivating students in information literacy instruction, and Small et al.'s[26] interview questions used in their study of student motivation at community colleges. I consulted question development best practices outlined by Robson[27] to minimize problems with question wording and bias in results.

A list of the survey questions is found in the Appendix 1A. The electronic survey included paired statements (see Appendix 1A, questions 17 through 30) which I designed to be opposite teacher behaviors or instructional strategies, and I asked students to choose the statement with which they agreed more. I selected these instructional strategies and behaviors because research shows that these factors relate to student motivation to learn,[28] and several are specific ARCS strategies or are based on other theories of motivation. Understanding whether those strategies resonate with students informs instructors about whether they should be used in future IL sessions. I report survey results only for those questions relevant to the scope of this chapter.

Survey review and administration

I asked the instructor of record for each class for permission to administer the survey and administered it using SurveyMonkey software in February and March 2015 at the end of ten undergraduate library instruction sessions I taught.[29] One hundred forty students were potential respondents in the following courses: Introduction to Speech (ENG 202; three sections), General Biology I (BIO 211; four sections), Media & Culture in America (HST 331; one section), English Composition (WR 121; one section) and Senior Thesis Preparation for English, History, and Theology majors (ENG/HST/REL 492; one section). I asked students seventeen or younger not to complete the survey, and I asked those students who had already completed the survey not to participate again.

Data analysis

SurveyMonkey automatically recorded questionnaire results and the software calculated response percentages for closed-ended questions. In open-ended questions, I asked students to elaborate on why they did or did not feel motivated to learn research skills. I worked with another librarian to code open-ended responses to identify common themes and patterns using a process described by the Cerritos College Office of Research and Planning.[30] Results from the survey provide a snapshot of CU student attitudes toward learning information literacy skills and their attitudes toward various types of instruction.

Results
Quantitative responses

One hundred nineteen of 140 students who participated in ten instruction sessions completed the survey. Seventy-eight percent of respondents were women and 22 percent were men. The response rate was 85 percent. However, I excluded results from two sections of General Biology I from the data analysis because of my possible influence on their responses; I graded a lab assignment in two of those sections. Thus, I report on responses from 91 students in this chapter. Most of those 91 respondents (53, or 58.2 percent) indicated they had not attended a library instruction session previously during the current semester, and over one-third (34, or 37.4 percent) had attended one or two sessions. When asked how many library sessions they had attended in the last year, 37 students (40.6 percent) responded they had not attended any, while 45 (49.5 percent) indicated they had attended one or two sessions. Eight students (8.8 percent) had attended three or four sessions within the last year.

Interest level. When asked to rate their interest level in learning research skills that day, most students responded positively. (See table 1.1.) The majority of students (55 percent) said they were interested, and an additional 14.3 percent said they were very interested in learning research skills. A smaller group (24.2 percent) was neutral, while 6.4 percent of students indicated they

Table 1.1. Students' interest level, confidence, anxiety, and beliefs about transferability of learning research skills (n=91).

Question	Very interested	Interested	Neither interested nor disinterested	Not interested	Really not interested
Rate your interest level in learning research skills today	13 (14.3%)	50 (55%)	22 (24.2%)	3 (3.2%)	3 (3.2%)
	Very confident	**Confident**	**Neither confident nor unsure**	**Unsure**	**Very unsure**
When you arrived to class, what was your confidence level in being able to complete the research for your assignment on your own?	17 (18.7%)	43 (47.2%)	21 (23.1%)	9 (9.9%)	1 (1.1%)
	Very anxious	**Anxious**	**Neither anxious nor relaxed**	**Relaxed**	**Very relaxed**
When you arrived to class today, what was your level of anxiety regarding completing your research assignment?	2 (2.2%)	24 (26.4%)	29 (31.9%)	24 (26.4%)	12 (13.2%)
	Strongly agree	**Agree**	**Neither agree nor disagree**	**Disagree**	**Strongly disagree**
Do you believe the information you learned today will help you complete your research assignment?	43 (47.3%)	41 (45%)	78 (7.7%)	0 (0%)	0 (0%)
Do you believe learning research skills will help you complete assignments in other classes?	53 (58.2%)	34 (37.4%)	3 (3.3%)	1 (1.1%)	0 (0%)

Table 1.1. Students' interest level, confidence, anxiety, and beliefs about transferability of learning research skills (n=91).

Do you believe learning research skills will help you solve problems in your life outside of school?	48 (52.7%)	24 (26.4%)	18 (19.8%)	1 (1.1%)	0 (0%)
When you arrived to class today, what was your level of anxiety regarding completing your research assignment?					

were either not interested or really not interested in learning research skills. The relatively high interest levels may be because, for many students, this was their first library instruction session of the semester. Other researchers have shown that students who have had previous library instruction tend to be less attentive in subsequent IL sessions,[31] but this factor did not seem to impact this group of students.

Confidence and anxiety. Students provided a greater range of responses to the questions about confidence and anxiety levels in being able to complete their research assignment independently. (See table 1.1.) Almost half of the students (47.2 percent) reported feeling confident when they arrived at class, and 18.7 percent felt very confident. Almost one-quarter of students (23.1 percent) felt neither confident nor unsure, and 11 percent felt either unsure or very unsure. Interestingly, while students generally felt confident, a notable number of students reported feeling anxious at the beginning of class about being able to complete their research assignment. The greatest number of students (39.6 percent) rated themselves as relaxed or very relaxed. However, 31.9 percent of students chose neither anxious nor relaxed, and 28.6 percent of students reported feeling anxious or very anxious.

Motivation. A large majority of students (78, or 85.7 percent) felt motivated to learn research skills. When asked if they thought the information they learned during the session would help them complete their research assignment, most responded affirmatively. More than 47 percent of students strongly agreed with the statement, and 45 percent agreed. Almost 8 percent of students were neutral, and no students disagreed. In addition, students recognized the transferability of learning research skills. When asked whether they believed learning research skills would help them complete assignments in other classes, 58.2 percent of students strongly agreed and 37.4 percent agreed. Students did not agree as strongly about whether learning research skills would help them to solve problems in life outside of school. Almost 53 percent of students agreed with that statement, but only 26.4 percent strongly agreed, and 19.8 percent were neutral.

The last group of questions in the survey asked students to select one of two statements with which they agreed more about instructional techniques or motivation. I included these questions to assess student attitudes about techniques that Small et al.[32] identified as effective in keeping students on-task during library instruction. I share responses to questions 17 through 30 in table 1.3 and discuss those results later in this chapter.

Qualitative responses

Reasons for students' motivation or lack of motivation to learn research skills. One hundred four students elaborated on why they were or were not motivated to learn research skills. I excluded twenty-five responses from General Biology I students, which yielded seventy-nine analyzed responses. Table 1.2 lists the broad categories that I identified from students' responses and the numbers of students whose responses fit into those categories. The table also shows which of those categories are related to intrinsic or extrinsic motivation. Most of the reasons students gave are based upon extrinsic motivations, such as accomplishing a general or specific goal. Of those students who were motivated to learn research skills, students cited academic reasons most frequently (thirty times). Specific motivations they mentioned (in descending order) included knowing the information would help them complete the current assignment or assignments in other classes (9, or 11.4%); become better writers or improve their papers (9, or 11.4%); become well-rounded students or improve general academic success (4, or 5.1%); and improve the quality, reliability or accuracy of their work (3, or 3.8%).

Table 1.2. Reasons students gave for their motivation to learn research skills (n=79)

Categories	Number of Students
Extrinsic Motivations	
Academic (complete assignments, become better writers, general academic success)	30
To improve their research skills (make research process easier, more efficient)	14
To use beyond academic life (future use, in other parts of life, helpful)	13
To acquire information (find scholarly or credible sources, investigate a topic)	8
To use in their career	5
Intrinsic Motivations (enjoy learning, interested in session content)	3
Related to Emotions (minimize frustration, improve confidence)	2

Examples of students' responses follow:

- Student 1: "I know that as I continue in college im [sic] going to have to do a lot of research papers, so learning to use it now will help me later on."
- Student 2: "It will help me write accurate pappers [sic] during my education."
- Student 3: "I believe that education is about learning through your exploration and experience of the material …so learning how to research from reputable sources is very important to begin the process of actively learning."
- Student 4: "It is a crucual [sic] skill for academic success."

The second most frequent explanation students gave about being motivated to learn how to research was to simply improve upon their skills. Fourteen students (17.7 percent) wrote about this idea. Five students wanted to learn how to make the research process easier, four students mentioned wanting to know how to research or improve upon skills they already had, two mentioned making research more efficient or quicker, and two noted the influence of technology in research. One student discussed organizing information. Examples of students' comments follow:

- Student 5: "The more I learn about research the easier it will be to find and use information for classes and projects."
- Student 6: "I have some skills already. But I would like to improve them."
- Student 7: "i [sic] want to learn how to do better reaserch [sic] and have my reaserch [sic] be more centralized and simple."
- Student 8: "I feel motivated because technology is always changing and it is important to keep up with the changes."

The third most frequent category included broader reasons students were motivated. Thirteen responses (16.5 percent) related to this category. Seven students mentioned future use (unspecified) of the information they learned, four students thought it would be helpful in all or other parts of life, and two students thought it was helpful or necessary but did not elaborate on that belief. Five students were motivated to learn because of their career goals. Examples of these types of statements follow:

- Student 9: "Because I will be participating in a lot of research over the years."
- Student 10: "I am interested in learning skills so I can apply them to doing research papers for future classes and my own interests."
- Student 11: "I am majoring in nursing (ie. [sic] the medical field) and feel this information will be important."

Eight students (10.1 percent) wrote about their motivation in terms of acquiring information. Three students wanted to find the best or scholarly

Table 1.3. Students' Source of Motivation and Preferences for Instruction Techniques (n=88)

Paired Statements	% Students
The instructor is primarily responsible for motivating me to learn course material.	14.8%
I am primarily responsible for motivating myself to learn course material.	85.2%
The instructor's enthusiasm about a topic makes me want to learn more about that topic.	90.9%
The instructor's enthusiasm about a topic does not affect my desire to learn more about that topic.	9.1%
I prefer to have opportunities to interact with the instructor during class (e.g., ask and respond to questions, get one-on-one help).	89.8%
I prefer to have minimal interactions with the instructor during class.	10.2%
When the instructor asks students questions in class, my interest in the material generally increases.	84.1%
When the instructor asks students questions in class, my interest in the material generally decreases.	15.9%
When I answer a question in class I prefer that the instructor provides immediate feedback to me.	96.6%
When I answer a question in class I do not want immediate feedback from the instructor.	3.4%
I prefer to have choices about how I learn in class (such as developing my own learning goals or being offered multiple ways to complete an assignment).	55.7%
I prefer that the instructor develop one clear way that we are to complete the learning in class.	44.3%
I like to see how the material I am learning can be applied to solve problems.	93.2%
I prefer more theoretical, abstract analyses of course concepts.	6.8%
I prefer that an instructor use a variety of teaching methods (such as lecture, demonstration, discussion, group work, video, games) during a class session.	90.9%
I prefer than an instructor use a single teaching method during a class session.	9.1%
I prefer to have hands-on practice when learning skills that involve technology, such as when learning how to use a new feature of Blackboard.	84.1%
I prefer to watch a demonstration without having hands-on practice when learning skills that involve technology.	15.9%

Table 1.3. Students' Source of Motivation and Preferences for Instruction Techniques (n=88)

I prefer that the instructor stresses collaboration and collegiality in the classroom.	83.7%
I prefer that the instructor stresses independence and competition in the classroom.	16.3%
I enjoy working with my classmates in small groups in the classroom.	62.5%
I enjoy working by myself in the classroom.	37.5%
Working with other students in the classroom helps me learn the material.	80.7%
Working with other students in the classroom does not help me learn the material.	19.3%
I prefer to be challenged when learning new material.	56.8%
I prefer to have my learning scaffolded in small steps by the instructor when learning new material.	43.2%
Feeling successful at a task keeps me motivated to learn more.	97.7%
Feeling successful at a task does not impact my motivation to learn more.	2.3%

or credible sources. Three students were motivated to find information on a specific topic (it is unclear whether for personal or academic purposes), and two students mentioned databases, search tools, or other resources in their response.

- Student 12: "It is helpful in being able to find the best resources."
- Student 13: "Yes, knowing about the different databases and search tools is helpful."

Finally, three students mentioned reasons that can be linked to intrinsic motivation. They responded either that they enjoyed learning about the topic or learning in general or that they were interested in the session content. In addition, two students mentioned emotions in their responses. These students wanted to either minimize their anxiety or frustration doing research or improve their confidence level.

- Student 14: "Research has become something like a treasurehunt [sic] of information."
- Student 15: "I was concerned about finding resources for my research topic. I knew there would be a lot, but that was the point—there was a lot—but now I feel my topic is more focused and the level of anxiety has been neutralized."

Students who indicated they were unmotivated to learn research skills shared their reasons for feeling this way. Ten responses from unmotivated students fell into six categories. Four students noted they had learned research skills in other classes or elsewhere, and two students mentioned they were not interested in research or do not like to do research. Two students believed their basic research skills were already adequate. One student wrote that she was not motivated, in general, and another student wrote she had been frustrated by past research experiences.

Students' instructional preferences. Students' preferences for particular instruction techniques were more uniformly aligned with each other. (See table 1.3.) In most cases, 88 students responded to the questions in this section of the survey. Regarding the social aspects of learning, most students preferred to work collaboratively in the classroom. Seventy-two students (83.7 percent) favored a collaborative and collegial classroom environment over one that was competitive and emphasized independence. A smaller majority of students (55, or 62.5 percent) enjoyed working in small groups in the classroom, and 71 students (80.7 percent) believed that working with other students helped them learn material.

A strong majority of students indicated they wanted instructors who engaged with them in the classroom. Eighty students (90.9 percent) thought an instructor's enthusiasm provoked their learning about a topic, and most students (79, or 89.8 percent) wanted opportunities to interact with the instructor during class. They generally agreed (74, or 84.1 percent) that their interest in materials increased when an instructor asked questions, and almost all students (85, or 96.6 percent) wanted immediate feedback from an instructor after answering a question.

Almost all students (86, or 97.7 percent) agreed that feeling successful at completing a task motivated them to want to learn more. However, students were more evenly split in their attitudes about choices in learning activities and level of challenge when learning new material. Most students (49, or 55.7 percent) preferred to have flexibility in the way they learned and completed assignments, but many (39, or 44.3 percent) wanted the instructor to develop one clear path for learning. In a similar split, most students (50, or 56.8 percent) liked to be challenged when learning, but 38 students (43.2 percent) desired learning to be scaffolded in small steps. These disparate attitudes underscore the challenge of meeting all student preferences and differentiating instruction for various skill levels through learning activities and assignments.

Discussion

I embarked on this project to assess students' motivations regarding research and to determine whether teaching methods that Keller[33] and Jacobson and Xu[34] have promoted as motivational are appealing to undergraduate students. The results from my survey of CU students cannot be generalized because I used non-random convenience sampling. However, the findings provide some evidence about

undergraduates' attitudes about learning research skills and preferred pedagogies and shed light on how librarians might approach ARCS-designed library
sessions. In the following sections, I remark on students' motivation, in general,
and then I highlight issues librarians might consider when planning their information literacy sessions and suggest strategies for addressing each of the four
ARCS components to improve student motivation.

Assessing students' motivation

It was surprising how many students indicated they were *interested* in learning research skills and that almost 86 percent of students were *motivated* to
learn research skills. The high numbers could be because many of the students
I surveyed were freshmen. Perhaps their motivation was due to their newness
to college and recognition that their academic habits needed to change. Head
found in her study of freshmen students that many in this group discovered
their high school research skills were insufficient for the rigors of college.[35]
In contrast, one group of students I surveyed was enrolled in a senior thesis
preparation class, and those students could have been motivated by their anxiety related to beginning a long-term, extensive research project. Students in
"high stakes" situations, such as those who have a significant project to complete or those students who are new to the library, are probably more motivated to learn. The timing of the sessions may have been a factor as well. I worked
with faculty to schedule the sessions close to when faculty introduced a research assignment or expected most students to begin their research. Thus,
many students may have readily perceived the sessions' relevance to them.

Moreover, it was surprising that more than 85 percent of students felt personally responsible for being motivated to learn in their courses. In a study
of college student interest and boredom during instruction, Small, Dodge,
and Jiang found that students identified their instructors as primarily being
responsible for their interest or lack of interest in learning.[36] While the survey
question I included in this study is slightly different, it indicates CU students
surveyed generally believed the opposite: that they (themselves) were responsible for motivating themselves to learn course material.

These results are encouraging and suggest librarians might not need to
be so intentional about using motivational strategies, but it is unrealistic to
expect every group of students will be generally motivated to learn about research. Even seasoned librarian instructors experience classes with low participation and a lack of apparent student interest. Thus, librarians should design instruction infused with motivational strategies to proactively address
motivational deficits that students may have when they arrive to class.

Keller emphasized that the key to effective implementation of the ARCS
model is to know the motivational characteristics of one's audience so one
may create concrete motivation objectives.[37] It may not be practical to survey

student attitudes in every instruction setting, and students would probably experience survey fatigue as a result. But librarians should consider assessing students about their motivation regularly to create appealing sessions for different groups of students. Librarians might use the following methods to determine audience characteristics:

- Reflect on past experiences with similar groups of students (e.g., year in school, students in a particular class or major), either in instructional settings or one-on-one interactions. When did students seem to be motivated? What factors seemed to impact their motivation?
- Ask your office of institutional research whether they have any data from institution-wide surveys related to students' attitudes about academics, the library, or motivation in general.
- If your library conducts a regular user experience survey, add a question about students' interest in learning research skills.
- Before a session, work with faculty to administer a brief survey about levels of motivation and reasons for being motivated, or question faculty about student characteristics and class dynamics to determine what pedagogies might work best with the group and if they have a sense of students' preferred learning styles.
- Administer a brief survey at the beginning of class that asks if and why students are motivated (may require on-the-fly adjustment of instruction plans!).

Intrinsic motivation

The fact that so few students I surveyed in this study indicated they were intrinsically motivated to learn research skills suggests librarians need to inject interesting and enjoyable elements into all sessions. In the following ARCS sections, I describe a few ways to boost students' intrinsic motivation by engaging students' curiosity and giving them personal control over learning. In addition, using humor and telling stories about serendipitous research discoveries in the real world can reveal fun and unexpected aspects of conducting research. Games that teach IL skills may work best with younger students, and librarians should consider audience characteristics when deciding whether to use games. Books and articles are available that help librarians gamify their sessions, including *Let the Games Begin! Engaging Students with Field-tested Interactive Information Literacy Instruction*.[38]

Attention

Keller asserted that getting and sustaining learners' attention is critical to successful instruction.[39] Tactics Keller promotes are based on stimulating students' curiosity, through either perceptual arousal (increasing interest) or inquiry arousal (encouraging an attitude of inquiry).[40] Instructional strategies he suggested include using humor, questioning learners, sharing personal or human interest examples, challenging learners' thinking, introducing a paradox, and using analogies.[41] Curiosity is another critical component of intrinsic motivation; thus, using curiosity-building strategies effectively will improve engagement and could lead to deeper learning.

A strong majority of undergraduates I surveyed in this study indicated they preferred instructors who use strategies that fall into Keller's attention category. They felt compelled to learn when instructors express enthusiasm about course content, provide opportunities for interactions with them and provide immediate feedback, ask questions, and use a variety of teaching methods. My research results echo findings from Latham and Gross's[42] research on students' preferred pedagogies.

Students in this study and in Latham and Gross's[43] study desired interacting with faculty regularly in class. My survey did not include specific questions about the quality of those desired interactions, such as an instructor's friendliness or other behaviors. Regardless, one simple way librarians can increase motivation is to exhibit behaviors that foster a welcoming learning environment. Mehrabian described "immediacy behaviors" people demonstrate that communicate warmth and a desire for closeness to others.[44] Examples of such behaviors, that are also attention strategies, are moving around the classroom, using vocal variety, calling on students by name, smiling, and making eye contact.[45] Kelley and Gorham's experimental study of undergraduate students showed that teacher immediacy improves cognitive learning and creates perceptual arousal, such as attentional focus, recall, and enhanced memory.[46] In addition, Christophel, in her study of graduate and undergraduate students in various classroom settings, found that immediacy has a positive impact on "all levels of learning."[47] Jacobson and Xu, in their recommendations for instruction librarians, promoted using immediacy strategies as well to increase motivation.[48] Librarians who would like additional tips about modifying their classroom behaviors might consult Artman, Sundquist, and Dechow's book *The Craft of Librarian Instruction: Using Acting Techniques to Create Your Teaching Presence*.[49] In it, the authors offer methods for enlivening sessions, connecting with students, and keeping their attention.

Because CU students indicated they want instruction with pedagogical variety, I have increased the number of strategies I use during a session. My sessions typically begin with using a comic, graphic, or quick quiz that relates to the session's content, a brief introduction of the session's activities, a hands-on activity that relates to the assignment, time for sharing findings in a plenary discussion, and a wrap-up activity, such as a minute paper. Examples of specific inquiry arousal strategies I have used to gain and keep students' attention follow:

- Begin a session asking students a "big picture" question, such as, "Is information power? Why or why not?"
- Share authentic examples of a professional's information-seeking behavior with students going into that field (such as nursing) and ask them to critique those strategies.
- Use creative media, the "Open Access Explained" video (https://www.youtube.com/watch?v=L5rVH1KGBCY), with students that describe a real-world information need and ask them to analyze the economic issues surrounding publication.

I have not formally assessed the effectiveness of using each of these strategies, but informal feedback from students has been positive, and student engagement is typically high in sessions I have designed using these strategies.

Relevance

No amount of motivational instruction techniques will motivate students to learn if they do not understand how the content of the lesson meets their needs. Gorham and Millette found that relevance was of primary importance to college students in influencing their motivation in classes.[50] Librarians should avoid teaching general orientation sessions, where students do not have an immediate need for the information shared. A strong majority of students surveyed in this study reported feeling motivated to learn research skills because they recognized learning about research would help them complete or do well on their coursework. Thus, spending much time convincing students of its importance related to their assignments may not be necessary.

Klentzin found that 33 percent of freshmen students surveyed were extrinsically motivated to conduct research, and 49 percent of students valued research solely based on whether the topic resonated with them.[51] Because of students' focus on extrinsic motivators, librarians must match session content with a course assignment. Students may have difficulty connecting library information to their academic work when it is not presented in the context of an assignment. This is not to say librarians should only focus on an assignment, but it should be apparent to students the session will help them advance their work. Fewer students in my study saw the applicability of learning research skills to life outside of academics, which means librarians might consider making more explicit connections between academic research and a broader life context. I reflect on ways librarians can help students make these broader connections later in this chapter.

Students judge a session's relevance based on both its content and pedagogy. Librarians can create motivating instruction and demonstrate its value by using group activities that tap into many students' psychological needs for social affiliation (or relatedness). Most students surveyed in this study indicated they enjoyed working with classmates in the classroom. An even larger majority thought working with other students helped them learn and preferred a collaborative and collegial classroom environment over one focused on competition and independence. However, librarians might give students choices about working individually or in a group; not every student enjoys working with classmates.

Jacobson and Xu recommended cooperative learning, a type of group activity where students learn from one another and are held accountable for teaching material to the entire class.[52] Loo, in his study of team-based activities in IL sessions for chemistry students, found that using collaborative learning engaged students (albeit different classes exhibited different levels of engagement) and required them to grapple with content and use metacognitive abilities, such as time and process management.[53] Teaching this way had the added benefit of providing opportunities for one-on-one instructor-student interactions and direct observation and evaluation of students' learning.[54] Drawbacks are that team learning activities require significant time to plan and may require more class time than a typical hour-long IL session.

I have used a cooperative learning activity successfully in two-hour biology classes (some of which I surveyed for this project), where students teach their classmates about scholarly communication in the sciences. The activity has been popular with students and they seem to take pride in being responsible for teaching about a particular topic and sharing their knowledge with other students. Giving students agency or control is one way to meet students' needs for autonomy and increase intrinsic motivation.[55] Hands-on, active learning provides an opportunity for students to direct their learning, and more than 84 percent of the students I surveyed preferred hands-on practice when learning technology-related skills, in particular.

The majority of students in this study liked to see how the material they are learning can be used to solve problems, so practical examples grounded in real-world case studies would likely appeal to them. Roberts[56] used the ARCS model to create problem-based learning scenarios and taught research sessions using freely available resources that students could use after college with the intent of encouraging the transfer of their research skills to non-academic contexts. Students in her study reported they would use research skills covered in the session to solve information problems in their everyday lives.[57] They could perceive the relevance of the sessions beyond their academic coursework.

Hoyer[58] recognized the importance of social context in IL and noted it is not enough for librarians to teach skills that will only help students succeed in an academic environment since most students will not have careers in academia. She suggested a more discipline-focused approach to IL instruction and that social connections and networking were more relevant to information seeking in the workplace.[59] Librarians need to consider how the realities of information seeking in work environments might impact their instruction and bridge academic literacies with other areas of life. Even though many students already seem to believe learning research skills will help them in the future, librarians can emphasize the value employers place on finding and using information.[60] Librarians might connect specific critical-thinking skills they teach, such as evaluating sources of information, with workplace values, such as maintaining credibility. Librarians need to share explicit examples with students that demonstrate developing their research skills will not only help them find information at libraries but learn to navigate the "information ecosystem in which all of us work and live."[61]

None of my research questions focused on students' desire for instruction that links to their personal experiences, but Keller asserted that connecting information with students' personal experiences or interests and infusing popular culture are ways to hook them into a session.[62] In Muddiman and Frymier's study, students indicated they were cued to instructions' relevance when their faculty used those particular strategies.[63] Students should be able to connect information seeking and IL concepts to themselves, personally. Using the familiar in instruction, such as connecting with students' prior learning, using analogies and metaphors, and common experiences, is a relevance strategy.[64]

Confidence

Confidence and anxiety are elements of the affective piece of learning and have been prominent topics in the library literature since Mellon's seminal research on students' feelings about academic libraries[65] and Kuhlthau's work on the Information Search Process.[66] Without confidence, students may not persist at a task. However, using ARCS strategies to address students' confidence in learning research skills must be done in a thoughtful way. Gustavson and Nall[67] and Latham and Gross[68] have noted that students tend to be overconfident in their information literacy skills, so librarians must be careful about how they bolster students' confidence.

My research was inconclusive about the nature of students' confidence and anxiety during a library session; to most effectively plan the confidence piece, it would be best for a librarian to measure students' confidence in advance of the session. More detailed information than that provided in my study is needed to understand students' confidence and anxiety levels regarding their research assignments to develop effective instructional interventions. In this study, most students were confident in their research abilities to complete their assignment, but almost 30 percent of students reported being anxious about doing the assignment. Were students anxious about aspects of the assignment that were unrelated to the library, such as their writing ability or the difficulty of the project? Regardless, library anxiety is a known phenomenon of which librarians should be aware, and using humor (an attention strategy) may be an antidote to help lessen students' anxiety during a session.[69] Polger and Sheidlower's research on instructional strategies librarians use to engage students in the classroom showed that most teaching librarians they surveyed use humor intentionally and felt it was effective.[70]

One way librarians could more accurately assess research confidence is to administer paired quiz questions that ask students to first answer a skill or knowledge question and then a question that asks them to reflect on their confidence regarding that specific research knowledge or skill (called an implicit-confidence test).[71] Ideally, a librarian would partner with the course instructor to administer this type of survey before the session. If the results indicate students are generally overconfident, librarians will need to be more thoughtful about how they reinforce students' confidence during a session. Moreover, an implicit-confidence test is a method librarians can use to help students become self-reflective and recognize when they might be overconfident about their skills in a particular area. Librarians might openly discuss with students how such tests can reveal flawed thinking and how overconfidence can hinder learning. Working with students one-on-one to discover gaps in knowledge and providing corrective feedback might be the most effective strategy and helps preserve students' egos.

Librarians need to incorporate self-reflection activities and expose the affective impacts of conducting research so students can overcome potential barriers to learning. For example, in order to decrease their anxiety, it might be helpful for librarians to share that feelings of frustration and confusion are common during the early stages of research. Librarians can help students tolerate and persist through the ambiguities of the research process. College students' beliefs about intelligence can be influenced, and students who believe intelligence is malleable are more likely to take on challenges in learning.[72] Thus, librarians should communicate an expectation that students will succeed and connect students' personal efforts, rather than innate intelligence, with success. By addressing these issues, librarians will help learners "value persistence, adaptability, and flexibility and recognize that ambiguity can benefit the research process."[73]

Addressing the affective side of research may be particularly important when librarians instruct millennial students (now in their twenties and early thirties); research shows millennials tend to fear ambiguity,[74] which typifies the first stages of research.[75] Cahoy and Schroeder developed a model, including worksheets based on Mellon's library anxiety model, for incorporating affective learning outcomes into library instruction.[76] Their model gives librarians strategies to help them "discover, articulate, and address students' self-efficacy, motivation, emotions and attitudes."[77] I plan to investigate its effectiveness when used in one-shot sessions.

To help students develop feelings of confidence, Keller stated that instructors need to provide the following pieces in their instruction: requirements for learning, opportunities for success, and personal control.[78] Opportunities for success and personal control correlate specifically with Ryan and Deci's self-determination theory, which suggests that intrinsic motivation is partially based on individuals' needs for competence and autonomy.[79] Learning requirements help students "develop realistic expectations for success"[80] and include a clear description of objectives, outcomes, or goals, and criteria that will be used to evaluate students' work. When librarians state clear goals and evaluation criteria, they may help keep students' overconfidence in check. Librarians should specify learning expectations and give students an overview of the plan for the session's activities that includes goals. Having students develop their own learning goals will increase their autonomy and buy-in during a session.

Keller promoted using hands-on activities that challenge at an appropriate level so students develop feelings of achievement or competence.[81] Jacobson and Xu also encouraged librarians to help learners develop confidence by giving them active, hands-on activities tailored to their skill level and by exhibiting positive teacher behaviors, such as encouraging participation, using praise, and responding to students' errors tactfully.[82] Polger and Sheidlower found in their survey of librarians that they rated hands-on experiences for students as the most effective engagement technique.[83] Hands-on activities may appeal to millennial students because of their "proclivity for exploration and discovery,"[84] and students in my study preferred hands-on practice when learning technology-related skills. Interestingly, just under 57 percent of students I surveyed liked to be challenged when learning new material, so librarians might need to be vigilant about monitoring students' skills and planning appropriately leveled and scaffolded instruction. Small suggested librarians give a periodic review or summary of content and adjust the difficulty of instruction to students' abilities.[85]

Librarians can provide the following opportunities for personal control:

- Give students time to search for sources on their topics independently and accomplish assignment-related goals in class.
- Create opportunities for autonomy with boundaries and clear expectations so they understand how to achieve their objectives or learning goals (to lessen ambiguity).
- Give learners positive, immediate, and meaningful feedback, which acknowledges their efforts. Feedback can help a student whose response is not quite accurate to come to a correct conclusion and bolster their feelings of efficacy.[86]

To help students build upon their existing search habits, librarians should model their own search strategies and narrate their behavior to make explicit their decision-making processes, such as those used to select a search tool, brainstorm keywords, construct a search phrase, and refine searches. Acknowledging barriers to searching and showing students how to overcome those barriers helps them internalize the idea that initial search attempts do not always produce the desired results, and mental flexibility and persistence are required for success.[87] Teaching students how to deal with challenges is a strategy that falls within Keller's description of personal control.[88] If librarians model their techniques effectively, students will see that success is directly connected to their efforts and ability to use more nuanced search strategies.

Satisfaction

Satisfaction, an affective component of motivation, relates to students' positive feelings about a learning experience and their desire to keep learning.[89] Keller identified the following concepts as central to learners' satisfaction: intrinsic reinforcement, extrinsic rewards, and equity.[90] Students will most likely feel satisfied if they recognize the skills or knowledge they are acquiring can be applied to achieve their academic goals (extrinsic rewards). Perhaps the most obvious way to fulfill "natural consequences," where students can implement learning in a meaningful way,[91] is to help them *progress* on their assignment. To indicate progress, librarians might use the following strategies in a session:

- Provide worksheets on which students can document keyword term selection for database searching, strategies for overcoming research roadblocks, ways of using sources in a paper, or a timeline of research goals for a long-term project.
- Ask students to email themselves search results or create a database account with saved searches or results.[92]
- Provide students with a written checklist of learning goals they can mark so they have a sense of what they have accomplished by the end of a class.
- Provide a handout that reinforces a session's content.

Even small indications of accomplishment might be effective. Giving students the opportunity to demonstrate their learning to other students by sharing the results of their group activities or individual work with the entire class provides an extrinsic reward.[93] This might be done more formally in a presentation format or through short voluntary reports to the group.

To encourage deeper reflection, at the end of a session, librarians might have students describe how instruction has helped them with an assignment, will help them in the future, or how their behavior might change as a result of learning. Roberts used the following self-reflective questions in her study to determine how students perceived a session's relevance, but asking these questions may encourage students to develop positive feelings about a session: How might you use the search strategies we talked about in your everyday life? What part of this workshop will you use outside academic work?[94]

Instructors can support learners' intrinsic enjoyment of an instruction session by giving feedback that connects students' efforts with their achievements and supports their pride in accomplishment.[95] Students crave feedback on their work, and librarians have the power to give feedback in a way that motivates. Dweck's work on types of feedback adults give to children has shown that students who are praised regarding their efforts or strategies used to approach a task expressed more of a mastery-orientation and persisted at tasks.[96] Those students with a mastery orientation tend to be optimistic about their prospects for success, work harder, and problem-solve to overcome obstacles.[97] Thus, librarians should praise students, not only for their correct responses but also for their efforts in class. Librarians should give students feedback when they do hands-on work and encourage them when they become frustrated or discouraged. Keller advised that feedback should be phrased to be informational and focused on the learner's actions versus controlling and focused on a result.[98] An example of an informational message is, "I am impressed by how you persisted in developing your search strategy." In contrast, a controlling message might be, "You applied my keyword selection technique and look at your great results!" Librarians should avoid praise that centers on traits, such as intelligence. Satisfaction relates to equity as well; instructors should strive to treat each student fairly and provide feedback that respects all learners.

Limitations of This Study

I used a student questionnaire in this study due to its ease of administration, completion, and scoring. However, self-report instruments, such as questionnaires, can result in the collection of unreliable data.[99] I asked students to rate their confidence and anxiety levels before and after library instruction at the end of the instruction session. These data may not be fully reliable because students may have had inaccurate recall of their feelings at the start of the session. In addition, the survey only measured motivation at a particular moment in time. Motivation is influenced by many factors, including mood, hunger, and fatigue, which may have impacted students' responses.

It is important to note that students' self-reported attitudes about pedagogy do not equate with observable classroom behaviors that indicate motivation, which was the focus of Small et al.'s research.[100] Expressed attitudes do not necessarily translate to actual behaviors, and this can result in data that is not externally valid.[101] A more valid method of assessing motivation would be to directly observe student behaviors in a class while they are completing research tasks. Measurement of students' effort and persistence can give an indication of motivation while learning a task.[102] However, because direct observation of my own IL instruction would require the assistance of another librarian in completing this thesis project, I chose to use a questionnaire. I used non-random convenience sampling to select participants to complete the survey because I desired feedback on my own instruction. Because I selected survey and interview participants non-randomly, the results may not be generalizable to a larger population.

Conclusion

An important step in implementing Keller's ARCS motivational model is examining an audience's motivations and understanding what content and pedagogy might be relevant to the group. That step is problematic for librarians because we typically meet our students on the day instruction takes place. Regardless, librarians should attempt to better understand their students to design engaging instruction. In the study this chapter describes, I sought to perform an audience analysis on a more general level by using a survey to ask undergraduate students why they were motivated or unmotivated to learn research skills and what instructional strategies they preferred. This type of survey is just one method librarians might use, which is relatively easy to implement to assess student characteristics. In contrast, Latham and Gross chose to acquire similar information using student focus groups, which may yield more holistic information from participants.

Not surprisingly, I discovered most students were motivated to learn research skills because they wanted to succeed academically, either on their immediate research assignments or more generally. Very few students indicated they were intrinsically motivated to learn research skills. Students' selections on the instructional methods portion of the survey revealed they preferred strategies that Keller promotes as being motivational, which reinforces their potential effectiveness with that particular group.

While my survey results are not generalizable, they suggest that the various attention strategies Keller describes, such as asking questions, using a variety of instructional methods, and providing opportunities for students to interact with their instructor, would be effective. Using the immediacy behaviors described in this chapter to help build a positive rapport with students does not require extensive planning and is arguably one of the best ways instructors can help students stay engaged and have a positive attitude about learning. To demonstrate relevance, instructors should base their teaching upon students' research assignments. However, because fewer students seem to perceive the broader relevance of learning research skills, it is important to show them (not just tell them) how those skills will benefit them both on the job and in other areas of life. Asking students to solve real-world research-based problems can help them draw that conclusion. Giving students constructive, immediate feedback, and praising them for their efforts meets their needs for efficacy and would most likely help students feel satisfied with instruction. Because most students do not seem to view doing research as inherently "fun," it is paramount to add elements that boost students' intrinsic motivation, such as piquing curiosity and giving them personal control over their learning—but with clear guidelines and expectations about learning outcomes. Infusing instruction with intrinsic strategies may help students focus on the task of learning, rather than extrinsic outcomes, such as completing coursework.

Additional research is needed to understand students' anxiety in library instruction settings. The question about anxiety that I asked in this study did not reveal whether students' anxiety was related to library research or their assignment. Because previous research has shown students tend to be over-confident about their research abilities, it would be prudent for library instructors to assess students' skills and share with students those results so they have an accurate understanding of their abilities and needs for improvement.

The process of gathering information about one's audience is not only useful for designing motivational instruction; it also fosters a student-centered teaching approach. Thinking about student characteristics shifts the focus from an instructor's preferences to pedagogy that appeals to students. In addition, students pay attention when instructors ask their opinions and are more likely to feel valued and respected as individual learners, which is an effective way to build rapport with them. By keeping students' needs at the forefront and learning about their preferences, an instructor might be encouraged to try new instructional methods that they may not have considered before. Not all of Keller's strategies may resonate with all instructors but they provide a foundation from which one may strategically plan engaging instruction that appeals to diverse groups of learners.

Appendix 1A.

Reflection on the Library Session

1. Name of course in which library instruction took place:
2. Approximately how many librarian-taught research sessions have you attended at CU this semester (not including today's session)?
   a. None, 1–2, 3–4, 5 or more, other (please explain).
3. Approximately how many librarian-taught research sessions at CU have you attended during the last year (not including today's session)?
   a. None, 1–2, 3–4, 5 or more, other (please explain).
4. Rate your interest level in learning research skills today.
   a. Very interested, interested, neither interested nor disinterested, not interested, really not interested
5. What did you like about the session?
6. Please describe how you feel the session could be improved.
7. The library session goals matched the assignment requirements.
   a. Strongly agree, agree, neither agree nor disagree, disagree, strongly disagree
8. The library session goals were attainable during the class period.
   a. Strongly agree, agree, neither agree nor disagree, disagree, strongly disagree
9. When you arrived to class today, what was your confidence level in being able to complete the research for your assignment on your own?
   a. Very confident, confident, neither confident nor unsure, unsure, very unsure
10. After this session, what is your confidence level in being able to apply the information you learned to complete your assignment?
    a. Very confident, confident, neither confident nor unsure, unsure, very unsure
11. When you arrived to class today, what was your level of anxiety regarding completing your research assignment?
    a. Very anxious, anxious, neither anxious nor relaxed, relaxed, very relaxed
12. After the session today, what is your level of anxiety regarding completing your research assignment?
    a. Very anxious, anxious, neither anxious nor relaxed, relaxed, very relaxed
13. Do you believe the information you learned today will help you complete your research assignment?
    a. Strongly agree, agree, neither agree nor disagree, disagree, strongly disagree

14. Do you feel motivated to learn research skills? Why or why not?
15. Do you believe learning research skills will help you complete assignments in other classes?
    a. Strongly agree, agree, neither agree nor disagree, disagree, strongly disagree
16. Do you believe learning research skills will help you solve problems in your life outside of school?
    a. Strongly agree, agree, neither agree nor disagree, disagree, strongly disagree

Student Preferences for Instructional Strategies

Please reflect on what helps foster your desire to learn during ANY classroom instruction (not just library instruction). Think of the instructor behaviors and classroom environment you prefer and select the statement with which you **most agree**.

1.
   a. The instructor is primarily responsible for motivating me to learn course material.
   b. I am primarily responsible for motivating myself to learn course material.
2.
   a. The instructor's enthusiasm about a topic makes me want to learn more about that topic.
   b. The instructor's enthusiasm about a topic **does not** affect my desire to learn more about that topic.
3.
   a. I prefer to have opportunities to interact with the instructor during class (e.g., ask and respond to questions, get one-on-one help).
   b. I prefer to have minimal interactions with the instructor during class.
4.
   a. When the instructor asks students questions in class, my interest in the material generally increases.
   b. When the instructor asks students questions in class, my interest in the material generally decreases.
5.
   a. When I answer a question in class, I prefer that the instructor provides immediate feedback to me.
   b. When I answer a question in class, I do not want immediate feedback from the instructor.

6.
   a.   I prefer to have choices about how I learn in class (such as developing my own learning goals or being offered multiple ways to complete an assignment).
   b.   I prefer that the instructor develop one clear way that we are to complete the learning in class.

7.
   a.   I like to see how the material I am learning can be applied to solve problems.
   b.   I prefer more theoretical, abstract analyses of course concepts.

8.
   a.   I prefer that an instructor use a variety of teaching methods (such as lecture, demonstration, discussion, group work, video, games) during a class session.
   b.   I prefer than an instructor use a single teaching method during a class session.

9.
   a.   I prefer to have hands-on practice when learning skills that involve technology, such as when learning how to use a new feature of Blackboard.
   b.   I prefer to watch a demonstration **without** having hands-on practice when learning skills that involve technology.

10.
   a.   I prefer that the instructor stresses collaboration and collegiality in the classroom.
   b.   I prefer that the instructor stresses independence and competition in the classroom.

11.
   a.   I enjoy working with my classmates in small groups in the classroom.
   b.   I enjoy working by myself in the classroom.

12.
   a.   Working with other students in the classroom helps me learn the material.
   b.   Working with other students in the classroom **does not** help me learn the material.

13.
   a.   I prefer to be challenged when learning new material.
   b.   I prefer to have my learning scaffolded in small steps by the instructor when learning new material.

14.
   a. Feeling successful at a task keeps me motivated to learn more.
   b. Feeling successful at a task does not impact my motivation to learn more.

Endnotes

1. Don Latham and Melissa Gross, "Instructional Preferences of First-Year College Students with Below-Proficient Information Literacy Skills: A Focus Group Study," *College & Research Libraries* 74, no. 5 (2013): 430, doi:10.5860/crl-343.
2. Latham and Gross, "Instructional Preferences," 432.
3. John M. Keller, *Motivational Design for Learning and Performance* (New York: Springer, 2010), 44–46.
4. Allan Wigfield and Jacquelynne S. Eccles, "Expectancy-Value Theory of Achievement Motivation," *Contemporary Educational Psychology* 25, no. 1 (2000): 68–81, doi:10.1006/ceps.1999.1015.
5. Keller, *Motivational Design*, 9, 29.
6. Dale H. Schunk, Judith L. Meece, and Paul R. Pintrich, *Motivation in Education: Theory, Research, and Applications* (Boston: Pearson Education, Inc., 2014), 253.
7. Keller, *Motivational Design*, 126.
8. Schunk, Meece, and Pintrich, *Motivation in Education*, 267.
9. Keller, *Motivational Design*, 126.
10. Keller, *Motivational Design*, 126.
11. Keller, *Motivational Design*, 3.
12. Carol C. Kuhlthau, "Inside the Search Process: Information Seeking from the User's Perspective," *Journal of the American Society for Information Science* 42, no. 5 (1991): 369–70, http://wp.comminfo.rutgers.edu/ckuhlthau2/wp-content/uploads/sites/185/2016/01/InsidetheSearchProcess.pdf.
13. Alison J. Head, "*Learning the Ropes: How Freshmen Conduct Course Research Once They Enter College*," December 4, 2013, accessed May 13, 2017, http://www.project-infolit.org/uploads/2/7/5/4/27541717/pil_2013_freshmenstudy_fullreportv2.pdf.
14. Association of College and Research Libraries, "Framework for Information Literacy for Higher Education," January 11, 2016, accessed February 2, 2017, http://www.ala.org/acrl/standards/ilframework.
15. Ruth V. Small, "Designing Motivation into Library and Information Skills Instruction," *SLMQ Online: School Library Media Quarterly Online* 1 (1998): 1–15, http://www.ala.org/aasl/sites/ala.org.aasl/files/content/aaslpubsandjournals/slr/vol1/SLMR_DesigningMotivation_V1.pdf; Ruth V. Small, "An Exploration of Motivational Strategies Used by Library Media Specialists during Library and Information Skills Instruction," *School Library Media Research* 2 (1999): 1–27, http://www.ala.org/aasl/sites/ala.org.aasl/files/content/aaslpubsandjournals/slr/vol2/SLMR_MotivationalStrategies_V2.pdf.
16. Ruth V. Small, Nasriah Zakaria, and Houria El-Figuigui, "Motivational Aspects of Information Literacy Skills Instruction in Community College Libraries," *College & Research Libraries* 65, no. 2 (2004): 96–121, doi:10.5860/crl.65.2.96.
17. Trudi Jacobson and Lijuan Xu, *Motivating Students in Information Literacy Classes* (New York: Neal-Schuman Publishers, Inc, 2004).

18. John M. Keller, "The Systematic Process of Motivational Design," *Performance & Instruction* 26 (1987): 4.
19. Ashley Muddiman and Ann Bainbridge Frymier, "What is Relevant? Student Perceptions of Relevance Strategies in College Classrooms," *Communication Studies* 60, no. 2 (2009): 133, doi:10.1080/10510970902834866.
20. John M. Keller, "The Systematic Process of Motivational Design," 4.
21. Muddiman and Frymier, 136.
22. Keller, *Motivational Design*, 60.
23. Latham and Gross, "Instructional Preferences," 430–49.
24. Diane M. Christophel, "The Relationships among Teacher Immediacy Behaviors, Student Motivation, and Learning," *Communication Education* 39 (1990): 323–40, http://www.tandfonline.com/loi/rced20#.VbJ2BkZvlr9.
25. Jacobson and Xu, *Motivating Students*.
26. Small, Zakaria, and El-Figuigui, "Motivational Aspects of Information Literacy," 120.
27. Colin Robson, *Real World Research: A Resource for Social Scientists and Practitioner-researchers* (Malden, MA: Blackwell Publishers Inc., 2002), 245–46.
28. Jacobson and Xu, *Motivating Students*, 44–63.
29. I submitted the survey and a description of the study to Concordia University's Institutional Review Board (the Concordia University Research Committee) to ensure they met federal guidelines regarding human participants. The Committee approved the project in January 2015.
30. Cerritos College Office of Research and Planning, "A Brief Guide to the Analysis of Open-Ended Survey Questions," http://cms.cerritos.edu/uploads/Researchand-Planning/Brief_Guide_to_Open-Ended_Survey_Questions.pdf.
31. Michelle Hudson, Laurie McGowan, and Cheri Smith, "Technology and Learner Motivation in Library Instruction: A Study of Personal Response Systems," *Indiana Libraries* 30, no. 1 (2011): 24, http://journals.iupui.edu/index.php/IndianaLibraries/article/view/1911/1822.
32. Small, Zakaria, and El-Figuigui, "Motivational Aspects of Information Literacy," 99, 109–11.
33. Keller, *Motivational Design*.
34. Jacobson and Xu, *Motivating Students*.
35. Head, *Learning the Ropes*, 3.
36. Ruth V. Small, Bernard J. Dodge, and Xiquiang Jiang, "Dimensions of Boredom and Interest in Instructional Situations," paper presented at the Convention of the Association for Educational Communications and Technology, Indianapolis, Indiana, 1996.
37. Keller, *Motivational Design*, 58.
38. Theresa R. McDevitt, *Let the Games Begin!: Engaging Students with Field-tested Interactive Information Literacy Instruction* (New York: Neal-Schuman Publishers, 2011).
39. Keller, *Motivational Design*, 92.
40. Keller, *Motivational Design*, 92.
41. Keller, *Motivational Design*, 92.
42. Latham and Gross, "Instructional Preferences," 443, 445.
43. Latham and Gross, 443, 445.

44. Ann Frymier and Gary M. Shulman, "What's in It for Me? Increasing Content Relevance to Enhance Students' Motivation," *Communication Education* 44 (1995), 40; Albert Christophel and Albert Mehrabian, "Attitudes Inferred from Non-immediacy of Verbal Communications," *Journal of Verbal Learning and Verbal Behavior* 6, no. 2 (1967).
45. Frymier and Shulman, "What's in It for Me?," 41.
46. Derek H. Kelley and Joan Gorham, "Effects of Immediacy on Recall of Information," *Communication Education* 37, no. 3 (1988), 198–207.
47. Diane M. Christophel, "The Relationships Among Teacher Immediacy Behaviors, Student Motivation, and Learning," *Communication Education* 39, no. 4 (1990), 335–40. This paraphrase, 335.
48. Jacobson and Xu, *Motivating Students*, 44–46, 55–58.
49. Julie Artman, Jeff Sundquist, and Doug Dechow, *The Craft of Librarian Instruction: Using Acting Techniques to Create Your Teaching Presence* (Chicago: Association of College and Research Libraries, 2016).
50. Joan Gorham and Diane M. Millette, "A Comparative Analysis of Teacher and Student Perceptions of Sources of Motivation and Demotivation in College Classes," *Communication Education* 46, no. 4 (1997): 254–55, doi:10.1080/03634529709379099.
51. Jacqueline Courtney Klentzin, "The Borderland of Value: Examining Student Attitudes towards Secondary Research," *Reference Services Review* 38, no. 4 (2010): 557, doi:10.1108/00907321011090728.
52. Jacobson and Xu, *Motivating Students*, 67.
53. Jeffery L. Loo, "Guided and Team-based Learning for Chemical Information Literacy," *The Journal of Academic Librarianship* 39, no. 3 (2013): 257, doi:10.1016/j.acalib.2013.01.007.
54. Loo, "Guided and Team-based Learning," 257.
55. Schunk, Meece, and Pintrich, *Motivation in Education*, 238.
56. Lindsay Roberts, "Research in the Real World: Improving Adult Learners Web Search and Evaluation Skills through Motivational Design and Problem-Based Learning," *College & Research Libraries* 78, no. 4 (2017): 534, doi:10.5860/crl.78.4.527.
57. Roberts, 540.
58. Jennifer Hoyer, "Information is Social: Information Literacy in Context," *Reference Services Review* 39, no. 1 (2011): 12. doi:10.1108/00907321111108088.
59. Hoyer, 20–21.
60. Alison J. Head, *Learning Curve: How College Graduates Solve Information Problems Once They Join the Workplace* (2012), accessed March 31, 2017, http://www.projectinfolit.org/uploads/2/7/5/4/27541717/pil_fall2012_workplacestudy_fullreport-1.pdf.
61. Association of College and Research Libraries, "Framework for Information Literacy."
62. Keller, *Motivational Design*, 126-132.
63. Muddiman and Frymier, "What Is Relevant?," 136.
64. Keller, *Motivational Design*, 126-32.
65. Constance A. Mellon, "Library Anxiety: A Grounded Theory and Its Development," *College & Research Libraries* 47, no. 2 (1986): 276–82, doi:10.5860/crl.76.3.276.

66. Kuhlthau, "Inside the Search Process."
67. Amy Gustavson and H. Clark Nall, "Freshman Overconfidence and Library Research Skills: A Troubling Relationship?," *College and Undergraduate Libraries* 18, no. 4 (2011): 302, doi:10.1080/10691316.2011.624953.
68. Latham and Gross, "Instructional Preferences," 432.
69. Mark Aaron Polger and Scott Sheidlower, *Engaging Diverse Learners: Teaching Strategies for Academic Librarians* (Santa Barbara, CA: Libraries Unlimited, 2017), 43.
70. Polger and Sheidlower, 42, 55.
71. Gustavson and Nall, "Freshman Overconfidence," 294–95.
72. Carol S. Dweck, *Self-theories: Their Role in Motivation, Personality, and Development,* (Philadelphia, PA: Psychology Press, 1999), 26.
73. Association of College and Research Libraries, "Framework for Information Literacy."
74. Andrea Hershatter and Molly Epstein, "Millennials and the World of Work," *Journal of Business and Psychology* 25, no. 2 (2010): 216, doi:10.1007/s10869-010-9160-y.
75. Kuhlthau, "Inside the Search Process."
76. Ellysa Stern Cahoy and Robert Schroeder, "Embedding Affective Learning Outcomes in Library Instruction," *Communications in Information Literacy* 6, no. 1 (2012), http://www.comminfolit.org/index.php?journal=cil&page=article&op=view&path%5B%5D=v6i1p73&path%5B%5D=146.
77. Cahoy and Schroeder., 73.
78. Keller, *Motivational Design*, 159.
79. Richard M. Ryan and Edward L. Deci, "Self-Determination Theory and the Facilitation of Intrinsic Motivation, Social Development, and Well-being," *American Psychologist* 55, no. 1 (2000): 68–78, doi:10.1037/0003-066X.55.1.68.
80. Keller, *Motivational Design*, 159.
81. John M. Keller, "Strategies for Stimulating the Motivation to Learn," *Performance & Instruction* 26, no. 8 (1987): 4, http://onlinelibrary.wiley.com/journal/10.1002/%28ISSN%291930-8272/issues.
82. Jacobson and Xu, *Motivating Students*, 8, 55, 66.
83. Polger and Sheidlower, *Engaging Diverse Learners*, 55.
84. Charles H. Becker, "Student Values and Research: Are Millennials Really Changing the Future of Reference and Research?" *Journal of Library Administration* 52, no. 6/7 (2012): 484, doi:10.1080/01930826.2012.707948.
85. Small, "An Exploration of Motivational Strategies," 26.
86. Dweck, *Self-theories*, 113–14.
87. Association of College and Research Libraries, "Framework for Information Literacy."
88. Keller, *Motivational Design*, 52.
89. Keller, *Motivational Design*, 45.
90. Keller, *Motivational Design*, 189.
91. Keller, "Strategies for Stimulating the Motivation to Learn," 6.
92. Krista M. Reynolds, Lindsay Michelle Krista M., Roberts, Lindsay Michelle, and Janet Hauck, Janet, "Exploring Motivation: Integrating the ARCS Model with Instruction," *Reference Services Review* 45, no. 2 (2017): 6, doi:10.1108/RSR-10-2016-0057.

93. Keller, *Motivational Design*, 189.
94. Roberts, "Research in the Real World," 540, 548.
95. Keller, *Motivational Design*, 189.
96. Dweck, *Self-theories*, 114, 121.
97. Dweck, *Self-theories*, 9–10.
98. Keller, *Motivational Design*, 176.
99. Paul R. Pintrich and Dale H. Schunk, *Motivation in Education: Theory, Research, and Applications* (Upper Saddle River, NJ: Pearson Education, Inc., 2002), 19.
100. Small, Zakaria, and El-Figuigui, "Motivational Aspects of Information Literacy."
101. Robson, *Real World Research*, 231.
102. Pintrich and Schunk, *Motivation in Education*, 14.

Bibliography

Artman, Julie, Jeff Sundquist, and Doug Dechow. *The Craft of Librarian Instruction: Using Acting Techniques to Create Your Teaching Presence*. Chicago: Association of College and Research Libraries, 2016.

Association of College and Research Libraries. "Framework for Information Literacy for Higher Education." January 11, 2016. http://www.ala.org/acrl/standards/ilframework.

Becker, Charles H. "Student Values and Research: Are Millennials Really Changing the Future of Reference and Research?" *Journal of Library Administration* 52, no. 6/7 (2012): 474–97. doi:10.1080/01930826.2012.707948.

Cahoy, Ellysa Stern, and Robert Schroeder. "Embedding Affective Learning Outcomes in Library Instruction." *Communications in Information Literacy* 6, no. 1 (2012): 73–90. http://www.comminfolit.org/index.php?journal=cil&page=article&op=view&path%5B%5D=v6i1p73&path%5B%5D=146.

Cerritos College Office of Research and Planning. "A Brief Guide to the Analysis of Open-Ended Survey Questions." http://cms.cerritos.edu/uploads/ResearchandPlanning/Brief_Guide_to_Open-Ended_Survey_Questions.pdf.

Christophel, Diane M. "The Relationships among Teacher Immediacy Behaviors, Student Motivation, and Learning." *Communication Education* 39 (1990): 323–40. http://www.tandfonline.com/loi/rced20#.VbJ2BkZvlr9.

Dweck, Carol S. *Self-theories: Their Role in Motivation, Personality, and Development*. Philadelphia: Psychology Press, 1999.

Frymier, Ann, and Gary Shulman. "What's in It for Me? Increasing Content Relevance to Enhance Students' Motivation." *Communication Education* 44 (1995): 40–50.

Gorham, Joan, and Diane M. Millette. "A Comparative Analysis of Teacher and Student Perceptions of Sources of Motivation and Demotivation in College Classes." *Communication Education* 46, no. 4 (1997): 245–61. doi:10.1080/03634529709379099.

Gustavson, Amy, and H. Clark Nall. "Freshman Overconfidence and Library Research Skills: A Troubling Relationship?" *College & Undergraduate Libraries* 18, no. 4 (2011): 291–306. doi:10.1080/10691316.2011.624953.

Head, Alison J. *Learning the Ropes: How Freshmen Conduct Course Research Once They Enter College* (2013). Accessed May 13, 2017. http://www.projectinfolit.org/uploads/2/7/5/4/27541717/pil_2013_freshmenstudy_fullreportv2.pdf.

———. *Learning Curve: How College Graduates Solve Information Problems Once They*

Join the Workplace (2012). Accessed March 31, 2017. http://www.projectinfolit.org/uploads/2/7/5/4/27541717/pil_fall2012_workplacestudy_fullreport-1.pdf.

Hershatter, Andrea, and Molly Epstein. "Millennials and the World of Work." *Journal of Business and Psychology* 25, no. 2 (2010): 211–23. doi:10.1007/s10869-010-9160-y.

Hoyer, Jennifer. "Information is Social: Information Literacy in Context." *Reference Services Review* 39, no. 1 (2011): 10–23. doi:10.1108/00907321111108088.

Hudson, Michelle, Laurie McGowan, and Cheri Smith. "Technology and Learner Motivation in Library Instruction: A Study of Personal Response Systems." *Indiana Libraries* 30, no. 1 (2011): 20–7. http://journals.iupui.edu/index.php/IndianaLibraries/article/view/1911/1822.

Jacobson, Trudi, and Lijuan Xu. *Motivating Students in Information Literacy Classes.* New York: Neal-Schuman Publishers, Inc., 2004.

Keller, John M. *Motivational Design for Learning and Performance.* New York: Springer, 2010.

———. "Strategies for Stimulating the Motivation to Learn." *Performance & Instruction* 26, no. 8 (1987): 1–7. doi:10.1002/pfi.4160260802.

———. "The Systematic Process of Motivational Design." *Performance & Instruction* 26, no. 9/10 (1987): 1–8. doi:10.1002/pfi.4160260902.

Kelley, Derek H., and Joan Gorham, "Effects of Immediacy on Recall of Information." *Communication Education* 37, no. 3 (1988): 198–207. doi:10.1080/03634528809378719.

Klentzin, Jacqueline Courtney. "The Borderland of Value: Examining Student Attitudes towards Secondary Research." *Reference Services Review* 38, no. 4 (2010): 557–70. doi:10.1108/00907321011090728.

Kuhlthau, Carol C. "Inside the Search Process: Information Seeking from the User's Perspective." *Journal of the American Society for Information Science* 42, no. 5 (1991): 361–71. http://www.asis.org/jasist.html.

Latham, Don, and Melissa Gross. "Instructional Preferences of First-Year College Students with Below-Proficient Information Literacy Skills: A Focus Group Study." *College & Research Libraries* 74, no. 5 (2013): 430–49. doi:10.5860/crl-343.

Loo, Jeffrey L. "Guided and Team-based Learning for Chemical Information Literacy." *The Journal of Academic Librarianship* 39, no. 3 (2013): 252–59. doi:10.1016/j.acalib.2013.01.007.

McDevitt, Theresa R. *Let the Games Begin!: Engaging Students with Field-tested Interactive Information Literacy Instruction.* New York: Neal-Schuman Publishers, 2011.

Mellon, Constance A. "Library Anxiety: A Grounded Theory and Its Development." *College & Research Libraries* 47, no. 2 (1986): 276–82. doi:10.5860/crl.76.3.276.

Muddiman, Ashley, and Ann Bainbridge Frymier. "What is Relevant? Student Perceptions of Relevance Strategies in College Classrooms." *Communication Studies* 60, no. 2 (2009): 130–46. doi:10.1080/10510970902834866.

Pintrich, Paul R., and Dale H. Schunk. *Motivation in Education: Theory, Research, and Applications.* Upper Saddle River, NJ: Pearson Education, Inc., 2002.

Polger, Mark Aaron, and Scott Sheidlower. *Engaging Diverse Learners: Teaching Strategies for Academic Librarians.* Santa Barbara, CA: Libraries Unlimited, 2017.

Reynolds, Krista M., Lindsay Michelle Roberts, and Janet Hauck. "Exploring Motivation: Integrating the ARCS Model with Instruction." *Reference Services Review* 45, no. 2 (2017): 1–17. doi:10.1108/RSR-10-2016-0057.

Roberts, Lindsay. "Research in the Real World: Improving Adult Learners Web Search and Evaluation Skills through Motivational Design and Problem-Based Learning." *College & Research Libraries* 78, no. 4 (2017): 527–51. doi:10.5860/crl.78.4.527.

Robson, Colin. *Real World Research: A Resource for Social Scientists and Practitioner-Researchers.* Malden, MA: Blackwell Publishers Inc., 2002.

Ryan, Richard M., and Edward L. Deci. "Self-Determination Theory and the Facilitation of Intrinsic Motivation, Social Development, and Well-being." *American Psychologist* 55, no. 1 (2000): 68–78. doi:10.1037/0003-066X.55.1.68.

Schunk, Dale H., Judith L. Meece, and Paul R. Pintrich. *Motivation in Education: Theory, Research, and Applications.* Boston: Pearson Education, Inc., 2014.

Small, Ruth V. "Designing Motivation into Library and Information Skills Instruction." *SLMQ Online: School Library Media Quarterly Online* 1 (1998): 1–15. http://www.ala.org/aasl/sites/ala.org.aasl/files/content/aaslpubsandjournals/slr/vol1/SLMR_DesigningMotivation_V1.pdf.

———. "An Exploration of Motivational Strategies Used by Library Media Specialists during Library and Information Skills Instruction." *School Library Media Research* 2 (1999): 1–27. http://www.ala.org/aasl/sites/ala.org.aasl/files/content/aaslpubsandjournals/slr/vol2/SLMR_MotivationalStrategies_V2.pdf.

Small, Ruth V., Bernard J. Dodge, and Xiquiang Jiang, "Dimensions of Boredom and Interest in Instructional Situations." Paper presented at the Convention of the Association for Educational Communications and Technology, Indianapolis, Indiana, 1996. http://files.eric.ed.gov/fulltext/ED397840.pdf.

Small, Ruth V., Nasriah Zakaria, and Houria El-Figuigui. "Motivational Aspects of Information Literacy Skills Instruction in Community College Libraries." *College & Research Libraries* 65, no. 2 (2004): 96–121. doi:10.5860/crl.65.2.96.

Svinicki, Marilla D. *Learning and Motivation in the Postsecondary Classroom.* Bolton, MA: Anker Publishing Co., 2004.

Wigfield, Allan, and Jacquelynne S. Eccles, "Expectancy-Value Theory of Achievement Motivation." *Contemporary Educational Psychology* 25, no. 1 (2000): 68–81. doi:10.1006/ceps.1999.1015.

CHAPTER 2

The Choice is Yours:
Guiding Graduate Students to Construct Meaningful and Motivating Learning Goals

Lindsay Roberts

Introduction

As adult learners, graduate students often bring rich life and work experiences to their studies. These students may have a wealth of experience in the field but may also be returning to academia for the first time in several years. Librarians who work with graduate students may struggle to find ways to engage students' lived experiences, show them the relevance of information literacy, speak openly about their gaps in knowledge and literature searching, and build confidence in new skills and ways of thinking. Very little literature exists addressing motivation as it relates to information literacy for graduate students. Much of the work on motivation in education focused on children and young adults prior to Knowles' pivotal work on andragogy in the 1970s. Knowles' work represented one of the first formal departures from a passive banking model, wherein students were viewed as knowledge repositories,[1] and toward more active, participant-centered learning. This work emphasizes the need for learners to see the relevance and importance of the material they are to learn (aligning with expectancy-value theory) and to connect this relevance with problems or opportunities in their own lives.[2]

Grounded in adult learning theory and drawing on goal setting theory, this chapter suggests best practices for librarians interested in using learning goals as a motivational tool during instruction and reports on my use of

43

student-defined learning goals in an exploratory study with a small group of education PhD students. In this chapter, I will explore students' reflections on their use of learning goals to improve their motivation and consider the related literature.

Related Literature
Needs of Education Graduate Students

Beyond deeper subject expertise, graduate students' needs differ from those of undergraduates. The needs of education graduate students were the particular focus of the small study described in this chapter. In education, graduate students may be returning to school after years spent teaching and may still be working full-time while taking courses or taking distance classes. In their research on outreach to graduate students, Cannady, King, and Blendinger used reference data to identify several challenging areas their education graduate students faced, including lack of awareness of tools like Google Scholar and subject-specific databases, difficulty discerning among format types, limited time, and distance from campus.[3] These authors found success in outreach methods such as orientations, flexible consultation scheduling during evenings and weekends, LibGuides, and faculty sharing librarian contact information.[4] They also emphasized the importance of keeping in mind the six assumptions for adult learners, based on Knowles' andragogy framework.[5] The six assumptions are paraphrased as (1) adults need to know why the learning is important, (2) adults need to be self-directed, (3) adults have their own life experiences, self-identities, mental models, and biases, (4) adults are ready to learn what they recognize they need to know, (5) adults are oriented toward problem-based or life-based learning that can be applied to solve problems or improve performance, and (6) adults have their own internal motivations and desires in addition to external motivators like grades or salary raises. While these assumptions are valuable for all college students, they may be particularly appropriate for graduate students in professional programs or who are juggling work and family priorities.

In their phenomenographic research, Blummer, Watulak, and Kenton identified similar barriers for education graduate students.[6] Their survey findings highlighted students' feelings of uncertainty and confusion about where to begin searching and which search tools were best.[7] Their interview findings showed that while students' research processes included identifying their topic, finding related sources, and developing a final product, students often revisited these steps rather than moving through them linearly.[8] The researchers noted that convenience was important to students, whether in full-text online access or in use of public or academic libraries close to home or that they were previously familiar with.[9] In addition to these needs, library anxiety may impact graduate students in education and other disciplines. Studies demonstrate that when students have high levels of library anxiety, they have lower levels of perceived self-competence and are more likely to procrastinate or avoid aspects of their research, with the result of lower educational outcomes.[10]

Goal Setting Theory

Goal setting can be a way of involving adult learners in the learning process and connecting material to their interests.[11] Goals are a key part of both expectancy-value theory and social cognitive theories of motivation; they diverged from earlier mechanistic views of human behavior and motivations.[12] Effective goals provide focus, direction, accountability to self and others, and a way to mark progress, and research indicates goals may also be linked to positive well-being.[13] Locke and Latham offer six summary points related to their many years of work on goal setting:

1. People use past experiences to help them in achieving a newly set goal.
2. If an individual is unable to correlate a goal with a past experience, they will draw from similar contexts and experiences to apply knowledge to the goal.
3. If a task is completely new to someone, they will spend time planning a strategy to help them achieve the goal.
4. Higher self-efficacy is associated with the increased likeliness of developing task strategies.
5. Specific, challenging learning goals yield better results than performance goals by preventing anxiety and performance pressure. When using learning goals, people often focus on finding effective strategies systematically rather than failing to perform or trying a range of effective/ineffective strategies rapidly.
6. Using high-performance goals can be effective when people are trained in a specific strategy. However, if people don't use the best strategy for a situation, their performance is likely to be worse.[14]

Instructors may want to consider how to help individuals set goals that are appropriately tailored for their interests and abilities, such as goals that have low-stakes of failure, and to consider whether team-based (rather than individual goals) would be more appropriate to encourage collaboration. Finally, instructors will want to maintain an awareness of individuals' intrinsic motivation levels;[15] this could be achieved through regular check-ins or student self-assessments.

Goal orientation

Investigations into goals have also centered on goal orientation theory, a trait-based understanding of motivation, with performance orientation and mastery/learning orientation thought of as opposing pairs at either end of a continuum.[16] Research has shown that with learning goals, "children are willing to risk displays of ignorance in order to acquire skills and knowledge" and are more likely to "analyze and vary their strategies."[17] In research with adults, individuals are also more likely to interpret constructive feedback more positively if they have a learning or mastery orientation.[18] Performance goals, in contrast, are often associated with displays of skill, competence, or achievement,[19] such as correctly solving a math problem in front of the class or meeting sales goals for a company's quarterly report. While they can be valuable motivators and accountability tools, performance goals can be limiting when individuals are focused more on appearing competent or avoiding criticism than when they are focused on growth and learning.[20] They can even be associated with unethical behavior and competition in business environments.[21]

Learning goals

In the instructional design field, learning goals and objectives have been used for decades in order to help instructors and learners understand the scope of material to be learned.[22] The types of learning goals discussed in instructional design focus on what learners are able to do at the end of instruction,[23] thus aligning more closely with performance or outcome goals as described in goal setting theory. This distinction is important for teaching librarians who are accustomed to using learning objectives or goals as part of lesson planning. In contrast to performance or outcome goals, a learning goal as defined in goal setting theory "frames the goal instructions in terms of knowledge or skill acquisition," with greater emphasis on processes and progress rather than concrete outcomes.[24] There is evidence that encouraging a focus on learning goals can help college students focus on growth rather than exclusively extrinsic rewards or outcomes.[25] Intriguingly, Hoyert and O'Dell examined the learning goal or performance goal orientations of undergraduates and found that 52 percent of traditional-aged undergraduates were oriented toward learning goals, compared to 76 percent of the nontraditional group (defined in this study as students twenty-four years and older).[26] This may reflect adult students' and graduate students' maturity and focus on learning over or in addition to grades.

Properties of effective learning goals

What makes for well-written learning goals? Schunk identified three goal properties that can enhance or detract from the outcomes: goals should be specific, relatively close or proximal (within, say, one semester rather than five years), and appropriately challenging.[27] Research has shown that students who set themselves challenging or difficult goals that are attainable may have a greater incentive to achieve the goal since the feeling of accomplishment would be greater than for an easier goal.[28] Latham and Seijts summarize four conditional variables which must be present in order for individuals to reach a goal successfully: (1) the goal must be within their ability level, (2) the resources to achieve the goal must be available, (3) the individual must be committed to the goal, and (4) the individual must have feedback on their progress toward the goal.[29] Learning goals work best when individuals are faced with acquiring new knowledge that is complex or takes time to learn and master.[30] Information literacy threshold concepts are ripe for learning goals since they are fundamentally complex, thorny, and transformative.[31]

One study has shown that when participants have pre-created goals assigned to them by others, their intrinsic motivation decreased, though a cause for the decrease was not fully understood.[32] Other studies suggest that performance can be similar between self-set and assigned goals when the level of challenge is the same and the reason for the goal is understood.[33] Though the literature on learning goals has not yet borne out this theory, a connection between self-set goals and high goal commitment may exist. Perhaps learners are more likely to "buy-in" to their goals when they create them, have control over the goals or participation in setting them, or at least understand and believe in the reasons behind setting the goal.[34]

Goal setting frameworks

Goal setting frameworks and advice abound in both practitioner-oriented and scholarly materials, blogs, and websites.[35] I found no evidence in the literature of empirically validated methods for instructing participants in creating their own learning goals, and the work of goal-setting theorists does not define a particular method.[36] In the scholarly literature, healthcare and mental health researchers have developed and validated a version of the SMART (Specific, Measurable, Assignable, Realistic, Time-related) goal-setting system for performance outcomes. The acronym, developed by Doran, is frequently adapted (variations in the acronym abound and have been expanded to SMARTER).[37] Researchers have explored SMART rubrics to evaluate goal setting quality and used these models in training with participants.[38] While SMART is widely used, it has been critiqued for not including affective components or environmental context.[39] SMART's focus on specificity and measurability seem to be better aligned for performance rather than learning goals.

I explored a method called QUEST for learning goals, developed by Tim Gallwey during his individual coaching of business leaders. QUEST stands for **Qualities** the individual would like to cultivate, **Understandings** they would like to improve, **Expertise** they would like to develop, **Specific** (such as a timeframe within the next few weeks), and **Time** they can reasonably commit to the goal.[40] Due to its flexibility and emphasis on growth rather than outcomes, an adapted version of the QUEST method was chosen for an exploratory study with graduate students who created their own learning goals for a literature review assignment.

Exploratory Study

This chapter contains qualitative findings related to learning goals from the exploratory study, with the following research questions: (1) How can information literacy instructors use learning goals as a motivational teaching tool? (2) How do education graduate students describe their interests in furthering their own information literacy practices through writing learning goals? Student participants attend a four-year public research institution in the Western United States and were recruited from a small graduate seminar offered in the education department. The total number of study participants was nine graduate students. Students were required to complete a major literature-based paper as 50 percent of their course grade. Though a small sample size (n=9) is not enough to generalize from, trends are noticeable and provide inspiration for further research and practice.

Table 2.1

Learning Goals Instructions

You may have had previous training or experiences with these skills in an academic or work context. You're encouraged to draw on these experiences as you complete the following questions, considering what you currently know and the areas you would like to focus on during the semester.

You will be asked to define 1 to 3 learning goals for yourself to focus on this semester. Think back on your experiences and strengths and think ahead to how you plan to use these types of research skills in the future. The questions below can be used to guide your planning. Keep goals specific enough to achieve within this semester rather than long-range goals that might need months or years to develop.

- Which qualities would you like to see more of in yourself as a researcher?
- What skills could you develop that would enable you to search the literature more effectively? What skills are you learning that you could apply to your present or future job?
- What would be helpful to develop within the next few weeks?
- How much time can you reasonably give to this goal?

Table 2.1 (continued)

Learning Goals Pre-Activity

- When you finish your graduate program, in what kind of positions or work environment do you see yourself?
- In your career, how important will the following skills be?
  - O Efficiently searching scholarly literature
  - O Critically evaluating sources for credibility and reliability
  - O Organizing, annotating, and synthesizing sources
- Tell me about your previous experiences searching the literature, writing literature reviews, or organizing and synthesizing several sources. What has been a struggle in the past? What has come easily for you in the past?

Given your prior experiences and future aspirations, what are 2 or 3 learning goals you would like to set for yourself to improve your literature review strategies and processes?

Example Learning Goal

Goal:		
Try several search strategies to improve targeted searching. I want to spend less time sorting through results and re-doing searches I've already done.		
Specific Strategy or Task	**Estimated Time to Complete**	**Date to Complete**
• Try using AND to narrow searches	10 mins	Jan. 28
• Create search log to track search strings and results	10 mins	Feb. 1
• Choose subject headings to use in addition to keywords in the databases	20 mins	Feb. 10
• Meet with librarian for feedback on search strings	30 mins	Feb. 15
What makes me care about this goal? I know that improving search efficiency and tracking will make me feel less stressed. I sometimes have to continue my searches several days apart and often feel like I'm repeating the same work. I think I would avoid searching and procrastinating less if I had better strategies for approaching searches.		

- Set between one and three goals
  - O List your first goal, followed by specific strategies, actions, or tasks that you could do to grow towards this goal. Think about a few tasks that could each fit within an hour or less

Goal:		
Specific Strategy or Task	**Estimated Time to Complete**	**Date to Complete**
What makes me care about this goal?		

Goal:		
Specific Strategy or Task	**Estimated Time to Complete**	**Date to Complete**
What makes me care about this goal?		

Goal:		
Specific Strategy or Task	**Estimated Time to Complete**	**Date to Complete**
What makes me care about this goal?		

- Is there anything else you'd like to share or feel that the librarian should know?

Table 2.1 (continued)

Mid-Semester Check-In

- Please describe your topic and scope of your project.
- What progress have you made so far?
- Revisiting the learning goals you set for yourself, what should your next steps be?
  - ○ What are specific strategies, actions, or tasks that you could do within an hour to grow towards these goals?
- What help do you need?

Learning Goals Post-Activity

- Think about your previous experiences searching the literature, writing literature reviews, or organizing and synthesizing several sources after the research workshops. What has changed about your approach, if anything, since completing the three research workshops?
- When organizing, annotating, and synthesizing your literature, what processes have you decided to change, if any?
- Thinking back on your experiences and strengths and thinking ahead to how you plan to use these types of research skills in the future, please briefly reflect on the 2 to 3 learning goals you set for yourself to focus on during this semester.
- Is there anything else you feel the librarian should know?

Students completed a pre-activity designed to help them generate their own learning goals and a post-activity that asked them to reflect on their learning goals. After the pre-assignment, I visited the class for three short research workshops throughout the semester, with the content of the workshops described in the Appendix 2A. I sent students a short list of questions as a mid-semester check-in after the second workshop. Personalized follow-up emails were sent to students after the third session to address individual questions and learning goal strategies. A revised copy of the learning goals exercises is shown in table 2.1.

Reflections on goal setting

In a post-activity, students reflected on their learning goals. Qualitative data from the surveys were coded during two phases: a first phase of hand-coding using descriptive, in vivo, and values coding methods,[41] and a second phase of coding used focused and pattern-coding.[42] Several students recognized a need for goals with manageable, intermediate steps. For example, one student said, "I don't think I set specific enough goals, so they weren't that helpful to me. I should work on writing more specific actionable goals" (participant 1). Two students reported having forgotten about their goals from the start of the semester (participants 2 and 5) and indicated in discussion that more frequent email or in-person follow-up from the librarian with specific strategy suggestions related to their goals would be helpful in the future. Others indicated they found the goal-setting experience helpful: "It was useful as a reflective tool," and one student noted "especially when [the librarian] checked in about them [the goals] and offered suggestions" (participants 2 and 4). Another student stated that her initial goals of efficiency and streamlining "will come with time possibly. Or they will not come at all and these are simply not efficient processes" (participant 5), referencing an in-class discussion of linear and nonlinear aspects of the research process.

Table 2.2 details students' metacognitive and affective perceptions of using learning goals as well as their changes to searching behavior from the post-activity. Students indicated they needed time and practice to continue working on their goals. One student confirmed the importance of finding a process that "works for me and still allows me to play the academic game" (participant 5). Another student realized their former approach of employing broad keywords often resulted in a glut of results and, ultimately, "too many articles that stay unread" (participant 2). Another student similarly recognized a need to focus on a few articles initially and then fill in the gaps, saying "[t]he alternative, that I am trying to avoid, is to follow the research in an interesting direction that is not actually productive" (participant 1). One student realized they had strong reactions against aspects of research and writing that felt dehumanizing, stating, "I don't think this process can be done well void of connection with other people …also the structure of academic writing is frustrating to me. It feels cold and inauthentic making the process horrible" (participant 5). As these quotes illustrate, when students reflect on these processes they are better able to put supports in place for themselves. Participant 5, for example, could consider research collaborations, rather than solo authorship, to honor her need for connection and collaboration.

Table 2.2. Post-Activity Metacognitive and Behavior Themes

Overarching Theme	Subcomponents
1. Metacognitive and affective awareness	• Recognizing progress may take time • Customizing research processes and workflows • Improving scope and avoiding overly broad searches • Recognizing parts of the research process as nonlinear • Conflicting emotions about academic writing • Valuing human network as part of the research process
2. Changes to behavior	• Recognizing strategies to refine searching • Increased knowledge of search operators • Considering switching citation managers

Students had similar comments about changes to their searching behavior becoming more focused after discussing strategies to refine searching, such as, "It has helped me to be more targeted rather than just putting my keywords into Google Scholar and scrolling through what comes up" (participant 2). Other students valued learning advanced strategies with search operators that they felt helped them with "utilizing the power of the database" (participant 1). Finally, after in-class discussions of pros and cons of citation managers, one student reported "thinking strongly about switching to Zotero" (participant 4) to better meet their needs. Students' comments and coded themes suggest the process of setting and reflecting on learning goals contributed to students' metacognitive and affective awareness of the research process. Students recognized where they might want to change strategies in the future, valued finding processes that work for them, and recognized the role of their emotions during the literature review project.

Discussion and Recommendations

This chapter explores learning goals as a motivational tool for library instruction. I conducted a small exploratory study with early career PhD students; the students set learning goals to strengthen their abilities to conduct research, annotate, and write a literature review. Qualitative responses show student awareness of growth in their research skills and that students valued the opportunity to improve. While not generalizable, the study suggests that learning goals can support student motivation through tracking growth and encouraging reflection. The exploratory study aligns with the existing literature on the benefits of goal setting and the use of learning goals.

Librarians may encounter limitations in trying to design instruction for students whose learning goals are vastly different. During the second workshop, I attempted a "choose your own adventure" structure so that students could work on areas of greatest interest or need related to their learning goals. In retrospect, more structure for the second workshop combined with one-on-one consultations with each student would have been more effective to address their individual needs and concerns. Ultimately, providing a range of resources for exploration outside of class time can be helpful when the needs and learning goals differ widely, as can individual email follow up or consultations with the students.

Seven Practices for Teaching Goal Setting with Graduate Students

How can we guide graduate students to create effective, motivating learning goals? The seven recommendations are intended to assist librarians' reflection and planning when using learning goals during instruction. While these recommendations were written with graduate students in mind, they lend themselves to adaptation for adult students or a general student population as well.

　1. **Discuss learning versus performance goals.** An emphasis on learning goals and an in-class discussion about the differences between learning and performance goals may help relieve anxiety and produce more productive goal setting and reflection.[43] Student comments in this exploratory study indicated that students valued thoroughness and completeness in searching; they were also deeply committed to social justice work, helping others, and understanding and contributing to the field. They wanted to perform well in their research and writing. In fact, affective analysis of qualitative comments suggests issues of perfectionism and lack of confidence may be paralyzing or limiting for some students who want to perform well. Onwuqgbuzie and Jiao identified both of these issues within their "Anxiety-Expectation Mediation model of library anxiety," a predictive model that was able to show the relationship between library anxiety and graduate students' performance on a written research proposal that required extensive library research.[44] To alleviate and mitigate these concerns, librarians could have a discussion with students about scholarly expectations in the field and their graduate student journey toward becoming professional scholars. This activity could help identify areas for students to focus on in improving their research abilities as well as validate students' prior educational and professional experiences, as Keller suggests in his work on motivation for adult learners.[45] Reframing prior notions of goal setting can also be a helpful way to refocus students toward a mastery frame where importance is placed on "practice, feedback, and errors are emphasized as learning opportunities."[46]

　2. **Break goals into specific, actionable pieces.** From thirty interviews with a range of graduate students who had left their program, successfully completed their program, or were current students in a program, Collins found "specific, documented goals, measurable goals, challenging goals, and goal assessment" to be impactful in students' perceptions of their persistence or lack of persistence in their graduate programs.[47] Librarians can guide graduate students toward focused, specific goals by helping them identify a super-ordinate goal, then engage in task analysis to break a large or vague goal such as "improve searching efficiency" into smaller component parts that could be tied to specific goals.[48] Reflections on what students perceived as strengths and struggles in the pre-activity showed differences in their metacognitive awareness. Some students initially had very clear, specific ideas of what they would like to work on, compared with others who wrote more generic goals. By the post-activity, students recognized the need for more specific, actionable goals. This finding is borne out in the literature through Latham's work on superordinate goals versus action step goals,[49] where super-

ordinate goals are big picture, such as "better note taking and record keep-ing," and action steps might be "use a synthesis matrix to record notes for the next week." Popular works and game-design literature on micro goals, mini goals, or daily goals also support this technique.[50]

3. **Show examples of goals.** In coaching students toward writing SMART goals, Dembo and Seli offer sample goals, giving a generic or overly broad version as a "poor" example and a "better" example that more closely fol-lows the SMART acronym.[51] These examples of goals are intended to help students write their own goal statements more effectively. Research with edu-cation graduate students also indicates that having students practice identify-ing qualities of strong goals may be helpful before they set their own goals.[52] These researchers and others also noted that even as adults, some students were not able to accurately evaluate their own capabilities. Therefore, increas-ing practice in metacognitive awareness and self-reflection alongside goal set-ting is crucial.[53]

4. **Make sure the goals are important to students.** Research indicates that a person's "goal commitment" is crucial to whether they will follow through with action toward accomplishing the goal.[54] Thus, activities that ground goal setting in graduate students' own values, interests, and career as-pirations may help ensure goal commitment and persistence.[55] A dissertation study with STEM graduate students found that priming students to reflect on what they would like to accomplish academically and professionally and how having strong research skills will help get them there.[56] Consider asking a Likert question such as, "On a scale of 1 to 5, how much do you care about this goal?" or a more open-ended question such as, "Why do you care about this goal?" Additionally, discussing commitment as a group or in consultations could help ensure that students only commit to working toward goals they are genuinely invested in. Participating in a community of practice around their research goals is also thought to help increase goal commitment for graduate students.[57]

5. **Discuss expectations of efficiency.** Help students understand that parts of the research process are inherently nonlinear and rely on creativity and insight. Such processes may resist efficient workflows. Efficiency was a frequent concern for students during each aspect of the research process in the exploratory study: searching, organizing and annotating, and synthesiz-ing. While teaching students a linear and fast research process would be ideal, librarians recognize that so much of searching, organizing, and synthesizing isn't straightforward at all. The findings of Blumer, Watulak, and Kenton sup-port this idea; they noticed their graduate students struggled to feel confident that they had found all of the relevant research on their topics and frequently went back to find additional materials during the writing stage.[58] Further, compromised information processing and task-unrelated thoughts and be-

haviors are thought to be two of the negative impacts of library anxiety.[59] Awareness of the hallmarks of being overwhelmed can help adjust students' expectations, help them recognize the affective highs and lows of research, encourage help-seeking behavior, and hopefully keep students feeling engaged in their learning goals and the research process even when they encounter challenges. This is one of the primary benefits of shifting from a performance to a mastery mindset for research strategies.

6. **Model coping and elicit task strategies.** Help students recognize that for a major project, such as a literature review, they are building and framing their own mental models for their field and integrating large amounts of new information while constructing these schemas, all of which take time. This approach can help students feel self-compassion and encourage them to feel comfortable seeking help from the librarian, instructors, or peers. Research suggests that librarians can model research-related coping and task strategies for students, such as looking for patterns in search results to inform the next iteration of a search string. Modeling responses to a messy or unsuccessful search can help students recognize when they may want to switch strategies.[60] Dembo and Seli suggest that after students have identified goals, they ask themselves three questions to consider which strategies they might use towards attaining the goal: "How would other people achieve this goal? Who can help me achieve this goal? How have I achieved similar goals in the past?"[61] Listing strategies that answer these questions may prevent students from getting stuck when things don't go perfectly.

7. **Build relationships through feedback.** Learning goals can help extend instruction in meaningful ways. Working closely with a group of graduate students over the course of an entire semester may feel like a luxury for librarians who are accustomed to one-shot research workshops or student-initiated research consultations. Regardless of the session length, Booth advocates for extending instruction through pre-session activities and post-session follow-up, where time permits.[62] Even with a one-shot, a librarian could use a pre-session survey asking students to define their specific goals for the workshop and provide names and email addresses. These data could allow the librarian to follow-up with personalized recommendations, strategies, or links to additional sources.

Since discussion with students is seen as a critical component of goal setting, guidelines for goal-setting conversations can be helpful for librarians, such as Symonds and Tapps' Goal Discussion Checklist for teachers.[63] If time allows, goal setting in person or during one on one appointments can be ideal to create well-formed outcomes and help build long-term coaching relationships with graduate students.[64] Zimmerman and Moylan suggest using microanalytic questions—short open- or closed-ended questions that could be used for written feedback from students—can help stimulate self-regulation and motivational beliefs. For example, a short question could be used to help a student reflect on whether their current research strategies or processes are successful or unsuccessful.[65] For managing progress and making adjustments once goals have been set, feedback from librarians and instructors on student progress is extremely important, as is students' self-reflection on progress toward the goal.[66] Goal setting for research skills could be an ideal way to partner with teaching faculty, who can help support goal setting and feedback throughout the semester.

Conclusion

Experimenting with learning goals as a motivational tool can be a rich area of exploration and growth for librarians, teachers, and graduate students. More research and practical studies are needed to show how best to coach adult students in crafting their own learning goals related to library research. Yet, the existing body of literature on goal setting suggests that benefits include greater engagement, persistence, and metacognitive awareness, qualities that align well with our profession's current focus on metaliteracy, metacognition, and threshold concepts. While not generalizable, the current exploratory study suggests goal setting may engage with students' lived experiences and future aspirations, increase their perceived relevance of information literacy through self-set goals, and build confidence in new skills and ways of thinking by encouraging a mastery instead of a performance mindset.

Appendix 2A. Contents of Three Research Workshops

First Workshop: Efficient Searching

30 minutes

- Search operators
- Subject headings in ERIC database
- Keyword matrix to organize search concepts
- Takeaway: Commit to spend 10 minutes this week exploring Subject Headings related to your literature review topic

Second Workshop: Analysis & Insight

1 hour

- Kuhlthau's Information Search Process
- Choose Your Own Adventure in small groups: "analysis" (such as search logs, synthesis matrices, and productivity tools) or "insight" (such as concept mapping and citation maps)
- Group discussion
- Takeaway: What one tool or strategy might you try in the next week? What would be most helpful as your next step?

Third Workshop: Synthesis

1 hour

- Common literature review problems
- Writing examples of literature review synthesis
- Discussion of students' research process and learning goals
- Takeaway: Individualized advice sent via email

Endnotes

1. Paulo Freire, *Pedagogy of the Oppressed* (New York: Bloomsbury Academic, 2000).
2. John M. Keller, "Development and Use of the ARCS Model of Instructional Design," *Journal of Instructional Development* 10, no. 3 (September 1987): 2–10, doi:10.1007/BF02905780.
3. Rachel E. Cannady, Stephanie B. King, and Jack G. Blendinger, "Proactive Outreach to Adult Students: A Department and Library Collaborative Effort," *The Reference Librarian* 53, no. 2 (April 2012): 164–65, doi:10.1080/02763877.2011.608603.
4. Cannady, King, and Blendinger, 164.
5. Cannady, King, and Blendinger, "Proactive Outreach to Adult Students"; Malcolm S. Knowles, Elwood F. Holton III, and Richard A. Swanson, *The Adult Learner: The Definitive Classic in Adult Education and Human Resource Development* (Houston, TX: Gulf Publishing Company, 1998).
6. Barbara Blummer, Sara Lohnes Watulak, and Jeffrey Kenton, "The Research Experience for Education Graduate Students: A Phenomenographic Study," *Internet*

Reference Services Quarterly 17, no. 3–4 (2012): 117–46, doi:10.1080/10875301.2012.747462.

7. Blummer, Watulak, and Kenton, 130.

8. Blummer, Watulak, and Kenton, 132.

9. Blummer, Watulak, and Kenton, 134.

10. Anthony J. Onwuegbuzie and Qun G. Jiao, "Information Search Performance and Research Achievement: An Empirical Test of the Anxiety-Expectation Mediation Model of Library Anxiety," *Journal of the American Society for Information Science and Technology* 55, no. 1 (2004): 41–54, doi:10.1002/asi.10342.

11. John M. Keller, *Motivational Design for Learning and Performance: The ARCS Model Approach* (New York: Springer, 2010), 126, doi:10.1007/978-1-4419-1250-3.

12. Jacquelynne S. Eccles and Allan Wigfield, "Motivational Beliefs, Values, and Goals," *Annual Review of Psychology* 53, no. 1 (February 2002): 109–32, doi:10.1146/annurev.psych.53.100901.135153; Edwin A. Locke and Gary P. Latham, "Building a Practically Useful Theory of Goal Setting and Task Motivation: A 35-Year Odyssey," *The American Psychologist* 57, no. 9 (2002): 705–17, doi:10.1037/0003-066X.57.9.705.

13. Andrew K. Macleod, Emma Coates, and Jacquie Hetherton, "Increasing Well-Being through Teaching Goal-Setting and Planning Skills: Results of a Brief Intervention," *Journal of Happiness Studies* 9 (2008): 185–96, doi:10.1007/s10902-007-9057-2; Gary P. Latham, "Goal Setting: A Five-Step Approach to Behavior Change," *Organizational Dynamics* 32, no. 3 (2003): 311, doi:10.1016/S0090-2616(03)00028-7; Locke and Latham, "Building a Practically Useful Theory of Goal Setting and Task Motivation: A 35-Year Odyssey."

14. Locke and Latham, 707.

15. Lisa D. Ordóñez et al., "Goals Gone Wild: The Systematic Side Effects of Overprescribing Goal Setting," *Academy of Management Perspectives* 23, no. 1 (February 2009): 6–16, doi:10.5465/AMP.2009.37007999.

16. Carol S. Dweck, "Motivational Processes Affecting Learning," *American Psychologist* 41, no. 10 (1986): 1040–48, doi:10.1037/0003-066X.41.10.1040; Elaine S. Elliott and Carol S. Dweck, "Goals: An Approach to Motivation and Achievement.," *Journal of Personality and Social Psychology* 54, no. 1 (1988): 5–12, doi:10.1037/0022-3514.54.1.5; G. P. Latham and G. H. Seijts, "Distinguished Scholar Invited Essay: Similarities and Differences Among Performance, Behavioral, and Learning Goals," *Journal of Leadership & Organizational Studies* 23, no. 3 (August 1, 2016): 227, doi:10.1177/1548051816641874.

17. Dweck, "Motivational Processes Affecting Learning," 1042.

18. Dale H. Schunk, Paul R. Pintrich, and Judith L. Meece, *Motivation in Education: Theory, Research, and Applications*, 3rd ed. (Upper Saddle River, NJ: Pearson/Merrill Prentice Hall, 2008), 190.

19. Carol S. Dweck and Ellen L. Leggett, "A Social-Cognitive Approach to Motivation and Personality," *Psychological Review* 95, no. 2 (1988): 256–73, doi:10.1037/0033-295X.95.2.256.

20. Dweck and Leggett, 259.

21. Ordóñez et al., "Goals Gone Wild: The Systematic Side Effects of Overprescribing Goal Setting," 10–11.

22. Walter Dick and Lou Carey, *The Systematic Design of Instruction* (Glenview, IL:

Scott, Foresman and Company, 1985), 15; Robert M. Gagne and M. David Merrill, "Integrative Goals for Instructional Design," *Educational Technology Research and Development* 38, no. 1 (1990): 23.

23. Dick and Carey, *The Systematic Design of Instruction*, 15.

24. Latham and Seijts, "Distinguished Scholar Invited Essay: Similarities and Differences Among Performance, Behavioral, and Learning Goals," 227.

25. Gerard H. Seijts, Gary P. Latham, and Meredith Woodwark, "Learning Goals: A Qualitative and Quantitative Review," in *New Developments in Goal Setting and Task Performance* (New York: Routledge, 2013), 207.

26. Mark Sudlow Hoyert and Cynthia D. O'Dell, "Goal Orientation and Academic Failure in Traditional Aged and Nontraditional Aged College Students," *College Student Journal* 43, no. 4 (2009): 1052–62.

27. Dale H. Schunk, "Goal Setting and Self-Efficacy during Self-Regulated Learning," *Educational Psychologist* 25, no. 1 (1990): 74.

28. Edward L. Deci and Richard M. Ryan, *Intrinsic Motivation and Self-Determination in Human Behavior* (New York: Springer Science, 1985), 218–19, doi:10.1017/CBO9781107415324.004; Latham and Seijts, "Distinguished Scholar Invited Essay," 225.

29. Deci and Ryan, 225–26.

30. Latham and Seijts, "Distinguished Scholar Invited Essay."

31. Lori Townsend, Korey Brunetti, and Amy R. Hofer, "Threshold Concepts and Information Literacy," *portal: Libraries and the Academy* 11, no. 3 (2011): 854, doi:10.1353/pla.2011.0030.

32. George Manderlink and Judith M. Harackiewicz, "Proximal versus Distal Goal Setting and Intrinsic Motivation," *Journal of Personality and Social Psychology* 47, no. 4 (1984): 918–28, doi:10.1037/0022-3514.47.4.918.

33. Locke and Latham, "Building a Practically Useful Theory of Goal Setting and Task Motivation," 708; Latham and Seijts, "Distinguished Scholar Invited Essay," 226.

34. Gerard H. Seijts and Gary P. Latham, "The Effect of Commitment to a Learning Goal, Self-Efficacy, and the Interaction Between Learning Goal Difficulty and Commitment on Performance in a Business Simulation," *Human Performance* 24, no. 3 (July 2011): 189–204, doi:10.1080/08959285.2011.580807; Latham and Seijts, "Distinguished Scholar Invited Essay."

35. Maurice J. Elias, "SMART Goal Setting With Your Students," *Edutopia*, 2014, https://www.edutopia.org/blog/smart-goal-setting-with-students-maurice-elias; Hyrum W. Smith, *The 10 Natural Laws of Successful Time and Life Management : Proven Strategies for Increased Productivity and Inner Peace* (New York: Warner Books, 1994); W. Timothy Gallwey and Robert Bull, *The Inner Game of Work: Focus, Learning, Pleasure, and Mobility in the Workplace* (New York: Random House, 2001); George T. Doran, "There's a SMART Way to Write Management's Goals and Objectives," *Management Review* 70, no. 11 (1981): 35–36.

36. Latham and Seijts, "Distinguished Scholar Invited Essay," 226.

37. Doran, "There's a SMART Way to Write Management's Goals and Objectives," 35–36; Trevor Day and Paul Tosey, "Beyond SMART? A New Framework for Goal Setting," *Curriculum Journal* 22, no. 4 (2011): 515–34, doi:10.1080/09585176.2011.627213; Robert S. Rubin, "Will the Real SMART Goals Please Stand Up?," *The Industrial-Organizational Psychologist* 39, no. 4 (2002): 26–27.

38. Julia Bowman et al., "The Development, Content Validity and Inter-Rater Reliability of the SMART-Goal Evaluation Method: A Standardised Method for Evaluating Clinical Goals," *Australian Occupational Therapy Journal* 62, no. 6 (December 2015): 422, doi:10.1111/1440-1630.12218; Elisabeth Marsland and Julia Bowman, "An Interactive Education Session and Follow-up Support as a Strategy to Improve Clinicians' Goal-Writing Skills: A Randomized Controlled Trial," *Journal of Evaluation in Clinical Practice* 16, no. 1 (February 2010): 3–13, doi:10.1111/j.1365-2753.2008.01104.x; Samantha P. Clarke et al., "Do Goal-Setting Interventions Improve the Quality of Goals in Mental Health Services?," *Psychiatric Rehabilitation Journal* 32, no. 4 (2009): 292–99, doi:10.2975/32.4.2009.292.299.

39. Day and Tosey, "Beyond SMART? A New Framework for Goal Setting."

40. Gallwey and Bull, *The Inner Game of Work.*

41. Johnny Saldaña, *The Coding Manual for Qualitative Researchers*, 3rd ed. (Los Angeles: SAGE Publications, 2016).

42. Saldaña, 236–44.

43. Locke and Latham, "Building a Practically Useful Theory of Goal Setting and Task Motivation."

44. Onwuegbuzie and Jiao, "Information Search Performance," 45.

45. Keller, *Motivational Design*, 49.

46. Latham and Seijts, "Distinguished Scholar Invited Essay," 228.

47. Robert Collins, Jill Coddington, and Dorothy Williams, "Do Graduate Students Who Set Formal Goals Really Graduate at Higher Rates?," in *Building a Sustainable Future for Adult Learners* (Charlotte, NC: Information Age Publishing, 2015), 62.

48. Barry J. Zimmerman and Adam R. Moylan, "Self Regulation: Where Metacognition and Motivation Intersect," in *Handbook of Metacognition in Education*, ed. Douglas J. Hacker, John Dunlosky, and Arthur C. Graesser (New York: Routledge, 2009), 301.

49. Latham, "Goal Setting: A Five-Step Approach to Behavior Change."

50. David P. Campbell, *If You Don't Know Where You're Going, You'll Probably End up Somewhere Else: Finding a Career and Getting a Life* (Sorin Books, 2007), 36; Smith, *The 10 Natural Laws of Successful Time and Life Management*; Taj Campbell, Brian Ngo, and James Fogarty, "Game Design Principles in Everyday Fitness Applications," in *Proceedings of the 2008 ACM Conference on Computer Supported Cooperative Work* (San Diego, CA: ACM, 2008).

51. Myron H. Dembo and Helena Seli, *Motivation and Learning Strategies for College Success*, 5th ed. (New York: Routledge, 2016), 109.

52. Linda S. Schwartz and Margaret E. Gredler, "The Effects of Self-Instructional Materials on Goal Setting and Self-Efficacy," *Journal of Research and Development in Education* 31, no. 2 (1998): 83–89.

53. Schwartz and Gredler, "The Effects of Self-Instructional Materials on Goal Setting and Self-Efficacy"; D. Scott Ridley et al., "Setting Self-Regulated Learning: The Interactive Influence of Metacognitive Awareness and Goal-Setting," *The Journal of Experimental Education* 60, no. 4 (1992): 293–306; Linda S. Garavalia and Margaret E. Gredler, "An Exploratory Study of Academic Goal Setting, Achievement Calibration and Self-Regulated Learning," *Journal of Instructional Psychology* 29, no. 4 (2002): 221–30.

54. Zimmerman and Moylan, "Self Regulation," 301; Latham, "Goal Setting."

55. Smith, *The 10 Natural Laws of Successful Time and Life Management*; Seijts and Latham, "The Effect of Commitment to a Learning Goal," 200.
56. Melissa Hurst, "An Exploratory Study of Goal Commitment among Graduate Students in Science, Technology, Engineering, and Mathematics Fields" (University of South Carolina, 2010), 95–96.
57. Hurst., 96.
58. Blummer, Watulak, and Kenton, "The Research Experience for Education Graduate Students," 138.
59. Onwuegbuzie and Jiao, "Information Search Performance," 50–51.
60. Dale H. Schunk, "Self-Efficacy for Reading and Writing: Influence of Modeling, Goal Setting, and Self-Evaluation," *Reading & Writing Quarterly* 19, no. 2 (2010): 169, doi:10.1080/10573560308219; Locke and Latham, "Building a Practically Useful Theory of Goal Setting," 708.
61. Dembo and Seli, *Motivation and Learning Strategies*, 111.
62. Char Booth, *Reflective Teaching Effective Learning* (Chicago, IL: American Library Association, 2011).
63. Matthew L. Symonds and Tyler Tapps, "Goal Prioritization for Teachers, Coaches and Students: A Developmental Model," *Strategies* 29, no. 3 (2016): 36.
64. Day and Tosey, "Beyond SMART?."
65. Zimmerman and Moylan, "Self Regulation," 305.
66. Schunk, "Self-Efficacy for Reading and Writing," 164–65.

Bibliography

Blummer, Barbara, Sara Lohnes Watulak, and Jeffrey Kenton. "The Research Experience for Education Graduate Students: A Phenomenographic Study." *Internet Reference Services Quarterly* 17, no. 3–4 (2012): 117–46. doi:10.1080/10875301.2012.747462.
Booth, Char. *Reflective Teaching Effective Learning*. Chicago, IL: American Library Association, 2011.
Bowman, Julia, Lise Mogensen, Elisabeth Marsland, and Natasha Lannin. "The Development, Content Validity and Inter-Rater Reliability of the SMART-Goal Evaluation Method: A Standardised Method for Evaluating Clinical Goals." *Australian Occupational Therapy Journal* 62, no. 6 (December 2015): 420–27. doi:10.1111/1440-1630.12218.
Campbell, David P. *If You Don't Know Where You're Going, You'll Probably End Up Somewhere Else: Finding a Career and Getting a Life*. Sorin Books, 2007.
Campbell, Taj, Brian Ngo, and James Fogarty. "Game Design Principles in Everyday Fitness Applications." In *Proceedings of the 2008 ACM Conference on Computer Supported Cooperative Work*. San Diego, CA: ACM, 2008.
Cannady, Rachel E., Stephanie B. King, and Jack G. Blendinger. "Proactive Outreach to Adult Students: A Department and Library Collaborative Effort." *The Reference Librarian* 53, no. 2 (April 2012): 156–69. doi:10.1080/02763877.2011.608603.
Clarke, Samantha P., Trevor P. Crowe, Lindsay G. Oades, and Frank P. Deane. "Do Goal-Setting Interventions Improve the Quality of Goals in Mental Health Services?" *Psychiatric Rehabilitation Journal* 32, no. 4 (2009): 292–99. doi:10.2975/32.4.2009.292.299.
Collins, Robert, Jill Coddington, and Dorothy Williams. "Do Graduate Students Who

Set Formal Goals Really Graduate at Higher Rates?" In *Building a Sustainable Future for Adult Learners*, 51–64. Charlotte, NC: Information Age Publishing, 2015.

Day, Trevor, and Paul Tosey. "Beyond SMART? A New Framework for Goal Setting." *Curriculum Journal* 22, no. 4 (2011): 515–34. doi:10.1080/09585176.2011.627213.

Deci, Edward L., and Richard M. Ryan. *Intrinsic Motivation and Self-Determination in Human Behavior*. New York: Springer Science, 1985. doi:10.1017/CBO9781107415324.004.

Dembo, Myron H., and Helena Seli. *Motivation and Learning Strategies for College Success*. 5th ed. New York: Routledge, 2016.

Dick, Walter, and Lou Carey. *The Systematic Design of Instruction*. Glenview, IL: Scott, Foresman and Company, 1985.

Doran, George T. "There's a SMART Way to Write Management's Goals and Objectives." *Management Review* 70, no. 11 (1981): 35–36.

Dweck, Carol S. "Motivational Processes Affecting Learning." *American Psychologist* 41, no. 10 (1986): 1040–48. doi:10.1037/0003-066X.41.10.1040.

Dweck, Carol S., and Ellen L. Leggett. "A Social-Cognitive Approach to Motivation and Personality." *Psychological Review* 95, no. 2 (1988): 256–73. doi:10.1037/0033-295X.95.2.256.

Eccles, Jacquelynne S., and Allan Wigfield. "Motivational Beliefs, Values, and Goals." *Annual Review of Psychology* 53, no. 1 (February 2002): 109–32. doi:10.1146/annurev.psych.53.100901.135153.

Elias, Maurice J. "SMART Goal Setting With Your Students." *Edutopia*, 2014. https://www.edutopia.org/blog/smart-goal-setting-with-students-maurice-elias.

Elliott, Elaine S., and Carol S. Dweck. "Goals: An Approach to Motivation and Achievement." *Journal of Personality and Social Psychology* 54, no. 1 (1988): 5–12. doi:10.1037/0022-3514.54.1.5.

Freire, Paulo. *Pedagogy of the Oppressed*. New York: Bloomsbury Academic, 2000.

Gagne, Robert M., and M. David Merrill. "Integrative Goals for Instructional Design." *Educational Technology Research and Development* 38, no. 1 (1990): 23–30.

Gallwey, W. Timothy, and Robert Bull. *The Inner Game of Work: Focus, Learning, Pleasure, and Mobility in the Workplace*. New York: Random House, 2001.

Garavalia, Linda S., and Margaret E. Gredler. "An Exploratory Study of Academic Goal Setting, Achievement Calibration and Self-Regulated Learning." *Journal of Instructional Psychology* 29, no. 4 (2002): 221–30.

Hoyert, Mark Sudlow, and Cynthia D. O'Dell. "Goal Orientation and Academic Failure in Traditional Aged and Nontraditional Aged College Students." *College Student Journal* 43, no. 4 (2009): 1052–62.

Hurst, Melissa. "An Exploratory Study of Goal Commitment among Graduate Students in Science, Technology, Engineering, and Mathematics Fields." University of South Carolina, 2010.

Keller, John M. "Development and Use of the ARCS Model of Instructional Design." *Journal of Instructional Development* 10, no. 3 (September 1987): 2–10. doi:10.1007/BF02905780.

———. *Motivational Design for Learning and Performance: The ARCS Model Approach*. New York: Springer, 2010. doi:10.1007/978-1-4419-1250-3.

Knowles, Malcolm S., Elwood F. Holton III, and Richard A. Swanson. *The Adult Learner: The Definitive Classic in Adult Education and Human Resource Development*.

Houston, TX: Gulf Publishing Company, 1998.

Latham, G. P., and G. H. Seijts. "Distinguished Scholar Invited Essay: Similarities and Differences Among Performance, Behavioral, and Learning Goals." *Journal of Leadership & Organizational Studies* 23, no. 3 (August 1, 2016): 225–33. doi:10.1177/1548051816641874.

Latham, Gary P. "Goal Setting: A Five-Step Approach to Behavior Change." *Organizational Dynamics* 32, no. 3 (2003): 309–18. doi:10.1016/S0090-2616(03)00028-7.

Locke, Edwin A., and Gary P. Latham. "Building a Practically Useful Theory of Goal Setting and Task Motivation: A 35-Year Odyssey." *The American Psychologist* 57, no. 9 (2002): 705–17. doi:10.1037/0003-066X.57.9.705.

Macleod, Andrew K., Emma Coates, and Jacquie Hetherton. "Increasing Well-Being through Teaching Goal-Setting and Planning Skills: Results of a Brief Intervention." *Journal of Happiness Studies* 9 (2008): 185–96. doi:10.1007/s10902-007-9057-2.

Manderlink, George, and Judith M. Harackiewicz. "Proximal versus Distal Goal Setting and Intrinsic Motivation." *Journal of Personality and Social Psychology* 47, no. 4 (1984): 918–28. doi:10.1037/0022-3514.47.4.918.

Marsland, Elisabeth, and Julia Bowman. "An Interactive Education Session and Follow-up Support as a Strategy to Improve Clinicians' Goal-Writing Skills: A Randomized Controlled Trial." *Journal of Evaluation in Clinical Practice* 16, no. 1 (February 2010): 3–13. doi:10.1111/j.1365-2753.2008.01104.x.

Onwuegbuzie, Anthony J., and Qun G. Jiao. "Information Search Performance and Research Achievement: An Empirical Test of the Anxiety-Expectation Mediation Model of Library Anxiety." *Journal of the American Society for Information Science and Technology* 55, no. 1 (2004): 41–54. doi:10.1002/asi.10342.

Ordóñez, Lisa D., Maurice E. Schweitzer, Adam D. Galinsky, and Max H. Bazerman. "Goals Gone Wild: The Systematic Side Effects of Overprescribing Goal Setting." *Academy of Management Perspectives* 23, no. 1 (February 2009): 6–16. doi:10.5465/AMP.2009.37007999.

Ridley, D. Scott, Paul A. Schutz, Robert S. Glanz, and Claire E. Weinstein. "Setting Self-Regulated Learning: The Interactive Influence of Metacognitive Awareness and Goal-Setting." *The Journal of Experimental Education* 60, no. 4 (1992): 293–306.

Rubin, Robert S. "Will the Real SMART Goals Please Stand Up?" *The Industrial-Organizational Psychologist* 39, no. 4 (2002): 26–27.

Saldaña, Johnny. *The Coding Manual for Qualitative Researchers.* 3rd ed. Los Angeles: SAGE Publications, 2016.

Schunk, Dale H. "Goal Setting and Self-Efficacy during Self-Regulated Learning." *Educational Psychologist* 25, no. 1 (1990): 71–86.

———. "Self-Efficacy for Reading and Writing: Influence of Modeling, Goal Setting, and Self-Evaluation." *Reading & Writing Quarterly* 19, no. 2 (2010): 159–72. doi:10.1080/10573560308219.

Schunk, Dale H., Paul R. Pintrich, and Judith L. Meece. *Motivation in Education: Theory, Research, and Applications.* 3rd ed. Upper Saddle River, NJ: Pearson/Merrill Prentice Hall, 2008.

Schwartz, Linda S., and Margaret E. Gredler. "The Effects of Self-Instructional Materials on Goal Setting and Self-Efficacy." *Journal of Research and Development in Education* 31, no. 2 (1998): 83–89.

Seijts, Gerard H., and Gary P. Latham. "The Effect of Commitment to a Learning Goal, Self-Efficacy, and the Interaction Between Learning Goal Difficulty and Commitment on Performance in a Business Simulation." *Human Performance* 24, no. 3 (July 2011): 189–204. doi:10.1080/08959285.2011.580807.

Seijts, Gerard H., Gary P. Latham, and Meredith Woodwark. "Learning Goals: A Qualitative and Quantitative Review." In *New Developments in Goal Setting and Task Performance*, 195–212. New York: Routledge, 2013.

Smith, Hyrum W. *The 10 Natural Laws of Successful Time and Life Management: Proven Strategies for Increased Productivity and Inner Peace.* New York: Warner Books, 1994.

Symonds, Matthew L., and Tyler Tapps. "Goal Prioritization for Teachers, Coaches and Students: A Developmental Model." *Strategies* 29, no. 3 (2016): 34–38.

Townsend, Lori, Korey Brunetti, and Amy R. Hofer. "Threshold Concepts and Information Literacy." *Portal: Libraries and the Academy* 11, no. 3 (2011): 853–69. doi:10.1353/pla.2011.0030.

Zimmerman, Barry J., and Adam R. Moylan. "Self Regulation: Where Metacognition and Motivation Intersect." In *Handbook of Metacognition in Education*, edited by Douglas J. Hacker, John Dunlosky, and Arthur C. Graesser, 299–315. New York: Routledge, 2009.

CHAPTER 3

"When Will I Ever Use This Again?"

Cultivating Motivation Through an Authentic Learning Environment

Chapel D. Cowden and Jenny Holcombe

Many library instruction programs encourage professors to schedule instruction close to the point of need so that instructional content can focus on the looming assignment. If the professor executes perfect timing, a certain level of external motivation may be created for the student during library instruction that is primarily geared toward succeeding at this assignment. The motivation is often fleeting, however, and the intended learning outcomes from the library instruction session are often obscured and unlikely to truly "take root" in a transformative way because students wonder, "When will I ever use this again?"

Library instruction approached from a different pedagogical perspective, however, has the potential to engender intrinsic motivation and create an environment where concepts and experiences become transformative. The ultimate goal of library instruction goes beyond a particular assignment or class and ends with a student capable of functionally navigating information sources to achieve better understanding of a topic. An authentic learning environment, where learning is situated in the "context of future use,"[1] creates the perfect conditions for engagement and critical thinking by demonstrating application of skills beyond the classroom. Immersing students in this carefully constructed environment actively involves them in the learning process, stimulates self-motivation, and prepares them not just for what's now but for what's next.

While the creation of authentic learning environments and their correlation to student engagement and motivation are well recorded in a wide variety of settings, they are not well represented in either the library literature or in the library instruction classroom. It is possible that librarians perceive the time investment is too steep and that a short (often an hour or less) one-shot class cannot be transformed into an authentic learning environment in a meaningful way. Given the shortage of literature on the subject, it is also likely that librarians are simply unaware of the many possibilities for creating such an environment.

Over the course of several semesters, the authors (a nursing research professor and a librarian) closely collaborated to take on these challenges and create a more authentic, forward-thinking learning environment for undergraduate, senior-level nursing students, with the goal to engage and motivate them to explore and address authentic problems using only tools available to them after they leave the university. Formerly, library instruction for these students followed the all-too-common path of database demos, medical subject headings, and advanced search tips. While these mechanical skills certainly have a place in library instruction, a lingering question remained: How do we create an environment, in a single library instruction session, where students are self-motivated and the purpose of the work and its connection to the nursing profession are clear?

This chapter addresses this question while exploring the pedagogical underpinnings and practical applications of authentic learning environments and their potential as a motivational tool in the library instruction classroom. Specifically, we detail the evolution of the aforementioned authentic learning environment created for senior-level nursing students, including practical planning strategies and teaching materials for reuse. The coauthors have seen the value of implementing an authentic learning environment and believe that librarians (and others) can utilize this approach in any discipline and see the same level of success.

The Roots of Student Motivation and the Need for Authenticity

Motivation, in the most basic sense, means "to be moved to do something; energized or activated toward an end."[2] More specifically, student motivation is focused on "the degree to which a student wants to learn" or is "energized" or "activated" toward learning in the classroom.[3] Student motivation is a key component of any classroom environment. Nurturing and promotion of student motivation are imperative to ensure that learning objectives are met. Students who are more motivated are also more engaged, which can lead to better learning outcomes.[4] Student motivation may be of particular interest in the university setting where the impact of student learning can be more directly linked to the subsequent professional work environment.

At this point, we find it necessary to differentiate between intrinsic and extrinsic motivation. When students engage in a learning activity because they want to participate in the activity, either because they enjoy the activity or understand the relevant value of the activity to their own current or future life, their engagement is said to be intrinsically motivated. Conversely, when students engage in learning activities simply because the activity is required of the course or they want to earn a good grade, their engagement is said to be extrinsically motivated.[5] Research has revealed positive relationships between motivation—particularly intrinsic motivation—and student engagement, interest, learning, achievement, and satisfaction.[6] As university students prepare to move from the classroom to the work environment, efforts should be made in the classroom to increase intrinsic motivation, especially as it applies to activities pertaining to potential problems encountered in the workplace/real-world setting. This is especially true in professional programs of study (i.e., nursing) where the development of expert thinking is essential to students' ability to solve novel problems.[7]

Self-determination theory (SDT) proposes three underlying components of intrinsic motivation: autonomy, relatedness, and competence.[8] When a student has a sense of control over an activity, has the opportunity for positive peer/professor interactions/collaboration, and can develop or demonstrate competence as a result of participation in an activity, motivation is enhanced.[9] Following this logic, intrinsic motivation would be more important to long-term learning and success since it should beget a higher level of sustained student engagement based on meaningful experiences.[10] The ability of an activity and/or instructor to influence one or more of these (SDT) components should serve to increase individual student intrinsic motivation, which should, in turn, enhance student engagement and learning. One such way for an instructor to influence these SDT components is through the development of an authentic learning environment.

Grounded in constructivist theory and student-centered learning, authentic learning environments are situated among a host of similar and related paradigms and processes—situated learning, authenticity, inquiry-based learning, problem or project-based learning, self-directed learning, etc. The natural origination point of some of these paradigms (problem- and project-based learning in particular) was the field of medicine. Nursing education is brimming with examples of authentic learning environments and problem-based learning scenarios in the form of simulation activities and student clinical placement. As a discipline, nursing (and other healthcare-related fields) understands the necessity of exposing students to situations that parallel those they will encounter post-graduation in a healthcare setting. These structured exposures in nursing education have been linked to higher levels of critical thinking, student satisfaction, problem-solving, self-directed learning, knowledge, confidence, and motivation.[11] The BSN Program at UTC is highly competitive, accepting approximately 20 percent of applicants as second-semester sophomores. The competitive nature of this program functions as a powerful self-motivator for students and fosters a greater desire for them to engage with and learn content that is more closely related to real-life situations. When presented with a problem in an authentic learning environment, student interest is likely to be elevated and motivation to engage with the content should be enhanced, both intrinsically (personally relevant curiosity, genuine interest) and extrinsically (desire to meet patient needs).

Motivation and motivational design are mainstays in the library instruction landscape as evidenced by comprehensive coverage in Jacobson and Xu's *Motivating Students in Information Literacy Classes*[12] as well as a wealth of academic journal articles dedicated to the subject. Related concepts such as problem-based learning, self-directed learning, etc. have also appeared to varying degrees in the library literature, but authentic learning environments and their cultivation in the library instruction classroom, especially as they relate to student-motivation, are sparse. Many articles have examined the role of authenticity in the virtual or physical library instruction classroom to varying degrees,[13] but few focus much attention upon the correlation between authentic learning and student motivation. While Klipfel tackles authenticity in library instruction for a freshman English class only so far as authentic topic selection, his work specifically explores the relationship between authenticity and motivation and concludes that authentic elements applied to library instruction can exert a positive impact on student motivation.[14]

Perhaps librarians already believe that the work done in the classroom is largely authentic. Shenton and Fitzgibbon assert, however, that information literacy instruction is most often comprised of isolated skills built into "exercise contexts" that have no bearing on authentic assignments or real-world situations.[15] This is problematic because it creates a vacuum in which skills are taught, used, and potentially dismissed/discarded as irrelevant beyond the scope of a particular assignment/class with no regard to future applicability. Consider that many of us provide relevant, perhaps even discipline-specific, searches in the classroom, but does this constitute authentic learning? Authenticity and the creation of a truly authentic learning environment cannot be achieved simply by shifting class examples in the direction of the discipline or assignment. True authenticity is achieved when students recognize and understand the connectivity between classroom instruction/activities and the future application of acquired skills.

Restructuring Library Instruction

As previously mentioned, the undergraduate nursing program at the University of Tennessee at Chattanooga (UTC) is a well-respected and rigorous program that only accepts approximately 20 percent of applicants each year based on stringent admissions criteria. Nursing Agency V: Research (NURS 4410) is a senior-level advanced research course taken in the penultimate semester prior to graduation. As described earlier, library instruction for these students traditionally followed the all-too-common path of database demos, medical subject headings, and advanced search tips. While a review of this instructional content may be necessary to some degree, much of it was previously covered in a sophomore-level nursing class, and avoiding repetition was important in the restructuring of the class.

Critical to the success of redesigning the information literacy components of NURS 4410 was a shared vision and close collaboration between the librarian and the disciplinary professor of record for the class. Collaborating with faculty is a necessary element of integrating a successful authentic learning environment and careful attention must be paid, by both parties, to establishing and nourishing the collaboration in order for a successful partnership to be realized. Disciplinary faculty are immersed in the culture and knowledge constructs of their disciplines, whereas librarians may not have advanced training or schooling in the content area required.[16] In addition, health science and science disciplines typically require very rigorous schedules that do not necessarily lend themselves to the integration of outside experts (such as librarians) when time is tight. With this in mind, a shared understanding of the requirements and subsequent impact of the information literacy intervention is crucial. Disciplinary faculty should understand the importance of sharing the information literacy instructional burden.[17] In this case, both the librarian and disciplinary professor recognized the need for a change and agreed to remain open to approaching the restructuring of the library components and providing instruction as a team.

Following several discussions between the co-authors, a shared philosophy emerged. We wished to create an environment in which (1) students would be intrinsically motivated, (2) classroom activities/actions would replicate "real-world" experiences, and (3) a clear connection to future practice (career) would be apparent. Obviously, a one-hour class would not suffice. In order to provide an authentic learning environment, 2.5 to 3 hours is desirable. Class content could also be frontloaded through applying a flipped design which requires students to engage with assigned pre-class materials. Additional elements, such as critical reflection, could be pushed to post-class discussion boards in the class online space.

We determined loose goals and time constraints and then constructed learning outcomes to serve as the pedagogical compass for the exploration. To fit with the aforementioned shared philosophies, we decided that the learning outcomes should reflect the elements of authenticity that we would be looking to build in the classroom environment while adhering to discipline and educational standards when possible. The ACRL Framework for Information Literacy, though not fully accepted at the time of our initial integration of this project, was useful in sparking more creative thinking about class elements and learning outcomes and allowed a certain freedom to exist. The frame Research as Inquiry was probably the most influential piece of the framework and led us to develop our overall class activity as a problem-based learning scenario.[18] Other frames, including Information Has Value and Authority is Constructed and Contextual, played a role as well but only in terms of creative thinking about the outcomes—not as strict directives. The finalized learning outcomes were:

Students will be able to

1. analyze sources for credibility and appropriateness for evidence-based medicine practice as it relates to the levels of evidence paradigm in order to make decisions based on the best level of evidence available at the time;

2. find effective pathways for locating quality information efficiently in order to ingrain behaviors necessary in the fast-paced medical environment;

3. utilize PubMed more effectively in order to research more comprehensively and be prepared for the future when subscription databases are no longer available; and

4. critically reflect upon the research process and its relationship to evidence-based medicine in order to translate skills and knowledge into new environments such as future projects and careers.

Constructing an Authentic Learning Environment

Following the construction of learning outcomes and the decision to create an authentic learning environment, the authors found it necessary to explore elements inherent in authentic learning environments and how those could be realized in the nursing class. Opinions, theories, and discussions abound regarding what makes an authentic learning environment,[19] but we found *Authentic Learning Environments* by Herrington, Reeves, and Oliver[20] particularly resonant. Herrington et al. provide a framework for an authentic learning environment that encompasses nine characteristics or elements (gleaned from their examination of many other models).[21] Specifically, their framework was proposed for technology-based learning environments but was built using a variety of models and, we believe, is applicable to most any environment, technology-based or not. It is worth noting that the class discussed in this chapter was a real-time, in-person class, but most of these elements have been applied in an online asynchronous graduate course as well.

In the following section, each of the nine characteristics is discussed as it relates to the authentic learning environment created for the nursing class. In addition, the motivational purpose of each element will be explored. Some elements were incorporated more fully than others and, as Herrington et al. note, these characteristics fall on a "spectrum" or "continuum" with implemented environments or tasks considered either more or less authentic.[22] These elements have a reasonable degree of overlap that is also evident in the explanation of the nursing class environment that follows. The elements are the following:

1. Authentic tasks

Herrington et al. call for "ill-defined tasks with real world relevance,"[23] also a hallmark of the problems utilized in problem-based learning. Problem-based learning surfaced early in class planning discussions and emerged as the best basis for an activity that would fit within our construction of the authentic learning environment. Ill-defined tasks are purposeful and represent realistic problems. Most problems that these students will face in professional practice will not be easy to solve and will often require some discussion or negotiation with doctors, patients, family caregivers, and administrators, potentially requiring them to seek further information prior to such conversations. In the problem-based activity in class, students negotiated ill-defined questions (or problems), assigned at the beginning of the activity, with their group members, determined an approach to the problem, and assigned individual roles in answering the problem. The problems were designed to mimic real-life questions the students might encounter in their current clinical placements and/or future employment as a nurse and were largely developed by the disciplinary faculty member who is, of course, immersed in the culture and knowledge of the discipline. Each group, consisting of approximately five members, was assigned a different problem. Group membership was determined by self-selection at the beginning of the semester for work throughout the course, culminating in a group research proposal and presentation on a topic of their choosing. An example of one of the problems: "Pain control is a major issue in a pediatric oncology unit. Physiological measures are currently used as indicators of pain. Are there other evidence-based ways to assess pain in children?" This problem is broad and unwieldy and would naturally require the students to determine an approach that might require narrowing, reconfiguring the question, or redefining/refocusing the major elements. The ill-defined nature of the question is necessary in order to simulate the "messy" problems that students will face in practice.

2. An authentic context that reflects the way the knowledge will be used in real life

As Herrington et al. note, "it is not enough to simply provide suitable examples from real-world situations to illustrate the concept or issue being taught."[24] As previously noted, providing specific search topics for database searching is not enough to constitute authenticity. This activity would be considered a rote, point-and-click task requiring little to no higher order thinking, one of the five standards of authentic instruction.[25] To create the proper environment, it was necessary to simulate some of the actual constraints of the search into their professional frame instead of merely providing real-life problems or questions that they might encounter. Once students graduate from the nursing program, they are unlikely to have many or any subscription databases to use for diagnostics, patient education, and research-based evidence. So, while nursing students at UTC are uniformly most comfortable with using CINAHL, they were encouraged to use only Google, Google Scholar, and PubMed for the in-class problem-based learning component. As the practice of evidence-based medicine is the guiding light of UTC's nursing program, students were required to find the highest levels of evidence to answer each of their "problems" using only these three tools. This exercise mimics the realities of their future practice as nurses. Students also worked under a time constraint to further mirror likely elements of working life. For example, when presented with a patient question during an initial conversation in a physician's office, the nurse will have approximately sixteen minutes to find a suitable answer for the patient.[26] Through this immersive experience, students should be more likely to exhibit a high level of motivation to engage in the process and succeed. One student discussion board comment following the in-class session shows understanding of the connection to future work life stating, "Due to these activities, we are becoming well prepared to not only research topics for this class, but we are becoming well prepared to do research on the job."

3. Access to expert performances and the modeling of process

The idea behind this element is that problem-solving in the real world usually has varying levels of novice, peer, and expert support available to assist in the problem-solving. During the nursing class session, students worked in groups providing the peer element to aid in negotiating the assigned problems. For the duration of the problem-based learning activity, the disciplinary professor and librarian circulated in the room, making themselves available as needed and providing "expert" support. A hallmark of student-centered learning is, however, for the teacher to serve as facilitator, not as the "expert," so while advice was provided when requested, it was not offered up unasked. Additionally, at the beginning of the class session and prior to the problem-based learning activity, there was a fifteen- to twenty-minute lecture in which the librarian modeled certain search practices within databases. This was not meant to replace what students had learned in previous semesters but simply to function as a refresher and a time to ask questions before the activity began. In general, while modeling could provide a basis for student confidence levels to improve, concern exists that it could stifle student creativity and critical thinking and might put more external motivational pressure on the students to perform in a "specified" way.

4. Multiple roles and perspectives

In problem-based learning, students must be able to consider a variety of different perspectives related to assigned problems. While this element of the framework was not directly addressed in the nursing class, the students were responsible, within their respective groups, for defining the elements of the problem they were assigned. This exercise involved negotiating what was most important to the patient/organization when determining the direction of their search. Additionally, students were asked to consider how locating information would be different when they are no longer in a university setting and will no longer have access to the library's subscription databases. This critical-thinking query is not so much an exploration of multiple perspectives directly related to the assigned problems but more a perspective related to the students and their views on their future careers.

5. Collaborative construction of knowledge

Herrington et al. recognized a very important point inextricably woven through the sciences: real-world problems are complex and require collaboration.[27] The National Science Foundation makes this statement eloquently: "Important research ideas often transcend the scope of a single discipline or program."[28] The nursing students represent a close-knit cohort and complete the majority of their projects throughout the curriculum in groups. A peer-evaluation system is in place in many of their classes (though not in this particular assignment) and all students are quite aware that each person must take an active role in any group work. Problem-based learning also necessitates this collaborative construction of knowledge. Students must work together to determine an approach to the problem assigned and then divvy up the necessary work. This process is organic, however, and students are not restrained in how they parse out the work, but their ingrained understanding of the expectations of group work serves as a motivating factor to participate fully.

6. Reflection

Authentic learning environments must apply a critical reflective component in some manner. Students in the nursing class offered some reflection via their presentations at the end of class (see the next section: Articulation), such as "Where did you search [for answers to your problems]? What worked best?" and "Did you identify any research gaps or missing evidence?" Reflection was most directly addressed in the course management system's discussion board. Students were required to answer several reflective questions and then comment on at least two other posts (extrinsically motivated with a grade). Sample questions included: "What was the biggest challenge that your group faced in answering their questions?" and "Did this activity change the way you plan to search in the future? If so, how?" in addition to others. Reviewing the student reflections yielded some interesting insights into the various motivating factors exhibited by the students.

Student 1 stated:

> The biggest issue, I believe, was not being able to have access to articles. We could search for and find works that were relevant but we normally did not have access to them and were approached with "GET IT AT UTC," [the library link resolver] which we obviously could not [use] for this exercise. Even with Pubmed it was very difficult to find relevant information that we [were] able to access. This really opened a lot of our eyes to the privilege that we have being able to use our libraries subscriptions to the databases. Also, I realized we are fortunate as a country to have access to www.nih.gov.

7. Articulation

Articulating concepts, ideas, and processes can increase understanding and retention of material.[29] Many who teach will recognize that never do we learn a concept better than when we have to teach it to others. In keeping with this point, each group of students was required to provide a brief presentation at the end of the class period. Each group was required to provide a visual aid (using markers and a large piece of paper) and discuss several questions related to their problems and searches in front of the class. Students could then ask questions and the professors would ask follow-up questions. It is the rare student who can remain unmotivated when asked to present in front of peers! Many students even worked hard to embellish their visual aids with drawings related to their problems.

8. Coaching and scaffolding

Herrington et al. emphasize the need for students to receive higher level assistance, whether from more experienced peers or from professors.[30] As previously discussed, in the nursing class, the professors function as facilitators, guiding, not coaching, the work of students when requested. Instruction, including a brief review of where to find necessary databases and a review of the "levels of evidence," is given at the beginning of class. Students are also prompted to complete several pre-class materials to prep them for the class discussions and activities. One purpose of this activity was to position students for success during the remainder of the course where they were later tasked with developing search strategies for their own group research projects.

9. Authentic assessment

Herrington et al. suggest that the assessment in an authentic learning environment be "tied directly to the successful solution of the task."[31] Therefore, the assessment should be the result of the in-class work (the problem-based learning scenario) and the correlation and meaning should be obvious to the students. In this case, the articulation and assessment are basically the same. After providing evidence in the form of a presentation, students are asked additional questions or for clarification by the professors. This report-out method is a way to provide immediate feedback and assessment of the work done by the group. Students are also assessed on their discussion board posts, but only in the form of added questions and discussion—the grade given is for completion only, not based upon performance. Assessments almost always represent a top motivating factor for students and the nursing class falls in line with this idea. While the stakes (points awarded) were relatively low, presenting in front of the class provides a motivating factor to do well in front of peers. The ability of students to assess evidence and properly identify types (levels) of evidence in the presentation was particularly important, and most student groups had evidently spent time on these determinations. As an additional motivating factor for process-oriented goals in this activity, we stressed to students that there was no "correct" answer to the problems presented because they could be defined and explored in multiple ways. Removing this barrier was a way to encourage students to negotiate and define the problem with their group members instead of trying to find the one correct answer.

Recommendations for Incorporating Authentic Learning Environments and Fostering Motivation for Information Literacy in any Discipline

Though we were able to implement all nine elements of an authentic learning environment (as described by Herrington et al.) to varying degrees, the reader should recognize that not all of these elements can or should be implemented in every setting. A fifty-minute one-shot library session is unlikely to contain all of these elements. It could, however, incorporate some of the elements, and Herrington et al. note that activities can be characterized simply as more or less authentic along a continuum. Room exists for variation.

To that end, we are providing a few additional recommendations for fostering an authentic learning environment for any library instruction occasion.

1. **Cultivate your own authenticity.** Part of mindfully providing space for authentic learning in the classroom is to be cognizant of the authenticity that you, the instructor, bring to your students. In her highly influential book, *Reflective Teaching, Effective Learning*, Char Booth states that "goal orientation, interpersonal connection, and genuine enthusiasm for the task at hand are all aspects of authenticity."[32] Authentic learning environments cannot be constructed when the instructor does not have a clear vision of the desired outcomes and a strong belief in what he/she is doing. Your students will pick up on your motivation to succeed in working with them and they will, in turn, be motivated themselves. Even the driest of topics can be engaging with the addition of an enthusiastic presenter who is able to make the students realize a personal connection and/or need for knowledge of the topic.

2. **Start small or big! Just start.** Maybe you choose to integrate only a single element into a single class—and that's OK. As with so many interesting projects, each semester could realize a new evolution of your project. To be realistic, not every class can or will have all of the authentic learning elements, but incorporating even a few makes instruction more authentic and leads to higher motivation among students. Additionally, students seem to favor non-traditional classroom activities that require them to engage with the content beyond the book and PowerPoint slides.

3. **Assess what you do.** You do not have to roll out a grand assessment plan, but you do need to plan some sort of assessment every time

you integrate authentic learning environment elements, whether it be a simple classroom assessment technique (CAT) or a full assignment. Assessment of how your students feel about the authentic learning environment and whether they see the connection to their profession is critical. Assisting your students in drawing this full-circle connection will help solidify the necessity of such authentic learning activities and potentially help them recognize future connections between content and professional responsibilities. Determining how the students feel will give insight into what motivates them and will allow you to alter and enhance your instruction to increase those motivational factors.

4. **Focus on the students.** Ensure that every decision made is student-centered. You will need to consider the composition of the students to be reached (learning abilities and needs, diversity, etc.), as well as their interests and needs. You will need to remember that sometimes the disciplinary professor is not functioning under these same principles. Navigating this disparity in approach will require excellent negotiation skills on the librarian's part to advocate for the students and their actual needs versus the perceived needs from the faculty perspective. Consensus can be reached and a successful partnership achieved.

5. **Don't underestimate planning time.** As instructors typically function as facilitators or serve as modelers in authentic learning environments, one might be tempted to think that there is no need to spend time planning. In fact, the opposite is true. Though the instructor's role is minimized, he/she needs to remain open and active, listening and encouraging and commenting when needed. Planning time is typically extensive. For example, co-author 1 of this article devoted approximately five hours per week for a month, excluding time meeting with the disciplinary faculty member, developing and re-developing a lesson plan for the nursing class described above. Though teaching time was only about fifteen to twenty minutes (of 2.5 hours), all elements of the environment needed to be carefully planned so that students could realize success.

6. **Loosen your grip.** While this advice may seem at odds with the previous section, wading into the authentic learning/student-centered learning waters means that you will have to loosen your grip in the classroom. The role of the instructor is decentralized and the larger burden of learning is on the student. This can, at times, yield unpredictable results. As an instructor, you must allow for many different paths to the same answer even if they were not the paths that you expected. Struggle is a defining element of the

problem-based learning method described above and the instructor must accept that student struggles are a normal and expected part of this learning method. The good news about encountering potentially unexpected outcomes is that they provide the basis for additional discussion and reflection with your students and exploration of differing strategies for approaching real-life problems they may see in the future.

Final Thoughts

Motivating students in any discipline can be challenging. The attempt to motivate them to engage with information literacy concepts and activities that they think they have already mastered and will never use again can feel like a fool's errand. We believe that the authentic learning environment elements discussed in this chapter are not just useful but are critical to successfully motivating students to develop sound information literacy skills and behaviors and, more important, to truly understand how these skills can be put to use in their chosen professions. With the thoughtful inclusion of authentic learning environments within the classroom, instructors are preparing students for the ill-defined, real-world problems they are sure to encounter post-graduation, thereby increasing students' capacity for expert thinking[33] and overall success.

The authors have provided access to additional resources, including a class plan, references to literature on problem-based learning, and authentic examples for a variety of disciplines at the following URL: http://bit.ly/motivationALEs.

Endnotes

1.   Jan Herrington, Thomas C. Reeves, and Ron Oliver, "Authentic Learning Environments," in *Handbook of Research on Educational Communications and Technology*, eds. M. Spector, M. D. Merrill, J. Elen, and M. J. Bishop (New York: Springer-Verlag, 2014), 401, doi:10.1007/978-1-4614-3185-5_32.
2.   Richard M. Ryan and Edward L. Deci, "Intrinsic and Extrinsic Motivations: Classic Definitions and New Directions," *Contemporary Educational Psychology* 25 (2000): 54, doi:10.1006/ceps.1999.1020.
3.   Kevin M. Klipfel, "Authentic Engagement: Assessing the Effects of Authenticity on Student Engagement and Information Literacy in Academic Library Instruction," *Reference Sciences Review* 42, no. 2 (2014): 230, doi:10.1108/RSR-08-2013-0043.
4.   Klipfel, "Authentic Engagement," 230.
5.   Klipfel, "Authentic Engagement"; Juliana L. D'Sa, "Effect of Problem-Based Learning on Motivation of Nursing Students," *International Journal of Current Research and Review* 7 no. 8 (2015): 34–8; Ryan and Deci, "Intrinsic and Extrinsic Motivations."

6. M. Bruce King, Fred, M. Newmann, and Dana, L. Carmichael, "Authentic Intellectual Work: Common Standards for Teaching Social Studies," *Social Education* 73, no. 1 (2009): 43, accessed April 13, 2017, http://www.ncss.org/; Klipfel, "Authentic Engagement"; Phyllis C. Blumenfeld, Toni M. Kempler, and Joseph S. Krajcik, *Motivation and Cognitive Engagement in Learning Environments* (na, 2006); Sevilla Bronson, *Autonomy Support Environment and Autonomous Motivation on Nursing Student Academic Performance: An Exploratory Analysis* 44 (2016), 103–8, doi:10.1016/j.nedt.2016.05.013.
7. Marilyn M. Lombardi, "Authentic Learning for the 21st Century: An Overview," *Educause Learning Initiative* 1, no. 2007 (2007): 1–12.
8. Edward L. Deci and Richard M. Ryan, "Optimizing Students' Motivation in the Era of Testing and Pressure: A Self-Determination Theory Perspective," in *Building Autonomous Learners: Perspectives from Research and Practice Using Self-Determination Theory*, eds. W. C. Liu, J. C. Wang, and R. M. Ryan (Singapore: Springer, 2016), 9–29, doi:10.1007/978-981-287-630-0_2.
9. Erika A. Patall, "Constructing Motivation through Choice, Interest, and Interestingness," *Journal of Educational Psychology* 105, no. 2 (2013): 522, doi:10.1037/a0030307; Blumenfeld, Kempler, and Krajcik, "Motivation and Cognitive Engagement."
10. Klipfel, "Authentic Engagement."
11. Young Sook Roh and Sang Suk Kim, "Integrating Problem-Based Learning and Simulation," *CIN: Computers, Informatics, Nursing* 33, no. 7 (2015): 278–84, doi:10.1097/CIN.0000000000000161.
12. Trudi E. Jacobson and Lijuan Xu, *Motivating Students in Information Literacy Classes* (New York: Neal-Schuman Publishers, 2004).
13. Rebecca K. Miller, "Social Media, Authentic Learning and Embedded Librarianship: A Case Study of Dietetics Students," *Journal of Information Literacy* 6, no. 2 (2012): 97–109; Anne R. Diekema, Wendy Holliday, and Heather Leary, "Re-Framing Information Literacy: Problem-Based Learning as Informed Learning," *Library & Information Science Research (07408188)* 33, no. 4 (2011): 261–68; Larissa Gordon and Eleonora Bartoli, "Using Discipline-Based Professional Association Standards for Information Literacy Integration: A Review and Case Study," *Behavioral & Social Sciences Librarian* 31, no. 1 (2012/01/01 2012): 23–38; Mary C. English and Anastasia Kitsantas, "Supporting Student Self-Regulated Learning in Problem-and Project-Based Learning," *Interdisciplinary Journal of Problem-Based Learning* 7, no. 2 (2013): 6; Klipfel, "Authentic Engagement."
14. Klipfel, "Authentic Engagement."
15. Andrew K. Shenton and Megan Fitzgibbons, "Making Information Literacy Relevant" (in English), *Library Review* 59, no. 3 (0 0, 2010 2016-09-27 2010): 165–74.
16. Carol A. Leibiger, "'Google Reigns Triumphant'?: Stemming the Tide of Googlitis Via Collaborative, Situated Information Literacy Instruction," *Behavioral & Social Sciences Librarian* 30, no. 4 (2011): 187–222.
17. Gordon and Bartoli, "Using Discipline-Based."
18. Association of College & Research Libraries, "Framework for Information Literacy for Higher Education," http://www.ala.org/acrl/standards/ilframework Association of College and Research Libraries.
19. Fred M. Newmann and Gary G. Wehlage, "Five Standards of Authentic Instruction," *Educational Leadership* 50, no. 7 (1993): 8–12; Daniel Callison and Annette

Lamb, "Authentic Learning," *School Library Media Activities Monthly* 21, no. 4 (2004): 34–39.
20. Herrington, Reeves, and Oliver, "Authentic Learning Environments."
21. Herrington, Reeves, and Oliver.
22. Herrington, Reeves, and Oliver.
23. Herrington, Reeves, and Oliver, 404.
24. Herrington, Reeves, and Oliver, 403.
25. Newmann and Wehlage, "Five Standards."
26. Ming Tai-Seale, Thomas G. McGuire, and Weimin Zhang, "Time Allocation in Primary Care Office Visits," *Health Research and Educational Trust* 45, no. 5 (2007): 1871–94. doi:10.1111/j.1475-6773.2006.00689.x.
27. Herrington, Reeves, and Oliver, "Authentic Learning Environments."
28. National Science Foundation, "Introduction to Interdisciplinary Research," accessed April 12, 2017.
29. Herrington, Reeves, and Oliver, "Authentic Learning Environments."
30. Herrington, Reeves, and Oliver.
31. Herrington, Reeves, and Oliver, 404.
32. Char Booth, *Reflective Teaching, Effective Learning: Instructional Literacy for Library Educators* (in English) (Chicago: American Library Association, 2011), 9–10.
33. Lombardi, "Authentic Learning."

Bibliography

Association of College & Research Libraries. "Framework for Information Literacy for Higher Education." http://www.ala.org/acrl/standards/ilframework.

Blumenfeld, Phyllis C., Toni M. Kempler, and Joseph S. Krajcik. *Motivation and Cognitive Engagement in Learning Environments*. na, 2006.

Booth, Char. *Reflective Teaching, Effective Learning: Instructional Literacy for Library Educators*. In English. Chicago: American Library Association, 2011.

Bronson, Sevilla. *Autonomy Support Environment and Autonomous Motivation on Nursing Student Academic Performance: An Exploratory Analysis* 44 (2016): 103–8. doi:10.1016/j.nedt.2016.05.013.

Callison, Daniel, and Annette Lamb. "Authentic Learning." *School Library Media Activities Monthly* 21, no. 4 (2004): 34–9.

D'Sa, Juliana L. "Effect of Problem-Based Learning on Motivation of Nursing Students." *International Journal of Current Research and Review* 7 no. 8 (2015): 34–8.

Deci, Edward L., and Richard M. Ryan. "Optimizing Students' Motivation in the Era of Testing and Pressure: A Self-Determination Theory Perspective." In *Building Autonomous Learners: Perspectives from Research and Practice Using Self-Determination Theory*, edited by W. C. Liu, J. C. Wang and R. M. Ryan, 9–29. Singapore: Springer, 2016. doi:10.1007/978-981-287-630-0_2.

Diekema, Anne R., Wendy Holliday, and Heather Leary. "Re-Framing Information Literacy: Problem-Based Learning as Informed Learning." *Library & Information Science Research (07408188)* 33, no. 4 (2011): 261–68.

English, Mary C., and Anastasia Kitsantas. "Supporting Student Self-Regulated Learning in Problem-and Project-Based Learning." *Interdisciplinary Journal of Problem-Based Learning* 7, no. 2 (2013): 6.

Gordon, Larissa, and Eleonora Bartoli. "Using Discipline-Based Professional Association Standards for Information Literacy Integration: A Review and Case Study." *Behavioral & Social Sciences Librarian* 31, no. 1 (2012/01/01 2012): 23–38.

Herrington, Jan, Thomas C. Reeves, and Ron Oliver. "Authentic Learning Environments." In *Handbook of Research on Educational Communications and Technology*, edited by M. Spector, M. D. Merrill, J. Elen, and M. J. Bishop, 401–12. New York: Springer-Verlag, 2014. doi:10.1007/978-1-4614-3185-5_32.

Jacobson, Trudi E., and Lijuan Xu. *Motivating Students in Information Literacy Classes.* New York: Neal-Schuman Publishers, 2004.

King, M. Bruce, Fred M. Newmann, and Dana L. Carmichael. "Authentic Intellectual Work: Common Standards for Teaching Social Studies." *Social Education* 73, no. 1 (2009): 43. Accessed April 13, 2017. http://www.ncss.org/.

Klipfel, Kevin M. "Authentic Engagement: Assessing the Effects of Authenticity on Student Engagement and Information Literacy in Academic Library Instruction." *Reference Sciences Review* 42, no. 2 (2014): 229–45. doi:10.1108/RSR-08-2013-0043.

Leibiger, Carol A. "'Google Reigns Triumphant'?: Stemming the Tide of Googlitis Via Collaborative, Situated Information Literacy Instruction." *Behavioral & Social Sciences Librarian* 30, no. 4 (2011): 187–222.

Lombardi, Marilyn M. "Authentic Learning for the 21st Century: An Overview." *Educause Learning Initiative* 1, no. 2007 (2007): 1–12.

Miller, Rebecca K. "Social Media, Authentic Learning and Embedded Librarianship: A Case Study of Dietetics Students." *Journal of Information Literacy* 6, no. 2 (2012): 97–109.

National Science Foundation. "Introduction to Interdisciplinary Research." Accessed April 12, 2017.

Newmann, Fred M., and Gary G. Wehlage. "Five Standards of Authentic Instruction." *Educational Leadership* 50, no. 7 (1993): 8–12.

Patall, Erika A. "Constructing Motivation through Choice, Interest, and Interestingness." *Journal of Educational Psychology* 105, no. 2 (2013): 522. doi:10.1037/a0030307.

Roh, Young Sook, and Sang Suk Kim. "Integrating Problem-Based Learning and Simulation." *CIN: Computers, Informatics, Nursing* 33, no. 7 (2015): 278–84. doi:10.1097/CIN.0000000000000161.

Ryan, Richard M., and Edward L. Deci. "Intrinsic and Extrinsic Motivations: Classic Definitions and New Directions." *Contemporary Educational Psychology* 25 (2000): 54–67. doi:10.1006/ceps.1999.1020.

Shenton, Andrew K., and Megan Fitzgibbons. "Making Information Literacy Relevant." In English. *Library Review* 59, no. 3 (0 0, 2010 2016-09-27 2010): 165–74.

Tai-Seale, Ming, Thomas G. McGuire, and Weimin Zhang. "Time Allocation in Primary Care Office Visits." *Health Research and Educational Trust* 45, no. 5 (2007): 1871–94. doi:10.1111/j.1475-6773.2006.00689.x.

CHAPTER 4

Using Motivation Theory and Research When Teaching Information Literacy Online

Nick Faulk and Alan Carberry

Introduction

Whether using a learning management system to reach students in online courses or deploying web or video to offer just-in-time assistance, librarians can use motivation theories and evidence-based practice to engage students and maintain their attention. A small but growing body of evidence investigates motivation in online information literacy instruction specifically, while a considerable wealth of literature explores motivation in the online context more generally. This chapter covers that library-focused material while providing an overview of particularly relevant literature from the areas of educational psychology, instructional technology, and e-learning. Through this review, three key themes emerge: the importance of instructional and visual design to shape a learner's sense of immediacy with the material and level of motivation, the power of interactivity to sustain learner attention and interest, and the influence of communication and feedback on learner motivation in both synchronous and asynchronous learning scenarios.

Librarians need to pay particular attention to synchronous and asynchronous learning for off-campus students because, as of fall 2015, 29 percent of higher education students were enrolled in at least one distance learning course, with about 12 percent of students taking distance learning courses exclusively.[1] Students enrolled in online education programs tend to be older than their peers enrolled in face-to-face programs, with undergraduate students over the age of thirty being four times as likely as their peers under the age of twenty-three to be enrolled in a program exclusively taught online.[2] In one study, about one out of three online-education-enrolled students expressed a low sense of self-efficacy with information literacy concepts, and between one quarter and one-third of students in online programs expressed interest in a range of workshops on several information literacy topics.[3] There was relatively little difference in the desire for workshops in high self-efficacy students and low self-efficacy students, suggesting that some of the students who most need information literacy instruction online lack active interest in it.[4]

Tutorials, online guides, and self-guided courses are common modalities for reaching both online and face-to-face students that provide an alternative to the embedded librarian model or a for-credit course. While learners in low-pressure scenarios such as these report a reduction in learning anxiety, the lack of extrinsic motivation to complete self-directed e-learning lessons makes it difficult for some learners to prioritize an extensive or long-running lesson.[5] This makes attention to motivation a concern that extends to unmediated teaching scenarios as well as more formal online teaching scenarios.

In their Self Determination Theory (SDT), Richard Ryan and Edward Deci distinguish between intrinsic and extrinsic motivation types, based on the different reasons that lead to action.[6] "Intrinsic motivation relates to an individual doing something because they find it enjoyable, while extrinsic motivation refers to doing something because it leads to a separable outcome."[7] According to Ryan and Deci, intrinsic motivation results in high-quality learning and creativity, with optimal challenges, feedback, and freedom from demeaning evaluations contributing to this motivation type.[8] According to Ryan and Deci, intrinsic motivation will only occur for activities that have intrinsic interest for the individual. Outside of this, individuals are impacted by extrinsic motivational factors. "Given that many of the educational activities prescribed in schools are not designed to be intrinsically interesting, a central question concerns how to motivate students to value and self-regulate such activities, and without external pressure, to carry them out on their own."[9] Ryan and Deci offer a continuum of motivational types that ranges from amotivation, or the state of lacking intent to act, toward self-determination and interest.[10] Key to moving toward self-determination is the movement away from externally regulated factors toward those that are self-regulated or autonomous.[11]

The work of Carol Kuhlthau may give us insight into the affective domains around extrinsic motivators, particularly in the information-seeking habits of students. Kuhlthau's Information Seeking Process (ISP) model outlines five stages of information seeking and details affective, cognitive, and physical domains along the process.[12] Kuhlthau's ISP model outlines a journey toward ownership and possession in the process of seeking information that leads to clarity and sense of direction and confidence, as well as increased interest in both process and research product.[13] According to Kuhlthau, students expect to become more interested in their research topic as the search for information progresses.[14] This suggests that intrinsic motivation generally develops later in the information-seeking process.

Motivation Design

Relatively little literature explores the motivational opportunities and challenges created by online teaching situations. The question of motivation as it relates to online, for-credit information literacy courses was tackled by Trudi Jacobson and Lijuan Xu as a chapter in their 2004 book, *Motivating Students in Information Literacy Classes*.[15] Their work draws attention to the importance of fundamental facets of motivation online, such as clarity in course design and incorporation of activities for different types of learners.[16] They also note that instructors can encourage active or problem-based learning as a technique for enhancing motivation, just as an instructor would in a face-to-face course.[17] Even in 2004, the work noted the need for additional research on motivation in the online information literacy sphere by encouraging readers to share and publish their own techniques for motivating students online.[18]

Despite the ongoing lack of scholarship dedicated to motivating students for online information literacy instruction, a growing body of literature pays some attention to online learning within the context of motivating students during information literacy instruction in general. These works provide lessons that are easily transferable to an exclusively online context. For example, Motivation Design through the ARCS (Attention, Relevance, Confidence, and Satisfaction) model of instructional design can empower librarians to incorporate motivation into their information literacy instruction regardless of a teaching scenario's modality.[19] Amanda Hess's literature review found that librarians can and should promote extrinsic motivation through lesson design, as students may lack intrinsic motivation for information literacy lessons incorporated into their program of study.[20] Using the ARCS model, Hess notes that an instructional designer can start by developing design objectives and then identify motivation techniques that align with those objectives and the teaching situation.[21] Hess also notes that, in 2015, research on motivation in online information literacy instruction is absent in a variety of its permutations, including the embedded librarian model and information literacy modules embedded directly into a course's structure and schedule.[22]

When incorporating motivation design into online courses, the instructional librarian might pay particular attention to the needs of older students, given their large population in distance education programs.[23] Adult learners, in particular, are looking for immediacy, engagement, and praxis in their learning.[24] These needs create numerous opportunities to design for motivation through student engagement, such as allowing students to co-create their learning opportunities with their instructors and providing them with the opportunity to bring their learning to action and see the implications of their choices first-hand.[25]

Librarians creating online learning objects should pay particular attention to visual design techniques as a method of sustaining learner attention.[26] Repetition of visual elements such as color and the location of navigational elements, thoughtful consideration of proximity of visual elements to those that are logically related, alignment of visual elements along an (invisible) grid, and use of contrast through color or shape are four considerations of visual design that help sustain attention.[27]

The influence of design choices on student motivation also figures heavily into education literature more generally. Maggie Hartnett's monograph-length case study, *Motivation in Online Education*, provides considerable insights into the motivational characters of students in online, for-credit classes.[28] Hartnett cites Ryan and Deci's self-determination theory, which places students' ability to establish motivation to learn on their sense of autonomy, sense of competence for the tasks they are asked to complete, and the relatedness of the learners to the broader social surrounding.[29] The relevance or importance of a learning activity both to professional and personal contexts is important for establishing autonomy, as are instructional techniques that center the meaningfulness of student choice.[30] In developing relatedness, the key factor is that students develop a relationship with both the instructor and other learners.[31] In applying this research to teaching and design scenarios, Hartnett's guidance is multi-faceted. Part of supporting autonomy means acquainting oneself with a learner's unique circumstances and using that knowledge to limit their constraints.[32] Thoughtful instructional design around a clear narrative can eliminate barriers that undermine a student's sense of competence.[33] To support relatedness, strive to develop a sense of community among all learners with techniques such as online discussion and synchronous sessions.[34]

Interactivity

Students in self-directed e-learning situations such as tutorials, online guides, and self-paced courses can face some specific challenges that differ from those in the classroom setting, and a key to maintaining motivation in those scenarios is interactivity.[35] Learners reported media-based interactivity such as "animations..., simulations..., and drag-and-drop quiz(zes)" as key to sustaining their engagement and attention, while the lack of human presence in self-directed learning was an impediment for users from academia but not necessarily users from industry.[36] As most study participants from academia were in their thirties and forties, adult students may experience motivation loss during self-directed learning in the academic context, even if they are also professionals.[37] The e-learning situations used by study participants also allowed for a high level of learner control, such as the ability to choose which lessons are most relevant to their needs and to complete a course at their own pace, something which learners reported as a factor that increased their motivation.[38]

In developing an interactive, online information literacy tutorial, Dominique Turnbow and Amanda Roth looked for strategies to embed engagement techniques into their instructional design process.[39] Turnbow and Roth used several pedagogical theories to inform their practice, including the Cognitive Theory of Multimedia Learning by Richard Mayer.[40] This informed their choice to use graphical representations of information when possible as opposed to text and audio alone.[41] Further, they found interactivity to be an important component of tutorial design, which influences their choice of instructional technology.[42]

Differentiated instruction in the form of an interactive tutorial can provide an opportunity to enhance student motivation. One study on the impact of differentiated instruction on students saw gains in students' level of motivation regardless of the level of motivation with which they started.[43] Despite those gains, a student's motivation before beginning a differentiated instruction tutorial does influence their interaction with it. Students who began their online differentiated instruction tutorial with higher levels of motivation spent more time reviewing the course materials.[44]

Library-produced videos are a common tool deployed both within online courses and as learner resources on a library's website or how-to guides. While it might seem counterintuitive to associate interactivity with a video, emerging and existing technologies create opportunities to create such learning objects. Designing a video with a responsive e-learning tool is one example of a method to raise a video's interactivity and with it a learner's engagement with the content.[45] E-learning production software such as Articulate Storyline allows designers to create multimedia course modules featuring an unmediated slide deck with regular pauses for quizzes, branched learner paths, and other interactive features.

Communication and Feedback

With online courses offering numerous opportunities for synchronous and asynchronous communication, Bas Giesbers led a research study into how students' motivation influences their participation in those communication modalities.[46] Students who took advantage of synchronous communication in the form of a live video chat with their instructor were more likely to participate in asynchronous communication—and participate with higher quality posts—than their peers who did not participate in the synchronous communication.[47] This finding held up for students with both autonomous and control-oriented motivation profiles.[48] Meanwhile, students with an autonomous motivation profile are more likely to participate in asynchronous communication than their control-oriented motivation peers, suggesting that the participation in synchronous communication was transformative for the control-oriented student who chose to participate in them.[49] To quote Giesbers et al., "synchronous communication afforded control-oriented learners to be equally engaged in knowledge construction as autonomy-oriented learners."[50] This research suggests that synchronous communication is an effective tool for librarians to use in engaging online students regardless of the students' specific motivation profiles.

Instructors should take advantage of their online settings by making their presence known to students through consistent messages on matters of process and expectation and by designing discussion board activities such that they include faculty feedback.[51] Guidance and constructive feedback along with clear expectations for the learner were key influencers on motivation due to those practices' role in reinforcing learner competence.[52] Intentional planning for feedback can help address the need for regular communication in support of competence.[53]

When it comes to engaging learners in online environments, William Cuthbertson and Andrea Falcone demonstrate that creating a community is essential to student success in online information literacy courses.[54] Creating space for students to interact informally with one another is one method for fostering this community, something that a librarian teaching a semester-long course might do with initial icebreakers and regular prompts for students to share their interests.[55] The authors also suggest that instructors allow students to take ownership of discussion board topics and consult with one another on assignments, practices reminiscent of Cooke's call for co-created learning.[56]

Even asynchronous learning provides numerous opportunities for motivating communication in the form of automatic feedback. Turnbow and Roth found that Gagné's Events of Instruction gave them a framework through which to analyze their tutorial, even though it was taught asynchronously, a choice which influenced the use of communication in their tutorial.[57] This framework allowed the authors to establish the ways that their tutorial would gain learner attention—in this case, through an audio component spoken in a casual tone—and provide feedback. Here, feedback would be embedded directly into the tutorial through regular quizzes.[58] Related instructional videos can be paired with short quizzes to provide learners with the instant feedback to enhance learners' sense of competence.[59]

Conclusion

The online environment creates numerous opportunities for the librarian looking to inspire students learning information literacy skills and dispositions. This review highlights several key instructional strategies the instructor may employ to increase motivation of students online. Librarians can design with motivation in mind through attention to the instructional and visual elements that shape a learner's sense of immediacy. Adult learners, in particular, seek engagement and praxis in their learning scenarios, leading to increased motivation. Interactive and engaging learning environments are important to sustaining learner attention and interest. Finally, effective communication and timely feedback positively impact learner motivation in both synchronous and asynchronous learning scenarios. Librarians use a wide range of tools and techniques to teach students online, creating many opportunities for further experimentation, research, and review on best practices at the intersection of motivation and information literacy.

Endnotes

1. Joel McFarland et al., U.S. Department of Education, National Center for Education Statistics, *The Condition of Education 2017*, NCES-2017-144 (Washington, DC, 2017), xxvi, https://nces.ed.gov/pubs2017/2017144.pdf.
2. U. S. Department of Education, National Center for Education Statistics, "Table 311.20: Number and percentage of undergraduate students taking night, weekend, or online classes, by selected characteristics: 2011–12," *Digest of Education Statistics: 2015*, accessed April 1, 2017, https://nces.ed.gov/programs/digest/d15/.
3. Yingqi Tang and Hung Wei Tseng, "Distance Learners' Self-Efficacy and Information Literacy Skills," *The Journal of Academic Librarianship* 39, no. 6, 2013: 519–20.
4. Tang, "Distance Learners' Self-Efficacy," 519.
5. Kyong-Jee Kim, "Motivational Challenges of Adult Learners in Self-Directed

E-Learning," *Journal of Interactive Learning Research* 20, no. 3, 2009: 330–31.

6. Edward L. Deci and Richard M. Ryan, *Intrinsic Motivation and Self-Determination in Human Behavior* (New York: Plenum, 1985); Richard M. Ryan and Edward L. Deci, "Intrinsic and Extrinsic Motivations: Classic Definitions and New Directions," *Contemporary Educational Psychology* 25, 2000: 54–67.

7. Deci, *Intrinsic Motivation and Self-Determination*, 55.

8. Deci, *Intrinsic Motivation and Self-Determination*, 58.

9. Deci, *Intrinsic Motivation and Self-Determination*, 60.

10. Richard M. Ryan and Edward L. Deci, "Self-Determination Theory and the Facilitation of Intrinsic Motivation, Social Development, and Well-Being," *American Psychologist* 55, no. 1, 2000: 68–78.

11. Ryan, "Self-Determination Theory," 73.

12. Carol Collier Kuhlthau, *Seeking Meaning: A Process Approach to Library and Information Services* (Connecticut: Libraries Unlimited, 2004).

13. Kuhlthau, *Seeking Meaning*, 82.

14. Kuhlthau, *Seeking Meaning*, 84.

15. Trudi E. Jacobson and Lijuan Xu, *Motivating Students in Information Literacy Classes* (New York: Neal-Schuman, 2004), 127–38.

16. Jacobson, *Motivating Students in Information Literacy Classes*, 128–29.

17. Jacobson, *Motivating Students in Information Literacy Classes*, 136–37.

18. Jacobson, *Motivating Students in Information Literacy Classes*, 138.

19. Amanda N. Hess, "Motivation Design in Information Literacy Instruction," *Communications in Information Literacy* 9, no. 1, 2015: 44–59.

20. Hess, "Motivation Design in Information Literacy Instruction," 56.

21. Hess, "Motivation Design in Information Literacy Instruction," 47.

22. Hess, "Motivation Design in Information Literacy Instruction," 56.

23. Nicole A. Cooke, "Becoming an Androgogical Librarian: Using Library Instruction as a Tool to Combat Library Anxiety and Empower Adult Learners," *New Review of Academic Librarianship* 16, no. 2, 2010: 208–27; "Table 311.20," *Digest of Educational Statistics*.

24. Cooke, "Becoming an Androgogical Librarian," 220.

25. Cooke, "Becoming an Androgogical Librarian," 220–22.

26. Char Booth, *Reflective Teaching, Effective Learner* (ALA Editions: Chicago, 2011), 59.

27. Booth, *Reflective Teaching, Effective Learner*, 128–29.

28. Maggie Hartnett, *Motivation in Online Education* (Singapore: Springer Science + Business Media, 2016).

29. Hartnett, *Motivation in Online Education*, 20–23.

30. Hartnett, *Motivation in Online Education*, 46–50.

31. Hartnett, *Motivation in Online Education*, 69–72.

32. Hartnett, *Motivation in Online Education*, 116–17.

33. Hartnett, *Motivation in Online Education*, 121–22.

34. Hartnett, *Motivation in Online Education*, 119–20.

35. Kim, "Motivational Challenges," 317–35.

36. Kim, "Motivational Challenges," 325–26.

37. Kim, "Motivational Challenges," 322. Four of the six participants from academia in Kim's study reported being in their thirties or forties.

38. Kim, "Motivational Challenges," 328–29.
39. Dominique Turnbow and Amanda Roth, "Engaging Learners Online: Using Instructional Design Practices to Create Interactive Tutorials," in *Distributed Learning: Pedagogy and Technology in Online Information Literacy Instruction*, eds. Tasha Maddison and Maha Kumaran (Cambridge, MA: Chandos Publishing, 2017), 123–34.
40. Turnbow, "Engaging Learners Online," 128.
41. Turnbow, "Engaging Learners Online."
42. Turnbow, "Engaging Learners Online," 131–32.
43. Raymond Flores et al., "The Impact of Adapting Content for Students with Individual Differences," *Educational Technology and Society* 15, no. 3, 2012: 253–54.
44. Flores, "The Impact of Adapting Content," 255–56.
45. Nichole A. Martin and Ross Martin, "Would You Watch It?: Creating Effective and Engaging Interactive Tutorials," *Journal of Library and Information Services in Distance Learning* 9, no. 1–2, 2015, 44.
46. Bas Giesbers et al., "A Dynamic Analysis of the Interplay Between Asynchronous and Synchronous Communication in Online Learning: The Impact of Motivation," *Journal of Computer Assisted Learning* 30, no. 1, 2014: 30–50.; Giesbers, "A Dynamic Analysis," 33. Autonomy-oriented learners are typically intrinsically motivated. Control-oriented learners are predisposed to be extrinsically motivated.
47. Giesbers, "A Dynamic Analysis," 43.
48. Giesbers, "A Dynamic Analysis," 46.
49. Giesbers, "A Dynamic Analysis," 43–45.
50. Giesbers, "A Dynamic Analysis," 45.
51. Jacobson and Xu, *Motivating Students in Information Literacy* Classes, 131–32, 134–35.
52. Hartnett, *Motivation in Online Education*, 59–60.
53. Hartnett, *Motivation in Online Education*, 118–19.
54. William Cuthbertson and Andrea Falcone, "Elevating Engagement and Community in Online Courses," *Journal of Library & Information Services in Distance Learning* 8, no. 3–4, 2014: 216–17.
55. Cuthbertson, "Elevating Engagement and Community," 217–18.
56. Cuthbertson, "Elevating Engagement and Community," 218–20; Cooke, "Becoming an Androgogical Librarian," 221.
57. Turnbow and Roth, "Engaging Learners Online," 125–26.
58. Turnbow, "Engaging Learners Online," 125.
59. Martin and Martin, "Would You Watch It?," 47.

Bibliography

Booth, Char. *Reflective Teaching, Effective Learning*. Chicago: ALA Editions, 2011.
Cuthbertson, William, and Andrea Falcone. "Elevating Engagement and Community in Online Courses." *Journal of Library & Information Services in Distance Learning* 8, no. 3–4 (2014): 216–24. doi:10.1080/1533290x.2014.945839.
Cooke, Nicole A. "Becoming an Andragogical Librarian: Using Library Instruction as a Tool to Combat Library Anxiety and Empower Adult Learners." *New Review of Academic Librarianship* 16, no. 2 (2010): 208–27.

Flores, Raymond, Faith Ari, Fethi A. Inan, and Ismahan Arslan-Ari. "The Impact of Adapting Content for Students with Individual Differences." *Educational Technology and Society* 15, no. 3, (2012): 251–61.

Giesbers, Bas, Bart Rienties, Dirk Tempelaar, and Wim Gijselaers. "A Dynamic Analysis of the Interplay between Asynchronous and Synchronous Communication in Online Learning: The Impact of Motivation." *Journal of Computer Assisted Learning* 30, no. 1, (2014): 30–50.

Hartnett, Maggie. *Motivation in Online Education*. Singapore: Springer Science+Business Media, 2016.

Hess, Amanda N. "Motivation Design in Information Literacy Instruction." *Communications in Information Literacy* 9, no. 1 (2015): 44–59.

Jacobson, Trudi E., and Lijuan Xu. *Motivating Students in Information Literacy Classes*. New York: Neal-Schuman, 2004.

Kim, Kyong-Jee. "Motivational Challenges of Adult Learners in Self-directed E-learning." *Journal of Interactive Learning Research* 20, no. 3 (2009): 317–35.

Kuhlthau, Carol C. *Seeking Meaning: A Process Approach to Library and Information Services*, 2nd ed. Connecticut: Libraries Unlimited, 2004.

Martin, Nichole A., and Ross Martin. "Would You Watch It? Creating Effective and Engaging Video Tutorials." *Journal of Library & Information Services in Distance Learning* 9, no. 1–2 (2015): 40–56. doi:10.1080/1533290x.2014.946345.

McFarland, Joel, Bill Hussar, Cristobal de Brey, Tom Snyder, Xiaolei Wang, Sidney Wilkinson-Flicker, Semhar Gebrekristos, et al. U. S. Department of Education. National Center for Education Statistics. *The Condition of Education 2017*, NCES-2017-144. Washington, DC, 2017. https://nces.ed.gov/pubs2017/2017144.pdf.

Ryan, Richard M., and Edward L. Deci. "Intrinsic and Extrinsic Motivations: Classic Definitions and New Directions." *Contemporary Educational Psychology* 25, 2000: 54–67.

———. "Self-Determination Theory and the Facilitation of Intrinsic Motivation, Social Development, and Well-Being." *American Psychologist* 55, no. 1, 2000: 68–78.

Tang, Yingqi, and Hung Wei Tseng. "Distance Learners' Self-efficacy and Information Literacy Skills." *The Journal of Academic Librarianship* 39, no. 6 (2013): 517–21. doi:10.1016/j.acalib.2013.08.008.

Turnbow, Dominique, and Amanda Roth. "Engaging Learners Online: Using Instructional Design Practices to Create Interactive Tutorials." In *Distributed Learning: Pedagogy and Technology in Online Information Literacy Instruction*, edited by Tasha Maddison and Maha Kumaran, 123–34. Cambridge, MA: Chandos Publishing, 2017.

U.S. Department of Education. "Table 311.20: Number and percentage of undergraduate students taking night, weekend, or online classes, by selected characteristics: 2011-12." *Digest of Education Statistics: 2015*. Accessed April 1, 2017. https://nces.ed.gov/programs/digest/d15/.

CHAPTER 5

Using Authentic Teaching in Information Literacy Instruction to Improve Student Motivation

Josefine Smith and Anna Kozlowska

Reflecting on one's teaching practices is important to becoming an effective teacher. Why am I a teacher? Why am I teaching information literacy? Why is it important to educate students about how to find, access, and evaluate information? What kind of impact do I want to have on my students?

The concept of authentic teaching encourages us to consider these questions. This concept was first defined by Clark Moustakas as a way that a teacher can "bring his own unique self to the classroom, facilitate actualization of potentialities in himself and in children" to enable "creative capacities and hidden potentials" for students.[1] Several aspects of authentic teaching theory and motivation research are applicable to information literacy instruction: establishing a clear vision and purpose, creating authentic relationships with learners, building trust and credibility, giving the freedom to pursue personal interests, encouraging creativity and risk taking, and seeking the sources of inspiration and cultivating collaborations. This chapter explores the concept of authentic teaching and learning and gives instructors practical ways to motivate students through the application of these practices.

Literature Review

The concept of authentic teaching and learning has been present in education literature since the1960s. The most well-known proponents of this theory are Carl Rogers, Clark Moustakas, and Stephen D. Brookfield. The basic premise is to approach students holistically as individuals with their own opinions, passions, and ideas, rather than as passive vessels. Therefore, while content knowledge and subject expertise are important, the authentic teacher puts an emphasis on creating relationships based on mutual respect between a teacher and a learner. In other words, "if college teachers define themselves only as content or skill experts within some narrowly restricted domain, they effectively cut themselves off from the broader identity as change agents involved in helping students shape the world they inhabit."[2] Our ability to connect with students in the classroom and during research consultations has implications for students' motivation and engagement.

Research has shown that student motivation is crucial to their ability to retain and implement learned material in other contexts. In "Motivation: A Literature Review," Emily Lai discusses motivation theory with particular attention to how motivation has been defined, how it develops, what teachers can do to motivate students, and the ways it could be assessed.[3] Student motivation is categorized as either intrinsic (self-directed) or extrinsic (externally reinforced). Initial approaches to student motivation focused on extrinsic reinforcement. B.F. Skinner, a major proponent of this theory, believed the best way to motivate students to better performance is through distribution of rewards and punishments.[4] His approach did not address the student's or teacher's identity, desires, or other motivators. However, relying on extrinsic motivation alone is not ideal. It is not equally effective for all students and the benefits of extrinsic rewards tend to decay over time. It also places a focus on the reward and how to get it rather than on learning.

The limitations of this approach led to development of Cognitive Behavior Modification (CBM) theory, according to which "students take more responsibility for their own learning by monitoring their behavior, setting goals, deploying metacognitive strategies, and administering their own rewards."[5] However, the researchers found disadvantages to this method. In research conducted with children, they observed that they choose between setting "low performance standards" or rewarding themselves undeservedly."[6]

Current research emphasizes intrinsic motivation and explores ways to encourage its development in students. Broussard and Garrison organize the current research on motivation into three questions:[7]

1. "Can I do this task? [positive expectancies]
2. Do I want to do this task and why? [value]
3. What do I have to do to succeed in this task? [goal-directed behavior]"[8]

According to Ambrose et al., in order to improve learning and performance it is imperative to motivate students by creating positive expectancies and value of the goal, which leads to goal-directed behavior.[9] They also argue that class climate impacts student motivation and that educators should approach students holistically as "intellectual, social, and emotional beings."[10] In this vein, Linnenbrink and Pintrich's research connects cognition and motivation, and highlights its impact on academic achievement.[11] This concept also acknowledges the relationship of social contexts like the students' intersectional identities, their backgrounds, etc. with the learning process.

There has been significant research exploring student motivation in the context of student learning and information literacy.[12] Authentic teaching aligns with ACRL's *Framework for Information Literacy for Higher Education*[13] and creates a natural method to increase student motivation and engagement in your information literacy (IL) classroom. This concept especially connects to the Framework's emphasis on a more holistic approach to information literacy in general. The Framework states, "This Framework depends on these core ideas of metaliteracy, with special focus on metacognition, or critical self-reflection, as crucial to becoming more self-directed in that rapidly changing ecosystem."[14] If we maintain and share awareness of who we are as teachers, we can more easily present ourselves as complex people in the classroom and, ultimately, open the door for students to do the same. In demonstrating our humanity and complexity, we also model for students the concept that self-reflection is an important component of information literacy practice. Intrinsic motivation is key to the Framework's concept of dispositional development toward information literacy, and its metacognitive underpinnings. The focus of "autonomy, competence and relatedness" when considering intrinsic motivation create clear connections to authentic teaching.[15]

Authentic Teaching and Learning Practices

As instructors, librarians and other IL practitioners are tasked with a unique set of challenges. A basic hurdle facing IL practitioners is that, though teaching is typically at least a small part of our day-to-day activities, often we do not have in-depth training in teaching, educational theory, or learning theories. In our teaching, we must contend with time constraints and limited opportunity to interact with students (one-shot instruction); a dependence on faculty members for creating class climate; and a lack of tools and incentives to hold students accountable for their learning. Authentic teaching's emphasis on individual identities, transparency, and teacher-student relationships could inform our pedagogy and be utilized in our day-to-day practice to bolster student engagement and motivation. Based on the research in authentic teaching theory and motivation, the following are practices that could be useful for IL practitioners.

1. Establishing a clear vision and purpose.

According to Brookfield, "Teaching is about making some kind of dent in the world so that the world is different than it was before you practiced your craft. Knowing clearly what kind of dent you want to make in the world means that you must continually ask yourself the most fundamental evaluative question of all—What effect am I having on students and on their learning?"[16] Reflecting on a broader purpose behind your teaching will help guide your teaching philosophy and practice. Your clear sense of purpose and direction "imbues the students with a sense of confidence. They realize they are under the guidance of someone who is experienced, insightful and, above all, committed."[17] It will also remind you of the value and meaning of your profession and why teaching information literacy skills and concepts is important. In addition, it will show your passion and enthusiasm for the discipline. According to Ambrose et al., "Your enthusiasm might raise students' curiosity and motivate them to find out what excites you about the subject, leading them to engage more deeply than they had initially planned or discover the value they had overlooked."[18] This can help your students to frame their response to why they should want to engage in information literacy instruction, giving support to their own value of those skills.

In addition, one could argue that allowing your personal identity to shape your performance in the classroom facilitates an approach that recognizes the student as a whole person.[19] By being transparent and modeling a way to personally assimilate knowledge into your understanding of information, you create an open and transparent classroom dynamic.

2. Creating authentic relationships with learners.

Once you articulate your purpose as an educator, you can start developing a relationship with your students. According to Laursen, "The authentic teacher does not distance herself from the students by hiding herself behind a detached and impersonal teacher role but views herself as well as the students as human beings with intentions, feelings and interests."[20] Furthermore, in his famous work "Questions I Would Ask Myself If I Were a Teacher," Rogers asks, "Do I dare to let myself deal with this boy or girl as a person, as someone I respect? Do I dare reveal myself to him and let him reveal himself to me? Do I dare to recognize that he/she may know more than I do in certain areas—or may in general be more gifted than I?"[21] This fosters student motivation on a few levels. First, it gives them a sense of confidence in the successful completion of their task: The more one is treated as a capable individual, the more confidence they have in their abilities. It also creates a space for the student to determine their connection to information and how it enriches their life or supports their goals.

3. Building trust and credibility.

Rogers emphasized the importance of revealing our fallibilities, though scholars agree that uncovering those imperfections too soon might undermine a teacher's credibility as an expert.[22] It is imperative to earn students' trust and respect first, before sharing our imperfections with them. This aspect of authentic teaching might be very challenging for information literacy professionals. We rarely have the opportunity to meet with students enough times to build a relationship where we can reveal our imperfections. Students often are not confident about the knowledge and expertise of the librarian; exposing fallibilities too soon could have a negative impact on our credibility as information experts. Thus, we might ask ourselves how this principle applies in our educational context. Sharing an honest confession too early in the session might not be the best idea, but as the session progresses being open about our vulnerabilities—like not knowing the answer to all questions off the top of our heads—is one way we can apply this principle. Other strategies include asking students about their topics, posing additional questions, and showing genuine interest to help build a positive rapport with your students. By modeling such behavior, you establish trust and a safe space for students to experience failure as part of the learning process. Being able to ask questions freely and make mistakes encourages students' further learning and exploration.

4. Giving the freedom to pursue personal interests.

Another important aspect of authentic teaching and learning theory is allowing your students the freedom to pursue their own interests. According to Moustakas, "The sources of health in the individual, in addition to the potentialities, talents and resources which are present at birth, are his freedom of being, his capacity to make choices and determine which experiences are positive and which are negative for his own growth, and his sense of responsibility for being true to his own self."[23] The freedom to "be," the capacity to make choices, and responsibility for those choices are all imperatives in authentic teaching practice. Many educators, librarians included, assume that they know better what their students need to learn than the students themselves, and design instruction based on their own goals rather than the desires and needs of their students. In turn, they are disappointed and frustrated when students find this instruction boring and irrelevant.

Authentic teaching does not mean that we need to bend to students' whimsical wishes, but to deliver instruction based on their interests and passions, to be a facilitator of learning and to trust that they are capable of making their own choices. In other words, "The authentic teacher respects the attitudes and intentions of students and she does not try to manipulate the students but to convince them by giving reasons for her proposals."[24] Kevin M. Klipfel demonstrates how this principle is applied in librarianship in his article "Authenticity and Learning: Implications for Reference Librarianship and Information Literacy Instruction," which shows how giving freedom to students to choose their own research topic influences their motivation and learning.[25] Other important strategies to increase student motivation include providing authentic, real-world tasks and demonstrating relevance to students' academic lives and/or future professional lives.[26] If you show students an explicit connection between information literacy in this course, other academic courses, their future professional lives, etc., it will make it easier for them to appreciate the value of your IL instruction and help them to perceive it as a building block and connection between their many courses.

5. Encouraging creativity and risk taking.

The authentic teacher fosters creativity in their students and encourages them to take risks. The best way to encourage risk-taking is by creating an inclusive class climate and modeling this behavior ourselves. Rogers encourages us to ask these significant questions: "Do I have the courage and the humility to nurture creative ideas in my students? Do I have the tolerance and humanity to accept the annoying, occasionally defiant, occasionally oddball qualities of some of those who have creative ideas? Can I make a place for the creative person?"[27]

When we establish a class climate that welcomes diverse ideas and comments, even those that force us to go outside of our comfort zone, this models risk-taking that fosters a more authentic learning experience. It is much easier to go with a prepared lesson plan, but deviating from our plan and being receptive to students' reactions and concerns are important features of authentic teachers. That does not mean coming to class unprepared and just going with the flow, but knowing when to stop, observe the room for reactions, and effortlessly switch gears in our lesson plan if the situation requires such an adjustment.

Another important premise is to take risks with different teaching methods and approaches. The authentic teacher recognizes that students do not arrive to a classroom as blank slates. They all bring their unique experiences and learning styles; therefore, it is important that we design our classes with consideration to diversity in the classroom. Authentic library instructors do not make assumptions about their students, but use diverse examples and methods to create an inclusive environment that is considerate of different learning styles, sexual orientation, or socio-economic backgrounds. Instead of approaching learning theory and methods as a strict set of rules, seeing their strengths and different applications can enrich your teaching practice. Then they can be combined and integrated creatively and seamlessly into your instruction. For example, debate over what is more effective—lecture, hands-on activities, discussion, etc.—is not productive, because for different students, different methods will be more suitable. Therefore, the authentic teacher experiments and uses diverse approaches in the classroom to acknowledge the individuality of each learner.

Using authentic teaching to incorporate flexibility and fluidity into your practice allows you to create an environment where students can explore the research process in a personal way. This is important on two levels. First, having a class environment that fosters exploration and a personal connection to the research process allows students to move beyond superficial or rote learning. Also, by enabling students to assimilate IL skills and dispositions into their personal identity, students experience the value of learning that process.

6. Seeking the sources of inspiration and cultivating collaborations.

Finally, the authentic teacher is an inspired teacher who never stops searching for ways to connect with students and better respond to their needs. In a study with Danish teachers, Laursen found that the "best" teachers are the ones who cooperate closely with their colleagues.[28] In other words, the authentic teacher does not hold her best ideas for herself but is open to creating a community of learning in the workplace. Such a teacher is not afraid of sharing her ideas and learning from others.

This indirectly improves student motivation, but is also instrumental in successfully applying creative and new theories and practices to impact that motivation. A better prepared and invigorated teacher creates a more vibrant classroom dynamic, which unquestionably is important when trying to foster student motivation. This tenet encourages us as instructors to continuously explore teaching methods, refresh our practices, and identify the best strategies to foster student engagement and motivation.

Authentic Teaching Theory in Practice

There are many ways to implement authentic teaching into your practice. In fact, the core of the theory is that it is authentic to *you*, and not a prescriptive methodology. The following examples are strategies we have experimented with successfully. Hopefully, through our experiences implementing authentic teaching, you the reader will identify ideas for your own practice. To frame these applications authentically, we share our strategies for general classroom use in lower-level and upper-level courses.

Authentic teaching can be used to shape the classroom dynamic. We will make small talk with the students and the professor before class starts and even for the first few minutes of class, to open up communication and ask students questions about their lives. The idea behind this is that it recognizes that we are people and not just instructors, and that they are people and not just one-dimensional students. Small purposeful moves like these always make a difference in the tone of the class; often students will loosen up and be more comfortable talking, and they act as if they feel more involved with the class—they make more eye contact, lean forward, etc. Attempting to use their names also shows that you see them as individual people. This can be difficult in one-shot instruction situations, but one way to attempt it is to write down their names in accordance with where they are sitting if you are teaching from a teacher station or podium. Taking time to create short icebreakers can frame their engagement around their own experiences, like going around the room and having each student identify something they use the library for, or an interesting piece of information they recently found in their everyday life, etc. This is especially effective when you start with your own contribution.

When teaching lower-level classes, like a first-year seminar, librarians often introduce concepts of information literacy for the first time. In these cases, authentic teaching allows the librarian to use their own connection to IL to illustrate how to conceptualize the importance and value of information literacy. For example, if your passion for information literacy lies within the context of building students' agency as individuals, use that to frame your lesson. If students are working on a research paper, then you can propose that the research that they do builds their expertise and knowledge of that subject and gives them the power to take part in a larger conversation. When you connect your lesson content to what you find exciting about information literacy, that passion shows when interacting with students.

Authentic teaching can also frame the examples you use to illustrate a concept. For example, when describing scholarly conversation, you can use the example of a group discussion. This example creates an interactive visual representation of a scholarly conversation that naturally shows how representing different points of view in a claim impacts its arguments and conclusions. It also engages the students when connecting that dynamic to the different potential voices in a conversation (i.e. popular/scholarly sources, primary/secondary, etc.).

In mid- and upper-level classes, as the content is more sophisticated and nuanced, you can bring in more formal or targeted elements of your background. When teaching upper-level French classes, Josefine shares that her father is French, which expands their perception of her as an instructor. In research method or senior seminar classes, she will use examples from her own research to model how individualized the research process can be, but also identify both best practices and the larger theory behind the process. She asks the students to perform a quick three- to five-minute free write to identify different scholarly conversations that they need to contextualize their thesis or question.

When teaching information literacy in Spanish, Anna uses her experience as a learner of the Spanish language at the same institution. It gives her a unique opportunity to be both a teacher and a student. She also appeals to their personal interests; for example, she designed games in Spanish based on the Trivia Crack app, which is popular among the students outside of their usual classwork. Staying abreast with students' interests beyond the classroom is a great way to build a good rapport. It also helps to foster more informal and personal connections.

Both Anna and Josefine teach information literacy sessions in foreign languages. Obviously, in order to do that, language proficiency is required; however, many of us are afraid to show our skills and talents because we do not believe they are perfect enough to be revealed. This elusive sense of perfection prevents us from taking risks in our teaching practices and deprives students of the opportunity to see an instructor learning as they go and incorporating new knowledge into their work. Neither Anna's Spanish nor Josefine's French are perfect, but both students and professors always appreciate their earnest efforts to use the language in their information literacy instruction.

Finally, in pursuit of professional development opportunities we often forget about the priceless resource that is in front of us—our own colleagues. At Dickinson, beyond our regular teaching responsibilities, we allocate time towards sharing ideas and learning from one another. Last year, Anna facilitated a teaching and learning workshop for all information literacy instructors. During the three-day workshop, the instructors discussed teaching and learning theories (among them authentic teaching), practiced presentation skills, applied instructional design models, reviewed assessment methods, and shared their personal classroom experiences and ideas. The goal of the workshops was not a top-down training. Instead, we all took responsibility for our own learning and ideas to contribute to our common goal—becoming better teachers.

Another idea for creating a learning community of information literacy professionals is classroom peer-observations. Notice the purposeful use of the term "observation" instead of peer-evaluation. When evaluated, we tend to switch to a performer mode and this is not consistent with authentic teaching theory. The goal of peer-observation is to obtain feedback on our practice and see our teaching persona through the eyes of our colleagues. In addition, in the maelstrom of our daily duties, we often forget about the most basic thing: the value of conversation. In order to be authentic teachers we need to reclaim the value of community in our workplace.

Conclusion

As there are few examples of literature exploring the application of authentic teaching to information literacy instruction, this chapter serves to introduce the topic, frame it within the context of information literacy instruction, and offer examples of how it can be applied to motivate students. Librarians increase student motivation in their IL instruction by establishing a clear vision and purpose, creating authentic relationships with learners, building trust and credibility, giving the freedom to pursue personal interests, encouraging creativity and risk taking, and seeking the sources of inspiration and cultivating collaborations.

Conscious application of those practices in both one-shot and multiple IL instruction sessions creates a positive class climate, promotes inclusiveness, and encourages students to draw connections to their personal interests as they develop ownership of IL skills. Obviously, establishing an authentic connection with students is easier during multiple instruction sessions because there is more time to build those relationships, but these principles can also be applied in one-shot instruction. Librarians can use personal and relevant examples, implement diverse teaching methods, and create activities that allow the student more autonomy in even the shortest one-shot.

There is still more to explore when applying this theory to information literacy instruction. One of the limitations is that motivation is very difficult to assess; therefore, there is mostly anecdotal evidence showing the relationship between authentic teaching and students' motivation. Lai identified several challenges in assessing motivation, most of them due to the inaccuracies of self-reporting or our inability to observe the cognitive elements of motivation in students directly.[29] Coming up with methods to assess student motivation during IL instruction would be the next step in exploring the relationship between authentic teaching theory and its impact on motivation.

Ultimately, as the *Framework for Information Literacy for Higher Education* is based on the idea of a "constellation" of documents to support the information literacy practitioner, so too is the theory of authentic teaching one star in the larger collection of methodology useful to the IL instructor.[30] It especially can be useful as a practical way to increase student motivation and engagement in your classroom.

Endnotes

1. Clark E. Moustakas, *The Authentic Teacher: Sensitivity and Awareness in the Class-room* (Cambridge, MA: HA Doyle Pub. Co., 1956), vi.
2. Stephen D. Brookfield, *The Skillful Teacher: On Technique, Trust, and Responsive-ness in the Classroom* (San Francisco: Jossey-Bass Publishers, 1990), 17.
3. Emily R. Lai, "Motivation: A Literature Review," *Pearson's Research Report* (2011), 4. Accessed July 26, 2017. http://images.pearsonassessments.com/images/tmrs/Mo-tivation_Review_final.pdf.
4. Deborah Stipek, "Motivation and Instruction," in *Handbook of Educational Psy-chology*, edited by David C. Berliner and Robert C. Calfee (New York: Routledge, 1996), 86.
5. Lai, "Motivation: A Literature Review," 6.
6. Speidel & Tharp, 1980, as cited in Stipek, "Motivation and Instruction," in *Hand-book of Educational Psychology*, ed. David C. Berliner, and Robert C. Calfee (New York: Routledge, 1996), 87; Shavaun Wall, "Children's Self-Determination of Stan-dards in Reinforcement Contingencies: A Re-Examination," *Journal of School Psy-chology* 21, no. 2, 1983: 128. http://dx.doi.org/10.1016/0022-4405(83)90037-71983.
7. Sheri C. Broussard and M. E. Betsy Garrison, "The Relationship Between Class-room Motivation and Academic Achievement in Elementary-School-Aged Children," *Family and Consumer Sciences Research Journal* 33, no. 2 (2004): 107. doi:10.1177/1077727X04269573, as cited in Lai, "Motivation: A Literature Review," 6.
8. Lai, "Motivation: A Literature Review," 7; Susan A. Ambrose, Michael W. Bridg-es, Marsha C. Lovett, Michele DiPietro, Marie K. Norman, *How Learning Works: Seven Research-Based Principles for Smart Teaching*, (Hoboken, NJ: John Wiley & Sons, 2010), 70.
9. Ambrose et al, *How Learning Works*, 70.
10. Ibid., 187.
11. Linnenbrink, Elizabeth A., & Paul R. Pintrich, "Motivation as an Enabler for Academic Success." *School Psychology Review* 31, no. 3 (2002): 313–327, and Paul R. Pintrich, "A Motivational Science Perspective on the Role of Student Motivation in Learning and Teaching Contexts." *Journal of Educational Psychology* 95, no. 4 (2003), as cited in Lai, "Motivation: A Literature Review," 17.
12. John M. Keller, "The Systematic Process of Motivational Design," *Performance & In-struction* 26, no 9-10 (1987): 1–8; Joy H. McGregor, "How Do We Learn," in *Learning and Libraries in an Information Age: Principles and Practice*, ed. Barbara K. Stripling (Englewood, CO: Libraries Unlimited, 1999): 25-53; Joseph Lowman, "Promoting Motivation and Learning," *College Teaching* 38 (1990); Eric Sotto, *When Teaching Be-comes Learning: A Theory and Practice of Teaching* (London: Cassell, 1994); John M. Keller, "Strategies for Stimulating the Motivation to Learn," *Performance & Instruc-tion* 26, no 8 (1987): 1-7; Susan L. Moyer and Ruth V. Small, "Building a Motivation Toolkit for Teaching Information Literacy," *Knowledge Quest* 29, no. 3 (2001):28-32; Morell D. Boone, "Motivation and the Library Learner," in *Bibliographic Instruction and the Learning Process: Theory, Style and Motivation*, ed. Carolyn A. Kirkendall (Ann Arbor, MI: Pierian Press, 1984): 37-47; Maureen Kilcullen, "Teaching Librari-ans to Teach: Recommendations on What We Need to Know," *Reference Services Re-view* 26, no 2 (1998): 7-18; Diane Nahl-Jakobovits and Leon A. Jakobovits, "Learning Principles and the Library Environment," *Research Strategies* 8, no 2 (1990): 74-81.

13. Association of College and Research Libraries, *Framework for Information Literacy for Higher Education* (Chicago, IL: Association of College and Research Libraries, 2015): 2. Accessed July 26, 2017. http://www.ala.org/acrl/standards/ilframework.
14. Association of College and Research Libraries, *Framework for Information Literacy for Higher Education.*
15. Richard M. Ryan, and Cynthia L. Powelson, "Autonomy and Relatedness as Fundamental to Motivation and Education," *The Journal of Experimental Education* 60, no. 1 (1991): 53.
16. Brookfield, *The Skillful Teacher*, 18-19.
17. Ibid, 19-20
18. Ambrose, *How Learning Works*, 85.
19. Carrie Donovan, "Sense of Self: Embracing Your Teacher Identity." *The Library with the Lead Pipe* (August 2009): 2. Library & Information Science Source, http://inthelibrarywiththeleadpipe.org/2009/sense-of-self-embracingyour-teacher-identity.
20. Per F. Laursen, ""The Authentic Teacher," in *Teacher Professional Development in Changing Conditions*, ed. Douwe Beijaard, Pauline C. Meijer, Greta Morine-Dershimer, Tillema Harm (Springer Netherlands, 2005), 203-204.
21. Carl R. Rogers, "Questions I Would Ask Myself If I were a Teacher," *Education* 95, no. 2 (1974): 135.
22. Rogers, "Questions I Would Ask Myself If I Were a Teacher;" Brookfield, *The Skillful Teacher*; Moustakas, *The Authentic Teacher.*
23. Clark E. Moustakas, *The Authentic Teacher*, 9.
24. Laursen, "The Authentic Teacher," 203.
25. Kevin M. Klipfel, "Authenticity and Learning: Implications for Reference Librarianship and Information Literacy Instruction." *College & Research Libraries* 76, no. 1 (2015): 19-30.
26. Ambrose, *How Learning Works*, 83-84.
27. Rogers, "Questions I Would Ask Myself If I were a Teacher," 138.
28. Laursen, "The Authentic Teacher," 210.
29. Lai, "Motivation: A Literature Review," 37, 31.
30. Lisa J. Hinchliffe, "The ACRL Information Literacy Constellation," June 19, 2016, https://lisahinchliffe.com/tag/information-literacy/.

Bibliography

Ames, Carole. "Classrooms: Goals, Structure, and Student Motivation." *Journal of Educational Psychology* 84, no. 3(1992): 261–271.
Association of College and Research Libraries. *Framework for Information Literacy for Higher Education.* Chicago, IL: Association of College and Research Libraries, 2015. http://www.ala.org/acrl/standards/ilframework.
Bandura, Albert. "Self-Efficacy Mechanism in Human Agency." *American Psychologist* 37, no. 2 (1982), 122–147.
Boone, Morell D. "Motivation and the Library Learner," in *Bibliographic Instruction and the Learning Process: Theory, Style and Motivation*, edited by Carolyn A. Kirkendall, 37-47. Ann Arbor, MI: Pierian Press, 1984.
Brookfield, Stephen D. *The Skillful Teacher: On Technique, Trust, and Responsiveness in the Classroom.* Hoboken, NJ: John Wiley & Sons, 2015.

Broussard, Sheri C. and M. E. Betsy Garrison. "The Relationship Between Classroom Motivation and Academic Achievement in Elementary-School-Aged Children." *Family and Consumer Sciences Research Journal* 33, no. 2(2004): 106-120. doi:10.1177/1077727X04269573.

Case, Roland. "Moving Critical Thinking to the Main Stage." *Education Canada* 45, no. 2 (2005): 45–49.

Connell, James P., and James G. Wellborn. "Competence, Autonomy, and Relatedness: A Motivational Analysis of Self-System Processes." *Minnesota Symposia On Child Psychology* 23 (1991): 43-77.

Covington, Martin V. *Making the Grade: A Self-Worth Perspective on Motivation and School Reform.* Cambridge, UK: Cambridge University Press, 1992.

Cranton, Patricia. *Becoming an Authentic Teacher in Higher Education.* Malabar, FL: Krieger, 2001.

Deci, Edward L., Richard Koestner, & Richard M.Ryan. A Meta-Analytic Review Of Experiments Examining the Effects of Extrinsic Rewards on Intrinsic Motivation. *Psychological Bulletin* 125, no. 6 (1999): 627–668.

Donovan, Carrie. "Sense of Self: Embracing Your Teacher Identity." *In The Library with the Lead Pipe* (August 2009): 1-5. *Library & Information Science Source*, http://inthelibrarywiththeleadpipe.org/2009/sense-of-self-embracingyour-teacher-identity.

Eccles, Jacquelynne S., & Allan Wigfield. "Motivational Beliefs, Values, and Goals." *Annual Review of Psychology* 53, no. 1(2002): 109–132.

Grassian, Esther S., and Joan R. *Kaplowitz. Information Literacy Instruction: Theory and Practice.* 2nd ed. New York: *Neal-Schuman,* 2001.

Hidi, Suzanne, & Harackiewicz, Judith M. "Motivating the Academically Unmotivated: A Critical Issue for the 21st Century." *Review of Educational Research* 70, no. 2(2000): 151–179.

Hinchliffe, Lisa J. "The ACRL Information Literacy Constellation," June 19 2016, https://lisahinchliffe.com/tag/information-literacy/.

Houtman, Eveline. "'Mind-Blowing:' Fostering Self-Regulated Learning in Information Literacy Instruction." *Communications in Information Literacy* 9, no. 1 (2015): 6-18.

Keller, John M. "Strategies for Stimulating the Motivation to Learn," *Performance & Instruction* 26, no. 8 (1987): 1-7.

Keller, John M. "The Systematic Process of Motivational Design," *Performance & Instruction* 26, no. 9/10 (1987): 1-8.

Kilcullen, Maureen. "Teaching Librarians to Teach: Recommendations on What We Need to Know," *Reference Services Review* 26, no. 2 (1998): 7-18.

Klipfel, Kevin M. "Authenticity and Learning: Implications for Reference Librarianship and Information Literacy Instruction." *College & Research Libraries* 76, no. 1 (2015): 19-30.

Lai, Emily R. "Motivation: A Literature Review." *Pearson's Research Report* (2011): 1-44. Accessed July 26, 2017. http://images.pearsonassessments.com/images/tmrs/Motivation_Review_final.pdf.

Laursen, Per F. "The Authentic Teacher." In *Teacher Professional Development in Changing Conditions*, edited by Douwe Beijaard, Pauline C. Meijer, Greta Morine-Dershimer, Tillema Harm, 199-212. Dordrecht, The Netherlands: Springer Netherlands, 2005.

Limberg, Louise, Mikael Alexandersson, Annika Lantz-Andersson, and Lena Folkesson.

"What Matters? Shaping Meaningful Learning Through Teaching Information Literacy." *Libri* 58, no. 2 (2008): 82-91.

Linnenbrink, Elizabeth A., & Pintrich, Paul R. "Motivation as an Enabler for Academic Success." *School Psychology Review* 31, no. 3 (2002): 313-327.

Lowman, Joseph. "Promoting Motivation and Learning"" *College Teaching* 38, no. 4 (1990): 136-139.

Matteson, Miriam L. "The Whole Student: Cognition, Emotion, and Information Literacy." *College & Research Libraries* 75, no. 6 (2013): 862-877.

McGregor, Joy H. "How Do We Learn," in *Learning and Libraries in an Information Age: Principles and Practice*, edited by Barbara K. Stripling, 25-53. Englewood, CO: Libraries Unlimited, 1999.

Moustakas, Clark E. *The Authentic Teacher: Sensitivity and Awareness in the Classroom.* Cambridge, MA: HA Doyle Pub. Co., 1956.

Moyer, Susan L. and Ruth V. Small, "Building a Motivation Toolkit for Teaching Information Literacy," *Knowledge Quest* 29 no. 3 (January/February 2001): 28-32.

Nahl-Jakobovits, Diane and Leon A. Jakobovits, "Learning Principles and the Library Environment," *Research Strategies* 8, no. 2 (Spring 1990): 74-81.

Pintrich, Paul R. "A Motivational Science Perspective on the Role of Student Motivation in Learning and Teaching Contexts." *Journal of Educational Psychology* 95, no. 4(2003): 667–686.

Rogers, Carl R. *Freedom to Learn; A View of What Education Might Become.* Columbus, OH: C. E. Merrill Pub. Co., 1969.

Rogers, Carl R. "Questions I Would Ask Myself If I Were a Teacher." *Education* 95, no. 2 (1974): 134-139.

Ryan, Richard M., and Cynthia L. Powelson. "Autonomy and Relatedness as Fundamental to Motivation and Education." *The Journal of Experimental Education* 60, no. 1 (1991): 49-66. http://envoy.dickinson.edu:2105/stable/20152311.

Schunk, Dale. H. "Ability Versus Effort Attributional Feedback: Differential Effects on Self Efficacy and Achievement." *Journal of Educational Psychology* 75, no. 6(1983): 848–856.

Shenton, Andrew K., and Megan Fitzgibbons. "Making Information Literacy Relevant." *Library Review* 53 no. 3 (2010): 165-174.

Sotto, Eric. *When Teaching Becomes Learning: A Theory and Practice of Teaching.* London: Cassell, 1994.

Stipek, Deborah J. "Motivation and Instruction," in *Handbook of Educational Psychology*, edited by David C. Berliner and Robert C. Calfee. New York: Routledge, 1996. 85-113.

Wall, Shavaun M. "Children's Self-Determination of Standards in Reinforcement Contingencies: A Re-Examination," *Journal of School Psychology* 21, no. 2(1983): 123-131. http://dx.doi.org/10.1016/0022-4405(83)90037-71983.

Weiner, Bernard. "'Spontaneous' Causal Thinking." *Psychological Bulletin* 97, no. 1 (1985): 74-84.

Willingham, Daniel T. "Critical Thinking: Why Is It So Hard to Teach?" *American Educator*, 31, no. 2(2007): 8–19.

CHAPTER 6

Teaching Motivation That Works:
Structuring Graduate-Level Research Support Workshops to Foster Centered, Focused, Self-Sufficient Learners

Wendy C. Doucette

All too frequently, instruction librarians' only opportunity to teach students distills down to the fifty-minute, one-shot, make-or-break experience. We disseminate the essential information as requested—how to use the library, how to search the databases, and so on—with little time to explain why all the pieces fit together and why they are important. Worse, well-intentioned librarians often strive to cover as much as possible in these sessions, oversaturating and frustrating their student audience.

Even in settings of brief duration with no follow-up, another approach is possible. Rather than attempting to demonstrate everything at once, we can interject effective, real-life motivational tactics into the session by highlighting the underlying purpose of the process demonstrated. In other words, we can focus not simply on "what" or "how" but on "why." Providing this context and structure not only grounds students, it clarifies and demystifies the process. Understanding that purpose and method are as important as data better empowers students with strategies to pursue their own needs independently. This chapter focuses on graduate students, particularly those in doctoral programs, but with a little creative thinking, these strategies could also be adapted for application with undergraduate learners.

The Problem of Motivation

Even for experts, evoking appropriate, directed student response is a dauntingly difficult task, as Dupont, Galand, and Nils demonstrate in their excellent overview of factors concerning motivation and engagement.[1] After much research and effort, Jayaraman Parameswari and K. Shamala conclude the same,[2] as do David Litalien, Frederic Guay, and Alexandre Morin over the intricacies of conflicting contexts for the external motivations of graduate students.[3] Elisabeth Mueller, Miriam Flickinger, and Verena Dorner, provide a helpful summary of the many facets of this question[4] and structure their investigation to include this complexity: "Based on *students' mixed arguments* in describing the relationship between extrinsic academic motivation and their decision *for or against* a PhD, we formulate the following *competing hypotheses*," namely whether "extrinsic academic motivation is negatively [or] positively related to the intention to earn a PhD."[5]

In creating our instruction program, our objective is not to analyze why our students behave as they do. While the topic is unquestionably interesting, we do not engage in the long debate known to all who have encountered Carol Dweck's (and others') career-spanning research over the effects of mastery (internal) orientation and goals versus those which are performance-oriented (external). Likewise, we leave the finer points of Self-Determination Theory and Achievement Goal Theory to others.

Empathy as a Core Value

When serving our own students, we begin with empathy.[6] The pursuit of higher education is difficult enough for traditional undergraduates; for graduates, the additional challenges of maintaining a home, holding other employment, and caring for children (or parents or both) are often overwhelming. In one-on-one consultation sessions with the author, a number of international students (usually male) have revealed the financial pressure on them not only to graduate and begin successful careers but to continue to send money home on the meager salary of a graduate student. American female single-parent graduate students likewise self-report the same financial pressure. The bottom line is that whatever the additional circumstances, graduate school is hard enough for everyone. Because we know graduate students are often stretched to the breaking point, we take a holistic approach and respect our students' motivations as their own private concerns.

With the onslaught of requirements and deadlines facing graduate students, we are well aware of the reluctance to commit to learning anything deemed "extra." As subject specialists, program professors fulfill the critical roles of instructor and mentor within the student's chosen program of study. As Niall Hegarty diplomatically states, "Although professors may be motivated by their realm of instruction, they are not however employed for their motivational skills."[7] Our graduate-level research support workshops incorporate multiple voices and perspectives into teaching what Nella Roberts and Maria Plakhotnik call the "'how-to' insights to navigate through [doctoral students'] long journey."[8] This commitment to teaching "everything else, or how to get out of grad school" fulfills a critical support role.[9] As Cheryl Polson states, "The quality of the graduate experience and success can vary significantly …and is a function, in part, of the student services made available to them."[10] Regardless of the bounty or surfeit of practical support given within individual programs, the graduate workshop series provides a common platform for learning the essential "how-to" skills necessary for completing graduate school.

Andragogy, Not Pedagogy

The most important role of the graduate research and instruction librarian and the embedded librarian for the Graduate Thesis and Dissertation Boot Camp is keeping students on track and moving forward in order to graduate on schedule. We serve students from every degree program. Ranging from their early twenties to their early fifties, our students, international and domestic, come from diverse backgrounds. They have extensive work experience or none at all. They have previous master's or other advanced degrees or are in graduate school for the first time. They possess a multiplicity of specialties, aptitudes, and differences, amounting to what Elaine Cox calls "an abundance of prior life and work experience."[11] Despite all these differences, they all share the same common goal: successful completion of coursework leading to capstone or thesis or dissertation and graduation. Even students with previous advanced degrees confess they don't know how graduate school works.

Like all academic librarians, we receive standing or ad hoc invitations from faculty to teach library instruction to graduate students. At East Tennessee State University,[12] we go one step further by supplementing these opportunities by offering our own permanent workshops. Given every semester, this comprehensive program of research-level support covers a wide spread of essential topics. Begun in Fall 2015 with six workshops, the series grew to nine in Spring 2016 and will expand to eleven in Fall 2017. The underlying framework of the entire program rests on the concept of andragogy.

Although he did not author the term, Malcolm Knowles popularized the concept of andragogy in his 1970 book, *The Modern Practice of Adult Education*.[13] Almost fifty years later, the essence of the theory is still valid: pedagogy as a slow, incremental model for the long-term education of children versus andragogy as a self-motivated, point-of-need response to the immediate learning requirements of adults. To the category of "adult," I include undergraduates as equally worthy beneficiaries of performance-based library instruction.[14] As Chan Sang puts it, "Active learning is more effective than passive learning, regardless of age."[15]

Contextualizing Content for Real Life
Structure

The adult-focused concept of andragogy allows us to structure our graduate-level research support workshops for graduate students and faculty in a way that meets their schedule. While the piloted additional weeknight session students begged us to offer were discontinued due to poor attendance, the mainstay Saturday five- to six-hour sessions remain the core of the program. After working together for most of a day, students form a de facto cohort. Meeting face-to-face in a high-tech, research-oriented space (the library's collaborative wireless classroom) creates a supportive learning environment with a social component and peer support especially beneficial for students in online-only programs. We schedule the workshops four to six weeks into the semester, aiming for the sweet spot after students have settled into classes and before midterms.

Our adult learners want to make enduring changes in the way they approach information literacy, engage with research, and create satisfactory work-life balance. Based on a "problem-centered orientation to learning,"[16] we strive to appeal to visual learners through presentations and posters, to auditory learners through discussion, and to kinesthetic learners through direct participation.[17] In the registration process, registrants are given the opportunity to state in their own words why they are coming and what they want us to cover. Through the sign-in sheet and initial introductions, we can begin to form a sense of the composition of the day's group. Zorn-Arnold and Conaway correctly stress the value of this seemingly insignificant step of getting to know the day's participants before beginning the session.[18] Feeling comfortable, relaxed, and heard, students are prepared to receive our message in a grade-free, advisor-free, committee-free, judgment-free zone.

The Library's ownership of the program allows us to showcase our knowledge base as subject specialists in our own domain. Although it is certainly not a prerequisite to offering any sort of workshop, all of the librarians who teach the workshops hold faculty status and are professional researchers and postgraduates. Faculty instructors who are subject specialists teach our workshops by invitation.

Content

Andragogy allows us to unify the seemingly disparate pieces of a large-scale academic writing project as part of a whole. For our stressed students, the best motivational strategy is to equip them not only with information but with solutions to the immediate practical challenges common to all graduate students. The content we deliver needs to be timely, relevant, and applicable to real-life. This deliberate grounding allows students to "consciously practice making insightful connections across their courses, organizing information into meaningful units, and finding personal relevance in what they learn."[19]

We contextualize every workshop we offer, demonstrating the import and value of each piece. There is, frankly, very little value in things that are extremely useful—citation management, for example—without explaining not only how to do it but why it is important and what larger function it serves.

The graduate-level research support workshops address points-of-need at various stages, from those of first-semester students to more seasoned graduates. Piloted first among a series of offerings in the Thesis and Dissertation Boot Camp in Spring 2015 with two workshops ("Organize Yourself" and "Academic Searching"), the series opened to all graduate students and faculty in Fall 2015 with six workshops. Content is evaluated every semester with edits and new offerings based on instructor and student feedback.

The Spring 2017 series consisted of the beginner workshops, "How Academic Research Works," "Academic Searching," "Time and Project Management," "Understanding Data," and "Formatting APA Papers," and advanced workshops, "Academic Publications and Presentations," "Establish Your Professional Identity," "Infographics for Academics," and "Medical Searching." Given on sequential Saturdays, students are free to choose as many workshops as they wish to attend. The designations of "beginner" and "advanced" are concessions to logistics; it is simply not possible to have a day longer than six hours without stressing both instructors and participants. Realistically, however, the separation makes sense. Attempting to teach medical searching without establishing some prior familiarity with academic searching overall is inadvisable. Students do tend to follow the full sequence and only rarely sign up for an advanced workshop without having taken one or more in the beginner series first.

After welcome and introductions, we begin the series by stating that no matter how well they did as an undergraduate, nobody really understands how to succeed in graduate school until after they've completed the degree. It remains true that one has to learn by doing, but there are rules. (This is, in fact, the content of the first slide of the first workshop.) The starting workshop of the series, "How Academic Research Works" (HARW), presents the basics, such as plagiarism, copyright, and—based on demonstrated student need—literature review, in a behind-the-scenes contextual view explaining how academic research actually works.

HARW was created using the ACRL Information Literacy Framework. Given and heavily edited five times, this workshop remains the launching point for situating the student's role in the process. Core concepts from the framework, such as "Scholarship is a Conversation," take on new meaning when faced with the irrefutable evidence of oneself as an active scholar. Interestingly, the information within this workshop, particularly concerning the nature and purpose of literature review, is considered revelatory not only to new students but even to advanced students who have already completed the methodology courses required by their own departments. By explicitly framing the thesis or dissertation as an academic *narrative*, students understand not only the function of the pieces which make up the structure or project (thesis or dissertation) but their own agency as creators.[20] This level of consciousness reinforces Werner and Rogers' belief that through better self-positioning, "adult learners may better construct first-time dissertations more *mindfully* or in a more conscious manner with recognition of themselves, as learner and researcher."[21]

All of the workshops actively reference problem- and scenario-based assignments to address everyday, professional issues. When piloted, the workshop, originally titled "Organize Yourself," focused only on computer-related issues such as version control, file storage, and backups. Over time and with a greater direct understanding of how students address their computer issues, but more importantly, their current ability to attain the level of organization required overall to finish a project as daunting as thesis or dissertation, the workshop has shifted into two main parts. Now called "Time and Project Management," the first half ("The Easy Part") still addresses computing. The second half ("The Hard Part"), offers strategies for altering personal behavior with proven techniques such as the Pomodoro method and the Japanese philosophies of Morita therapy, naikan, and kaizen.[22]

Dupont, Galand, and Nils categorize two types of perfectionism: "Adaptive perfectionism, which refers to the setting of high personal standards, and maladaptive self-perfectionism, which refers to high levels of self-criticism and doubt about actions."[23] This distinction is intellectually interesting, but for our purposes, perfectionism of any kind tends to go hand-in-hand with procrastination. Perhaps the strongest anti-procrastination philosophy we recommend is Constructive Living. Popularized by Dr. David K. Reynolds, this application of Japanese Morita therapy distills down to a "just do it" mindset, where progress is made despite one's emotional mindset.[24] In other words, wanting to or "feeling like" researching, writing, or making any type of progress toward a thesis or dissertation becomes irrelevant. By working regardless of emotional state, breaking unmanageable goals into small, achievable milestones, and understanding how all of the disparate pieces required to complete a graduate program come together, prospective graduates matriculate. Beyond establishing a self-directed, targeted, time-sensitive mindset capable of addressing impending academic goals and deadlines, this shift in personal ideology can result in changed lives as well.

Partnerships and Satisfaction Ratings

The graduate-level research support workshops allow us to offer specialized services year-round to any interested graduate student or faculty member. Beginning our initial offerings as part of Thesis and Dissertation Boot Camp increased our value to the Graduate School, the organizer of Boot Camp. We leverage this partnership to successfully market the series each semester to all graduate students, graduate program coordinators, and faculty via the Graduate School's mailing lists. In our exit surveys, 70 percent said they heard about workshops through the Graduate School. Eleven percent heard the Graduate Research and Instruction Librarian speak about them at Graduate Orientation, an event to which we are invited by the Graduate School. The remainder are recommendations via graduate coordinators, other faculty, or friends. As a result of personal contact with a graduate coordinator or after in-class library instruction, some coordinators and faculty have begun requiring students in specific programs to attend the beginner series. As a given, we advertise the workshops on the library's webpage.

The majority of those attending are graduate students (92.2 percent versus 7.8 percent faculty). While we warmly welcome our fellow faculty, graduate students are the intended audience. These students frequently make individual follow-up appointments with us as a result of this contact. This, in turn, often leads to appointments with "friends of friends." International students, especially, leverage this peer network, bring unregistered friends to workshops and repeat topics as needed.

Of the 180 students who voluntarily completed exit surveys in Academic Years 2015–16 and 2016–17 (a 94.7 percent completion rate), only one person said the information learned in the workshops was not valuable to them. We are extremely pleased with our 99.994 percent satisfaction rating.

We also gauge participant readiness to implement the techniques discussed in the workshops. To the exit survey question "How likely are you to act on what you learned today?," 77 percent responded, "I'm starting today"; 23 percent answered, "I will eventually"; and (happily) 0 percent selected, "I'll never get around to it."

Fostering Self-Sufficient Learners

Our definition of successful student motivation is a practical one. Our goal is to provide support to graduate students about the process of becoming successful master's and doctoral candidates. By teaching the skills to fully own and manage the project and timetable, understand the parts of a thesis or dissertation, and write steadily and incrementally, regardless of the desire to do so or not, we hope to ingrain structure and method to what can otherwise seem a chaotic and random process. The stress on work-life balance is a healthy reminder to preserve the integrity of one's personal support system of good health and strong relationships.

In addition to having formed a collegial, professional relationship with us as a result of participating in the workshops, participants receive access to a LibGuide that includes all of the links and references covered within the series.

Starting in Summer 2016, we created a motivation shelf of books on writing, research methodology and design, data visualization, combating procrastination, the neuroscience of creative work, kaizen, constructive living, and related topics. These titles are selected because of their clear "how-to" message. We have found the Palgrave Study Skills[25] series particularly helpful and have ordered a large part of this collection.[26] Many students, particularly international, have stated their preference for a how-to book they can read and study at leisure when they have free time.

The motivation shelf provides the additional service traditionally expected of libraries by going beyond merely providing an array of databases that can be accessed on demand. Putting the right book into the right person's hand at the right time is a tangible manifestation that help is available here and now, not parceled out into academic articles or floating about in the internet's ether. In addition to brightly colored signage, the motivation shelf is equipped with marketing information about the workshops and contains our contact information.

Roberts and Plakhotnik point out that "at times just knowing that actual and potential resources are available is comforting."[27] We have found this to be true. Throughout the first semester we launched them, students nervously asked if the workshops would be offered again. We assured them that the workshops would return later in the semester, next semester, next year, and that there would be plenty of time for students to take them. We also promptly remind them that we are available on demand for individual appointments at any time of the year, including summer.

The exponential and reciprocal benefits of motivation

Turning motivation into something practical that can be taught, learned, and made immediately relevant has allowed us to grow beyond the micro role of librarian helping with reference and citations to fully engaging with the macro role of student service provider. We furnish students with the help they need when they want it. As Cox states, "The majority of learners are not ready for coaching until the easiness and familiarity of their everyday life is interrupted in some way."[28] It is difficult to imagine any educational situation with higher stakes and less guidance than graduate school. Not only is it our commitment and our honor to provide the services we do, we are perpetually touched by the depth of gratitude we receive from our students for helping them attain their educational goals and move on to the next chapter of their lives. Unexpectedly, we have become the recipients of the enduring rewards of this endeavor by finding our own motivation renewed.

Endnotes

1.   Serge Dupont, Benoît Galand, and Frédéric Nils, "Factors Predicting Postponement of a Final Dissertation: Replication and Extension," *Psychologica Belgica* 54, no. 1 (2014): 33–54, http://doi.org/10.5334/pb.ac; for more on motivation and self-determination theory, see: David Litalien, Frederic Guay, and Alexandre J. S. Morin, "Motivation for PhD Studies: Scale Development and Validation," *Learning and Individual Differences* 41 (2015): 1–13, http://dx.doi.org/10.1016/j.lindif.2015.05.006.
2.   Jayaraman Parameswari, and K. Shamala, "Academic Motivation and Locus of Control Among Engineering Students," *Journal of Psychosocial Research* 7, no. 1 (2012): 163.
3.   Litalien, Guay, and Morin, "Motivation for PhD Studies," 11.
4.   See their table: Elisabeth F. Mueller, Miriam Flickinger, and Verena Dorner, "Knowledge Junkies or Careerbuilders? A Mixed-Methods Approach to Exploring the Determinants of Students' Intention to Earn a PhD," *Journal of Vocational Behavior* 90 (2015): 81, http://doi.org/10.1016/j.jvb.2015.07.001.
5.   Mueller, Flickinger, and Dorner, "Knowledge Junkies or Careerbuilders?," 78.
6.   For more on the importance of empathy as a means of reaching students, see: Fiona Murphy, "Motivation in Nurse Education Practice: A Case Study Approach," *British Journal of Nursing* 15, no. 20 (2006): 1133, http://dx.doi.org/10.12968/bjon.2006.15.20.22300.
7.   Niall Hegarty, "Adult Learners as Graduate Students: Underlying Motivation in Completing Graduate Programs," *Journal of Continuing Higher Education* 59, no. 3

(2011): 146, http://dx.doi.org/10.1080/07377363.2011.614883.

8. Nella A. Roberts and Maria S. Plakhotnik, "Building Social Capital in the Academy: The Nature and Function of Support Systems in Graduate Adult Education," *New Directions for Adult & Continuing Education* 122 (2009): 49, http://dx.doi.org/10.1002/ace.333.

9. Dupont, Galand, and Nils, "Factors Predicting Postponement," 35; Litalien, Guay, and Morin, "Motivation for PhD studies," 12.

10. Cheryl J. Polson, "Adult Graduate Students Challenge Institutions to Change," *New Directions for Student Services* 102 (2003): 59, http://dx.doi.org/10.1002/ss.90.

11. Elaine Cox, "Coaching and Adult Learning: Theory and Practice," *New Directions for Adult & Continuing Education* 2015, no. 148 (2015): 29, http://dx.doi.org/10.1002/ace.20149.

12. Located in Johnson City, Tennessee, East Tennessee State University (ETSU) has approximately 11,000 undergraduate and 2,400 graduate students.

13. Malcolm Knowles, *The Modern Practice of Adult Education* (New York, NY: Association Press, 1970), 305–06.

14. For more on performance-based active learning, see: Jonathan Stolk and Janie Harari, "Student Motivations as Predictors of High-Level Cognitions in Project-Based Classrooms," *Active Learning in Higher Education* 15, no. 3 (2014): 231–47, http://dx.doi.org/10.1177/1469787414554873.

15. Chan Sang, "Applications of Andragogy in Multi-Disciplined Teaching and Learning," *MPAEA Journal of Adult Education* 39, no. 2 (2010): 33.

16. Tracy Carpenter-Aeby and Victor G. Aeby, "Application of Andragogy to Instruction in an MSW Practice Class," *Journal of Instructional Psychology* 40, no. 1 (2013): 10.

17. Doris Lee, John McCool, and Laura Napieralski, "Assessing Adult Learning Preferences Using the Analytic Hierarchy Process," *International Journal of Lifelong Education* 19, no. 6 (2000): 551, doi:10.1080/02601370050209078.

18. Barbara Zorn-Arnold and Wendy Conaway, "The Keys to Online Learning for Adults," *Distance Learning* 13, no. 2 (2016): 2.

19. Meera Kommeraju, Steven Karau, Ronald Schmeck, and Alen Advic, "The Big Five Personality Traits, Learning Styles, and Academic Achievement," *Personality and Individual Differences* 51 (2011): 476, http://dx.doi.org/10.1016/j.paid.2011.04.019.

20. Goddu references the importance of narrative learning as the inclusion of "reflect[ion] on his or her own life experiences." Kevin Goddu, "Meeting the CHALLENGE: Teaching Strategies for Adult Learners," *Kappa Delta Pi Record* 48, no. 4 (2012): 173, http://dx.doi.org/10.1080/00228958.2012.734004.

21. Thomas P. Werner and Katrina S. Rogers, "Scholar-Craftsmanship: Question-Type, Epistemology, Culture of Inquiry, and Personality-Type in Dissertation Research Design," *Adult Learning* 24, no. 4 (2013): 163, http://dx.doi.org/10.1177/1045159513499549.

22. Developed by Francesco Cirillo, the official home of the Pomodoro Technique is https://cirillocompany.de/. Dr. David K. Reynolds has devoted his career to writing about Morita therapy and naikan. Dr. Robert Maurer has written clearly and concisely on kaizen.

23. Dupont, Galand, and Nils, "Factors Predicting Postponement," 34–35.

24. Nearly thirty years after the fact, the author continues to sincerely acknowledge

David K. Reynolds' 1984 *Constructive Living* as the book that prevented me from leaving graduate school when I was struggling to write my dissertation.

25. "Palgrave Study Skills," Macmillan Publishers LTD, www.palgravestudyskills.com.
26. One caveat: this British series occasionally refers too specifically to details about O Levels for our comfort. If the advice is too UK-specific and no longer general recommendations about research or writing, we will choose to not purchase a title for fear of confusing students in our American university.
27. Roberts and Plakhotnik, "Building Social Capital in the Academy," 48.
28. Cox, "Coaching and Adult Learning," 33.

Bibliography

Carpenter-Aeby, Tracy, and Victor G. Aeby. "Application of Andragogy to Instruction in an MSW Practice Class." *Journal of Instructional Psychology* 40, no. 1 (2013): 3–13.

Cox, Elaine. "Coaching and Adult Learning: Theory and Practice." *New Directions for Adult & Continuing Education* 2015, no. 148 (2015): 27–38. http://dx.doi.org/10.1002/ace.20149.

Dupont, Serge, Benoît Galand, and Frédéric Nils. "Factors Predicting Postponement of a Final Dissertation: Replication and Extension." *Psychologica Belgica* 54, no. 1 (2014): 33–54. http://doi.org/10.5334/pb.ac.

East Tennessee State University. "University Headcount 2016." Accessed April 19, 2017. https://www.etsu.edu/opa/factbooks/Fact%20Book%202016%20PDF/01.2%20%20University%20Enrollment/01.2.0%20University%20Headcount.pdf.

Goddu, Kevin. "Meeting the CHALLENGE: Teaching Strategies for Adult Learners." *Kappa Delta Pi Record* 48, no. 4 (2012): 169–73. http://dx.doi.org/10.1080/00228958.2012.734004.

Hegarty, Niall. "Adult Learners as Graduate Students: Underlying Motivation in Completing Graduate Programs." *Journal of Continuing Higher Education* 59, no. 3 (2011): 146–51. http://dx.doi.org/10.1080/07377363.2011.614883.

Knowles, Malcolm. *The Modern Practice of Adult Education*. New York: Association Press, 1970.

Kommeraju, Meera, Steven Karau, Ronald Schmeck, and Alen Advic. "The Big Five Personality Traits, Learning Styles, and Academic Achievement." *Personality and Individual Differences* 51 (2011): 472–77. http://dx.doi.org/10.1016/j.paid.2011.04.019.

Lee, Doris, John McCool, and Laura Napieralski. "Assessing Adult Learning Preferences Using the Analytic Hierarchy Process." *International Journal of Lifelong Education* 19, no. 6 (2000): 548–60. doi:10.1080/02601370050209078.

Litalien, David, Frederic Guay, and Alexandre J.S. Morin. "Motivation for PhD studies: Scale Development and Validation." *Learning and Individual Differences* 41 (2015): 1–13. http://dx.doi.org/10.1016/j.lindif.2015.05.006.

Mueller, Elisabeth F., Miriam Flickinger, and Verena Dorner. "Knowledge Junkies or Careerbuilders? A Mixed-Methods Approach to Exploring the Determinants of Students' Intention to Earn a PhD." *Journal of Vocational Behavior* 90 (2015): 75–89. http://doi.org/10.1016/j.jvb.2015.07.001.

Murphy, Fiona. "Motivation in Nurse Education Practice: A Case Study Approach." *British Journal of Nursing* 15, no. 20 (2006): 1132–35. http://dx.doi.org/10.12968/bjon.2006.15.20.22300.

Parameswari, Jayaraman, and K. Shamala. "Academic Motivation and Locus of Control Among Engineering Students." *Journal of Psychosocial Research* 7, no. 1 (2012): 159–67.

Polson, Cheryl J. "Adult Graduate Students Challenge Institutions to Change." *New Directions for Student Services* 102 (2003): 59–68. http://dx.doi.org/10.1002/ss.90.

Roberts, Nella A., and Maria S. Plakhotnik. "Building Social Capital in the Academy: The Nature and Function of Support Systems in Graduate Adult Education." *New Directions for Adult & Continuing Education* 122 (2009): 43–52. http://dx.doi. org/10.1002/ace.333.

Sang, Chan. "Applications of Andragogy in Multi-Disciplined Teaching and Learning." *MPAEA Journal of Adult Education* 39, no. 2 (2010): 25–35.

Stolk, Jonathan, and Janie Harari. "Student Motivations as Predictors of High-Level Cognitions in Project-Based Classrooms." *Active Learning in Higher Education* 15, no. 3 (2014): 231–47. http://dx.doi.org/10.1177/1469787414554873.

Werner, Thomas P., and Katrina S. Rogers. "Scholar-Craftsmanship: Question-Type, Epistemology, Culture of Inquiry, and Personality-Type in Dissertation Research Design." *Adult Learning* 24, no. 4 (2013): 159–66. http://dx.doi. org/10.1177/1045159513499549.

Zorn-Arnold, Barbara, and Wendy Conaway. "The Keys to Online Learning for Adults." *Distance Learning* 13, no. 2 (2016): 1–5.

CHAPTER 7

Tagging and Sticky Notes:
Two Exercises for Teaching Students to Synthesize Prior Research

Rebecca Price

Introduction

Once students have accumulated piles of articles, what should they do next? As academic and research librarians, we most commonly teach research skills. As a start, we help students learn to find the background literature in their disciplines, and literature reviews are often the beginning or culmination of their academic projects. But when it comes time to turn sources into synthesis, students often do not know where to start.

This chapter presents two learning exercises that engage students in the process of synthesis: tagging and sticky notes. In the chapter, I relate the exercises to the Association of College and Research Libraries (ACRL) framework for information literacy, present preparation details and learning outcomes, share lesson plans and adaptation ideas, and briefly discuss the motivational techniques in play.

Lesson Plan
Overview, Including ACRL Framework Frames/Concepts

The ACRL Framework for Information Literacy in Higher Education recognizes that information generation is an iterative process that leads novice learners to "recognize the significance of the creation process."[1] The concept of synthesis is sometimes difficult to grasp since it involves transforming prior research into something entirely new. The ACRL Framework asks librarians to help students synthesize.[2] Just as we teach students to retrieve, analyze, critique, and organize information, we can also teach them what to do with that information. This includes teaching students how to conceptualize and visualize synthesis. By implementing the exercises presented in this chapter, librarians can encourage students to synthesize prior research and to thoroughly immerse themselves in research inquiry.[3] With these exercises, the librarian becomes the facilitator who helps students incorporate practices essential to the ACRL Framework, namely: monitoring gathered information and assessing for gaps or weaknesses, organizing the information in meaningful ways, and synthesizing ideas from multiple sources.[4] In addition, these librarian-facilitated exercises lead students to demonstrate "persistence, adaptability, and flexibility" and "seek multiple perspectives" during an iterative, sometimes frustratingly ambiguous research process.[5] Finally, as recommended by the framework, these exercises enable librarians to lead students into the conversations inherent in scholarship: conversations with prior research, with classmates, with librarians, with instructors, and with themselves.[6]

Learning Outcomes

Completing the tagging exercise will teach students to
- identify themes and concepts present in the literature and
- complete an initial synthesis which serves as the foundation for a written paper.
- Completing the sticky notes exercise will teach students to
- construct a "road map" or outline structure of their papers and
- refer to this structure while they write their first drafts.

Lesson Preparation

To prepare for each of these exercises, students should have found the majority of the prior research on their topic and organized their findings. In some courses with which I have worked, instructors have incorporated reference management software (e.g., EndNote or Mendeley) into assignments throughout the semester. Of course, this is not always the case. When this kind of preparation has not occurred, it may be helpful for instructors to assign homework prior to the librarian-led session, having students organize their articles into an Excel or Google spreadsheet with columns for author, article title, journal title, and publication date.[7] No matter how students choose to organize the research they have found, the entries need to be searchable by author, article title, publication date, and journal title.[8]

Since the goal is that students begin to conceptualize synthesis and see first-hand how the process works, all is not lost if they arrive unprepared. Ways to prepare for the unprepared student include providing a sample literature review spreadsheet (shareable in the course management system or Google) or to have the students partner with those who are prepared. In either case, students can still achieve the goal of grasping the idea of synthesis as it plays out in a literature review.

Lesson Plans
Exercise One: Tagging (#) to Conceptualize Synthesis

The tagging exercise engages students in conceptualizing synthesis by using the social media concept of tagging. Put into play, these social media skills allow librarians to guide novice researchers through the essential steps of synthesis: critical analysis, recognizing themes, and grouping, using a language and thought process that is familiar to their everyday lives.[9] Emphasizing connections to personal utility and meaningfulness increases student interest and motivation to understand the content of a lesson.[10]

Time to complete

This exercise is suitable for a one-shot workshop or classroom session. Depending on the size of the class and the length of time available, it can range from twenty minutes to an hour to complete.

Part 1

Timing is important in order to keep students from getting lost in the murky world of synthesis. As the very first step, refer to the students' prepared article organization. Take three to five minutes to demonstrate how one might annotate an article entry on the table/Mendeley/EndNote, etc. Using one student's organizational tool as an example, annotate an entry in front of the class. Ask, "Why did you choose this article?" "In what ways is it like other articles?" "What's special about it?" Write or type a notes field for this article to demonstrate what it might look like. Then, give the students about ten minutes to add "notes" fields to their organizational systems. Wander among the students as they work and ask the sorts of prompt questions you demonstrated with the group.

Students add their own notes for each article. Similar to analytic memos used in data analysis, adding notes prompts students to document thought processes and decisions made.[11] Each note can be a few words or a few sentences—just enough to capture the essence of why the student selected that article for the literature review. Depending on the level of the student and the extensiveness of the literature review, students may need to complete this exercise with just a sample of the literature that they have found. The instructor should take into consideration the amount of time allotted and instruct students to annotate an appropriate portion of the literature that they have found. Another variation could be to add annotation to the organization task they complete before class.

At this point, take a few moments to discuss the concept of hashtags with the class. It may be helpful to ask, "Who uses Instagram [or other trendy social media site]? Why do you tag? Why do you think other people tag? How do you choose the tags that you use?"

Part 2

Instruct students to work individually and add tags (#) that they deem appropriate for each paper. These tags serve as tools that will help them structure their syntheses.[12] To prevent students from getting stuck, gently interrupt their progress. As students begin to tag their papers, visit with individuals and prompt their thought processes with probing questions. The following list is a good place to start:
- How would you tag this article?
- What category does this tag represent?
- Which articles would have the same tags?
- Which tags would differ?
- What groups are these tags starting to create?
- What themes are starting to emerge?
- What different ways could you organize your paper, based on the tags you applied?[13]

Part 3

After allowing the students several minutes to tag their papers, instruct students to share their findings with their neighbors, or ask some students to share with the class.

Evidence-based rationale

This activity is built upon aspects of multiple and interactive literacies, problem-based learning, and personal utility and meaningfulness. According to Anderson and May, librarians who teach a broad concept of information literacy should "include multiple and interactive literacies recognizing the influence of social and cultural contexts."[14] In this case, the contexts include students' comfort with and attachment to social media. The universality of students' social media usage includes aspects that translate to instruction.[15]

In their 2014 book, *Teaching Crowds: Learning and Social Media,* Dron and Anderson discuss how the concept of tagging can help students learn the vocabulary of a subject area and the different ways in which that subject is conceptualized. Tagging also helps students create value for their classmates, and eventually the readers of their papers, as they choose categories and tags that they deem relevant and contextually meaningful. Perhaps most important, "tagging is a meta metacognitive tool that encourages the tagger to think about the things that matter to him or her, helping the process of sense-making, embedding reflection in the process of creation, and thus enhancing learning."[16]

Finally, tagging reflects an example of problem-based learning (PBL) in which students receive a task, reflect and identify problems, and formulate methods to solve them, noting and explaining the strategies that they use.[17] According to Savery, PBL increases motivation by handing over responsibility for both the process and the solution to the learner.[18] PBL motivates students by prompting them to take ownership of their own learning.[19] Students who come unprepared may find motivation by partnering with others and seeing their progress.

Exercise Two: Sticky Notes to Visualize Synthesis

The sticky notes exercise actively engages novice researchers in a visual synthesis of the literature. The librarian facilitates collaborative synthesis, and team members help each other organize and visualize the structures of their draft literature reviews.

Time to complete

Sticky notes can be completed in forty-five minutes or fill more than an hour, depending on the students and time available.

Setup

Sticky notes help students to visualize themes and begin to structure a synthesis. Begin by dividing the class into groups of two to four students and equipping each student with a pad of sticky notes. Each student should have his or her organizational tool (e.g., Mendeley, Excel, or EndNote) available and open. Allot enough wall space to each group so that each member has an area roughly a foot wide and three feet high.

Part 1

Start by giving students some time to write main points from each article on separate sticky notes, along with enough information to identify the source.

Part 2

After a few minutes, instruct each group to work on one team member's paper at a time, adhering sticky notes to the wall. Instruct the group members to work together to begin to organize each student's sticky notes together by themes. Give the groups time to alter and play with paper organization. To ensure that everyone gets a chance to work on this collaborative synthesis, divide class time so that each group member gets an equal number of minutes, and remind the groups when it is time to switch to someone else's project.

Gentle guidance will help groups create "road maps" or sticky note structures of each group member's paper. As the groups work, visit each group. To facilitate synthesis, ask questions like the ones listed below:

- Step back and look. What goes with what?
- What if you moved this note? What would change about your paper?
- Where is the start of your paper?
- Where is the end?
- Can you get to the end directly from the start?
- Is there anything missing in the middle?

If time permits, allow each group to select one member's paper to discuss with the class.

Part 3

At the end of the class period, remind students to document the final organization of their sticky notes for future reference while they write their papers. Students often choose to take pictures of their sticky note syntheses with their phones.[20]

Evidence-based rationale

The sticky note exercise uses aspects of concept mapping in which abstract ideas are transformed into concrete visual representations.[21] Concept mapping exercises help students break away from the idea of learning as a linear process or rote memorization of facts. Instead, students begin to embrace the many possibilities that arise in meaningful learning experiences.[22] Similar to the previous exercise, sticky notes uses concepts of problem-based learning, and students are responsible for the outcome of the exercise.[23] In addition, this exercise implements cooperative learning practices, including guiding questions that librarians use to provide the structure necessary for improved student outcomes.[24]

Motivational Techniques in Play

The exercises presented in this chapter share some motivational techniques, while each contains unique methods that set it apart. Shared motivational techniques include those suggested by the dynamic theory of personality and problem-based learning.[25] In each exercise, students begin a task only to face interruptions from the instructor, who asks guiding questions. These interruptions provide the motivational tension endorsed by Lewin, and the questions spur students to focus renewed efforts on successfully completing the task at hand.[26] In addition, both exercises prompt students to take responsibility for the outcome, a motivational feature of problem-based learning.[27] According to Savery, "Critical to the success of [problem-based learning] is the selection of ill-structured problems (often interdisciplinary) and a tutor who guides the learning process and conducts a thorough debriefing at the conclusion of the learning experience."[28] Ill-structured problems reflect the messiness that is present in everyday life; they have unclear goals (e.g., What is synthesis?) and incomplete information (e.g., How will we turn these articles into a cohesive contribution?). With PBL techniques, the instructor guides the learning process, helping students turn messy stacks of articles into well-planned literature reviews. And in both of these exercises, the instructor guides students to think through the process of synthesis, debriefing them at the conclusion of the learning experience.

While these exercises share some motivational techniques, each contains some unique aspects. The tagging exercise mimics real life, a connection that is recognized by many motivational theories as critical for student learning.[29] In prior research, librarians have found that tying classroom instruction to students' real-life interests and experiences increased the perceived value of the exercises.[30] When students perceive that a task directly translates to their everyday lives (or feeds their social media addictions), they become increasingly motivated to participate.[31] Interests like social media, of which almost every student has multiple accounts, allow instructors to integrate students' real lives into learning.[32]

How to Adapt/Possible Adaptations

Both of the techniques presented in this chapter are adaptable to different settings. As an individual exercise, teaching tagging works at a library information desk, as an online course exercise, or as an in-class exercise. Similarly, the sticky notes exercise can be adapted for use in online classrooms. For example, in one hybrid in-person/online course, students mapped out their papers at home using sticky notes (or scraps of paper taped to a wall) and documented these structures with digital pictures. They shared these pictures on the group discussion board and other students responded with questions or comments. In a variation for the tagging exercise, students working in groups can each tag the same set of articles and then discuss the tags they have chosen. This approach is even more like social media and opens students' minds to the myriad ways in which the same item (in this case, an article) might be categorized.[33] As is essential for problem-based learning, the instructor debriefs the groups of students, keeping them on topic and their research question in mind.[34]

When led by a facilitating librarian, the exercises can help students conceptualize and visualize the nebulous concept of synthesis. With these exercises, students learn how to critically analyze and find themes within prior research and how to begin to synthesize that information into high-quality literature review write-ups.[35] While a due date can motivate students to write, it cannot guide them through a synthesis. These exercises equip librarians to employ motivational techniques and structured guidance as students learn to synthesize the literature.

Endnotes

1. Association of College and Research Libraries, "Framework for Information Literacy for Higher Education," January 11, 2016, http://www.ala.org/acrl/standards/ilframework.
2. Association of College and Research Libraries, "Framework."
3. Association of College and Research Libraries, "Framework."
4. Association of College and Research Libraries, "Framework."
5. Association of College and Research Libraries, "Framework."
6. Association of College and Research Libraries, "Framework."
7. For more about supporting organization of references, see: Jenny Emanuel, "Users and Citation Management Tools: Use and Support," *Reference Services Review* 41, no. 4 (2013): 639–59; and Don MacMillan, "Mendeley: Teaching Scholarly Communication and Collaboration Through Social Networking," *Library Management* 33, no. 8/9 (2012): 561–60.
8. Rebecca H. Price, "The Four-Part Literature Review Process: Breaking it Down for Students," *College Teaching* 65, no. 2 (2017): 90.
9. Price, "The Four-Part Literature Review Process," 90.
10. Amanda M. Durik and Judith M. Harackiewicz, "Different Strokes for Different Folks: How Individual Interest Moderates the Effects of Situational Factors on Task Interest," *Journal of Educational Psychology* 99, no. 3 (2007), 597–610; Suzanne Hidi and Judith M. Harackiewicz, "Motivating the Academically Unmotivated: A Critical Issue for the 21st Century," *Review of Educational Research* 70, no. 2 (2000), 151–79.
11. For more about analytic memos, see: Johnny Saldaña, *The Coding Manual for Qualitative Researchers* (Thousand Oaks, CA: Sage, 2009), 32–44.
12. Price, "The Four-Part Literature Review Process," 90.

13. Price, 90.
14. Karen Anderson and Frances A. May, "Does the Method of Instruction Matter? An Experimental Examination of Information Literacy Instruction in the Online, Blended, and Face-to-Face Classrooms," *Journal of Academic Librarianship* 36, no. 6 (2010): 499.
15. Khe Foon Hew and Wing Sum Cheung, "Use of Web 2.0 Technologies in K-12 and Higher Education: The Search for Evidence-Based Practice," *Educational Research Review* 9 (2013): 51; Jon Dron and Terry Anderson, *Teaching Crowds: Learning and Social Media* (Edmonton, AB: AU Press, 2014), 181.
16. Dron and Anderson, 181.
17. John R. Savery, "Overview of Problem-Based Learning: Definitions and Distinctions," *International Journal of Problem-Based Learning* 1, no. 1: 9–20; Karl A. Smith et al., "Pedagogies of Engagement: Classroom-Based Practices," *Journal of Engineering Education* 94, (2005): 96.
18. Savery, "Overview of Problem-Based Learning," 13.
19. Savery, "Overview of Problem-Based Learning," 13; John R. Savery, "Enhancing Motivation and Learning Through Collaboration and the Use of Problems," in *Inspiring Students: Case Studies in Motivating the Learner,* eds. Stephen Fallows and Kemal Ahmet (London: Kogan Page Limited, 1999), 40.
20. Price, "The Four-Part Literature Review Process," 91.
21. David Hay, Ian Kinchin, and Simon Lygo-Baker, "Making Learning Visible: The Role of Concept Mapping in Higher Education," *Studies in Higher Education* 33, no. 3 (2008): 302–03.
22. Hay, Kinchin, and Lygo-Baker, "Making Learning Visible," 302–03.
23. Smith et al., "Pedagogies of Engagement," 96.
24. Smith et al., 96; and Steven Yamarik, "Does Cooperative Learning Improve Student Outcomes?," *Journal of Economic Education* 38, no. 3 (2007): 275.
25. Kurt Lewin, *A Dynamic Theory of Personality* (New York, NY: McGraw-Hill, 1935); Savery, "Overview of Problem-Based Learning," 13; Savery, "Enhancing Motivation and Learning," 40.
26. Lewin, *Dynamic Theory of Personality*, 243–45.
27. Savery, "Overview of Problem-Based Learning," 13; Savery, "Enhancing Motivation and Learning," 40.
28. Savery, "Overview of Problem-Based Learning," 12.
29. Lewin, *A Dynamic Theory of Personality*, 247; Durik and Harackiewicz, "Different Strokes," 598; Hidi and Harackiewicz, "Motivating," 154.
30. Sarah Steiner and M. Leslie Madden, "Integrating Current Media Sources to Improve Student Interest in the Credit IL Course," in *Best Practices for Credit-Bearing Information Literacy Courses*, ed. Christopher V. Hollister (Chicago: Association of College and Research Libraries, 2010): 160.
31. Durik and Harackiewicz, "Different Strokes," 598.
32. Kaveri Subrahmanyam et al., "Online and Offline Social Networks: Use of Social Networking Sites by Emerging Adults," *Journal of Applied Developmental Psychology* 29, no. 6 (2008): 426; Chris Evans, "Twitter for Teaching: Can Social Media be Used to Enhance the Process of Learning?," *British Journal of Educational Technology* 45, no. 5 (2014): 902–15; Dron and Anderson, "Teaching Crowds," 181.
33. Dron and Anderson, "Teaching Crowds," 181.

34. Savery, "Overview of Problem-Based Learning," 12.
35. Price, "The Four-Part Literature Review Process," 90-91.

Bibliography

Anderson, Karen, and Frances A. May. "Does the Method of Instruction Matter? An Experimental Examination of Information Literacy Instruction in the Online, Blended, and Face-to-Face Classrooms." *Journal of Academic Librarianship*, 36, no. 6 (2010): 495–500.

Dron, Jon, and Terry Anderson. *Teaching Crowds: Learning and Social Media*. Edmonton, AB: AU Press, 2014.

Durik, Amanda M., and Judith M. Harackiewicz. "Different Strokes for Different Folks: How Individual Interest Moderates the Effects of Situational Factors on Task Interest." *Journal of Educational Psychology* 99, no. 3 (2007): 597–610.

Emanuel, Jenny. "Users and Citation Management Tools: Use and Support." *Reference Services Review* 41, no. 4 (2013): 639–59.

Evans, Chris. "Twitter for Teaching: Can Social Media be Used to Enhance the Process of Learning?" *British Journal of Educational Technology* 45, no. 5 (2014): 902–15.

"Framework for Information Literacy for Higher Education," Association of College and Research Libraries (ACRL). Accessed March 24, 2017. http://www.ala.org/acrl/standards/ilframework#process.

Hay, David, Ian Kinchin, and Simon Lygo-Baker. "Making Learning Visible: The Role of Concept Mapping in Higher Education." *Studies in Higher Education* 33, no. 3 (2008): 295–311.

Hew, Khe Foon, and Wing Sum Cheung. "Use of Web 2.0 Technologies in K-12 and Higher Education: The Search for Evidence-Based Practice." *Educational Research Review* 9 (2013): 47–64.

Hidi, Suzanne, and Judith M. Harackiewicz. "Motivating the Academically Unmotivated: A Critical Issue for the 21st Century." *Review of Educational Research* 70, no. 2 (2000): 151–79.

Lewin, Kurt. *A Dynamic Theory of Personality*. New York: McGraw-Hill, 1935.

MacMillan, Don. "Mendeley: Teaching Scholarly Communication and Collaboration Through Social Networking." *Library Management* 33, no. 8/9 (2012): 561–60.

Price, Rebecca H. "The Four-Part Literature Review Process: Breaking it Down for Students." *College Teaching* 65, no. 2 (2017): 88–91. http://www.tandfonline.com/doi/full/10.1080/87567555.2016.1276042.

Saldaña, Johnny. *The Coding Manual for Qualitative Researchers*. Thousand Oaks, CA: Sage, 2009.

Savery, John R. "Enhancing Motivation and Learning Through Collaboration and the Use of Problems." In *Inspiring Students: Case Studies in Motivating the Learner*, edited by Stephen Fallows and Kemal Ahmet, 33–41. London: Kogan Page Limited, 1999.

Savery, John R. "Overview of Problem-Based Learning: Definitions and Distinctions." *International Journal of Problem-Based Learning* 1, no. 1: 9–20. Accessed May 18, 2017. https://doi.org/10.7771/1541-5015.1002.

Smith, Karl A., Sheri D. Sheppard, David W. Johnson, and Roger T. Johnson. "Pedagogies of Engagement: Classroom-Based Practices." *Journal of Engineering Education*

94 (2005): 87–101.

Steiner, Sarah, and M. Leslie Madden. "Integrating Current Media Sources to Improve Student Interest in the Credit IL Course." In *Best Practices for Credit-Bearing Information Literacy Courses*, edited by Christopher V. Hollister, 160–72. Chicago, IL: Association of College and Research Libraries, 2010.

Subrahmanyam, Kaveri, Stephanie M. Reich, Natalia Waechter, and Guadalupe Espinoza. "Online and Offline Social Networks: Use of Social Networking Sites by Emerging Adults." *Journal of Applied Developmental Psychology* 29, no. 6 (2008): 420–33.

Yamarik, Steven. "Does Cooperative Learning Improve Student Outcomes?" *Journal of Economic Education* 38, no. 3 (2007): 259–77.

CHAPTER 8

Designing a Collaborative Cross-Campus Drop-in Workshop Series to Motivate Lifelong Learners

Tim Miller and Sarah Fay Philips

Introduction

The Humboldt State University Library decided to redesign library instruction and programming; we hoped to make our offerings more scalable and engaging for our students. To that end, we cultivated campus partnerships and designed a workshop program to motivate students to participate in co-curricular learning. Implementing a successful drop-in workshop program is challenging; many librarians have experience with poorly attended drop-in workshops, inadequate campus support, and insufficient student interest. Our library's initial experience was no different, yet with planning, partnerships, and some useful tools, we were able to address these issues and build a cross-campus collaborative workshop series that not only found marked success but is also sustainable and manageable by a handful of library staff. In this chapter, we discuss a few important strategies that helped us administer our program. We will also share an effective and easy to use instructional design tool for helping ensure that our program's pedagogical goals will be met when working with a wide array of facilitators.

In 2013, our library started offering drop-in information literacy workshops in addition to in-class instruction. We had received anecdotal feedback from students and faculty that these types of workshops were needed. For example, students seeking help at the reference desk would remark that the library should offer workshops on navigating databases. Similarly, faculty would say they wanted students to learn specific research skills or technologies but did not have the flexibility to provide instruction during class time. To meet these requests, the library developed and promoted drop-in information literacy workshops but had far fewer attendees than expected. Faculty and librarians worried that students lacked the interest or motivation to learn outside of their required classes. However, those of us involved with the program were enthusiastic about our encounters with workshop participants who expressed appreciation for and interest in this type of co-curricular learning. We needed to find a way to make the program sustainable and ensure the learning experience was motivating for students.

An early strategy was to partner with staff from the Learning Center, which is co-located in the library. The Learning Center shares the library's goal of supporting the academic success of students, and they were close to ending their drop-in workshop program due to low attendance. We began working together on lesson plans and marketing strategies for the coming semester. This collaboration, which came to be known as SkillShops, has grown over the course of three years to include facilitators from two dozen departments across the university and has nearly 1,600 attendees per year. The Skill-Shops program offerings have expanded to include academic, personal, and professional skills. SkillShops topics are varied and include basic research, citation management, financial literacy, test preparation, grammar, résumé writing, relationship skills, grant writing, digital media, and time management. (For a list of most frequently attended SkillShops titles, see Appendix 8B). SkillShops are facilitated by faculty and staff from various departments, including the Learning Center, Writing Studio, Academic and Career Advising Center, English Department, Youth Educational Services, and the African American Center for Academic Excellence. (For a list of which departments our facilitators come from, see Appendix 8C).

SkillShops are fifty-minute drop-in workshops facilitated by faculty, staff, and students. They are structured to allow for at least twenty-five minutes of active learning and immediate application of new skills. The SkillShops program is designed to cultivate lifelong learners through the encouragement of play, discovery, and social interaction. A key aspect of the SkillShops model is that students have the agency to choose the workshops most relevant to them and their needs. We work with faculty and staff to identify topics that aren't covered in the curriculum, and SkillShops attendance is voluntary.

When we began offering information literacy workshops, many other academic and student support units on campus were also offering their own workshops. While discussing our initial attendance problems, we learned that every other department was also experiencing lackluster success. As we set out to determine how to improve our marketing and promotion on campus, we quickly discovered a crippling lack of communication across departments. This deficiency reflected our heavily siloed campus culture. Over time, however, we found that by engaging and ultimately collaborating with these departments, we could break through the silos to market and promote our workshops as a team rather than scattered units. We have found the Skill-Shops program to be efficient, and the campus community also greatly appreciates that the library is the central place to organize and market workshops. The administration of the campus-wide SkillShops was scalable because of the resources in place for library event management (such as online registration and calendar management through Springshare's LibCal platform). Promotion for each workshop reached a larger audience because we used a shared print and online calendar created by the library. This means that when Counseling and Psychological Services promote their workshops (such as Mind Over Mood), they also promote workshops by the Career Center (such as Preparing for Graduate School) as well as workshops by other SkillShops partners.

The SkillShops program has created a centralized collaborative co-curricular environment managed by the library and built on the work already being done across campus. The SkillShops program is organized to continuously improve and expand existing workshop offerings by sharing resources and gathering student feedback. Some of this collaborative work increases the workload of SkillShops partners but also adds demonstrable value, such as significantly increased attendance and participation in a community of learners with other facilitators. The library has shouldered most of this extra work but has also gotten the most value from SkillShops, with the library recognized as the home of cross-campus programming focused on student success.

To ensure that SkillShops were meeting the needs of our students, we gathered student feedback after each workshop. We used this feedback to improve the program as a whole. For example, we included a question about what other topics students would like to learn about to determine where to expand our offerings. During facilitator training, we shared this feedback with the facilitators and discussed strategies for refining and developing their lessons.

SkillShops facilitators bring expertise in a wide variety of topics and teaching styles, providing a depth of skill sets which we use to continuously improve the program. Facilitators are part of an active team that collaborates to develop and model supportive learning environments where students are motivated to design their own learning experiences. As such, SkillShop lesson plans need to be designed to be relevant to students, connect to their coursework, promote their independence as learners, and support their personal and professional growth. To help facilitators build lessons that motivate students, we have created a lesson planning template and toolkit that is based on the ARCS Model of motivation developed by John Keller.[1]

The Role of Motivation in Learning

People are more likely to be intrinsically motivated, or at least have a higher autonomous level of extrinsic motivation, if they know they have a positive relationship with a person with whom they feel secure, such as a mentor or peer.[2] Facilitators, which can be faculty, staff, graduate students, or undergraduate peer educators, serve as either—and sometimes both—mentor or peer. The presence of student facilitators helps establish a student-centered classroom where the student facilitator acts as a model of what can be learned and accomplished, and where student participants are more active because they see the student teacher as more accessible.[3] Learners are also more likely to be intrinsically motivated if they feel they have autonomy or a choice in performing the task,[4] such as choosing which workshop to attend based on interest.

Since SkillShops facilitators have varying degrees of instructional experience, we needed to find a framework that was easy to understand and apply. In order to help facilitators use the ARCS model, our toolkit and lesson planning template is shared at regular meetings and training.

Skillshops are designed to focus on learner motivation and active learning, both of which promote independence and lifelong learning.[5] Facilitators also focus on incorporating activities that help ensure that learners have a chance to apply what they are learning during the workshop. SkillShops facilitators are required to include at least twenty-five minutes of active learning in each workshop because, as Crow suggested in "What Motivates a Lifelong Learner," students will experience increased intrinsic motivation and/or autonomy through this immediate application.[6] Dunlap and Grabinger describe the lifelong learner as a collaborative learner who is self-directed, intrinsically motivated, and in possession of metacognitive awareness.[7] McCombs states "the motivated person is a lifelong learner, and the lifelong learner is a motivated person."[8]

SkillShops facilitators provide meaningful feedback to students about the activity, and that feedback helps students understand what was accomplished during the workshop and lets them know how they can improve or expand on what they learned. Most SkillShops are smaller (ten students average) than traditional classroom instruction, so the instructor can personalize the experience for the students. This smaller workshop size also makes it easier for facilitators to spend time providing specific feedback, which goes a long way to ensuring that learners gain confidence and leave the workshop satisfied with their ability to perform the new skill(s).

Overview of ARCS
General Overview

Our SkillShops toolkit was intended to help facilitators incorporate the four categories of Keller's ARCS Model of motivation (attention, relevance, confidence, and satisfaction) into their lessons. We found the ARCS model to be an effective pedagogical tool, yet simple enough to use with a large number of facilitators with a wide range of instructional experience. ARCS is a condensed and simplified model that draws upon many other motivational theories and is described by Keller as "a synthesis of motivational concepts and characteristics."[9]

The four ARCS categories of motivation are the product of John Keller's synthesis of motivational literature into simple and useful macro-level concepts.[10] These categories provide a basis for understanding and implementing various concepts, theories, strategies, and tactics around learning motivation. Stimulating and sustaining learner motivation can be challenging. Finding reliable and valid methods for motivating learners can also be difficult. The ARCS model meets these challenges by providing guidance in analyzing the motivational characteristics of a group of learners and designing motivational strategies based on this analysis.[11]

Keller acknowledges that ARCS does not provide simple, prescriptive solutions to motivational problems. Instead, ARCS offers a problem-solving approach that leads instructors to solutions appropriate for a given situation. Keller describes ARCS as "an evolving model" and that the "goal of the model, like the goal of many educators, is to assist in helping learners want to learn and develop in ways that help them build satisfying lives that contribute something positive to their world."[12]

Why We Like ARCS

Keller's ARCS model includes a ten-step system to guide the instructional design process. Since we have limited time to work with the dozens of Skill-

Shops facilitators, we developed a simplified lesson planning tool that addresses three general instructional concepts: learning outcomes, active learning, and action plan steps. As part of our process in overseeing and managing the SkillShops program, we meet with our campus partners for regular facilitator meetings and occasional department training. During these meetings and training, facilitators share their strategies, lessons and activities, and any challenges they have experienced. Many facilitators who attend SkillShops training are new to teaching and find the ARCS model easy to apply and useful in lesson planning. Our campus has recently been without a Center for Teaching and Learning and the accompanying professional development opportunities. We have found that many staff and faculty are eager to engage in training and discussions to improve their teaching and learning practices.

How We Adapted ARCS
The ARCS Grid

	Attention	**R**elevance	**C**onfidence	**S**atisfaction
Objective	From the start of the SkillShop, grab learners' attention to get them curious and engaged.	Establish relevance in order to motivate learners.	Instill a sense of confidence in learners by helping them to believe that they can succeed.	Learners should be proud and satisfied of what they have achieved throughout the SkillShop.
Strategy	Stimulate inquiry Variety	Choice Present or future usefulness	Positive goals Realistic goals Focus on *their* efforts (control)	Feedback showing that learning was achieved and will be achievable in the future Immediate application
Lesson Planning Questions	How will you help the learners *want* to learn? What different methods and activities have you incorporated? How many?	How did you design the lesson to be useful to them now? How might the lesson prepare them for the future?	What is the goal? How will you structure the workshop to give learners the agency to achieve the goal?	What will you do so the learners know that they achieved the goal? How will you confirm that they know how to proceed in the topic?

Adapted from: Keller, J. M. (2000). How to integrate learner motivation planning into lesson planning: The ARCS model approach. *VII Semanario, Santiago, Cuba*, 1-13.

FIGURE 8.1: ARCS LESSON PLANNING GRID

We created a simple grid of our revised ARCS categories to aid facilitators in lesson planning. Facilitators can use the grid to ensure that the motivation of the learners is taken into consideration when designing a workshop or selecting an activity.

Objectives
ATTENTION

Objective: From the start of the SkillShop, grab the learner's attention to get them curious and engaged.

SkillShops facilitators are encouraged and coached to use active learning techniques that involve students in play and discovery. Students practice the new concepts in a safe and fun environment where they are encouraged to explore new ideas. Facilitators employ a variety of practices to engage students, including the use of media, discussion, small group work, and peer-to-peer learning.

RELEVANCE

Objective: Establish relevance and allow choice in learning opportunities in order to motivate learners.

Facilitators use various strategies to demonstrate the relevance of the Skillshop, but more importantly design the workshop to be relevant to student academic, professional, and personal goals. Facilitators also allow students to choose learning opportunities relevant to them and to share their thoughts and questions to ensure their specific needs are addressed.

CONFIDENCE

Objective: Instill a sense of confidence in learners by helping them to believe that they can succeed.

The SkillShops provide co-curricular support for student learning. Skill-Shops allow students to explore and try out new concepts and strategies during the workshops, which help them to gain the confidence to be independent learners. SkillShops facilitators provide feedback to students about what was achieved in the workshop in order to reinforce a sense of accomplishment.

SATISFACTION

Objective: Learners should be proud and satisfied of what they have achieved throughout the SkillShop.

Through active learning exercises, students are given the opportunity to apply new strategies and concepts during the workshops and are given meaningful feedback from the facilitators. Students leave the workshops with direct experience as to how the content can be useful to them. Facilitator and peer feedback can be helpful in this as well, providing the student with encouragement, correction, and recognition.

Strategies

The second row provides sample strategies for each component of ARCS. All SkillShops include at least twenty-five minutes of active learning in which students get to try out and explore the concepts covered during the session. Any activity can be tailored to include one of the ARCS categories. An activity can be designed to allow the students to try out the skill during the workshop, giving them confidence. For example, during a workshop on learning how to read a scholarly article, students work in small groups and practice active reading techniques. After the groups have had time to do the activity, all participants engage in a discussion about how they applied the active reading techniques and whether or not they worked. Students gain confidence because they will leave the session not only having learned about active reading but having had the chance to try it out and get feedback from the facilitator and their peers.

Lesson Planning Questions

The last row is a list of questions to help the facilitator develop a lesson plan that incorporates all of the different motivation categories. After a lesson plan is drafted, the facilitator can use the questions to make sure that they are incorporating a variety of pedagogical techniques to motivate students.

For example, the questions "What different methods and activities have you incorporated? How many?" remind a facilitator to add variety to their lesson plan. Using only one mode to share information (e.g., lecture) or only one type of activity (e.g., discussion) can make some students who do not engage with that mode feel left out. Even in a short fifty-minute workshop, learners can lose their focus. Adding another mode for sharing information, like a video or pair-share activity, can add variety to keep learners' attention. An individual activity, like a one-minute write, can reach those folks who might be less comfortable sharing in a group discussion or need time to process their thoughts first.

Lesson Planning Worksheet

The lesson planning worksheet (see figure 8.2) is designed to be used in coordination with the grid as a planning and brainstorming tool for capturing ideas. A facilitator can use the grid to help identify different elements of the lesson and then use the worksheet to generate ideas for motivating learners.

Humboldt State University
Arcata, California

SkillShops Lesson Plan with ARCS

Workshop title: ____________________

Brief description: ____________________

Design the Activities	Look at the ARCS Lesson Planning Questions (gray paper) and answer the questions below.
Describe how you will share the SLOs with the learners:	Explain how sharing these outcomes will encourage learner motivation. When will you restate/check-in about the SLOs
Describe a specific activity that will encourage discovery, exploration and/or social connections during the SkillShop:	Identify which objective this activity addresses (gray paper, first row). How is the activity designed to improve learner motivation?
Describe how you will help learners develop an action plan (what they will do after the workshop):	What will you do so the learners know that they achieved the goal? How will you confirm that they know how to proceed in the topic?

www.library.humboldt.edu

FIGURE 8.2: ARCS LESSON PLANNING TOOL

The worksheet is a simplified lesson plan with two columns and three rows. In the first column, the facilitator identifies three components of the lesson: the learning outcomes, planned activities or exercises, and the action plan activity for the learner. The facilitator then uses the lesson planning questions in the grid to identify how each of these components will address learner motivation.

Facilitator Toolkit

The lesson activity toolkit is a list of activities that address one or more of the ARCS components. We collect these activities during our SkillShops facilitator meetings and training. The toolkit is distributed to aid in the sharing of best practices and to provide facilitators who have less teaching experience with tools to help them create meaningful activities and lessons.

Case Studies

Included below are three examples of SkillShops that have been facilitated by the co-authors and the strategies for incorporating ARCS: Zotero Citation Management (software), Basic Research, and Shooting 360-degree Video.

Table 8.1. Attention Skillshops

Attention	Zotero	Basic Research	360-degree Video
Strategy	Stimulate Inquiry Variety	Stimulate Inquiry	Stimulate Inquiry
Activity that encourages discovery, exploration, and/or social connection	Demonstrate how quickly Zotero will create citations and bibliographies. Students have negative experience creating citations, so when they see how easy it is to create citations and bibliographies with Zotero, their curiosity is stimulated. During every step of the process, we use relevant examples from students' current research.	Ask attendees about their experiences reading multiple papers for a large research assignment, such as a capstone paper. How can they manage to read so many scholarly papers? How can they quickly determine if a paper is relevant? During the presentation, include quiz questions that address the learning outcomes.	Begin by asking students, "How is 360 video different from traditional video?" Facilitator leads discussion, with examples, demonstrating how they are different. Show what 360 video looks like on a desktop computer as well as through VR viewers.

Table 8.2. Relevance Skillshops

Relevance	Zotero	Basic Research	360-degree Video
Strategy	Choice (Present or future use)	Present or future usefulness	Choice (Present or future use)
Activity that encourages discovery, exploration, and/or social connection	During introductions, students name a citation style they use. The instructor uses each style mentioned so students know they will have current and future use for what they are learning. Students use their style when creating bibliographies.	Quick survey of students to see who has had to conduct research for an assignment, who has upcoming assignments. Survey students to see what techniques they currently use to read papers.	Talk about and ask students how they normally shoot video. What are some differences with 360 video that they will encounter? Show video and other content that SkillShops attendees have created in past.

Table 8.3. Confidence Skillshops

Confidence	Zotero	Basic Research	360-degree Video
Strategy	Realistic goals	Focus on their efforts	Focus on their efforts
Activity that encourages discovery, exploration, and/or social connection	At the beginning of the workshop, the instructor demonstrates how Zotero creates dynamic bibliographies and explains that they will learn how to do this. The workshop provides multiple opportunities to create citations with Zotero.	Students work in small groups to read an academic article and identify the hypothesis, findings, discussion, and suggestions for future research. Groups will report out and reflect on the fact that they have determined what the article is about and if it is relevant to a particular research question.	Allow students to use the camera and view the preview of their footage. Ask them how it has turned out and what they can do differently. Post video to Digital Media Lab Showcase page to recognize their work and allow them to share it.

Table 8.4. Satisfaction Skillshops

Satisfaction	Zotero	Basic Research	360-degree Video
Strategy	Immediate application Feedback showing learning was achieved	Feedback showing learning was achieved	Feedback showing learning was achieved
Activity that encourages discovery, exploration, and/or social connection	Have many opportunities for students to add to their library and create citations. We do not move on until everyone has been successful.	After reading the article in groups (see activity in Confidence above), discuss the answers and provide feedback.	Recap and highlight peer feedback and observations during and after shooting video.

Outcomes
Growth

Since 2013, the SkillShops program has grown from 150 to nearly 1,600 attendees per year.

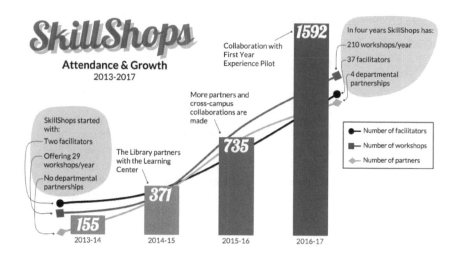

FIGURE 8.3: SKILLSHOPS GROWTH

We attribute the program's growth to the development of cross-campus partnerships and the collaborative spirit of the SkillShops facilitators, who are motivated to continuously improve the program. As our partnerships and collaborations deepen, the number of campus departments and the number of facilitators who want to offer SkillShops grow. This has led to an increase in workshop topics and the number of workshops offered. (For a list of the most frequently attended SkillShops, see Appendix 8B).

Feedback

Early on, we gathered feedback from learners individually. Facilitators created their own written surveys and chose how often to distribute them. Since the surveys were handed out during the workshops, the response rate was stellar, but many of us felt that the feedback was not very meaningful. It seemed that students were rushing off to class and were most frequently writing kind words and thank yous even when we, as facilitators, knew that things did not go quite so well.

As we gained more department partnerships and more facilitators, we began scheduling monthly meetings to coordinate and plan. Many facilitators already had experience and anecdotal knowledge about what was and was not working, but we did not have a lot of accessible data to share and analyze. After a year of growth, we had so many facilitators that we struggled to find the time to gather and analyze simple data such as our attendance statistics. We knew that even if we could coordinate the collection of paper feed-back surveys, we would neither have the time nor the resources to input and analyze that data. These factors led us to create an online survey system that would be easier for us to administer, provide consistent questions and for-mat, and would also give students sufficient time to consider their responses thoughtfully and provide them with confidentiality so they would feel secure in providing honest responses.

We worked with the facilitators and our campus Institutional Research office to develop a standard set of questions designed to get the answers that each of us was looking for. (For a list of the assessment questions emailed to each participant, see Appendix 8A). Using Google Forms, we created an on-line survey that was emailed out to attendees after each workshop. This system enabled us to be more efficient and accurate in gathering student responses and streamlined the process of analyzing the SkillShops program data.

As the weeks went by, we sent out hundreds of surveys via email after each workshop. Initially, we sent out reminders a week following the first email but decided to discontinue that in order to avoid overwhelming participants at-tending multiple SkillShops. Though our earlier paper survey response rate was considerably higher, our online survey response rate, 16 percent, was more than double the campus average of 7 percent for online surveys.

At the end of that semester, we had a large amount of informative data that we could efficiently and effectively share with SkillShops facilitators. We provided each facilitator with the anonymized survey responses for their own SkillShops as well as responses to SkillShops on similar topics. For exam-ple, someone who offered basic research and citation workshop got their own feedback as well as the feedback for all of the information literacy workshops. We felt it was important to provide them with an idea of the types of feed-back that their colleagues were getting in order to destigmatize negative feed-back but also to provide them with an understanding of how students were perceiving their learning experiences across a range of topics and teaching methods. Facilitators have expressed an appreciation for this larger context and have frequently identified ways to improve from comments given to other facilitators.

Reflections

Through our experience over the past three years, we have learned the value of gathering feedback and using it to guide our next steps. Gathering and analyzing feedback has allowed us to find solutions to specific problems but has also provided us with insights that were otherwise unknown to us. We often found this type of unexpected information helped give us a better un-derstanding of our students' perspectives. For example, during our second year of collaborating, after we had gained a diverse group of facilitators from across campus, students expressed their excitement to be in a co-curricular environment where they were exposed to different areas of campus and were given the opportunity to explore concepts that seldom come up in their course of study.

The survey question "What made you want to attend this SkillShop?" elicited reasons why students attend a specific SkillShop:

- They recognized a gap in their knowledge about applying for graduate school, jobs, or internships.
- They had an assignment they did not know how to complete, such as "Never done an annotated bibliography so I wanted to know how."
- People using new technology or software (e.g., Google Drive, Camtasia, WordPress) for work or class but wanted training to use it more effectively.
- Students recognized personal challenges with finances, stress, and social anxiety and attended a SkillShop to get resources to help themselves.
- Many students returned to another workshop because "I have taken SkillShops before and they have been helpful for the most part." They also picked a workshop when the topic was "a real-world applicable skill shop [rather] than just another 'how to use the library' type of deal."

Next Iterations

As new initiatives are developed on campus, such as our newly grant-funded peer-health educator workshop program, SkillShops is sought out as the partner and venue for learning. As the campus designs a new First-Year Experience program, each new student will identify and attend relevant SkillShops during their transition to the university. The library and SkillShops are at the center of co-curricular learning.

Appendix 8A: Assessment emailed to each participant after they attend a SkillShop

1. What motivated you to attend this SkillShop?
2. Please check all the places that you heard about this SkillShop.
   a. from Professor
   b. Facebook
   c. whiteboard in Library
   d. printed flyer
   e. weekly email announcements
   f. Humboldt State event calendar
   g. Library website
   h. from a friend
   i. Other (fill in answer)
3. Would you recommend this SkillShop to a friend?
4. Is there anything that you would change about this SkillShop to improve it? Please explain.
5. What did you learn in the SkillShop that you didn't know before?
6. What additional topics would you like to see as a SkillShop?

Appendix 8B: List of most frequently attended SkillShops (2014—2017)

Test Preparation (various discipline and test-specific topics)

Reading Scholarly Articles (L)

Discussing White Privilege (L)

Zotero Citation Management (L)

Financial Skills for College and Beyond

Wikipedia Edit-a-thon (L)

Hour of Code (L)

Time Management

Google Drive Basics (L)

Finding Internships

Let's Eat Grandma: Using Commas, Colons, and Semicolons Correctly

Résumé and Cover Letters

Writing Clearly and Concisely

Finding Grants and Fellowships (L)

(L) = Librarian lead SkillShop

Appendix 8C: List of where our facilitators come from (2014—2017)

Academic & Career Advising Center*
African American Center for Academic Excellence
Anthropology
Chemistry
Clubs & Activities Office
College of eLearning and Extended Education
Counseling & Psychological Services*
English
Environmental Resource Engineering
Environmental Studies
Educational Opportunity Program (EOP)
Financial Aid
Health and Wellbeing Services
Learning Center*
Math
Office of the Registrar
Retention through Academic Mentoring Program
School of Business
Social Work
Student Engagement and Leadership*
Supplemental Instruction
University Library
Writing Studio*
YES House (Youth Educational Services)

* SkillShops Partners

Endnotes

1. John M. Keller, "How to Integrate Learner Motivation Planning into Lesson Planning: The ARCS Model Approach," paper presented at VII Semanario, Santiago, Cuba, 1–13, 2000. http://apps.fischlerschool.nova.edu/toolbox/instructionalproducts/itde8005/weeklys/2000-Keller-ARCSLessonPlanning.pdf.
2. Roy F. Baumeister and Mark R. Leary, "The Need to Belong: Desire for Interpersonal Attachments as a Fundamental Human Motivation," *Psychological Bulletin* 117, no. 3 (May 1995): 497–529, http://dx.doi.org/10.1037/0033-2909.117.3.497.

3. Tara Gray and Sami Halbert, "Team Teach with a Student," *College Teaching*, v. 46, no. 4 (Fall 1998): 150–53.
4. Richard M. Ryan and Edward L. Deci, "Self-Determination Theory and the Facilitation of Intrinsic Motivation, Social Development, and Well-Being," *The American Psychologist* 55, no. 1 (January 2000): 68–78.
5. Joanna C. Dunlap and Scott Grabinger, "Preparing Students for Lifelong Learning," *Performance Improvement Quarterly* (October 22, 2008).
6. Sherry R. Crow, "What Motivates a Lifelong Learner?," *School Libraries Worldwide* 12, no. 1 (January 2006): 22–34.
7. Dunlap and Grabinger, "Preparing Students for Lifelong Learning."
8. Barbara L. McCombs, "Motivation and Lifelong Learning," *Educational Psychologist* 26, no. 2 (Spring 1991): 117, https://doi.org/10.1207/s15326985ep2602_4.
9. Keller, "How to Integrate Learner Motivation Planning."
10. John M. Keller, "Development and Use of the ARCS Model of Instructional Design," *Journal of Instructional Development* 10, no. 3 (1987): 2–10, https://www.jstor.org/stable/30221294.
11. Keller, "How to Integrate Learner Motivation Planning."
12. Keller, "How to Integrate Learner Motivation Planning."

Bibliography

Baumeister, Roy F., and Mark R. Leary. "The Need to Belong: Desire for Interpersonal Attachments as a Fundamental Human Motivation." *Psychological Bulletin* 117, no. 3 (May 1995): 497–529. http://dx.doi.org/10.1037/0033-2909.117.3.497.

Crow, Sherry R. "What Motivates a Lifelong Learner?" *School Libraries Worldwide* 12, no. 1 (January 2006): 22–34.

Dunlap, Joanna C., and Scott Grabinger. "Preparing Students for Lifelong Learning." *Performance Improvement Quarterly* (October 22, 2008).

Gray, Tara, and Sami Halbert. "Team Teach with a Student." *College Teaching*, v. 46, no. 4 (Fall 1998): 150–53.

Keller, John M. "Development and Use of the ARCS Model of Instructional Design." *Journal of Instructional Development* 10, no. 3 (1987): 2–10. http://www.jstor.org/stable/30221294.

———. "How to Integrate Learner Motivation Planning into Lesson Planning: The ARCS Model Approach." Paper presented at VII Semanario, Santiago, Cuba, 1–13, 2000. http://apps.fischlerschool.nova.edu/toolbox/instructionalproducts/itde8005/weeklys/2000-Keller-ARCSLessonPlanning.pdf.

———. *Motivational Design for Learning and Performance: The ARCS Model Approach.* Springer Science & Business Media, 2009. https://doi.org/10.1007/978-1-4419-1250-3.

McCombs, Barbara L. "Motivation and Lifelong Learning." *Educational Psychologist* 26, no. 2 (Spring 1991): 117. https://doi.org/10.1207/s15326985ep2602_4.

Roth, Amanda, and Dominique Turnbow. "Drab to Fab: Elevated Practices for Active Learning Online." Presentation at the Library Instruction West 2016, Salt Lake City, UT, June 8–10, 2016. http://digitalcommons.usu.edu/liw16/Libraryinstructionwest2016/ThursdayJune9/10.

Ryan, Richard M., and Edward L. Deci. "Self-Determination Theory and the Facilitation of Intrinsic Motivation, Social Development, and Well-Being." *The American Psychologist* 55, no. 1 (January 2000): 68–78.

CHAPTER 9

Grinnell Science Project:

Motivating First-Year Students to Persist in Scientific Inquiry

Kevin R. Engel, Rebecca Ciota, Elizabeth Rodrigues

Introduction

When institutional data from the early 1990s showed Grinnell College students from underrepresented groups were abandoning science courses and majors at a higher-than-average rate, faculty and staff knew they needed to help. Many of these students were leaving the major after doing poorly in introductory courses. As a result, a pre-orientation program, the Grinnell Science Project (GSP), was created. The program is "committed to developing the talents of all students interested in science and mathematics, especially those from groups underrepresented in the sciences—students of color, first-generation college students, and women in physics, mathematics and computer science."[1] Shifting the focus of intervention from academic preparation to academic motivation, the GSP develops self-efficacy and social integration to enable students to persist in STEM study. GSP's approach arose from data that suggest that the reasons these students left science courses and majors seemed not to be academic but rather socioeconomic and environmental. Specifically, it identified the factors of "unsuccessful acclimation to college life; learning styles that do not respond to traditional pedagogy; and a lack of mentoring and role models."[2] Rather than focusing on remediation, then, GSP focuses on acclimation to college life, community building, and sustained mentoring. These areas of focus align with the insights of the social cognitive model of educational motivation, which suggests, broadly, that academic achievement is not determined by intellect alone but is instead the product of a complex web of personal and environmental factors.[3] One factor is the students' sense of self-efficacy, defined as "a judgment of one's ability to accomplish a certain level of performance."[4] Another such factor is the students' perception of social integration, including the accessibility of faculty and staff, connection with other students, and educational paths that resonate with students' educational values. Researchers have connected all these factors to students.[5] The program has seen great successes. From 1992–1994 to 2015, the number of women science graduates has increased 82 percent and the number of students of color science graduates has increased over 300 percent. Over two multi-year periods since the mid-2000s, the average grades of students of color in introductory STEM courses in relation to the average grades of all students have reduced from 1.0 GPA unit to approximately 0.2 GPA units. And the percentage of women physical and computational science majors doubled from the low 20 percents in the early 1990s to about 40 percent in 2016.[6] The GSP has been evolving over the past 20-plus years and we're reporting on the latest version, which we have updated as ACRL frameworks have changed and as our experience and research has directed.

From the program's inception, the Grinnell College Libraries have been a collaborative partner in the design and implementation of a core component of the GSP pre-orientation program: a small "research-like" project designed to foster self-efficacy in doing college-level research, activate students' intrinsic motivation to engage with the scientific information landscape by connecting information literacy to their academic interests, and foster academic and social integration by catalyzing a sense of membership in a community of researchers.

Library instruction in GSP is scaffolded around a mini-research project that all students must complete. The mini-research project was developed in order to introduce students to undergraduate library research. First, librarians lead an introductory session focused on information-seeking using the open web. This ninety-minute session addresses the first frame of the ACRL Framework, or Authority Is Constructed and Contextual. The students discuss how they decide what source is "best" or most authoritative to answer scientific and academic questions. Then, students are given a quick overview of key library resources followed by a brief tour of the science library, which prepares them for the second stage, independent information-seeking on a topic of their choosing. This independent information-seeking addresses the frame that positions Research as Inquiry; students think of a question and use research in order to answer it. Finally, at the end of the pre-orientation week, students present on their topic and include an account of the sources they used. This final section of the mini-project highlights the fifth frame of Scholarship as Conversation by having the students discuss their research and findings. In keeping with a focus on developing self-efficacy and social integration, the outcomes sought include not only increased awareness of and comfort with library resources but also a sense of research as a site of community.

Literature Review

The Grinnell Science Project focuses on motivating students with a demonstrated interest in studying science and mathematics to continue to pursue those fields of study. Literature in psychology and education discusses student motivation and has more recently turned to understanding the differential effects of motivational factors on students from underrepresented groups. Researchers at Stanford University and the University of California Santa Barbara write that stress and self-protection against experiences that threaten an individual's values and aspirations can hinder learning. Self-affirmation, however, can reduce the negative outcomes by minimizing the threat against personal aspirations and values. Self-affirmation can have lasting effects if linked with positive feedback from the individual and the social group around them.[7] At a university in the southern United States, 680 undergraduates in a variety of majors responded to the Science Motivation Questionnaire II. The questionnaire assessed the motivation of the students by various components: intrinsic motivation, self-determination, career motivation, grade motivation, and self-efficacy. The results of the questionnaire revealed a relation between motivation and students' grades in the sciences.[8] In "Self-Efficacy and Academic Motivation," Dale H. Schunk discusses academic motivation in terms of self-efficacy, or the individual's perception of their own capabilities. Schunk discusses goal setting, information processing, role-models, rewards, attributional feedback, and predictive utility in relation to motivation and self-efficacy.[9] Xueli Wang from the University of Wisconsin Madison investigated the reasons that motivate students to choose STEM majors. The greatest motivation for pursuing STEM majors is achievement in high school math, exposure to math and science classes, and a belief in one's self-efficacy in math.[10]

Our work with GSP draws on active learning practices coupled with close collaboration with science faculty. Librarians working with STEM classes have typically found that a combination of self-directed learning and librarian follow-up or support is the best way of heightening student engagement in library-based scientific research. Thomas Kirk tested two different teaching methods—a lecture- or demonstration-based approach or "guided exercises"—and evaluates student learning based on their subsequent bibliographies, exams on library skills, and students' attitudes. He concludes that both methods can be effective with careful planning and clear goals.[11] In "A Comparison of Six Versions of Science Library Instruction," published in 1973, Frank Kuo evaluates lecture, audio-recorded instruction, audio-recorded instruction coupled with slides, slides presented via a television, a combination of the audio-recorded instruction and slides with a follow-up session with a librarian, and no instruction. He finds that the audiovisual tutorial and then follow up with a librarian to be the most effective form of library instruction.[12] More recent studies (not science-specific) affirm that a focus on active learning using a combination of independent or group work and direct instruction or support is a more effective mode of engagement than direct instruction alone. Brian Detlor et al., for example, found that students who received information literacy instruction sessions incorporating active learning, defined as instruction that "encourages students to engage in activities that require the use of higher order thinking skills such as analysis, synthesis and evaluation,"[13] made gains in key areas relevant to GSP's goal of increasing a sense of confidence and belonging in the scientific community. These gains included "greater reductions in anxiety using online library resources, higher increases in self-efficacy using online library resources, improved perceptions of online library resources, improved use of librarians, improved perceptions of librarians being more helpful and valuable, and greater time savings and reduction in effort in finding information."[14]

Through a collaborative approach, we seek to align library instruction with disciplinary goals, making its relevance clear to students. Authors Flaspohler, Rux, and Flaspohler[15] as well as Huerta and McMillan[16] stress the effectiveness of collaboration between librarians and other faculty. Others attempt to link library instruction and use to students' success. In "Identifying and Articulating Library Connections to Student Success," Lisa Massengale, Pattie Piotrowski, and Devin Savage found that the Paul V. Galvin Library at the Illinois Institute of Technology fostered learning and student success through research services, information literacy instruction, providing electronic resources, and interlibrary loan services.[17] These seemingly ancillary skills can also bolster a student's self-efficacy for navigating college work.

The Grinnell Science Project

The Grinnell Science Project seeks to "foster acclimation to college life and a community of scientists, and improvement of student achievement."[18] The pre-orientation week of GSP works to build a community of support for the incoming first-year students, and to help those students recognize the various members of their support network. GSP introduces students to activities they will be asked to do in class in the context of this budding community of peers and faculty. These activities include visits to Grinnell College's Reading and Writing Labs, a foray into a chemistry lab or a physics lab, an introduction to the library, an independent project combining information-seeking and evaluation skills, and an oral presentation.

This independent project and the Libraries have been a part of GSP since its inception. The inclusion of an accessible, small, and authentic research experience provided a clear opportunity for collaboration between the program and the Libraries. Over time, the science librarian has offered significant input into the design and scaffolding of the project. Specifically, he has advocated for a focus on source evaluation, a blend of group and individual work, and in-person instruction by librarians. In a series of structured encounters with information-seeking, a significant amount of students' time during the pre-orientation week is spent in the library and doing research.

The library portion of GSP begins with a ninety-minute instruction session on the Monday of the pre-orientation week. The GSP participants are split into two groups (to make the number manageable; typically, there are twenty-two to twenty-five students per library session). One of those groups participates in the library session in the morning, the other in the afternoon. These sessions are at the heart of GSP's fostering of library engagement. The librarians have an exceptional opportunity to emphasize and teach critical source evaluation, a skill and mindset that undergraduate students will need throughout their education (and the rest of their lives). Plus, these sessions are timed to maximize students' excitement at embarking on their college career. Particularly for the morning group, this library instruction session is the first academic task to which the students are exposed at Grinnell College. Information literacy provides an excellent way to begin this intellectual transition.

As an example, in fall 2017, the Monday instruction sessions looked like this: the students met in a computer lab near the Science Library and were given a short introduction, then they were welcomed to the college and to the idea of research literacy. They were given an agenda for the session. They were assured that they were not expected to know it all at this point in their academic careers—that searching for, finding, thinking about, and using information was not some incredibly easy process that they should have learned all about in high school. Information literacy is part of what they come to college for. The students were also assured that they would have more contact with librarians in subsequent semesters. In particular, they were very likely to meet with a librarian during one or more of their first-semester classes. The students were also encouraged to keep in mind the other academic support departments at Grinnell College—the Writing Lab, Science Learning Center, Math Lab, Information Technology Services, Student Affairs, Reading Lab, etc. The students were encouraged to talk to human beings when they had questions (rather than rely solely on Google or even the college website). Finally, they were reminded how to contact the librarian and were given a quick tour of the library website.

The students were then separated randomly into five groups of four or five. They were told that they would be doing a group exercise as a way for the librarian to get an idea of how they searched for information. The group exercise was explained and each group was given a question (the same question; in fall 2017, one of the questions used was, "Are autonomous cars practical?"). The groups were told that they must work together within their groups to find the best answer they can to the question within approximately twenty-five minutes. They were told that each member of a group must agree with their group's answer (to begin to promote group collaboration—an emphasis in Grinnell College's science curriculum). The students could use any information they had access to from or within that room; they did not have enough time to leave the room and seek information elsewhere (so, for example, they could not leave the room to go to the nearby Science Library). It was mentioned (but just once) that it was fair game to also seek information from the human beings in the room—that is, the librarian, the student mentors (that work with the GSP students and accompany them to the various activities), and, sometimes, one of the GSP faculty directors (besides their fellow group members).

It is always interesting to see how open students are to seeking guidance from other human beings as opposed to typing questions on a keyboard; students are strongly encouraged at Grinnell College to utilize professors' office hours and to seek assistance from the library and other academic support units.

What the groups needed to produce in twenty-five minutes was then explained (and had been written on the board):
- an answer to the question
- at least two pieces of evidence to support that answer and enough information about the sources of the evidence so that another person could find them
- process—how did the group find that evidence? Where did group members look?
- Why is that evidence authoritative? Why did group members choose it over other sources?

During the twenty-five minutes of the group exercise, the librarian circulated about the room, announcing when the students had five minutes left, two minutes left, etc. Occasionally, while looking over a student's shoulder, the librarian would offer advice if the student seemed at sea. Generally, though, the librarian would not assist unless asked.

After the twenty-five minutes ended, there was a short, large-group discussion about the best ways to start work, whether it's a short exercise or a longer project. Based on observation of the students during that session, the librarian suggested ways to initially define the question at hand: What specific interpretation of the question had the students chosen to answer? Did the students understand what the terms/words involved in the question meant? The librarian showed one of Grinnell College's Library Subject Guides (https://libweb.grinnell.edu/sp/subjects/guide.php?subject=BIO) to provide a visual context to the tips and the process.

The librarian then debriefed each of the groups—one-at-a-time—jotting on the board their responses to the points above. As the groups responded, the librarian would occasionally circle pieces of information as a marker for further discussion. After all groups had been debriefed, the librarian led a large group discussion relating the group responses to important points about source evaluation.

After the conclusion of the group exercise, the librarian presented and explained the independent project. (Each student had received a handout with the question from the group exercise on one side and a description of the independent project on the other.) As part of this explanation, the librarian again used one of the Library Subject Guides to briefly describe and show a few resources that would be useful. The librarian was also careful to stress the scope of the independent project—that it was intended as practice for the kinds of academic work the students would be doing "for real" when classes started in two weeks.

After a quick review of important points from the session and emphasizing to the students how to contact the librarian and that the librarian would be there to support them now and down the road, the librarian and student mentors led the GSP students to the nearby Science Library for a short tour. And then the students were off to the next activity on the GSP schedule.

Generally, the introduction, group exercise, and debriefing take approximately fifty-five to sixty minutes, with the rest of the time left for the presentation and explanation of the independent project, everyone moving to the Science Library, the short tour, and then possibly a few minutes for the students to begin work on their projects.

In these sessions, the librarian briefly introduces the students to information-seeking skills and resources pertinent to undergraduate-level research. In line with the change from the ACRL Standards to the ACRL Framework, our GSP sessions have also shifted focus over the years from instruction intended to impart specific skills in database navigation to activities designed to invite active learning. These revised library sessions give students hands-on experience with information-seeking as strategic inquiry and authority as constructed and contextual.

The debriefing and the large group discussion that follows, in particular, begin to give a sense of the world of information, including its realities, risks, and benefits; many students come out of high school with little formal instruction or practice in critical source evaluation and other important areas of information literacy.[19] The discussion also helps students organically articulate the difference between popular and scholarly texts. In addition, the debriefing allows students to discuss how they evaluate the sources they encounter on a particular topic. For example, many students tend to gravitate toward government publications or university websites due to a perceived trustworthiness of those sources. The students are challenged during the debriefing to articulate why they think those sources may be more trustworthy than others. Because the questions are focusing on the sciences, discussions of source timeliness also arise; for instance, is a study on the environmental impact of alternative fuels from 2008 as relevant and valuable as one from 2017 to answer a particular question? Why or why not? This discussion helps students begin to engage with sources as authored documents, rather than collections of transparently true facts, and lays the groundwork for understanding authority as constructed and contextual.

In addition to source evaluation, the session and the independent project provide an introduction to a more scholarly orientation toward research. Instead of being pointed toward a single, all-purpose database, students are introduced to a range of options, from reference to scholarly literature to the open web, and then asked to make their own decisions about where and how to look. Once they have begun to find relevant entries, articles, and sites, they are then asked to select what to pay attention to and what not to pay attention to. Instead of being asked to find the "right" answer, students are asked to come up with *an* answer, but one that is defended with evidence. Students are asked to begin reckoning with the world of information as it really is. After conducting these GSP library sessions for over twenty years, the science librarian consistently finds the GSP library sessions to be one of the most purely intellectual and enjoyable teaching experiences that he encounters. Excited to be at college and delve into real "college" work, and as yet unjaded by other college experiences, the students approach these sessions with a motivation and curiosity that is refreshing to behold.

As mentioned, the Monday session closes with students receiving their independent project assignment (see Appendix 9A). The assignment is designed to be both accessible and challenging. Its requirements are straightforward but multi-pronged. Students are instructed to "find two sources that provide enough information about a scientific topic of interest for you to give an approximately two-minute talk on Thursday." The constraints of two sources and two minutes to present are intended to balance out the open-end-edness of the prompt and force thoughtful selection of sources and concision of presentation. Perhaps most important, it asks the students to first examine their own interests and choose a topic for themselves. The assignment attempts to make a connection between passion and practice, inviting students to "nerd out" on anything that interests them while asking them to fulfill, in miniature, the basic stepping stones of academic research.

On Tuesday and Wednesday of the GSP pre-orientation week, the students have sixty-minute timeslots in which to return to the library and/or the librarian to do research for their independent project. A librarian is nearby during these two independent research sessions in order to assist. These designated times for library research affirm the centrality of the library in their work as scientists, give them additional opportunities to access resources and support, and highlight the library as not only a physical space but a place that is central to the social life of the science building.

On Thursday, the pre-orientation program culminates in the independent project—an oral presentation on an individual research topic. Over the years, the independent project has evolved to focus more heavily on source evaluation in both the research and the final presentation. The librarians have found that this focus is a better way to frame the world of information as it is rather than how we might like it to be. Genuine questions connected to personal interest activates intrinsic motivation.[20]

The independent project allows the new students to get a sense of creating a research question, practice finding information, begin developing disciplinary rubrics for evaluation, and understand that the librarians can help at every step of the process. It supplies a small but genuine experience of mastery that contributes to self-efficacy.[21] It brings students together around a task, beginning to connect them to each other as resources for learning.

Discussion and Key Takeaways

Programs like the GSP are common across the country as colleges seek to bolster the persistence of underrepresented students in STEM fields. Libraries could potentially seek out a similar collaborative opportunity in these contexts, with the complementary goal of supporting student persistence and student engagement with academic libraries. Some characteristics of a mutually beneficial collaboration in this context could include:

- **A known need for supporting underrepresented students in ways that go beyond academic remediation.** A campus initiative to expand support allows the wider motivational potential of a strong relationship to the library and librarians to become visible. It helps

shine a light on what librarians have to teach beyond a set of database skills.

- **Inclusion in (pre)orientation programming.** It is perhaps not
  so much time as *timing* that is of the essence: When are students
  primed to connect information literacy with their incipient identity
  as scholars? Ideally, there is a mutual benefit as the program taps into
  the library's cache as a locus for the community and the library taps
  into the program's population of students in search of community.
- **Opportunity to connect students' interest in scientific inquiry
  to their larger educational goals.** Because the GSP pre-orientation takes place outside of formal coursework, the focus can be on
  building self-efficacy and encouraging intrinsic motivation rather
  than formal assessment. It is a low-stakes environment in which
  excitement can have a freer rein. At the same time, students are encouraged to see their work in GSP as a prelude to successful work in
  the classroom, making the completion of the mini-research project a
  meaningful achievement.
- **Opportunity to maintain relationships with student participants,
  especially through curricular research literacy instruction.** Librarians may have additional bandwidth to contribute to the desire for
  sustained mentorship. In their capacity as a faculty/staff member,
  the librarian can serve as what Yu et al. call a "socializer," who "may
  provide support, for example, through encouragement or endorse-
  ment of academic and career choices."[22] Seeing the librarian again
  throughout their courses can help students draw on the motivational
  resources they developed during pre-orientation.

Once a potential program partnership has been identified, the key steps
are:

1. demonstrating the potentials of a structured introductory research
   experience to the faculty or student affairs staff developing the
   program;
2. working with those leaders to design a mini-project that prompts
   students to connect with their own academic interests and their
   future disciplinary research needs;
3. planning appropriate sessions, ideally combining components of direct instruction, active learning, independent work during commu-
   nally designated times in library space, and final presentation; and
4. remaining in communication with program leaders to assess and
   refine the program for future iterations.

The faculty and staff who run this pre-orientation program hope GSP
motivates students to develop a sense of community within the sciences at
Grinnell College so that when setbacks inevitably occur, students find the

strength and support to persevere and to pursue scientific study and research. The library portion of GSP combines independent research and group activities, encouraging relationship- and community-building as well as offering students an opportunity to build research literacy and connect with an important person resource, the science librarian.

Future Directions and Conclusion

The Grinnell Science Project has been a successfully run program for over twenty years, designed to foster a community among students from underrepresented groups who are interested in the sciences. The program includes multiple curricular and extracurricular experiences. One of the most prominent experiences is the library portion of GSP which includes a ninety-minute instructional session, two sixty-minute independent research sessions, and a sixty-minute session to present the findings of that research. This totals to four and a half hours during the week doing library-related activities—a significant amount in a packed schedule. Taking into account this amount of time, it is clear that information literacy and the libraries are an important feature of the Grinnell Science Project.

Institutional data show that GSP has been successful in reducing the rate of attrition for students in groups underrepresented in the sciences. We have not yet formally assessed how the library component contributes to student success or how participation in GSP correlates to students' future library use or research efficacy in other disciplines. The compact nature of the GSP pre-orientation program and the desire to expose new students to a wide range of academic and social services, activities, and processes in the space of one week means that adding formal assessment activities during that week is difficult.

However, future work could include following a cohort of these students through their first semester of college to see if their pre-orientation library experience led to outcomes such as greater likelihood to ask librarians for assistance (an indicator of academic integration), greater comfort in utilizing the library as a community space (an indicator of social integration), and greater success in utilizing information resources to identify and track down information needed for class (a demonstrable skillset that should foster self-efficacy). Another possibility could be a comparison of the pre-orientation week two-item bibliography with a required bibliography in a first-semester class—having the student and a librarian compare the bibliography entries on authority, validity, and timeliness—accompanied by a survey that asks students to reflect in some way on their self-efficacy and sense of social integration. Our experience working with GSP students over many years during and after the pre-orientation program suggests that the research experience as shared experience catalyzes a sense of identification with a community of practice, heightening students' motivation to persist in both the study of science and the use of the library as a home base for learning.

Ultimately, the goal of the Grinnell Science Project is to create community that a new student can rely on to overcome obstacles and continue their interest and passion for science. The library is a part of that support community. The library sessions and the independent project during the pre-orientation week help students begin to make the long and significant transition from student to scholar.

Appendix 9A. Pre-Orientation Week Grinnell Science Project

August 2004

Information Literacy
Group 1

Do normal childhood vaccinations—particularly using vaccines containing mercury—cause disorders such as autism, language and speech delay, and ADHD?

Group 2

Since 1945, fluoride has been routinely added to public water supplies in many areas of the United States to help prevent tooth decay, especially in children and young adults. Does fluoridated drinking water also lead to increased risks for bone cancer, hip fractures, birth defects, Alzheimer's Disease, and other maladies?

Individual Project

Find an article (*Scientific American* level) or chapter in a book on a scientific topic of personal interest. Read the article/chapter carefully. Find a couple of more in-depth *references* (must be available in our library); you do not need to read these but have them as supplementary resources. Write a one-page summary of the article/chapter on a word processor. Make sure to clearly credit the article in the body of your paper or in a footnote. Append the list of references to your paper. Your references should include at least one book and at least one article which you found yourself using some of the skills the reference librarians helped you learn. It is completely fair to have a librarian help you with finding those references. On Thursday, you will make a microscopically (2 minutes) short oral presentation on your topic.

Grinnell Science Project

August 2017

Information Literacy
Group 1

Are autonomous cars practical?

Group 2

Is corn-based ethanol a feasible alternative to regular gasoline?

Individual Project

Find two sources that provide enough information about a scientific topic of interest for you to give an approximately two-minute talk on Thursday.

In addition to preparing your talk, you should create an annotated bibliography (double-spaced; use APA format) of your sources. The annotation for each source should be one to two sentences summarizing the information contained in the source, plus one additional sentence discussing the value and importance of the source.

Your talk will consist of a brief summary of your topic and then a brief discussion of why you chose to use those information sources. Why do you consider them more valuable than other sources you may have come across?

Endnotes

1. "Grinnell Science Project," Grinnell College, accessed March 20, 2017, https://www.grinnell.edu/academics/areas/science/gsp.
2. "Grinnell Science Project: Background," Grinnell College, accessed March 20, 2017, https://www.grinnell.edu/academics/areas/science/gsp/background.
3. Elizabeth Linnenbrink and Paul Pintrich, "Motivation as an Enabler for Academic Success," *School Psychology Review 31.3* (2002): 313.
4. Albert Bandura, *Social Foundations of Thought and Action: A Social Cognitive Theory*, (Englewood Cliffs, NJ: Prentice-Hall, 1986), 391.
5. Kelly A. Rodgers, "Retention vs. Persistence: A Self-Determination Analysis of Students Underrepresented in STEM," in *Race and Ethnicity in the Study of Motivation in Education*, ed. Jessica T. Decuir-Gunby and Paul A. Schutz (New York: Routledge, Taylor & Francis Group, 2017), 38.
6. "Grinnell Science Project: Outcomes of Grinnell Science Project," Grinnell College, accessed November 16, 2017, https://www.grinnell.edu/academics/areas/science/gsp/outcomes.
7. Geoffrey L. Cohen and David K. Sherman, "The Psychology of Change: Self-Affirmation and Social Psychological Intervention," *Annual Review of Psychology 65* (2014): 361, https://doi.org/10.1146/annurev-psych-010213-115137.
8. Shawn M. Glynn, Peggy Brickman, Norris Armstrong, and Gita Taasoobshirazi, "Science Motivation Questionnaire II: Validation with Science Majors and Nonscience Majors," *Journal of Research in Science Teaching 48*, no. 10 (2011): 1159–76.
9. Dale H. Schunk, "Self-Efficacy and Academic Motivation," *Educational Psychologist 26*, no. 3&4 (1991): 207–31.
10. Xueli Wang, "Why Students Choose Stem Majors: Motivation, High School Learning, and Postsecondary Context of Support," *American Educational Research Journal 50*, no. 5 (October 2013): 1081–121.
11. Thomas Kirk, "A Comparison of Two Methods of Library Instruction for Students

in Introductory Biology," *College & Research Libraries* 32, no. 6 (November 1971): 465–74.

12. Frank Kuo, "A Comparison of Six Versions of Science Library Instruction," *College & Research Libraries* 34, no. 4 (July 1973): 278–90.

13. Brian Detlor et al., "Student Perceptions of Information Literacy Instruction: The Importance of Active Learning," *Education For Information* 29 (2012): 153.

14. Ibid.

15. Molly R. Flaspohler, Erika M. Rux, and John A. Flaspohler, "The Annotated Bibliography and Citation Behavior: Enhancing Student Scholarship in an Undergraduate Biology Course," *CBE—Life Sciences Education* 6 (Winter 2007): 350–60.

16. Deborah Huerta and Victoria E. Mcmillan, "Collaborative Instruction by Writing and Library Faculty: A Two-Tiered Approach to the Teaching of Scientific Writing," *Issues in Technology Librarianship* 28 (Fall 2000), doi:10.5062/F4Q23X69.

17. Lisa Massengale, Pattie Piotrowski, and Devin Savage, "Identifying and Articulating Library Connections to Student Success," *College & Research Libraries* 77, no. 2 (2016): 227–35, doi:10.5860/crl.77.2.227.

18. "Grinnell Science Project," Grinnell College.

19. See Heidi Julien, Susan Barker, "How High-School Students Find and Evaluate Scientific Information: A Basis for Information Literacy Skills Development," *Library & Information Science Research* 31, no. 1 (2009): 12–17, https://doi.org/10.1016/j.lisr.2008.10.008.

20. Susan A. Ambrose, Michael W. Bridges, Michele DiPietro, Marsha C. Lovett, and Marie K. Norman, "What Factors Motivate Students to Learn?," in *How Learning Works: 7 Research-Based Principles for Smart Teaching* (San Francisco: Jossy-Bass, 2010), 83.

21. Shirley Yu, Danya M. Corkin, and Julie P. Martin, "STEM Motivation and Persistence Among Underrepresented Minority Students: A Social Cognitive Perspective," in *Race and Ethnicity in the Study of Motivation in Education*, ed. Jessica T. Decuir-Gunby and Paul A. Schutz (New York: Routledge, 2017), 76.

22. Yu, Corkin, and Martin, "STEM Motivation and Persistence," 75–76.

Bibliography

Ambrose, Susan A., Michael W. Bridges, Michele DiPietro, Marsha C. Lovett, and Marie K. Norman. "What Factors Motivate Students to Learn?" In *How Learning Works: 7 Research-Based Principles for Smart Teaching*, 66–90. San Francisco: Jossy-Bass, 2010.

Bandura, Albert. *Social Foundations of Thought and Action: A Social Cognitive Theory.* Englewood Cliffs, NJ: Prentice-Hall, 1986.

Cohen, Geoffrey L., and David K. Sherman. "The Psychology of Change: Self-Affirmation and Social Psychological Intervention." *Annual Review of Psychology* 65 (2014): 333–71. https://doi.org/10.1146/annurev-psych-010213-115137.

Detlor, Brian, Lorne Booker, Alexander Serenko, and Heidi Julien. "Student Perceptions of Information Literacy Instruction: The Importance of Active Learning." *Education for Information* 29, no. 2 (2012): 147–61.

Flaspohler, Molly R., Erika M. Rux, and John A. Flaspohler. "The Annotated Bibliography and Citation Behavior: Enhancing Student Scholarship in an Undergraduate

Biology Course." *CBE—Life Sciences Education* 6 (Winter 2007): 350–60.

Glynn, Shawn M., Peggy Brickman, Norris Armstrong, and Gita Taasoobshirazi. "Science Motivation Questionnaire II: Validation with Science Majors and Nonscience Majors." *Journal of Research in Science Teaching* 48, no. 10 (2011): 1159–76.

Grinnell College. "Grinnell Science Project." https://www.grinnell.edu/academics/areas/science/gsp.

———. "Grinnell Science Project: Background." https://www.grinnell.edu/academics/areas/science/gsp/background.

———. "Grinnell Science Project: Outcomes of Grinnell Science Project." https://www.grinnell.edu/academics/areas/science/gsp/outcomes.

Huerta, Deborah, and Victoria E. McMillan. "Collaborative Instruction by Writing and Library Faculty: A Two-Tiered Approach to the Teaching of Scientific Writing." *Issues in Technology Librarianship* 28 (Fall 2000). doi:10.5062/F4Q23X69.

Julien, Heidi, and Barker, Susan. "How High-School Students Find and Evaluate Scientific Information: A Basis for Information Literacy Skills Development." *Library & Information Science Research* 31, no. 1 (2009): 12–1. https://doi.org/10.1016/j.lisr.2008.10.008.

Kirk, Thomas. "A Comparison of Two Methods of Library Instruction for Students in Introductory Biology." *College & Research Libraries* 32, no. 6 (November 1971): 465–74.

Kuo, Frank. "A Comparison of Six Versions of Science Library Instruction." *College & Research Libraries* 34, no. 4 (July 1973): 278–90.

Linnenbrink, Elizabeth A., and Paul R. Pintrich. "Motivation as an Enabler for Academic Success." *School Psychology Review* 31.3 (2002): 313–27.

Massengale, Lisa, Pattie Piotrowski, and Devin Savage. "Identifying and Articulating Library Connections to Student Success." *College & Research Libraries* 77, no. 2 (2016): 227–35. doi:10.5860/crl.77.2.227.

Rodgers, Kelly A. "Retention vs. Persistence: A Self-Determination Analysis of Students Underrepresented in STEM." In *Race and Ethnicity in the Study of Motivation in Education*, edited by Jessica T. Decuir-Gunby and Paul A. Schutz, 36–49. New York: Routledge, 2017.

Schunk, Dale H. "Self-Efficacy and Academic Motivation." *Educational Psychologist* 26, no. 3&4 (1991): 207–31.

Wang, Xueli. "Why Students Choose Stem Majors: Motivation, High School Learning, and Postsecondary Context of Support." *American Educational Research Journal* 50, no. 5 (October 2013): 1081–121.

Yu, Shirley, Danya M. Corkin, and Julie P. Martin. "STEM Motivation and Persistence Among Underrepresented Minority Students: A Social Cognitive Perspective." In *Race and Ethnicity in the Study of Motivation in Education*, edited by Jessica T. Decuir-Gunby and Paul A. Schutz, 67–81. New York: Routledge, 2017.

CHAPTER 10

Level Up the One-Shot:

Empowering Students with Backward Design and Game-Based Learning

Tarida Anantachai and Camille Chesley

Designed to be interactive and intrinsically motivating, games seek to create absorbing experiences for players. As librarians struggle with the challenge of teaching information literacy concepts within the time constraints of the "one-shot" library instruction session, game-based learning and gamified activities have garnered increased attention in instructional design discourse as dynamic approaches for enhancing students' learning experiences.

For first-year and other incoming students still adjusting to the college experience, games invite their active participation in a non-threatening and positive format and ease them into the rigors of a college course. Games can offer an empowering, democratizing experience that encourages students' engagement with the session's material, each other, and even with their own learning processes. In fact, games have been cited as an effective way of engaging students in the classroom, particularly those whose communication styles are not as compatible with the one-way delivery of standard lectures.[1] Games are also inherently designed to create opportunities for enhanced interactivity, peer-to-peer engagement, and trial-and-error experimentation.[2]

This chapter outlines some of the ways in which the integration of games and gamified activities can directly impact student motivation in the classroom. We will first discuss how games naturally align with the principles of both motivational design and backward design and offer an overview of some of the free and open source options that can assist instruction librarians in creating their first games. We will also include some examples of games that we have created and tools that we have customized to enrich student engagement in one-shot instruction sessions.

Motivation and Student Empowerment: The Case for Gaming

Before discussing games more specifically, we will briefly explore the connections between student agency and motivation and how gaming helps to promote these concepts in the classroom. Thirty years ago, Paulo Freire, an influential Brazilian educator, popularized the concept of a society and educational system that is complicit in the systemic oppression of student agency. He argued against the prevailing notion that students were "merely an empty receptacle to be 'filled,'"[3] viewing the ideal formal education as one which encouraged critical thinking and discouraged the elevation of educators, schools, and educational institutions to an unimpeachable pedestal. Building off of Freire's concepts, Kirk et al. note that schools have the potential to be a uniquely motivating environment for students, arguing that when teachers use power equitably and foster the creation of a positive sense of community in the classroom, they contribute to student empowerment.[4]

Academic librarianship shares a similar philosophy; for instance, the ACRL Framework for Information Literacy in Higher Education encourages students to critically engage with their own relationship to information by understanding how "authority is constructed and contextual."[5] However, as instructors, we must first engage with the reality of our own constructed authority by acknowledging the historical forces that concentrate power and authority in our hands, from the layout of our classrooms to the demographics of our profession (statistically, 88 percent white—much whiter and much older than our student bodies[6]). The significant homogeneity of our profession also directly impacts who makes the decisions regarding the design of classroom and library spaces as well as the "shared cultural understanding of what the work of faculty and students [within these spaces] is and should be."[7] Gaming, which, by its very nature, motivates players to assume control,[8] creates space for the democratization of the classroom and a more equal distribution of power and authority by empowering students to challenge the historically white structures and norms of the traditional classroom environment. While the typical library one-shot rarely allows librarians the opportunity to establish a long-term instructional relationship, a one-shot game-based session can still provide an empowering burst that dynamically shifts students' perceptions of their roles in the classroom, increases their sense of agency, and motivates their own self-learning processes. Even though the instructor still assumes the role of the "gamemaster" by introducing and facilitating the classroom game, the mechanics and the inexorable nature of the gameplay creates an environment in which the instructor can step back and invite the students to autonomously explore.

James Paul Gee's significant research on game-based learning is also worth acknowledging, particularly his examination of how effective games facilitate learning by tapping into players' cognitive abilities. Gee provides thirty-six learning principles that educators can take away from gaming, including how games encourage active and critical (i.e., not passive) learning, integrate self-knowledge activities that invite learners to reflect upon their abilities and potential capacities, and allow learners to independently experiment and make their own discoveries through their engagement in the gaming environment.[9] Though Gee's work focuses mostly on video games, his principles still offer insights into the parallels between game design and successful course design.

The concept of game design is closely reminiscent of motivational design theory; indeed, one of the key elements to successful gameplay itself is motivation.[10] John Keller's ARCS Model, one of the most influential motivational design theories, tasks instructors to design their instruction based on four main elements: gaining and maintaining their students' *attention*, demonstrating the material's *relevance*, creating an environment that builds their *confidence*, and providing them opportunities to feel *satisfaction* for their learning achievements.[11] Building upon this model as it relates to library instruction, Amanda Nichols Hess provides a comprehensive literature review of the benefits of and methods in which motivational design can and has been employed in a number of library instructional settings. Hess notes that even pedagogical principles such as the ACRL Framework evoke elements of motivational design, further validating the significance of actively incorporating this design theory in library instruction.[12]

In a related framework, Malone's Theory of Intrinsically Motivating Instruction posits three criteria for examining what makes games motivational: they must have a challenge stemming from meaningful goals, a fantasy that inspires players to enter an environment outside of their actual experience, and a curiosity that is aroused by the feedback structures in place.[13] Other similar theories can also be applied to gaming, including Ryan and Deci's Self-Determination Theory, which suggests that people are generally motivated by three psychological needs: their own autonomy, the relatedness they feel to others, and the competence of meeting a challenge.[14] When considering how these concepts relate to gaming in library instruction, Maura Smale provides an extensive overview that includes a number of applications of gaming in information literacy instruction and how they have helped to successfully increase student engagement and motivation.[15] Indeed, already one can see the many overlaps among motivational design, gaming, and information literacy instruction.

Backward Design: Putting Motivational Design and Gaming into Practice

Motivational design, in and of itself, could provide a solid framework for designing games for library instruction. However, even the most exciting, empowering game will not be nearly as successful if it is created simply for the sake of inspiration. Rather, it also has to be, as per the ARCS model, relevant to the course material and learning goals. In other words, in order to better ensure that a game-based one-shot session is not just an isolated burst of energy, instruction librarians must intentionally choose and design appropriate games that are tied to the learning goals of the session and, ideally, the deeper objectives of the course. Instructional design theory can provide an actionable framework at the nexus where multiple theories of motivational design, game design, and student agency converge.

Backward design, as popularized by Jay McTighe and Grant Wiggins, is an instructional design framework which emphasizes planning for enduring understanding rather than the simple acquisition of knowledge. Echoing Freire, McTighe and Wiggins note that the culture of schools frequently stifles students' spirit of inquiry.[16] To combat this state of affairs, they argue that educators should design backward, using "essential questions" to provide a framework[17] in order to avoid the pitfalls of classroom activities that are "hands-on without being minds-on."[18]

Backward design consists of three main design stages: first, the instructor identifies a set of desired results and core understandings. Second, the instructor works backward from there to determine assessment measures that ensure learners produce evidence of meeting these results, and third, the instructor develops an appropriate learning plan and experiences aligned to both these results and assessments.[19] While this general outline is a much-abridged version of McTighe and Wiggins' comprehensive framework, it provides a good structure for approaching and planning game-based learning activities. In practical terms, utilizing backward design in the course of designing games takes added importance. Advanced games, such as simulations or other computer-based applications, often require an incredible investment in time, software, and human capital; thus, it is especially important to ensure that the games chosen match the learning outcomes of both the one-shot session as well as the course overall. More "low-tech" games, such as scavenger hunts or games utilizing pre-existing resources such as board games, social media, or other templates, may take relatively less investment to adapt and keep up to date. However, these must still be intentionally integrated in order to more effectively contribute to student learning and motivation, to articulate the game's contribution to them, and to assess outcomes afterward.

Assessment

We would be remiss to conclude this introduction to backward design without a more in-depth discussion of assessment, particularly as it relates to the second and third stages of the backward design. Assessment itself can be high-stakes; increasingly, in primary and secondary schools, measures of student performance are tied to promotions, teacher evaluations, or even school funding. In librarianship, the focus centers around assessment as a tool to demonstrate value by linking the library to institutional student learning outcomes.[20] For the purposes of this chapter, we will limit the discussion to the assessment of learning and its implications for gaming and gamification in the classroom.

As previously noted, the second and third stages of backward design involve generating learning outcomes and assessment measures and creating corresponding lesson plans. McTighe and Wiggins argue that assessment is a critical component of demonstrating institutional values but caution that poorly-designed assessment measures also have the power to undermine.[21] If one's goal is to create an educational environment that encourages critical thinking, inquiry, and enduring understanding, then assessments and learning outcomes that focus on the acquisition of information over understanding will show students that "'what counts' is recall and recognition."[22] In the context of game design, this might look like the difference between students who can regurgitate a university policy on academic integrity and recite the definition of plagiarism, and students who are presented with an activity where they can articulate how citations contribute to an ongoing scholarly conversation.

Many games are naturally structured to gather assessment-level data within player-centered learning experiences, making them well-positioned to aid in the second and third stages of the backward design process. The very nature of gameplay itself requires continual player input and the progression of skills mastery.[23] Games provide a valuable opportunity to gather in-class student feedback and observe in real-time which concepts students find challenging. By thoughtfully choosing, designing, and exploiting the assessment measures embedded within games and designing lesson plans accordingly, instructors can not only immediately gauge student learning, they can also demonstrate the unique value of games in gathering instruction data. They better ensure that the games contribute to the course's goals beyond the one-shot session, rather than forcing the course to adapt to an isolated session and the games showcased within them.

Getting Started: Example Applications

At first glance, game design can seem like a daunting undertaking. However, instruction librarians can easily discover, customize, and utilize a number of freely available, open source software and templates to get started. Many of these resources come with built-in gaming interfaces that lend themselves well to librarians interested in taking their first steps into game-based instruction. Below are some freely available options and their potential applications in the classroom.

Game Shows and Other Preexisting Gaming Systems

Pre-established gaming systems, such as those within popular game shows and board games, are easy entry points for incorporating gaming into classroom instruction. Pre-existing game structures ease students into a gaming environment that is more recognizable to them, providing instructors with prototypes that have already incorporated core elements of motivational game design within them (e.g., as per Malone's framework, challenges and goals by striving to earn points, a "fantasy" that transports them from a more formal classroom environment into a self-driven game show, and the curiosity of revealing more information as they play). Since many students are often already familiar with these games, they do not require lengthy explanations or world-building, which can eat up valuable class time.

For example, many librarians have utilized the long-standing game show staple *Jeopardy!* for a variety of instructional settings.[24] Numerous templates, including those made in PowerPoint or designed within a web interface, are freely available online. *Jeopardy!*'s quiz-like format can be employed as an ice-breaking opening activity to pre-assess students' prior knowledge or as a fun closing activity to reinforce content presented earlier in class; reinforcement can be especially important for one-shot sessions when librarians are unlikely to visit future class sessions. The overarching question categories can be customized according to the learning objectives (e.g., identifying key terminology, types of information resources, search strategies, etc.) and each of the category "clues" can be scaffolded to become gradually more challenging as students make their way down the board. Designing questions accordingly can provide an instant assessment of students' comprehension of the material. For students, *Jeopardy!*'s continued presence in popular culture, as well as its fundamental points-based structure, invite them into a friendly, competitive activity that continually rewards them for their active contributions. Students can be grouped into teams to foster classroom collaboration and invite them to drive their own learning. Each team can autonomously select their "clues" (and thus, the level of difficulty of them) and then discuss and collectively agree upon their response.

Jeopardy! is perhaps the most widely known example that we have utilized; however, librarians can draw inspiration from other games in popular culture. For example, *Family Feud* or *Who Wants To Be A Millionaire* can be used to introduce students to a variety of resources and concepts at once (e.g., "According to a poll of your friendly campus librarians, name the top four business databases provided by our library.") or to review material previously discussed (e.g., "Which of the following is NOT a reason to properly cite your sources?"). Comedy Central's panel game show, *@midnight*, is also ripe with adaptable activities. For example, librarians can tweak one of its recurring mini-games, #Hashtagwars, by giving students a themed hashtag (e.g., #ClimateChangeIn5Keywords) for generating their own related keywords or phrases. Similarly, Heads Up!, a charades-like game popularized on *The Ellen DeGeneres Show*, can also be used as a keyword-generating activity. In this game, a player is tasked with guessing a mystery word or phrase they cannot see based on other words or actions provided by their teammates. Indeed, the highly interactive nature of game shows provides great opportunities for librarians to present information in an engaging format, to collect immediate feedback, and to embolden students to take part in both their own and their fellow students' learning processes.

Gamified Social Media

While the pre-existing structures of game shows offer a great starting point, game-based opportunities exist in other less obvious contexts. For instance, many smartphone apps incorporate user experiences that can be gamified into a classroom activity. One such example is Instagram (https://www.instagram.com), a popular photo-sharing app. Although it is most commonly recognized as a social media tool, its inherent features as a user-generated and social space lend themselves to creating a gamified, student-driven activity. Using the example of a one-shot library orientation session, below is one potential application of gamifying Instagram in instruction, which we adapted from an activity at the University of Montevallo.[25]

After starting with a brief overview of the library and providing students with some foundational knowledge and context (e.g., introducing them to certain areas of the library, how to navigate to the online catalog, etc.), students are placed in groups and given a short list of discovery prompts that task them to post photos of items throughout the library. The prompts may ask students to seek out unique study spaces, their favorite books, or even library staff members they encounter. Open-ended prompts which invite students to document something surprising, confusing, or interesting in the library allow students the freedom to proactively explore, record, and then later inform their fellow classmates about other areas and ideas that intrigued them. Encouraging the students to simultaneously insert descriptive captions to further elaborate on why they documented a particular item adds an element of reflection while introducing them to concepts such as keyword generation. For first-year students, in particular, this photo-journalistic activity can empower them to teach each other about an unfamiliar space on their own terms and within a medium that is familiar to them. It also builds their confidence within their new environment and helps to reduce library anxiety and information overload. At the same time, the real-time updates visible through students' postings introduces an element of competition, motivating them to seek out other resources or services that their fellow students have not yet posted.

While we have used this particular example in one-shot library orientations, Instagram and other gamified social media activities can be implemented in other settings. For example, a shared class account or hashtag can be created for semester-long projects in which students regularly post photos of primary resources or even quotes or passages of interest from their readings. Rather than posting on the discussion board of a learning management system, students can be tasked with commenting on their fellow students' Instagram posts. This activity encourages instructors and students to value the information and contributions that the students bring to their learning experience and gives them additional opportunities outside of the classroom to construct their own collaborative community of practice.

Instructors have several options to consider when implementing social media-based activities in the classroom. For instance, they can create a shared class account that all the students can temporarily access on library-owned devices distributed during class. Alternatively, they can opt to share a temporary password to this account, which students can then access on their own personal mobile devices. Another option is to assign a unique class hashtag to the activity, which students, with their own (public) accounts, can use to tag their contributions for later discoverability and viewing. While a detailed discussion of the other implications of introducing social media in the classroom is beyond the scope of this chapter, we recommend instructors provide a quick overview the game's basic rules in order to outline expectations and prevent inappropriate content or behaviors. For further information, instructors may also want to consult with resources such as the Electronic Frontier Foundation (https://www.eff.org), the Electronic Privacy Information Center's Social Media Privacy section (https://epic.org/privacy/socialnet), and the Pew Research Center's Internet & Technology reports (http://www.pew-internet.org). These resources offer a number of news and updates related to social media and privacy that can be introduced into classroom discussions beforehand. Indeed, gamified social media activities present librarians with opportunities to cultivate digital citizenship skills with their students. They can also engage students with broader concepts, such as those from the ACRL Framework. For example, social media projects could open up discussions on how scholars can discover trending conversations within their respective disciplines as well as some avenues for entering and contributing to these scholarly communities.

Open Source Tools

The rise of educational technology has opened doors for librarians interested in taking their first steps into game design. It has also led to an increase in open source tools—some of which require little to no prior coding experience—that can aid in this transition. One such example is Twine (http://twinery.org), a freely available storytelling tool developed by Chris Klimas. As a visual, highly customizable, and interactive medium, it is a user-friendly way to engage students with humor and targeted institutional and cultural references. Twine offers a web interface or downloadable application. We highly recommend downloading the application, as games created using the web interface are saved within one's browser and accidentally clearing browser data will also delete the game.

More than just a software program, Twine is better viewed as a storytelling tool. Users can create simple stories or stories with an infinite number of branches and variables. Thus, we highly recommend storyboarding and keeping detailed records of file names and other components. While advanced users can incorporate CSS or JavaScript, the game's basic functions allow conditional formatting and easy incorporation of images, making it possible to create games without any knowledge of coding.

The impetus behind utilizing Twine in this instance was a common frustration: the desire to push the limitations of one-shot information literacy sessions in response to an instruction request for an introduction to academic integrity. Teaching sessions on academic integrity (which is often conflated with plagiarism) are a familiar request for most libraries and a source of frustration for librarians and teaching faculty alike. Compounding this frustration, these sessions are often requested at the beginning of students' college careers in English, writing, or first-year experience courses, when students may not yet have a firm enough conceptual framework in which to place such ideas. In other words, they lack the specific context for the discussion and its applicability, leaving the classroom with only vague memories of warnings. The question then became: How can we provide students with this framework in a way that encourages discussion and exploration, allowing students to meaningfully engage with new concepts and build upon their own experiences?

To address this problem, we used Twine to create a Choose-Your-Own-Adventure (CYOA) novel. In the game, students are hanging out in our library when, after a sudden earthquake, they black out and wake up in an enchanted forest. After meeting a kind fairy who offers to take them home, they discover that an evil wizard has stolen her gems of power and sold them to the five great scholar-monsters of the realm. Much like the students, the scholar-monsters are hard at work writing papers, but they find citations quite confusing, and they are willing to trade great wealth for answers to their questions. Students must journey through the forests and caves of this strange land and answer citation-related questions.

Arguably, Twine's most valuable feature in the classroom is its ability to incorporate conditional logic in storyboarding. The game designer can easily create and interweave connections across different branches of a story, setting students on an inexorable path toward a pre-set conclusion, removing pressure and shifting the focus of the activity to exploration. Much like a reader with a CYOA novel using their finger to reserve their place in case they met a bad end on a particular page, Twine offers the ability to learn from mistakes and self-correct in real time. For example, when faced with the following question:

> Which of the following is the CORRECT way to cite a passage from page 46 of Dr. Swift's ground-breaking text, *Players and Haters: 26 Years of Shaking It Off*?

students are directed to choose among several versions of a quote and citation and must select one answer to continue. Using another medium, such as a paper scavenger hunt, students would have to wait until the end of the activity to learn the answer and unpack the explanation. Thanks to Twine's conditional formatting, students receive immediate feedback based on their answers. If students select the correct answer:

> Swift notes that the nature of players and haters is inflexible, stating "the players gonna play, play, play, play, play, And the haters gonna hate, hate, hate, hate, hate." (46)

they immediately see a screen which notes:

> According to the MLA format for in-text citations, this is correct! The author's last name and the page number where the quote can be found must appear in the same sentence. The paper writer mentions the author's last name in a sentence, so all that is required for an in-text citation is the page number in parentheses.

Twine is a powerful tool for democratizing learning because it removes the instructor from the place of power as the arbiter of right and wrong. The instructor's influence is still present, as they have created the story, the quest, and programmed the answers. However, the CYOA format taps into the motivational theories of self-determination. In other words, it provides students the agency (and, by extension, the authority) to collaborate, confer, debate their own paths, and ultimately learn at their own pace. It also creates a narrative structure and places students into a first-person perspective. These instructional strategies have proven effective for knowledge transfer and retention.[26]

Twine is just one example of open source software that can be used by educators to create educational games. Quest (http://textadventures.co.uk/quest), another open source tool for creating text-based games, and Adventure Game Studio (http://www.adventuregamestudio.co.uk) and GDevelop (http://compilgames.net), two systems that can be used to create simple platform games, are other powerful tools for game creation if one has the imagination and time to invest. Additionally, the recently released ACRL Framework for Information Literacy Sandbox[27] has the potential to serve as an open repository of information literacy games as it continues to grow. As of this writing, at least one game has already been submitted.

Conclusion

Game-based learning and gamified techniques present a natural fit for instruction librarians looking for creative ways to "level up" their one-shot sessions. The self-driven, motivational structure of games encourages students to autonomously engage with their own knowledge creation and reflective practices and to acknowledge the value they offer in the classroom. Games embolden students to take control of and develop confidence in their learning process, and they provide instruction librarians with inventive new approaches to assessment and lesson planning. They can also provide opportunities to break down the traditional classroom structures that have been historically shaped by the homogenous culture of librarianship and academia.

For those who are approaching games for the first time, getting started may seem intimidating. While many educators may not have the programming or technical skills to build games from scratch, they can often repurpose other games, tools, or software for their own purposes. However, they must also be cognizant of the fact that the games they utilize may not have been initially created with educators, let alone librarians, in mind. Furthermore, game-based learning and gamification can be particularly vulnerable to "mission creep." Yet by (backward) designing their lesson plans by first focusing on the learning outcomes and then intentionally selecting and adjusting games accordingly, instruction librarians can better ensure that these tools are focused on the course goals. They are able to better envision student learning and success beyond the one-shot session, articulate gaming's contribution to these goals, and ultimately create an empowering classroom environment that both inspires their students and motivates their own creative pedagogical practices.

Endnotes

1. Guy J. Leach and Tammy S. Sugarman, "Play to Win! Using Games in Library Instruction to Enhance Student Learning," *Research Strategies* 20 (2006): 193–94.
2. Justine Martine and Robin Ewing, "Power Up! Using Digital Gaming Techniques to Enhance Library Instruction," *Internet Reference Services Quarterly* 13, no. 2–3 (2008): 210–11.
3. Paulo Freire, *The Politics of Education: Cultural, Power, and Liberation* (South Hadley, MA: Bergin & Garvey, 1985), 114.
4. Chris M. Kirk, Rhonda K. Brown, Brittany Karibo, and Elle Park, "The Power of Student Empowerment: Measuring Classroom Predictors and Individual Indicators," *Journal of Educational Research* 109, no. 6 (2016): 589–95.
5. "Framework for Information Literacy in Higher Education," last modified January 11, 2016, http://www.ala.org/acrl/standards/ilframework.
6. "Diversity Counts 2009–2010 Update," last modified September 2012, http://www.ala.org/offices/diversity/diversitycounts/2009-2010update.
7. Freeda Brook, Dave Ellenwood, and Althea Eannace Lazzaro, "In Pursuit of Antiracist Social Justice: Denaturalizing Whiteness in the Academic Library," *Library Trends* 64, no. 2 (2015): 257.
8. Martine and Ewing, "Power Up!," 215–16.
9. James Paul Gee, *What Video Games Have to Teach Us About Learning and Literacy*, rev. and updated ed. (New York: Palgrave MacMillan, 2007), 207–13.
10. Karl M. Kapp, "Chapter 3—Theories Behind Gamification of Learning and Instruction," *The Gamification of Learning and Instruction: Game-Based Methods and Strategies for Training and Education* (San Francisco: Pfeiffer, 2012), Books24x7.
11. John M. Keller, "Development and Use of the ARCS Model of Instructional Design," *Journal of Instructional Development* 10, no. 3 (1987): 2–10.
12. Amanda N. Hess, "Motivational Design in Information Literacy Instruction," *Communications in Information Literacy* 9, no. 1 (2015): 44–59.

13. Thomas Malone, "Toward a Theory of Intrinsically Motivating Instruction," *Cognitive Science* 4 (1981): 333–69.
14. Richard M. Ryan and Edward L. Deci, "Self-Determination Theory and the Facilitation of Intrinsic Motivation, Social Development, and Well-Being," *American Psychologist* 55, no. 1 (2000): 68.
15. Maura A. Smale, "Learning Through Quests and Contests: Games in Information Literacy Instruction," *Library Innovation* 2, no. 2 (2011): 36–55.
16. Grant P. Wiggins and Jay McTighe, *Understanding by Design* (Alexandria, VA: Association of Supervision and Curriculum Development, 2005), 81.
17. Wiggins and McTighe, *Understanding by Design*, 4.
18. Wiggins and McTighe, *Understanding by Design*, 16.
19. Wiggins and McTighe, *Understanding by Design* 17–32.
20. Megan Oakleaf, "Value of Academic Libraries: A Comprehensive Research Review and Report," *Association of College & Research Libraries*, accessed April 28, 2017, http://www.ala.org/acrl/files/issues/value/val_report.pdf.
21. Grant P. Wiggins and Jay McTighe, *Essential Questions: Opening the Doors to Student Understanding* (Alexandria, VA: Association of Supervision and Curriculum Development, 2013), 81–101.
22. Wiggins and McTighe, *Essential Questions*, 101.
23. Hess, "Motivational Design in Information Literacy Instruction," 38–39.
24. Kristine Fowler, "Jeopardy in the Library: The University of Minnesota Library's Science Quiz Bowl," *College & Research Libraries News* 69, no. 9 (October 2008): 526–29, https://doi.org/10.5860/crln.69.9.8059; Leach and Sugarman, "Play to Win!," 191–203; Billie E. Walker, "This is Jeopardy! An Exciting Approach to Learning in Library Instruction," *Reference Services Review* 36, no. 4 (2008): 381–88.
25. Lauren Wallis, "#selfiesinthestacks: Sharing the Library with Instagram," *Reference Services Quarterly* 19, no. 3/4 (2014): 181–206.
26. Martine and Ewing, "Power Up!," 219–21.
27. "ACRL Framework for Information Literacy Sandbox," accessed April 24, 2017, http://sandbox.acrl.org.

Bibliography

American Library Association. "Diversity Counts 2009-2010 Update." Last modified September 2012. http://www.ala.org/offices/diversity/diversitycounts/2009-2010update.

Association of College & Research Libraries. "ACRL Framework for Information Literacy Sandbox." *American Library Association*. Accessed April 24, 2017. http://sandbox.acrl.org.

———. "Framework for Information Literacy in Higher Education." *American Library Association*. Last modified January 11, 2016. http://www.ala.org/acrl/standards/ilframework.

Brooke, Freeda, Dave Ellenwood, and Althea Eannace Lazzaro. "In Pursuit of Antiracist Social Justice: Denaturalizing Whiteness in the Academic Library." *Library Trends* 64, no. 2 (2015): 246–84.

Fowler, Kristine. "Jeopardy in the Library: The University of Minnesota Library's

Science Quiz Bowl." *College & Research Libraries News* 69, no. 9 (October 2008): 526–29. https://doi.org/10.5860/crln.69.9.8059.

Freire, Paulo. *The Politics of Education: Cultural, Power, and Liberation.* South Hadley, MA: Bergin & Garvey, 1985.

Gee, James Paul. *What Video Games Have to Teach Us About Learning and Literacy.* Rev. and updated ed. New York: Palgrave MacMillan, 2007.

Hess, Amanda N. "Motivational Design in Information Literacy Instruction." *Communications in Information Literacy* 9, no. 1 (2015): 44–59.

Kapp, Karl M. *The Gamification of Learning and Instruction: Game-Based Methods and Strategies for Training and Education.* San Francisco: Pfeiffer, 2012. Books24x7.

Keller, John M. "Development and Use of the ARCS Model of Instructional Design." *Journal of Instructional Development* 10, no. 3 (1987): 2–10.

Kirk, Chris M., Rhonda K. Brown, Brittany Karibo, and Elle Park. "The Power of Student Empowerment: Measuring Classroom Predictors and Individual Indicators." *Journal of Educational Research* 109, no. 6 (2016): 589–95.

Leach, Guy J., and Tammy S. Sugarman. "Play to Win! Using Games in Library Instruction to Enhance Student Learning." *Research Strategies* 20 (2006): 191–203.

Malone, Thomas. "Toward a Theory of Intrinsically Motivating Instruction." *Cognitive Science* 4 (1981): 333–69.

Martine, Justine, and Robin Ewing. "Power Up! Using Digital Gaming Techniques to Enhance Library Instruction." *Internet Reference Services Quarterly* 13, no. 2-3 (2008): 210–11.

Oakleaf, Megan. "Value of Academic Libraries: A Comprehensive Research Review and Report." *Association of College & Research Libraries.* Accessed April 28, 2017. http://www.ala.org/acrl/files/issues/value/val_report.pdf.

Ryan, Richard M., and Edward L. Deci. "Self-Determination Theory and the Facilitation of Intrinsic Motivation, Social Development, and Well-Being." *American Psychologist* 55, no. 1 (2000): 68–78.

Smale, Maura A. "Learning Through Quests and Contests: Games in Information Literacy Instruction." *Library Innovation* 2, no. 2 (2011): 36–55.

Walker, Billie E. "This is Jeopardy! An Exciting Approach to Learning in Library Instruction." *Reference Services Review* 36, no. 4 (2008): 381–88.

Wallis, Lauren. "#selfiesinthestacks: Sharing the Library With Instagram." *Reference Services Quarterly* 19, no. 3/4 (2014): 181–206.

Wiggins, Grant P., and Jay McTighe. *Essential Questions: Opening the Doors to Student Understanding.* Alexandria, VA: Association of Supervision and Curriculum Development, 2013.

———. *Understanding by Design.* Alexandria, VA: Association of Supervision and Curriculum Development, 2005.

CHAPTER 11

Examining Good-Game Design Mechanics that Enhance Student Motivation:

A Case Study of "The Research Race" Game

Ngoc-Yen Tran

Introduction

The Research Race (hereon referred to simply as The Race) is an active learning game played in one-shot information literacy sessions. It is an exercise that has students working together in teams to find answers and to locate materials in a friendly competition with their classmates, while also introducing them to the physical and digital spaces of the library. This chapter outlines how to play The Race and gives rationale for how The Race can enhance motivation through the use of good game design mechanics.

Development and Learning Outcomes

Inspired by a presentation seen at LOEX of the West,[1] I developed the first rendition of The Race[2,3] for first-year seminar courses as a way to get students to actively explore the physical and online aspects of the library in a friendly competition. In this way, The Race embraces the ACRL Framework of Research as Inquiry because the instructors present students with questions and problems to solve; each question builds on skills acquired during the activity and the answers suggest additional lines of inquiry.

The goal of the session is to introduce first-year students in a seminar course to library resources, services, and spaces. Students who attend the session should be able to use the library website to locate library hours and research guides, search for a book and to find it on the library shelves, search and find an article using a library database, make an interlibrary loan request, and to identify ways to get help. The focus of the entire session is on bringing awareness and giving students hands-on experiences with library resources, services, and spaces. The structure and the content of the game allow for adaptations for different courses.

Lesson Preparation, Setup, and Gameplay

The Race can best be described as a combination of a scavenger hunt and a relay race. To play the game, students working in teams of three to five are given tasks on small sheets of paper that introduce them to the library's resources, spaces, and services. These tasks (otherwise known as "legs" of The Race) are given out and completed in sequential order. In order to advance to the next leg of The Race, teams have to bring up their completed sheets of paper (and any additional requirements, such as a book or a picture) and check in with the librarian to make sure that they have answered the questions or completed the task correctly. The first team to complete all of the legs of The Race win a prize (though, everyone wins something).

The first pre-session task for the librarian is to create the legs of the race. Each leg consists of the questions that the teams need to answer, what tasks they need to complete, and what they need to bring up to complete the leg. Developing a version of The Race for the first time can take a couple of hours. However, once the parts have been created, updating them with different topics or requirements takes minimal time. I recommend printing the legs on different colored paper to help the instructor easily identify which step each team is working on during the game, especially in sessions where time is limited. Depending on the length of the session and the topics of the course, legs can be removed or added; however, the standard legs for an introductory first-year seminar course are described here. An example of each leg can be found in Appendix 11A.

Leg 1: Finding basic information on the library's website. In this leg of The Race, you can ask students to find answers to questions that can be found on the library's website. Questions for this leg can include finding the library's hours, finding your subject librarian, reserving a group study room, finding a research guide, etc. Generally, you will be able to fit in five to eight questions and students should be able to complete this first leg in about five to ten minutes.

Leg 2: Finding a book in the catalog and on the shelves. For this leg, give students a specific topic and a building map, then ask them to search the library catalog to identify a relevant book. You can task them (as a team) to locate it on the shelves and to bring it to the librarian. If the book title is acceptable, the team will progress to the next leg. This part can take a team ten to fifteen minutes to complete.

Leg 3: Searching a library database to find articles. This leg has two parts. First, give students a specific database to go to and specific terms to search, then asked to identify one relevant article. They will then write an APA or MLA citation for the article. In the second part, ask the teams to find an article for which they will need to make an interlibrary loan request. In this task, they need to identify the article, sign in to their interlibrary loan account, and take a photo of the interlibrary loan request page as evidence. This multi-part leg can be completed in fifteen to twenty-five minutes.

Leg 4: Getting help from a librarian. In this leg, task students with identifying the different ways they can get help from the library or the librarian. For institutions that have an instant messaging or texting service, the task can be to have students message the service while the librarian leading the session is signed-in to intercept these instant messages. This leg generally takes less than five minutes to complete and is often the last leg of The Race.

Depending on the course and the length of the session, you may want to create and add more legs. The additional legs can also be used as bonus round legs for teams that complete the required legs quickly. Examples include having the teams locate an encyclopedia to find an answer to a question, using the building map to visit various locations in the library and taking selfies as evidence, or searching more databases in order to familiarize themselves with them.

Other pre-session preparations include creating and having available a handout to give to students at the end with information they will need to know, printing legs and cutting them up (enough for everyone in the session), creating an answer sheet, gathering maps of the library building for each team, and buying or creating prizes. (I recommend a small prize, like candy, for everyone who participates in playing in the game, as well as a prize for the winner(s).)

Lesson Overview

Students can play the entire game in a fifty-minute one-shot but it can also be adapted (details below). In a typical instruction session, students are briefly introduced to the game and told the two rules: (1) they may not ask for external help and (2) every team member has to fill in each sheet of paper. Then, they can be formed into teams and asked to select a team name and a leader who will bring the completed tasks to the librarian. Once teams select a leader and present their team names, The Race begins with each team being given the first leg of the race, faced down. When a team believes that they have completed the leg, they bring all of the completed sheets from every team member to the librarian to check for correctness. If an answer is incorrect, or the book or article is not relevant to the topic, the team is asked to correct their mistake. Once they have all of the correct answers, they can advance to the next leg. The Race ends when all teams have completed every leg or when five minutes of the class session remain. Teams that finish early can begin searching for their assignment or work on bonus round legs to keep them occupied. The last five minutes of class are used for a short wrap-up where specific points are emphasized (such as interlibrary loan and subject librarian support) and to answer any remaining questions. Lastly, a handout with pertinent information is distributed and then small prizes are given out to the winning team(s) and candy for all participants.

Brief Review of Libraries and Educational Games

Using quest-based games, such as scavenger hunts,[4] treasure hunts,[5] and mysteries to solve[6,7] for orientations or information literacy courses is not a new approach in libraries. With the adoption of course management systems such as Blackboard and Canvas, libraries have also integrated their games into them. One such example is Fresno State University's HML-IQ game within Blackboard in which students have one task to complete per week for six weeks.[8] With further technological developments such as smartphones, iPad, and other tablets, librarians have adjusted their pedagogical approaches to use these platforms. For example, Wells exposed students to the physical music collection through a QR code scavenger hunt activity.[9] Likewise, at the University of California-Merced Libraries, librarians collaborated with affiliate groups to use the mobile platform SCVNGR to provide a game that had students completing a number of challenges within a twenty-five-mile radius.[10]

Adapting games for library instruction has had mixed results in terms of student learning gains. Marcus and Beck compared a traditional librarian-led tour to a self-guided treasure hunt and found through a questionnaire that students learned better using the self-guided tour.[11] Wells' QR code activity also had positive responses from students about whether or not the activity helped them get acquainted with library and library services.[12] On the other hand, McCain concluded through a study of library literature and information found on college and university libraries' websites that revealed conflicting views and effectiveness of library scavenger hunts.[13] Bailin, a librarian at Lafayette College ran a library version of *The Hunger Games* competition (based on the books by Suzanne Collins) and found that afterward students said they would prefer traditional library tours instead.[14] Nevertheless, games have and will continue to gain traction in higher education, especially if they are designed well because they can be used to motivate learners. The rest of this chapter gives rationale for how The Race uses good game design mechanics to enhance motivation.

How The Race Motivates Students with Good Game-Design Mechanics

Goals, Feedback, and Progress Reports

One aspect of good game design that motivates continued play and learning is clear and specific goals or objectives.[15,16] In The Race, the goals are explicitly given to students; the teams know that in order to win the game, they need to successfully complete a number of tasks or legs and that these deal with aspects of using the library for information and research. To determine if a leg has been completed successfully, the teams are told what a completed leg entails and given directions to bring their completed sheets up to the librarian to check for correctness before moving to the next task. In receiving immediate feedback from the librarian, the teams know what they did correctly and what needs improvement.[17] Not only are there goals, the teams are given a progress report of where they are in working toward their goal, an element that contributes to motivation and continued play. At the top of every leg, the teams are told which leg they are on and the total number of legs so that they can see how close they are to winning or completing the game.

Incremental Challenges

Designing a game that is at the appropriate level of challenge for the players is an important game design aspect for enhancing learner motivation.[18] As you design the legs of The Race, you can keep the students' skill levels and library knowledge in mind. Because first-year students are the target audience, clear and detailed instructions for each leg of the race can ensure the teams are able to complete the tasks successfully. By having legs that are achievable and goal-driven, the teams are encouraged to continue playing the game and are more likely to be engaged in the learning; if the legs were overly difficult, they may choose to abandon the game completely and not learn what they need to know.

Having achievable goals and objectives that are designed to be at the level of the players does not mean that the game should be easy. Good game design mechanics also include incrementally challenging players in order to keep them engaged and learning.[19] The legs of The Race can be ordered to increase in difficulty as the teams progress. For example, the first leg of The Race introduces the students to library basics, but as the groups progress to the third leg on finding an article, they are asked to recall and to apply knowledge or skills that they learned or experienced in a previous leg. Expanding on the last example, in order to know where to go to find an article, the teams need to remember that in the first leg they were asked to locate the library's A–Z databases list on the library's website. This recall encourages learning by creating experiences that are useful for future problem-solving or task completion,[20] and by continually being challenging, students stay engaged in playing the game.

Practice and Safe Failure

Since The Race requires students to use their bodies and their minds, it encourages students to be active participants in their learning.[21] This pedagogical approach has been proven beneficial to student learning in both the traditional classroom format[22] and in the design of games because players are allowed to practice their skills.[23] The legs, as they are designed in The Race, give the students opportunities to practice their information-seeking skills in a format that is novel and fun. In The Race, teams practice searching the library catalog, looking for an article, making an interlibrary loan request, writing a citation, and asking for help from a librarian. In some cases, the skills are practiced multiple times. Students also get additional practice when their teams answer questions or complete tasks incorrectly.

Besides having the opportunity to practice their skills, The Race gives learners time to use their knowledge or to practice their newly learned skills in a low-risk environment where failure is mitigated and successes are encouraged—another good game design mechanic.[24] As with any game, players may not get the correct answer the first time, but by having multiple opportunities for success, they have time to try different methods or to test different theories and to gain confidence in their abilities. Additionally, failure, or the mitigation of failure, is designed into the game. As students play through The

Race, they are given constant feedback regarding their answers and they have many opportunities to build their skills in a low-risk environment. Since they are working in a group environment, mistakes can be seen as a fault of the team and not of the individual. In this way, they can support one another and divert themselves from total disaster that could be detrimental to their confidence or motivation to continue.

Competition and Collaboration

Competition is a ubiquitous mechanic in games, whether it be the players competing against one another or themselves or the players working collaboratively to compete against a computer or other teams.[25] The Race is designed as a competitive game in that the teams are trying to beat one another in order to win the prize. However, because no grades are attached with winning or losing the game, the competition is friendly and low-stakes. Burguillo's study of games and competition-based learning discovered that games with a bit of friendly competition motivated students and increased their learning performance.[26] Even so, the lure of winning the prize or being recognized as the winner can be a motivating element. Although some students may be motivated by beating the other teams and by winning the prize, the social aspects associated with collaborating and interacting with other classmates can also be engaging and a motivate continued play.[27] This social aspect can be especially important for students in a first-year seminar course who are looking to make new friends and to learn from each other's experiences.

Choice and Control

Students' ability to make decisions, develop strategies, and to have general control within a game has been shown to lead to increased motivation and greater learning.[28,29] Admittedly, the amount of control in The Race is limited because the order of the legs is predetermined by the librarian and the goal of each task is specific, but there are some choices and decisions that the teams can make; the teams get to decide who will bring the completed sheets to the librarian and choose the strategies they will use to complete the legs. For example, in the first leg where students are asked to answer questions using the library website, some teams will divide the questions among each other and then share their answers with the rest of the team, and others will have each person work on their own and then share what they find with their teammates. By giving the students some control within the game, they understand that their choices and contributions matter to the overall outcome of the team.

Possible Adaptations

The Race is flexible because it can be adapted in different ways depending on the length of the class session, goals and objectives of the instructor or assignment, and the skill level of the students. In a fifty-minute class session, I recommend no more than four or five race legs, but if the class session is seventy-five or ninety-minutes, an additional one to three relevant legs can be included to fill in the time. If the goal of the instructor or the assignment is to visit the library and introduce students to library spaces, the legs can include having students visit specific locations in the library and take selfies there. Lastly, more or less detailed instructions can be given depending on the skill level or course level of the students in the class.

Conclusion

Librarians have long played games in one-shot information literacy sessions. The Research Race ties that tradition to game design best practices with clear goals, objectives and goals, acceptance and celebration of failure as part of learning, the provision of immediate feedback, practice and scaffolded learning, and student control. In The Research Race, these attributes can help improve pedagogical outcomes, student engagement, and motivation, while introducing them to both the physical and digital spaces of the library. Games as a form of teaching and learning will continue to be prominent in higher education and are an opportunity for libraries and librarians to engage game design mechanics as pedagogical strategies for developing new ways to teach students information literacy concepts in a way that is engaging, motivating, and encourages future learning and success.

Appendix 11A

Below is an example of The Research Race played by first-year seminar course.

Leg 1 of 4: Website / Basics   **Team name:** _____

In this leg of the race, explore the San Jose State University Library website (library.sjsu.edu) to answers these questions! Bring up the completed sheet to get the next leg.

1. What are today's hours for the library?_____
2. How long can most undergraduates borrow library books?

   _____

3. "CSU+" and "Interlibrary Loan" are: (circle one)
   a. Characters on Adventure Time
   b. Free ways to get books from other libraries
   c. Library Cats
4. Librarians create Research Guides by subject area to help students get started with research. If you're in the Biological Sciences research guide, what is the first suggested database for finding peer-reviewed articles? _____
5. Some professors & instructors put readings for their classes on Course Reserves so that everyone can use the material. For the class HIST 480: Mexico, how long can you check out the book *Planet Taco: A Global History of Mexican Food*? _____

Bring this completed sheet to the librarian to see if your team advances to the next leg of the race.

Leg 2 of 4: Finding a book   **Team name:** _____

In this leg, you are asked to use the OneSearch box on the main library homepage to look for a book.

1. Use the drop-down menu to select "San Jose State University Collections"
2. Find a book on the topic of: _popular Japanese culture_____ .
3. Complete the following:

Title_____

Author_____

Call Number _____

4. Use the map provided to find the floor of Knight Library where the book should be. Floor #_____

As a group, go find the book on the shelves and bring it back. (Note: If the book you're looking for turns out to be missing, grab a book next to where yours should be.)

Turn in this completed sheet and the book to the librarian to complete this leg and to move onto the next leg.

Leg 3 of 4: Finding a journal article   Team name: _____

In this leg, go to the Articles by Subject tab on the homepage and choose Psychology as the subject. Select PyscINFO. You are asked to find a scholarly (peer-reviewed/academic) article on the topic of: <u>gender in Argentina</u>.

Type in: Argentina gender into the search box.

<<instructor inserts screenshot here>>

Part 1:

1. Fill in the information below for the most relevant article that is peer-reviewed (remember, the most relevant articles may not always be at the top. Articles not deemed relevant will be returned. Article cannot be the one mentioned in Part 2):

Article title: _____

Author(s): _____

Name of journal article was published in: _____

     Year of publication: _____
     Volume number: _____
     Issue number: _____
     Page numbers: _____

2. Is the entire article available in full-text online? (hint: find the "FindText" link for best results)

If so, from what database? _____

If not, how can you get the full-text of the article? _____

Part 2:

1. Find the article: "Teaching Gender and Sexuality at Public Universities in Argentina."

2. Is it available electronically through the FindText link? _____

If yes, from which database? _____

If no, how can you get the full-text of the article? _____

Turn in this completed sheet to the librarian. If your answers are correct, you will move onto the last leg of the race.

Leg 4 of 4: Getting Help   **Team name:** _____
1. There is a librarian assigned to each subject or major. Who is the subject librarian for Geology? _____
2. Name one way you can Ask a Librarian for help! _____

Great job! This is the last leg of the race! Turn in this completed sheet to the librarian and (maybe) claim your prize.

Endnotes

1. Katherine O'Clair, "The Amazing Library Race," presentation at the LOEX of the West 2012 Conference, Burbank, CA June 6–8, 2012.
2. Ngoc-Yen Tran and Miriam Rigby, "Racing to Learn: Engaging First-Year Students by Gaming Library Instruction," virtual presentation for the American College & Research Libraries 2015 Virtual Conference, March 25–27, 2015.
3. Ngoc-Yen Tran, Miriam Rigby, and Annie Zeidman-Karpinski, "The Students Run the Session: Hands-Off One-Shots with a Library Game," workshop presentation for 2016 Librarians' Information Literacy Annual Conference (LILAC), Dublin, Ireland, March 21–23, 2016).
4. Davita Silfen Glasberg, Judy Harwood, Roland Hawkes, and Catherine Martinsek, "The Library Scavenger Hunt: Teaching Library Skills in Introductory Sociology Courses," *Teaching Sociology* 18 no. 2 (1990): 231.
5. Sandra Marcus and Sheila Beck, "A Library Adventure: Comparing a Treasure Hunt with a Traditional Freshman Orientation Tour," *College & Research Libraries* 64, no. 1 (2003): 23.
6. Nancy M. Foasberg, "Spyfall: Information Games and Scholarly Conversation," *College & Research Libraries News* 78 no. 7 (2007): 218.
7. Anna-Lise Smith and Lesli Baker, "Getting a Clue: Creating Student Detectives and Dragon Slayers in your Library," *Reference Services Review* 39, no. 4 (2011): 628.
8. Monica Fusich, Amanda Dinscore, Kimberley Smith, and Vang Vang, "HML-IQ: Fresno State's Online Library Orientation Game," *College & Research Libraries News* 72, no. 11 (2011): 626.
9. Veronica A. Wells, "Hunting for QR Codes: Linking Students to the Music Collection," *Music Reference Services Quarterly* 15, no. 3 (2012): 137.
10. Elizabeth McMunn-Tetangco, "If You Build It...? One Campuses' Firsthand Account of Gamification in the Academic Library," *College & Research Libraries News* 74, no. 4 (2013): 208.
11. Marcus and Beck, "A Library Adventure," 28.
12. Wells, "Hunting for QR Codes," 146.
13. Cheryl McCain, "Scavenger Hunt Assignments in Academic Libraries," *College & Undergraduate Libraries* 14, no. 1 (2008): 30.
14. Kylie Bailin, "From 'The Research Games' to Tours," *College & Research Libraries News* 76, no. 11 (2015): 589.

15. Atif Waraich, "Using Narrative as a Motivating Device to Teach Binary Arithmetic and Logic Gates," paper presented at the 9th annual SIGCSE Conference on Innovation and Technology in Computer Science Education, Leeds, United Kingdom, June 28–30, 2004.
16. Marc Prensky, *Digital Game-Based Learning* (New York: McGraw-Hill, 2001), 120.
17. Prensky, *Digital Game-Based Learning*, 120.
18. James Paul Gee, *What Video Games Have to Teach Us about Learning and Literacy* (New York: Palgrave Macmillan, 2007), 66; Rosemary Garris, Robert Ahlers, and James E. Driskel, "Games, Motivation, and Learning: A Research and Practice Model," *Simulation & Gaming* 33, no. 4 (2002): 449.
19. Gee, *What Video Games Have to Teach*, 122.
20. James Paul Gee, "Learning and Games," in *The Ecology of Games: Connecting Youths, Games, and Learning*, ed. Katie Salen and The John D. and Catherine T. MacArthur Foundation Series on Digital Media and Learning (Cambridge, MA: The MIT Press, 2008), 23.
21. Gee, *What Video Games Have to Teach*, 208.
22. Elisa L. Park and Bo Keum Choi, "Transformation of Classroom Spaces: Traditional Versus Active Learning Classrooms in Colleges," *Higher Education: The International Journal of Higher Education and Educational Planning* 68, no. 5 (2014): 768.
23. Gee, *What Video Games Have to Teach*, 114.
24. Gee, *What Video Games Have*, 114
25. Prensky, *Digital Game-Based Learning*, 122.
26. Juan C. Burguillo, "Using Game Theory and Competition-Based Learning to Stimulate Student Motivation and Performance," *Computers & Education* 55, no. 2 (2010): 573.
27. Gee, "Learning and Games," 26. Garris et al., "Games, Motivation, and Learning," 451.
28. Gee, *What Video Games Have to Teach*, 208.
29. Mark R. Lepper, and Diana I. Cordova, "A Desire to be Taught: Instructional Consequences of Intrinsic Motivation," *Motivation and Emotion* 16, no. 3 (1992): 197.

Bibliography

Bailin, Kylie. "From 'The Research Games' to Tours." *College & Research Libraries News* 76, no. 11 (2015): 586–89. Accessed December 5, 2016. http://crln.acrl.org/index.php/crlnews/article/view/9413/10614.

Burguillo, Juan C. "Using Game Theory and Competition-Based Learning to Stimulate Student Motivation and Performance." *Computers & Education* 55, no. 2 (2010): 566–75. https://doi.org/10.1016/j.compedu.2010.02.018.

Garris, Rosemary, Robert Ahlers, and James E. Driskel. "Games, Motivation, and Learning: A Research and Practice Model." *Simulation & Gaming* 33, no. 4 (2002): 441–67. https://doi.org/10.1177/1046878102238607.

Gee, James Paul. *What Video Games Have to Teach Us about Learning and Literacy.* New York: Palgrave Macmillan, 2007.

———. "Learning and Games." In *The Ecology of Games: Connecting Youths, Games, and Learning,* edited by Katie Salen and The John D. and Catherine T. MacArthur Foundation Series on Digital Media and Learning, 21–40. Cambridge, MA: The

MIT Press, 2008.

Glasberg, Davita Silfen, Judy Harwood, Roland Hawkes, and Catherine Martinsek. "The Library Scavenger Hunt: Teaching Library Skills in Introductory Sociology Courses." *Teaching Sociology* 18 no. 2 (1990): 231–34. http://www.jstor.org/stable/1318497.

Foasberg, Nancy M. "Spyfall: Information Games and Scholarly Conversation." *College & Research Libraries News* 78 no. 7 (2007): 218–19. Accessed December 5, 2016. http://crln.acrl.org/index.php/crlnews/article/view/9653/11094.

Fusich, Monica, Amanda Dinscore, Kimberley Smith, and Vang Vang. "HML-IQ: Fresno State's Online Library Orientation Game." *College & Research Libraries News* 72, no. 11 (2011): 626–30. Accessed December 5, 2016. http://crln.acrl.org/index.php/crlnews/article/view/8667/9122.

Lepper, Mark R., and Diana I. Cordova. "A Desire to be Taught: Instructional Consequences of Intrinsic Motivation." *Motivation and Emotion* 16, no. 3 (1992): 187–208. https://doi.org/10.1007/BF00991651.

Marcus, Sandra, and Sheila Beck. "A Library Adventure: Comparing a Treasure Hunt with a Traditional Freshman Orientation Tour." *College & Research Libraries* 64, no. 1 (2003): 23–44. https://doi.org/10.5860/crl.64.1.23.

McCain, Cheryl. "Scavenger Hunt Assignments in Academic Libraries." *College & Undergraduate Libraries* 14, no. 1 (2008): 19–31. http://dx.doi.org/10.1300/J106v14n01_02.

McMunn-Tetangco, Elizabeth. "If You Build It…? One Campuses' Firsthand Account of Gamification in the Academic Library." *College & Research Libraries News* 74, no. 4 (2013): 208–10. https://doi.org/10.5860/crln.74.4.8935.

O'Clair, Katherine. "The Amazing Library Race." Presentation at the LOEX of the West 2012 Conference, Burbank, CA, June 6–8, 2012.

Park, Elisa L., and Bo Keum Choi. "Transformation of Classroom Spaces: Traditional Versus Active Learning Classrooms in Colleges." *Higher Education: The International Journal of Higher Education and Educational Planning* 68, no. 5 (2014): 749–71. https://doi.org/10.1007/s10734-014-9742-0.

Prensky, Marc. *Digital Game-Based Learning.* New York: McGraw-Hill, 2001.

Smith, Anna-Lise, and Lesli Baker. "Getting a Clue: Creating Student Detectives and Dragon Slayers in Your Library." *Reference Services Review* 39, no. 4 (2011): 628–42. https://doi.org/10.1108/00907321111186659.

Tran, Ngoc-Yen, and Miriam Rigby. "Racing to Learn: Engaging First-Year Students by Gaming Library Instruction." Virtual presentation for the American College & Research Libraries 2015 Virtual Conference, March 25–27, 2015.

Tran, Ngoc-Yen, Miriam Rigby, and Annie Zeidman-Karpinski. "The Students Run the Session: Hands-Off One-Shots with a Library Game." Workshop presentation for 2016 Librarians' Information Literacy Annual Conference (LILAC), Dublin, Ireland, March 21–23, 2016.

Waraich, Atif. "Using Narrative as a Motivating Device to Teach Binary Arithmetic and Logic Gates." Paper presented at the 9th annual SIGCSE Conference on Innovation and Technology in Computer Science Education, Leeds, United Kingdom, June 28–30, 2004.

Wells, Veronica A. "Hunting for QR Codes: Linking Students to the Music Collection." *Music Reference Services Quarterly* 15, no. 3 (2012): 137–48. http://dx.doi.org/10.1080/10588167.2012.700831.

CHAPTER 12

"You're Batman's Only Hope":
Escape Room Activities in Academic Libraries

Kristen Lemay

Introduction

> *The clock is counting down, and your team is one clue away from opening the last combination lock and discovering the location where Batman is being held hostage. Together, you and your team must use the research skills you have learned to solve clues to the final lock's combination. The other teams in your class cheer you on and help search for objects in this themed room, as "2m 45s" flashes on the projector screen. With a minute to spare, your team finds the last combination lock number under a Spider-Man figurine. You open the mystery box and learn that the Riddler has hidden Batman in a local warehouse. Your class has saved the day!*

Themed escape rooms have become popular outings for friends and coworkers who are looking for a fun activity to test their logic and puzzle-solving skills. Players may crawl through tunnels, find rooms behind bookcases, or decipher secret codes from sheet music. In a higher education context, we can adapt escape rooms to create entertaining and educational spaces in which students can practice their research skills. This instruction exercise will guide you through the process of designing a thirty-minute escape room activity with combination locks for classes with fewer than twenty-five students, from the creation of clues to the selection of props. Examples shown are from an escape room activity which was planned for a popular culture studies class.

Overview

The activity is meant to complement skills and resources that students are introduced to at the beginning of the library session. Students either start the class with an information literacy session or a brief recap of a previous session where the students were introduced to Boolean operators, databases, and any other information that they will need in order to solve the room. Given that the escape room activity requires students to race around a room looking for objects, this activity is best suited for seminar groups with a small number of students. The space, be it a classroom or a computer lab, is transformed into a stage through the placement of some simple props. Books that might be relevant for students' research topics are set up around the room, alongside other objects that contribute to the theme of the room. Dramatic music can play softly in the background to build atmosphere. The librarian, acting as the room's host, helps immerse students in this "world" by telling them a story about why they must find an important object or secret information in the room.

As the clock counts down, students work together to open boxes within the room which contain clues. Each clue will ask them to work with a resource or practice a skill which was introduced to them earlier in the session. Clues may lead students to search for information to assess an author's credentials or to test multiple search strategies in a database to understand how Boolean operators work. By completing the task, students will discover answers which relate to objects in the room; for example, a task that points students to a monograph written by a given author may lead students to find this book or another book written by the same author. These objects, in turn, hold combination lock numbers for the locked boxes. When all of the groups have found their individual combination lock numbers, the groups come together to unlock the first combination lock. For example, if the correct combination is 10-31-2, the first group would have the number ten, the second group would have thirty-one, and the third group would have two. Each group is responsible for the class's overall success.

Once the students unlock the first box, they uncover another box inside and another set of clues. The process begins again with new clues that focus on different research skills. Once they have opened the second (and final) box, the students find the important object or secret information and win the game—assuming that the clock hasn't run out.

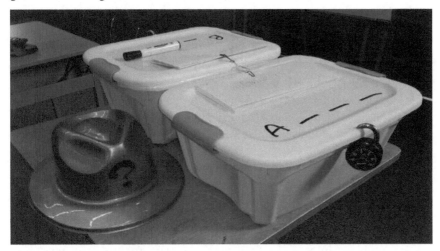

Figure 12.1: Each group receives a clue in an envelope. Each group solves a riddle and finds a combination lock number in the room. The groups come together and use their numbers to open the first box.

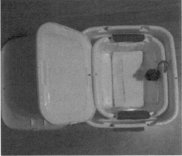

Figures 12.2 and 12.3: The groups will find a second set of clues on top of the smaller box. After solving these clues, the groups will find the combination lock numbers to open the final lock. The "solution" to the room (important object or secret information) will be inside this smaller box.

Depending on the clues within the game, this activity can have students work through the knowledge practices and dispositions of multiple frames within the Framework for Information Literacy for Higher Education. Since the activity focuses on searching, the librarian should build tasks that encourage students to build skill sets that emphasize searching as strategic exploration. Students will need to "exhibit mental flexibility and creativity" throughout the activity and may come to "understand that first attempts at searching do not always produce adequate results."[1]

Learning Outcomes

The specific outcomes for the activity will depend on the needs which the librarian identifies during consultation with the course instructor. Sample learning outcomes for the clue-solving portion of the activity could include:
By the end of this session, students will be able to
- identify multiple channels for scholarly conversation in order to understand how ideas are communicated within their discipline; and
- analyze how Boolean operators refine search strategies in order to retrieve relevant results.

For the group discussion, which follows the escape room, students should be able to
- identify that tackling complex research problems requires breaking problems into smaller, manageable tasks in order to understand that strategic thinking is crucial to the research process.

Lesson Preparation

Creating an escape room activity does require a fair bit of preparation on the librarian's part. Be prepared to carve out a few hours of prep time in the week leading up to the scheduled instruction session so that you are able to consult with the course instructor, design clues, and set the stage.

1. Consult with the Course Instructor

The Association of College and Research Libraries identifies collaboration between librarians and instructors throughout the planning and implementation of instruction as a key best practice for information literacy programs.[2] For this activity, students will benefit from the librarian and course instructor collaborating to develop specific learning outcomes and content for the escape room which will fit with the course's syllabus.[3] Once you have a better idea of the course's content, the parameters of an upcoming assignment, and the resources that the course instructor would like the students to learn, you will be able to develop an appropriate theme for the room.

Learning about the students' academic backgrounds will also help you to develop reasonable clues for the escape room. If the students are midway through a specialization in the course's subject, the learning outcomes and clues should challenge their greater familiarity with research in the discipline.

2. Design Clues

Students will have varying levels of experience with escape room problem-solving and with using library resources. Since students must solve the clues quickly, the tasks within each clue must be laid out as clearly as possible for the students so that they do not miss important steps. Students may experience accidental roadblocks when they jump ahead to a search engine instead of beginning with the database or website listed in the clue. Visual cues, such as bolding and numbered lists, will encourage students to slow down and read through the clue. If appropriate, add contextual information, a riddle that supports the room's theme, or information that will help students tie the answer to an object in the room. To avoid having one group finish four minutes ahead of another group, the clues should have a similar level of complexity or number of steps.

Examples:

The PCA (Popular Culture Association) offers cultural studies scholars an outlet for discussing new developments in their field.
1. Go to **pcaaca.org** and find the "**Journals**" webpage.
2. Which two journals are published by the PCA?

    Answer 1: _____ Answer 2: _____

3. Check out the **submission guidelines** for the **first journal** listed.
4. This journal has a "_____ _____" process, meaning that a copy of the article will be sent to reviewers _____.

(Most superheroes have a secret identity too…)

Eat exclusively in its restaurants and you'll add to your girth. Can you tell me, where is the happiest place on earth?

A: Disney World.

1. Go to the **Popular Culture Research Guide** on the library's website (**URL**).
2. Click on the encyclopedia tab and open the *St. James Encyclopedia of Popular Culture*.
3. Find the entry for **Disney (Walt Disney Company)**.
4. Look at the **bibliography** for this entry.
5. Which **1997 title** might help us understand how Disney's theme parks were designed and the criticism which they have received?

Answer: _____

Each group will have two rounds of clues, meaning that you can create clues that cover the same skills as long as these clues are given to different groups. If the ability to adjust search strategies is a learning outcome for the activity, clues can incorporate different research topics for the same database. If you choose not to duplicate similar skills in your clues, the concluding group discussion will allow students to share their experiences with one another. The resources with which the groups work, such as specialized databases or subject research guides, will have been showcased in the preceding information literacy session.

Create a Master Clue Sheet which includes all of the clues with their answers, corresponding objects and lock numbers, and notes about the skills or concepts that the students will be learning through the clue. To facilitate a rich group discussion at the end of the game, this escape room activity benefits from having different groups work through unique research tasks that demonstrate how to use diverse strategies and resources so that students can learn from each other about research in their discipline. The Master Clue Sheet will help you guide the students through this discussion process.

BreakoutEDU, a company which has created "an immersive games platform for learners of all ages,"[4] also encourages instructors to organize the flow of the game through a worksheet. Breakout EDU sells starter kits for escape room-style games and operates an online library where teachers can showcase the games that they create. Popular with K-12 educators, these kits include locks and other materials, such as invisible ink pens, UV flashlights, and hasps, and many of the games in the library include ready-to-go clues and handouts for different subjects and grade levels.[5] Like this escape room activity, Breakout EDU games have students break into a box instead of disarming a locked door and encourage the class to debrief using pre-made reflection cards.[6] Breakout EDU offers a game template to help educators organize the logical sequence of a game by outlining the lock/item type, how students will know the combination lock number, and where the lock/item will lead them.[7] The Master Clue Sheet from this escape room activity contains all of the relevant information you will need in one place. Since this activity requires you to set up multiple items, it is helpful to have one document to consult while you are assisting students who need help with answers or finding objects, and while you are prompting students to identify the skills that they used in the concluding group discussion.

Sample Master Clue Sheet:

Clue	Answer	Object/ Lock #	Skill/Concept
Which superhero is like a microwave dinner? *A: Captain America! He is more effective when thawed.*	Board Member 1, **University X** Board Member 2, **University Y**	University mug Blue Lock: 30	Become familiar with channels for scholarly conversation
1. Find the website for the **journal** which published this review for *Captain America: The Winter Soldier.*			Identify experts in the field
2. On the website, look at "**Journal Information**."			
3. Which two Canadian universities are represented by members of the journal's editorial board?			

Final Preparation:

1. Recruit a colleague or, better yet, a student to test the clues to make sure that the task instructions are clear. Work-study students can offer feedback about wording and the amount of time that students will need to complete the task.
2. Finalize the clues and decide which clues will be paired together for the different groups. Having a group complete two clues which use identical skills may not be as beneficial to the students' learning experiences as having them work through clues which encourage the students to apply two distinct concepts.
3. Print each group's clues on colored paper (Group 1 has purple clues, Group 2 has yellow clues, etc.). Write out the combination lock numbers on the same colored paper so that the clues and corresponding lock numbers match. Having the clues and combination lock numbers match will help ensure that groups do not take numbers which belong to other groups when they go searching for objects.

4. Print out a few false numbers to act as "red herrings" so that groups cannot simply pick up an object with a colored paper in their color and know that the number is correct without completing the research task. Attaching false numbers to objects which do not relate to answers will help ensure that students are actively working to find the answer, not just pieces of paper with numbers.
5. Place clues in envelopes and label them with group numbers.
6. Leave the first set out and put the second set of clues inside the large box.

Set the Stage

Imagine opening the first set of locks on an antique wardrobe and stepping through to discover a snow-covered room that looks suspiciously like Narnia, complete with a glowing lamppost. What an adventure!

Realistically, post-secondary institutions do not have the budgetary capacity to build the temporary sets for library instruction which would facilitate a totally immersive experience for escape room activities. Instead, classrooms can be transformed into themed rooms through music and objects which build ambiance.

Unless your library has a dedicated instruction room, you may be traveling to a classroom. Select objects that will have a large impact but will be manageable for you to transport and set up in the room. Not every object in the room will have a combination lock number on the back of it; part of the fun of the escape room is that students will encounter red herrings in the form of random objects and false numbers. Having students discern which objects do not contribute to their quest helps emphasize the value of persistence in the search process.

Sample materials:
- One large plastic tote and one small plastic tote
  O Drill holes through the lid on both sides. Secure one side with a zip tie and the other with the combination lock.
- Two combination locks
- Envelopes for clues
- Dry-erase marker
- Secret information or object (for when the final box is opened)
Objects (in which lock numbers can be hidden):
- Books which relate to the field of study (e.g., *Spider-Man and Philosophy: The Web of Inquiry* by Jonathan J. Sanford)
- Dollar store items (e.g., superhero masks, coloring book, and Spider-Man mini Frisbee)
- Poster or banner (e.g., *Game of Thrones* banner)

The number of combination locks and boxes you select will depend on the class size and the size of the groups. The benefit of using plastic totes is two-fold: groups can use dry-erase markers to write the combination lock numbers on the totes, and the totes are lightweight, making transportation easier. When the groups come together to open the locks, having spaces on the boxes for the groups to write down their numbers will save them precious time.

For larger classes, split the secret information or object(s) between the two small boxes so that solving the room is dependent on the successful completion of tasks by each group.

Example:

Class Size	Group Size	Combination Locks	Boxes
10–12 students	3–4 students (3 groups)	2 locks (3 numbers per lock)	1 small box 1 large box
20–24 students	3–4 students (6 groups)	4 locks (3 numbers per lock)	2 small boxes 2 large boxes

Executing the Lesson
Part 1: The Prologue

Time: 2 minutes

Instructions: Deliver opening speech, and distribute first set of envelopes

Activity:

Congratulations! As the librarian and host of the room, you will be embracing your inner thespian. To set the stage for the escape room, deliver a compelling tale that will provide your students with an impetus for working together to unlock the boxes and escape the room in a timely manner.

Build a world in which your students play a vital role, be they heroes or villains, and give them a quest. Do the students need to find a rare artifact in a museum before a homicidal thief arrives? Or, as Dracula's minions, will the students be retrieving a secret scroll containing an ancient spell to raise an undead army before Van Helsing hunts them down?

Sample script for a popular culture studies course:

> *Who's afraid of the Big Bad Bat? Not me. But perhaps you ought to be afraid FOR him. Captain Courageous is hanging out ...over a vat of acid. My henchmen are gleefully waiting for your hero to take a dip, but I like to keep things interesting. You have twenty minutes to solve my Mystery Room with*

your clever research skills. Think you know more about pop culture research than I do? I seriously doubt it.

I've left clues for you to solve, so divide yourselves into three groups and get cracking. These boxes hold the location where your hero is hanging about, so if you want the city's finest to find him before he's little more than a pile of goo, you'd better beat the clock.

Sample note for a British history course:

I don't have much time—this is happening much sooner than any of us had anticipated. Elite Solutions has been working on a time machine for decades. The corporation finally cracked it. Their top client has demanded that the first voyage should be to send an assassin back to the 1530s to kill Anne Boleyn before Elizabeth I is born—whatever sinister plan they've concocted all stems from there. We can't let this happen. Along with a team of specialists, I'm headed to the time machine facility. We have everything we need to operate the machine and complete the mission.

As the team's historians, you and I will be helping the team to maintain its cover in the 1530s so that we can capture the assassin before anyone in Henry VIII's court captures us. I have secured the fob to the facility in a box in my office and given you clues to help you break into the boxes. These clues will help prepare you for court life in the 1530s and ensure that unwanted visitors can't steal the fob.

We don't have much time—I need you to join me as soon as possible.

A strong opening narrative will establish the students' mission and connect the theme of the room with the clues and tasks that the students will be completing. Challenging the students' knowledge of research methods in popular culture, the villain in the first scenario constructs the room to prove his superiority, including research tasks which will determine whether the students' skills can compete with his own. Preparing students to survive court politics in the 1530s, the professor in the second scenario leaves clues which are relevant to understanding historical context. Maintaining a consistent theme through the opening narrative and the tasks will help students immerse themselves in the escape room's story.

In his discussion of storytelling and consistency in escape rooms, Nicholson emphasizes how the challenges within a room should be consistent with and contribute to the overall narrative; the challenges can "help players better understand the world in which the game exists."[8] According to Nicholson, only half of the Breakout EDU games which he analyzed with game design students incorporated challenges that "made sense within the presented narrative and world."[9] Constructing an opening narrative which forges a relationship between the room's world and its research tasks will allow students to remain engaged throughout the activity; if the tasks seem unrelated to the overall quest, "the player can be forgetful of the role they are supposed to be taking."[10]

After establishing the setting of the room, outline any additional information about the logistics of the activity that your students may require, such as the types of locks being used. (This is also an ideal time to remind any nervous students that the doors are not locked.)

Split the students up into smaller groups of three or four, based on the class size. Unlike a traditional escape room where the players go in and have to search around the room for their first clue, each group of students will start with an envelope which has the first clue inside.

Part 2: The Game is Afoot

Time: 20 minutes

Instructions: Troubleshoot issues

Activity:

To begin, groups will open their envelopes to start on their first clues. Each clue involves a task which asks students to work with a resource or to practice a skill that was introduced in the preceding information literacy session. If your clues involve online resources, make sure that there is at least one computer with access to the internet for each group.

While the students will be busy solving clues, racing around the room, and picking up objects, the librarian's role during this part of the escape room activity will be minimal. The librarian will circulate through the room to

- time the activity (or have a countdown clock);
- assist groups who are lagging behind; and
- troubleshoot clues and/or locks.

Part 3: A Period of Reflection

Time: 8 minutes

Instructions: Facilitate a group discussion

Activity:

As in a jigsaw activity where students investigate different resources and then come together to share their findings with the class, this group discussion allows the different groups to share their learning experiences with one another and to reflect on what they achieved during the activity.

Sample questions to prompt the conversation:
- Describe the tasks that you had to complete.
- What did you learn about research in your discipline?
- Why do you think this task was included in the activity?

Ask the students to discuss one or both of the tasks that they completed and to propose how the tasks and resources relate to the previous information literacy session or an upcoming assignment. Giving students time to discuss what they learned through the escape room activity gives them a chance to brainstorm about the different aspects of research in their discipline. By reflecting on how each task contributed to their understanding of the research process, students will be challenged to use higher-order thinking skills and to reason how their experiences during the activity will impact their research process for the upcoming assignment.

When students experience a twenty-minute game wherein they complete two research tasks, they are being shown that getting started on their research does not have to be intimidating or time-consuming, as they can accomplish quite a bit in less than half an hour if they set their minds to it.

Motivational Techniques

From an instructor's point of view, an escape room activity is "active learning" at its most active. Students apply the skills that they have learned during the lesson while running around the room to pick up objects and unlock physical locks. The activity is highly collaborative and encourages students to be active participants; the locks can only be unlocked and the room solved if all groups pull their weight and complete the research tasks. If each task is not completed, the groups cannot find the correct numbers to unlock the combination locks.

Part of the attraction of escape rooms to potential players is the theme of the room. In an escape room activity, students can imagine themselves as part of the adventure story as they complete research tasks that allow them to practice information literacy skills. Just as Brier and Lebbin used storytelling in information literacy instruction as "a tool to meet several of our goals without resorting to mere amusement," escape room activities are "interesting, playful, and substantive" learning opportunities that allow students to play the role of researcher and hero/heroine.[11]

With the clock ticking down, students are motivated to remain focused during the escape room activity and to think of the exercise as a game. Outlining elements of game design which contribute to successful gamification, Stott and Neustaeder propose that the inclusion of the freedom to fail, rapid feedback, progression, and storytelling in the classroom can raise student engagement.[12]

As previously discussed, an escape room activity encourages storytelling as a frame for the game, providing students with a narrative impetus for solving the room. As students try to complete the tasks, the locks operate as mechanisms for rapid feedback; if the lock numbers are incorrect, the students know that they have found false objects and should try to solve the task again. Students "progress" through the room by unlocking one box at a time to release a new set of clues, but the extent to which learning is scaffolded through the clues is at the discretion of the librarian. The freedom to fail and retry tasks is available to students so that they can experiment or seek intervention from the librarian; however, due to the timed nature of escape rooms, students cannot retry "levels" (or a box) more than a few times.

Librarians have integrated popular culture examples into information literacy instruction as a means of successfully engaging students' interest; Springer and Yelinek witnessed increased enthusiasm from students after incorporating *Jersey Shore*-themed activities into their instruction,[13] just as Tewell found that the inclusion of television comedies in instruction sessions "may have the capacity to increase undergraduate learning in library instruction and prove to be an effective means of familiarizing first-year students with information literacy."[14] For Stahura and Milanese, retooling their required information literacy course around the theme of a zombie apocalypse resulted in a radical improvement in the quality of their students' projects; students were engaged throughout the course and came to the consensus that the theme had "made research fun."[15] Using an adapted escape room game format for instruction taps into a growing popular culture trend and motivates students to participate, in part, because of their familiarity with this trend and its perceived entertainment value. Including popular culture examples within the room may increase the impact of this motivational technique further. Springer and Yelinek claim that popular culture examples can "evoke strong reactions in students, and these emotions allow deeper learning to occur"; their students exhibited an "infectious" comfort level with *Jersey Shore* topics and became animated in discussions about library resources.[16] An escape room activity which takes a popular figure as its theme, then, may cause positive affective reactions and increase students' enthusiasm for the clues and research tasks by tapping into their pre-existing interests.

Suggesting that librarians should make the beneficial aspects of an instruction activity obvious to students, Booth explains that the better students comprehend what an "experience will do for them in terms of attaining goals or completing tasks, the more they will perceive its intrinsic value."[17] Having students determine the value of the escape room activity for themselves through the final group discussion provides the extrinsic motivation of group work and the benefit of allowing students to hear one another's perspectives as they reflect on their learning experiences. Inviting students to consider the "why?" and "so what?" of the exercise gives them the chance to make meaning of the learning outcomes for their individual contexts and to consider the "now what?" of how their experience will impact their work going forward (e.g., how the clues match up with how they envision conducting research for an upcoming assignment).[18]

Possible Adaptations

- Scaffold learning by designing clues that build on previous tasks.
  - Example: Students first search in a database using Boolean operators and keywords (the clue would supply the search strategy), then add in additional subject headings to the search for the second clue.
- For smaller group sizes, select locks with four or five digits.
- If you are running the activity in a library instruction room, try adding a scavenger hunt element where students must find books or other objects in the library space outside of the room (stacks, service desk, etc.). Allow extra time for students to travel between the stacks and the instruction room.
- If time permits, demonstrate how to work through any of the clues which were troublesome for groups. Explain how the research process could be pushed further for the clue; for example, a specific search in a database could be explored using different limiters.

Endnotes

1. Association of College and Research Libraries, *Framework for Information Literacy for Higher Education* (Chicago: American Library Association, 2016), www.ala.org/acrl/standards/ilframework.
2. Association of College and Research Libraries, *Characteristics of Programs of Information Literacy that Illustrate Best Practices: A Guideline* (Chicago: American

Library Association, 2012), www.ala.org/acrl/standards/characteristics.

3. Victor, Otto, and Mutschler confirm the positive impact of collaboration and tailoring information literacy instruction to course content on student learning in their study of a collaboration between an instructor, a university archivist and librarians in a social sciences research methods course; after these collaborative sessions, students exhibited greater self-confidence in their ability to locate resources. See Paul Victor, Jr., Justin Otto, and Charles Mutschler, "Assessment of Library Instruction on Undergraduate Student Success in a Documents-Based Research Course: The Benefits of Librarian, Archivist, and Faculty Collaboration," *Collaborative Librarianship* 5, no. 3 (2013): 169, http://digitalcommons.du.edu/collaborativelibrarianship/vol5/iss3/2.

4. Breakout EDU, "Welcome," accessed June 5, 2017, http://www.breakoutedu.com/welcome.

5. Phil Goerner, "Breakout EDU Brings 'Escape Room' Strategy to the Classroom," *School Library Journal*, September 7, 2016, http://www.slj.com/2016/09/reviews/tech/breakout-edu-brings-escape-room-strategy-to-the-classroom-slj-review.

6. Breakout EDU, "Reflection Cards," accessed June 5, 2017, http://www.breakoutedu.com/reflectioncards. Sample questions on the website prompt students to examine group dynamics.

7. Breakout EDU, "Design a Game," accessed June 5, 2017, http://www.breakoutedu.com/create.

8. Scott Nicholson, "Ask Why: Creating a Better Player Experience through Environmental Storytelling and Consistency in Escape Room Design," paper presented at Meaningful Play 2016, Lansing, Michigan, 2016, 10, http://scottnicholson.com/pubs/askwhy.pdf.

9. Nicholson, 2.

10. Nicholson, 7.

11. David J. Brier and Vickery Kaye Lebbin, "Teaching Information Literacy Using the Short Story," *Reference Services Review* 32, no. 4 (2004): 385, doi:10.1108/00907320410569734.

12. Andrew Stott and Carman Neustaedter, *Analysis of Gamification in Education*, (Technical Report 2013-0422-01) (Surrey, BC: Connections Lab, Simon Fraser University, 2013), 1, http://clab.iat.sfu.ca/pubs/Stott-Gamification.pdf.

13. Amy Springer and Kathryn Yelinek, "Teaching with The Situation: *Jersey Shore* as a Popular Culture Example in Information Literacy Classes," *College & Research Libraries News* 72, no. 2 (2011): 80, http://crln.acrl.org/content/72/2/78.full.pdf.

14. Eamon C. Tewell, "Tying Television Comedies to Information Literacy: A Mixed-Methods Investigation," *The Journal of Academic Librarianship* 40, no. 2 (2014): 140, doi:10.1016/j.acalib.2014.02.004.

15. Dawn Stahura and Erin Milanese, "Teaching with Zombies: Bringing Information Literacy Back from the Dead," *College & Research Libraries News* 74, no. 7 (2013): 354, http://crln.acrl.org/index.php/crlnews/article/view/8976/9740.

16. Springer and Yelinek, "Teaching with The Situation," 7.

17. Char Booth, *Reflective Teaching, Effective Learning: Instructional Literacy for Library Educators* (Chicago: American Library Association, 2011), 58.

18. For further information, see Kolb's experiential learning cycle in David Kolb, *Experiential Learning: Experience as the Source of Learning and Development* (En-

glewood Cliffs, NJ: Prentice-Hall, 1984), and the ORID model in Brian Stanfield, *The Art of Focused Conversation: 100 Ways to Access Wisdom in the Workplace* (Toronto: ICA Canada, 1997). For further information on strategies for modeling and facilitating self-regulated learning in information literacy instruction, see Eveline Houtman, "'Mind-Blowing': Fostering Self-Regulated Learning in Information Literacy Instruction," *Communications in Information Literacy* 9, no. 1 (2015): 6–18, http://www.comminfolit.org/index.php?journal=cil&page=article&op=view&path%5B%5D=v9i1p6&path%5B%5D=203.

Bibliography

Association of College and Research Libraries. *Characteristics of Programs of Information Literacy that Illustrate Best Practices: A Guideline.* Chicago, IL: American Library Association, 2012. http://www.ala.org/acrl/standards/characteristics.

———. *Framework for Information Literacy for Higher Education.* Chicago, IL: American Library Association, 2016. http://www.ala.org/acrl/standards/ilframework.

Booth, Char. *Reflective Teaching, Effective Learning: Instructional Literacy for Library Educators.* Chicago: American Library Association, 2011.

Breakout EDU. "Design a Game." Accessed June 5, 2017. http://www.breakoutedu.com/create.

———. "Reflection Cards." Accessed June 5, 2017. http://www.breakoutedu.com/reflectioncards.

———. "Welcome." Accessed June 5, 2017. http://www.breakoutedu.com/welcome.

Brier, David J., and Vickery Kaye Lebbin. "Teaching Information Literacy Using the Short Story." *Reference Services Review* 32, no. 4 (2004): 381–85. doi:10.1108/00907320410569734.

Goerner, Phil. "Breakout EDU Brings 'Escape Room' Strategy to the Classroom." *School Library Journal*, September 7, 2016. http://www.slj.com/2016/09/reviews/tech/breakoutedu-brings-escape-room-strategy-to-the-classroom-slj-review.

Houtman, Eveline. "'Mind-Blowing': Fostering Self-Regulated Learning in Information Literacy Instruction." *Communications in Information Literacy* 9, no. 1 (2015): 6–18. http://www.comminfolit.org/index.php?journal=cil&page=article&op=view&path%5B%5D=v9i1p6&path%5B%5D=203.

Kolb, David. *Experiential Learning: Experience as the Source of Learning and Development.* Englewood Cliffs, NJ: Prentice-Hall, 1984.

Nicholson, Scott. "Ask Why: Creating a Better Player Experience through Environmental Storytelling and Consistency in Escape Room Design." Paper presented at Meaningful Play 2016, Lansing, Michigan, 2016. http://scottnicholson.com/pubs/askwhy.pdf.

Springer, Amy, and Kathryn Yelinek. "Teaching with The Situation: *Jersey Shore* as a Popular Culture Example in Information Literacy Classes." *College & Research Libraries News* 72, no. 2 (2011): 78–80, 85, 118. http://crln.acrl.org/content/72/2/78.full.pdf.

Stahura, Dawn, and Erin Milanese. "Teaching with Zombies: Bringing Information Literacy Back from the Dead." *College & Research Libraries News* 74, no. 7 (2013): 354–56. http://crln.acrl.org/index.php/crlnews/article/view/8976/9740.

Stanfield, Brian. *The Art of Focused Conversation: 100 Ways to Access Wisdom in the Workplace.* Toronto: ICA Canada, 1997.

Stott, Andrew, and Carman Neustaedter. *Analysis of Gamification in Education* (Technical Report 2013-0422-01). Surrey, BC: Connections Lab, Simon Fraser University, 2013. http://clab.iat.sfu.ca/pubs/Stott-Gamification.pdf.

Tewell, Eamon C. "Tying Television Comedies to Information Literacy: A Mixed-Methods Investigation." *The Journal of Academic Librarianship* 40, no. 2 (2014): 134–41. doi:10.1016/j.acalib.2014.02.004.

Victor, Paul, Jr., Justin Otto, and Charles Mutschler. "Assessment of Library Instruction on Undergraduate Student Success in a Documents-Based Research Course: The Benefits of Librarian, Archivist, and Faculty Collaboration." *Collaborative Librarianship* 5, no. 3 (2013): 154–76. http://digitalcommons.du.edu/collaborativelibrarianship/vol5/iss3/2.

CHAPTER 13

The List and the Spine:
Poetry, Information Literacy, and Motivation

Sarah Kortemeier

Introduction

What does the writing of poetry have to do with information literacy? As a working poet and teaching librarian, I answer: plenty! The writing of a poem is a research process that synthesizes extremely diverse pieces of information. When I write poetry, I ransack my memory and I call older relatives to ransack theirs. I use translation dictionaries. I fall down Wikipedia rabbit holes. I access primary sources via digitized archives, I look up statistics, I read feminist theology …and so on, and so on. I experience high levels of motivation during this process, both in terms of intrinsic motivation ("doing something because it is inherently interesting or enjoyable") and extrinsic motivation ("doing something because it leads to a separable outcome"—in this case, a finished poem).[1] Here, I have drawn on that personal experience to develop two exercises (a list poem and a spine poem) designed to build student motivation in information literacy instructional sessions.

The two activities presented here spring from the premise that people, with their individual passions and experiences, are the heart of research. Though it is certainly true that the "I" is infrequently privileged in professional scholarly writing, the individual interests of the researcher have enor-

213

mous motivational importance. As Dane Ward reminds us, "We discover and connect to the world from the inside out."[2] Ward argues compellingly for a "holistic" view of information literacy that incorporates both analysis and imagination. Under his proposed model, students learn not only how to evaluate information but "how to be engaged and why to care."[3] The list and spine poem exercises I have developed here are inspired by, and build upon, Ward's thinking about holistic information literacy as well as Jeremy J. Shapiro and Shelley K. Hughes's earlier, influential proposal for a broadened definition of information literacy as a liberal art.[4] Ward, for example, suggests that students might listen to music and create drawings in order to help them engage with a research topic on a personal level.[5] Here, I posit that writing poetry can also help students connect with their "inwardness," explore personal connections to research topics, and help them to deepen their analytical writing.[6] Writing poetry can also productively disrupt a "monolithic" (disciplinary/academic) approach to knowledge. If "the learning process is essentially a gateway to the universe," as Shilpa Shanbhag has argued, educators must acknowledge that the universe is larger than the classroom.[7] By exposing learners to multiple methods of knowledge production (in addition to purely academic knowledge production), teachers can help students make connections between their academic work and their personal, lived experience outside the academy.[8] The spine poem activity and the list poem activity invite students to combine scholarly knowledge with other ways of knowing.

I have made use of a number of currents in the contemporary thinking on learning and motivation in the development of these exercises. First, I have been influenced by the constructivist theory of learning, which holds that learners create both knowledge and meaning based on their current and past experience.[9] Second, I owe a great deal of my thinking in this chapter to self-determination theory, which holds that people have three basic needs for psychological well-being: competence, relatedness (a sense of security and social connection), and autonomy (the latitude to make choices).[10] Though all three have effects on motivation,[11] autonomy (particularly intellectual autonomy) may be an "essential link" that promotes deep-level engagement, perceptions of competence, and intrinsic motivation in students.[12] My own teaching reflects the assumption that autonomy-supportive instructional practices are important motivational tools.[13] Third, I have also made repeated use of John M. Keller's influential ARCS (Attention, Relevance, Confidence, Satisfaction) theory of motivation.[14] Keller holds that learners become motivated to learn when their *attention* is aroused by a "perceived gap in current knowledge," when the knowledge presented in a lesson is *relevant* to the learners' goals, when learners feel *confidence* in their ability to learn the material, and when learners experience *satisfaction* with the outcome of a task.[15] Below, I show how the components of each poetry writing exercise correspond to these theoretical frameworks.

Both the list poem activity and the spine poem activity put a new spin on a familiar technique. The list poem is beloved in creative writing pedagogy for its accessibility and its motivational power. The form of the list is familiar and comfortable[16] for writers of all experience levels, and list-making can lend itself to intensely musical, imaginative language.[17] Pioneering poet and educator Kenneth Koch also observed that list poems motivated his students to write. His *I Wish* list poems, for example, "gave [his students] something to write about which really interested them: the private world of their wishes."[18] List-making is also a natural fit for information literacy instruction since lists are a time-honored form of documentation for information-gathering.[19] The "Collaborative List Poem" activity presented here uses list-making to encourage students to synthesize multiple kinds of information from diverse sources, including personal experience and scholarly sources.

The second activity uses a "spine poem" (a type of found poem derived from the titles of books on a shelf) to encourage students to explore their personal connections to a research topic. The spine poem is fun, accessible,[20] and, I argue, a useful motivational tool. Recent work on the pedagogical uses of found poetry documents its motivational power. Lisa Patrick, for example, found that writing found poetry made participants in her study feel not only more confident in their ability to write poetry but more confident and engaged *as readers* (since the writing of found poems required participants to read, re-read, and re-experience texts in a creative, pleasurable way).[21] I use spine poems frequently as an engagement activity in my own teaching practice.

I originally developed these two activities to support a "controversy analysis" research paper assignment at The University of Arizona, though I have used both the "list" and "spine" techniques in support of a very wide range of writing assignments. The list poem and the spine poem can be done independently or in sequence. As written, they are designed to be placed quite early in the research process (ideally, just after students have chosen a research topic). I offer some ideas for possible adaptations after each exercise.

Exercise I: Collaborative List Poems
Overview

In this lesson, students work together to collect and list information on a controversial topic. These lists incorporate anaphora, concrete sensory detail, and a multiplicity of voices, resulting in musical text that echoes centuries of list-based poetry. In the process, students are encouraged to think of "scholarship as conversation," reflecting multiple points of view and a diverse cast of voices.[22] This lesson also prompts students to consider what they don't know about a topic, encouraging them to think about "research as inquiry."[23]

Learning Outcomes

By the end of this lesson, students will be able to

1. identify facts, personal memories, information needs, emotional responses, and stakeholders related to a research topic;
2. synthesize these lists collaboratively to create a group poem that reflects what they know (both affectively and cognitively) about a controversial topic; and
3. evaluate the appropriateness of the language they have generated for various types of rhetorical situations and/or appeals.

Lesson Preparation

This lesson requires the following materials to be set up before class: a writing surface large enough for the whole class to work on simultaneously (large whiteboard or sheet of butcher paper); index cards with prompts (see below); and excerpts from list poems by Sei Shōnagon (*The Pillow Book*)[24] and/or Joe Brainard (*I Remember*)[25] (see below). Students will not require any prior preparation to complete this activity. As written, this lesson serves as an introduction to a research unit.

Lesson Plan

Introduction: 10 minutes

Tell students that they will spend the class period investigating the different types of information researchers might synthesize for diverse purposes. Ask students: Why might researchers need more than one kind of information? In what situations might a researcher need a personal story instead of (or in addition to) a graph, for example?

Then, introduce list-making as a poetic tool that accomplishes just this kind of synthesis of diverse pieces of information. For centuries, poets and writers have used lists to capture complexity, nuance, and detail. Read an excerpt from an extended list poem aloud, such as Sei Shōnagon's Heian Court-era classic *Pillow Book* or Joe Brainard's *I Remember*.[26] Both works are notable for the way they use specific, concrete sensory detail to transport the reader inside another person's experience.

For example, Sei Shōnagon gives us an intimate portrait of her world through the use of multi-sensory detail in her "List of Infuriating Things":

> A hair has got onto your inkstone and you find yourself grinding it in with the inkstick. Also, the grating sound when a bit of stone gets ground in with the ink...

A baby who cries when you're trying to hear something...

...I hate people who don't close a door that they've opened to go in or out...[27]

And Joe Brainard draws a vivid picture of childhood with specific sensory details in *I Remember*:

I remember the only time I saw my mother cry. I was eating apricot pie.[28]

I remember the chair I used to put my boogers behind.[29]

I remember planning to tear page 48 out of every book I read from the Boston Public Library, but soon losing interest.[30]

I remember wooden forks hard to handle a big potato salad lump with.[31]

Read an extended selection from one (or both) of these poems aloud and ask students: What details in these lists stand out to you? What effect do these details have on the reader? Why might a writing technique designed to capture details like this be useful to researchers?

Evidence-based rationale:

The purpose of the introductory discussion and literary model(s) is to "hook" student *attention* (part of John M. Keller's ARCS theory of motivation) by introducing a new, incongruous, or surprising idea (students do not necessarily expect to encounter poetry in a research unit).[32]

Writing Activity: 15 minutes

Tell students that they will create a group list poem, like the one in the literary model(s), in order to explore a contemporary research topic.

Divide students into teams of two or three. Position each team around a large whiteboard or sheet of butcher paper. As a class, brainstorm and select a group research topic, preferably one that is at least somewhat controversial, timely, and complex. Ideally, there should be more than two possible sides to the controversy. The instructor may also pre-select a topic if this seems useful, particularly if the class has recently discussed a particular controversy. (I have worked with classes on topics such as cultural appropriation, the Black Lives Matter movement, border issues, and so on. This activity works best when the topic is something students know and care about.) When possible, ask students to focus on a single recent news story or incident that illustrates the controversy. This approach tends to result in more specific writing.

Give each team of two or three students a different prompt related to the group topic. Ask students to work together to brainstorm and list at least ten responses to their given prompt on the butcher paper or whiteboard and encourage them to include as many specific, concrete details (like those in the literary models) as possible in their list items. To save time and give each group a reference point, I recommend writing or copying each prompt onto an index card. Give each team one of the folowing cards:

Card 1.

I remember...
- Where were you when you heard about this topic for the first time?
- What is the most memorable thing you've ever heard said about this topic?
- Do you recall any events from your childhood that have a connection to this topic?
- Etc. Your final list should take the form "I remember X..."; "I remember X..."

Card 2.

I know...
- Facts you know already about this topic: e.g., How much does such-and-such program cost? When and where did a specific incident related to this controversy occur? Who does this controversy affect? Describe the controversy in terms of who, what, when, where, how, and why. Be as specific as you can!
- Your final list should take the form "I know X..."; "I know X..."

Card 3.

I don't know...
- What do you *not* know that has bearing on this topic? Think of the controversy in terms of who, what, when, where, how, and why (who does this controversy affect, when and how did this controversy become an issue, etc.). What gaps exist in your knowledge? What questions arise in your mind? List them.
- Your final list should take the form "I don't know X..."; "I don't know X..."

Card 4.

> *I've heard...*
> - What comments have people in your circle made concerning this topic? Try to quote them exactly, as best you can remember.
> - Your final list should take the form "I've heard X..."; "I've heard X..."

Card 5.

> *I need...*
> - What specific facts do I need to understand this topic better? What individual sources would I consult to find them?
> - What stories do I need to hear to write effectively about this topic? Who would I approach to find them? List specific individuals.
> - What "props" do I need to write well? A laptop? Music? Chips?
> - Your final list should take the form "I need X..."; "I need X..."

Card 6.

> *Silly things...*
> - List five "things" (can be objects, events, or people) associated with this topic that you find silly.
>
> *Interesting things...*
> - List five more things associated with this topic that you find interesting.

Card 7.

> *Beautiful things...*
> - List five "things" (can be objects, events, or people) associated with this topic that you find beautiful.
>
> *Infuriating things...*
> - List five more things associated with this topic that you find infuriating.

Card 8.

> *X wants...*
> - Make a list of people who have a stake in this controversy (caution: these should be *individuals*! List them by name, if possible. Do not list groups.)
> - What does each person want? Your final list should take the form "X wants..."; "X wants...

Discussion: 15 minutes

Go around the room and have each group read their list aloud, beginning each list item with the signal phrase on the top of their index cards: "I remember... I remember..." "X wants... X wants..." The result should be a musical collage, similar in effect to the list poems read at the beginning of the activity.

Then have each group quickly annotate their lists. Which of these list items might be appropriate to use in an introduction to a research paper? A conclusion? A thesis statement in an academic paper? An argument at a family dinner? Why? Have each group report back to the class and quickly explain their reasoning.

Evidence-based rationale:

This group activity is based on constructivist learning theory and on autonomy-supportive teaching practices. It builds on students' previous experience and encourages them to take ownership of a question, finding multiple possible answers.[33] This kind of activity encourages students to make meaningful intellectual choices, promoting intrinsic motivation.[34] The activity also reflects four of the components of Keller's revised ARCS model of motivation. First, the activity provides classroom task variety, which Keller cites as a key factor in creating and sustaining student curiosity and *attention*.[35] Second, the activity builds student *confidence* as students build a visual record of what they already know about a topic. Ideally, the list-making process reveals knowledge students either did not know they possessed or had not considered as essay-worthy material before completing the activity.[36] Third, the reading of the collaborative group poem (with its musical language and the opportunities afforded for the discovery of new ideas) contribute to student *satisfaction*.[37] Fourth, the final evaluation (which kinds of information are appropriate in different rhetorical situations?) establishes *relevance* to the upcoming research assignment and the overall goals of the course.[38]

Conclusion: 5–10 minutes

Discuss with students: This activity encourages us to compile both empirical facts and personal observations about a topic. Are both important to our understanding of a controversy? Why or why not? What are the uses of each type of information?

Evidence-based rationale:

This brief, final discussion is intended to firmly establish the *relevance* of the list-making activity to students' larger experience as well as to their learning and course goals (again, making use of the ARCS model of motivation).[39]

Possible Adaptations:

Educators might also use this activity later in the research process as students are working on fleshing out their individual research essays. In this case, each student would work on all eight of the list prompts independently (perhaps providing five responses to each prompt instead of ten), and students might share their list poems as time allows at the end of class. (If students are working on similar research topics, they could also do this activity in pairs or small groups, divided according to research topic.) In this version, the activity would incorporate more extrinsic motivators, in that the material generated in the list poem would have more direct application to the research paper.

Exercise II: Spine Poems
Overview

In this activity, students use a spine poem (a found poem composed of text gleaned from book titles) to explore and express their emotional connections to a research topic. In the course of this activity, students experience "search as a strategic exploration" (a decidedly non-linear, occasionally serendipitous process).[40] This activity also encourages students to think about how information from various sources, including the self, helps them to negotiate and understand the world. Students are asked to consider non-transactional ways in which "information has value."[41]

Learning Outcomes

By the end of this lesson, students will be able to

1. discover language that echoes their own personal emotional connections to individual research topics;
2. create poems about their research topics by assembling and collaging the language they find; and
3. reflect on and evaluate the uses of emotion in the research process.

Lesson Preparation

This lesson requires a library collection of printed books. Literary collections (fiction, creative non-fiction, poetry) produce best results. It's helpful to do this activity near the beginning of a research unit as students are narrowing down (or immediately after they have chosen) a research topic.

Lesson Plan

Introduction: 10 minutes

Tell students that they will be exploring the role of personal/emotional connections to research topics. (This may be a new angle on research for many
students. When I introduce this activity, especially in first-year composition
classes, I often frame it as part of a "bridge" between high school work and
higher-level scholarship. As students advance in a discipline, their work is
increasingly guided by their interests and undertaken in a spirit of inquiry.
This activity is designed to help students explore their personal connections
to potential research topics.)

Have students write down their research topic and a few notes on why
they chose it. Encourage students to be honest here; these notes are for their
own use and no one else will see them.

Evidence-based rationale:

The purpose of the introductory discussion, as in the first activity, is to "hook"
student *attention* (part of Keller's ARCS theory of motivation) by introducing
a new and surprising idea (in this case, the idea that emotion has a role in the
research process).[42]

Browsing Activity: 20 minutes

Ask students to go into the library collection and write down 10 titles that reflect their emotional responses to their research topics. Students should write
down one title that sounds funny in relation to their research topic, one that
sounds sad in relation to their research topic, and eight more that have some
connection to the reason they chose their research topics (the connection can
be very loose and/or metaphorical).

Evidence-based rationale:

The browsing activity is self-directed, promoting student feelings of autonomy and choice. In addition, this activity asks students to make choices based
on their individual feelings and values. Meaningful choice (that reflects "one's
personal goals, interests, or values"[43]) tends to boost student feelings of autonomy and intrinsic motivation.[44]

Writing Activity: 10 minutes

When students return with their ten titles, ask them to remix the language in
those titles to create a poem about their topic. These "spine poems" need not
use every word in every title, and they can present the words from the titles
in any order. They can take any form and they can be either long or short.

Ask students to stick with the language in the titles as far as possible, without adding in extra words of their own. (This constraint is usually fun and productive. However, individual students sometimes get inspired and want to write more, combining their own words with the language from the titles. I always allow this when students specifically ask for it. The poem is the point; the constraint is only important as a writing aid.)

Solicit volunteers to read their spine poems aloud. (The instructor can also collect poems and read them anonymously. Alternatively, go around the room and have each student read a single line from their spine poems. This lessens performance anxiety and creates a gorgeous, ephemeral group poem in the process, especially if everyone reads their lines in quick succession, without explanation, one after the other.)

Evidence-based rationale:

The writing activity is essentially an episode of linguistic play. When students have a sense of the *relevance* of this playful work (that is, its intersections with either their personal experience or an academic assignment), the play activity becomes a powerful motivational tool. Relevance is a key component of Keller's ARCS theory of motivation.[45]

Reflection Activity: 10 minutes

Conclude the lesson with a brief reflection paper to be handed in at the end of class. Ask students to write responses to the following questions:

- What kinds of language provoke emotion in us?
- In what contexts are emotional reactions useful to us?
- How do our emotions help us understand the world?
- List two occasions when you had to do research: one for a class and one because you needed information about something (the latter can be a very simple information need: Where should I go for dinner tonight?, etc.) Which of those two research processes did you feel a more personal connection to? How did that personal connection affect the research process?
- Why is it important to care about our research topics?

Evidence-based rationale:

The final reflection privileges students' personal experience and independent thought in an autonomy-supportive framework.[46] Students are free to think through their responses without fear of giving a "wrong" answer. Such frameworks tend to promote intrinsic motivation.[47] Additionally, this reflection activity asks students to discover and articulate the *relevance* of what they have just done to their upcoming assignment and their lives outside the classroom.[48]

Closing: 10 minutes

Discuss reflection questions briefly as a class, soliciting one or two student responses for each question. Conclude with the final question: as a class, why do we think it's important to care about research topics?

Evidence-based rationale:

This closing activity, in tandem with the previous reflection, attempts to combat negative student attitudes toward research by demonstrating the utility of passion in the research process. The goal is to "encourage [students] to see the inherent worth of the secondary research process by making the topic research more personal," since the presence of a personal connection to a research topic has dramatically positive implications for intrinsic motivation.[49]

Possible Adaptations:

Educators might use this activity in the closing class period of a research assignment instead of at the beginning of the unit. Here, the activity would become a reflection on the research project the class has just completed, rather than a means of encouraging students to pick research topics they care about. In this case, the activity might take a "pre/post" framework: *How did you feel about this topic when you started and how have your feelings changed? Go into the collection and choose five titles that express your earlier feelings about your topic and five that reflect the way you feel now. Use the language in those titles to write a poem about your topic.* The reflection activity at the end of the class period could stand as-is or could be changed so that some of the questions reflect the emotional process of research *(How did your emotional connection to this topic change over time and how did that affect your work on this project?).* In this adaptation, the focus shifts to intrinsic motivation almost exclusively, inviting students to think about how they might use their emotions and research interests to motivate future study.

The spine poem activity could also be used independently, without tying it to a specific assignment. This exercise could, for example, be used as part of an orientation designed to reduce library anxiety (feelings of being overwhelmed, unsure where to begin, and afraid to admit incompetence in the library).[50] Dale J. Vidmar has shown that brief ten- to twenty-minute "warmth"-oriented pre-sessions (held before a full library instruction session) can improve students' affective experiences in the library, which has positive implications for subsequent library instruction.[51] Though Vidmar did not measure student motivation specifically, motivation is part of the affective domain.[52] In addition, library anxiety is a major motivational obstacle (students in Constance A. Mellon's landmark study "discussed feelings of fear that kept them from beginning to search or that got in the way of their staying in the library long enough to master search processes"[53]). Alleviating library anxiety may well have positive results for student motivation. To adapt this activity for a "warmth" pre-session, instructors might ask students to think about a research topic that interests them, find several titles that speak in some way to *why* the topic interests them, write a poem about the topic using that language, and reflect at the end of the lesson on why it's important to care about research topics. The goal in this instance would be to provide a relaxed, welcoming introduction to the library, the librarian, and the research process, setting students up for a positive relationship with the library overall.

Motivational Techniques in Play

"To be motivated," Richard M. Ryan and Edward L. Deci remind us, "means *to be moved* to do something"[54]—yet educators traditionally skip over the role emotion plays in the research process when we teach research in higher education. I offer these exercises, then, as a counterpoint to this tendency and as a pedagogical response to the growing calls for attention to students' affective needs in IL instruction. These activities make an effort to help students explore *what moves them* to do research, understand and produce information, and learn. The spine poem activity attempts to help students locate intrinsic motivation by exploring their personal, emotional connections to research topics. The collaborative list poem addresses emotion more obliquely by incorporating personal information, stories, and memories into the process of information collection. Both activities, however, treat students' memories, experiences, and emotions as valid and useful information sources: "The information universe exists within us as much as it does beyond us."[55] By affirming students' creativity and personhood, educators can create space for deep intrinsic motivation to grow.

This approach to motivation is fundamentally constructivist. It is student-centered, grounded in inquiry, and based on the premise that the learner constructs both meaning and knowledge.[56] The enormous motivational importance of personal choice and agency in the research process—a "person-centered" or "student-centered" approach to information literacy instruction—has been widely discussed in the literature (though it is recognized that some IL instruction still follows a more didactic pattern focused on teacher-generated research topics).[57] As noted in the rationales for each of these exercises, I have been particularly influenced by theories of autonomy-supportive instruction, which hold that classroom opportunities for independent problem-solving and meaningful choice promote intrinsic motivation.[58] The collaborative list poem activity asks students to investigate their own memories and experiences to discover unique information about a given topic and then to evaluate how they might deploy that information in an original piece of writing. The spine poem lesson plan incorporates a self-directed browse activity and a playful found poetry exercise, both directed toward the inward exploration of affective responses. Both exercises, then, are largely student-directed. They also privilege students' lived experience in ways that are designed to build student confidence, a very powerful component of motivation.

John M. Keller's influential ARCS (Attention, Relevance, Confidence, Satisfaction) theory of motivation has also played a major role in the development of these lesson plans.[59] First, these activities capture learner *attention* through introducing variety in the classroom routine.[60] The spine poem activity involves a visit to a print library collection, while the collaborative list poems utilize props (index cards, butcher paper, or other centralized writing surface) to stimulate student interest.

Second, both activities are designed to be *relevant* to learners, drawing connections among students' personal experience, their immediate course-related goals (that is, the successful completion of their research papers), and their long-term intellectual interests. This is particularly important because relevance is traditionally one of the major challenges facing librarians who deliver information literacy instruction. Students do not always understand how a one-shot library instruction session connects with either their coursework or their broader lives.[61] Relevance comes up particularly frequently in these particular lessons because they were originally designed for use in a special-collections poetry library, where it is crucially important to establish relevance early and often for general-education class visits (since it's not always immediately clear to students how the materials in a poetry library can help them write papers). These activities make those connections explicit.

Third, both activities are designed to help build student *confidence* in their own writing ability. Both the spine poem and the collaborative list poem use students' own memories, knowledge, and interests to build poetic text, and the writing tasks in each activity are accessible.

Finally, these activities are designed to help students achieve a sense of *satisfaction* in their writing, which is especially important for *continuing* motivation.[62] In particular, both activities offer opportunities near the end of the lesson for students to hear their poems read aloud (an exercise that tends to surprise everyone with its beauty) and reflect on how the text they have generated might figure into their research papers.

The spine and list poem activities attempt to deepen students' intrinsic motivation while simultaneously providing effective extrinsic motivation. The exploration of personal connection to a research topic in both lessons is designed to lead not only to subjective, intangible outcomes (such as feelings of fascination or a desire to know more) but concrete, tangible *outputs* in the form of language students can use to improve the research essays they write. I emphasize both types of motivators when I teach these exercises. For example, when I introduce these activities to students, I usually outline the motivational goals of the lesson specifically: I open with a brief discussion of how our personal experiences and/or intellectual fascinations inform, drive, and make research enjoyable ("we would all prefer to *enjoy* the process of researching and writing this essay, right?!"). Then I explain what we'll be doing and how the text students generate during the lesson could be useful in an upcoming research assignment. Later in the lesson, I am also careful to point out the ways in which the writing students are generating might fit into an introduction, a conclusion, a title, a persuasive anecdote in the body of an essay, etc. The instructing librarian is best positioned to make use of these extrinsic motivators, of course, when s/he is familiar with a class's specific research assignment. (Familiarity with specific research assignments has other motivation-related benefits. For example, when the librarian works with faculty members to tailor library instruction to specific assignments, faculty members tend to place a high value on the library instructional session. Faculty investment in the lesson is an extrinsically motivating factor for students, who can tell.)[63]

The combination of intrinsic and extrinsic motivators in these activities is particularly important because of the way motivation can shift over time and from student to student, even within the bounds of a single class session. It is perfectly possible and natural for students to find some activities "more relevant or rewarding or just more interesting than others."[64] When I ask students to do a poetry activity (or any activity), I cannot realistically expect that all parts of the lesson will be perceived as equally useful by every student. Likewise, I cannot realistically expect that the intrinsic joy of writing poetry or doing research will provide sufficient motivation for everyone all the time. Furthermore, intrinsic and extrinsic motivators are not necessarily dichotomous or discrete. As Barbara A. H. Harmes reminds us, intrinsic and extrinsic motivation exist on a continuum.[65] If, for example, a student describes a childhood memory in one of these two activities that later becomes part of the introduction to her research paper, she may well use an "extrinsic" motivator to achieve greater personal connection to, and intrinsic satisfaction in, the writing process. (My anecdotal experience certainly bears this out. Students will occasionally rush joyfully up to me or to their instructor in the middle of one of these lessons to announce that they've found a title for their research paper or that they've remembered a personal story they can use to introduce their topic.) By giving students opportunities to exercise personal volition and choice in an exploratory atmosphere, I can help them create a positive school experience and discover sources of intrinsic motivation.[66] These single-session activities, then, have motivational goals that extend beyond the individual class meeting in which they are completed.

The work of poetry is a work of meaning-making and it is therefore eminently suited to a constructivist learning environment—in information literacy and beyond. These activities frame the writing of poetry as a matter of autonomy, exploration, and practical utility, as well as meaning-making, and these factors are key to my own understanding of student motivation: "Students experience academic engagement through feelings of relevance and choice, the knowledge that their work and learning *matters* and is valued by themselves and by others" (italics mine).[67] Poetry gives us one set of tools to help students engage in this way. There are, of course, many others. I look forward to a continued exploration of the potential intersections of arts education and information literacy instruction as the IL field evolves.

Endnotes

1. Richard M. Ryan and Edward L. Deci, "Intrinsic and Extrinsic Motivations: Classic Definitions and New Directions," *Contemporary Educational Psychology* 25, no. 1 (January 2000): 55, doi:10.1006/ceps.1999.1020.
2. Dane Ward, "Revisioning Information Literacy for Lifelong Meaning," *The Journal of Academic Librarianship* 32, no. 4 (July 2006): 398, http://dx.doi.org.ezproxy3.library.arizona.edu/10.1016/j.acalib.2006.03.006.
3. Ward, "Revisioning Information Literacy for Lifelong Meaning," 398.
4. Jeremy J. Shapiro and Shelley K. Hughes, "Information Literacy as a Liberal Art," *Educom Review* 31, no. 2 (March 1996).
5. Ward, "Revisioning Information Literacy for Lifelong Meaning," 399.
6. Ward, "Revisioning Information Literacy for Lifelong Meaning," 399.
7. Shilpa Shanbhag, "Alternative Models of Knowledge Production: A Step Forward in Information Literacy as a Liberal Art," *Library Philosophy and Practice* 8, no. 2 (Spring 2006), http://digitalcommons.unl.edu/libphilprac/.
8. Shanbhag, "Alternative Models of Knowledge Production."
9. *The SAGE Glossary of the Social and Behavioral Sciences,* s.v. "Constructivist Learning Theory," accessed July 19, 2017, http://zp9vv3zm2k.search.serialssolutions.com/?ctx_ver=Z39.88-2004&ctx_enc=info%3Aofi%2Fenc%3AUTF-8&r-fr_id=info%3Asid%2Fsummon.serialssolutions.com&rft_val_fmt=info%3Aofi%2Ffmt%3Akev%3Amtx%3Abook&rft.genre=bookitem&rft.title=The+SAGE+Glossary+of+the+Social+and+Behavioral+Sciences&rft.atitle=Constructivist+Learning+Theory&rft.date=2009-01-01&rft.isbn=9781412951432&rft.externalDocID=9756569&paramdict=en-US.
10. Richard M. Ryan and Edward L. Deci, "Self-Determination Theory and the Facilitation of Intrinsic Motivation, Social Development, and Well-Being," *American Psychologist* 55, no. 1 (January 2000): 68, 70, 71, http://dx.doi.org/10.1037/0003-066X.55.1.68; Candice R. Stefanou et al., "Supporting Autonomy in the Classroom: Ways Teachers Encourage Student Decision Making and Ownership," *Educational Psychologist* 39, no. 2 (2004): 99, doi:10.1207/s15326985ep3902_2.
11. Ryan and Deci, "Self-Determination Theory," 71.
12. Stefanou et al., "Supporting Autonomy in the Classroom," 100–101; Edward L. Deci

and Richard M. Ryan, "Conceptualizations of Intrinsic Motivation and Self-Determination," in *Intrinsic Motivation and Self-Determination in Human Behavior* (New York: Plenum Press, 1985), 29.

13. Stefanou et al., "Supporting Autonomy in the Classroom," 99; Deci and Ryan, "Conceptualizations of Intrinsic Motivation," 29; Edward L. Deci and Richard M. Ryan, "Optimizing Students' Motivation in the Era of Testing and Pressure: A Self-Determination Theory Perspective," in *Building Autonomous Learners: Perspectives from Research and Practice Using Self-Determination Theory*, ed. Woon Chia Liu, John Chee Keng Wang, and Richard M. Ryan (Singapore: Springer Science+Business Media, 2016):12–13, doi:10.1007/978-981-287-630-0_2.

14. John M. Keller, "First Principles of Motivation to Learn and e³-Learning," *Distance Education* 29, no. 2 (July 2008): 176–78, doi:10.1080/01587910802154970. This is a revised/expanded version of a motivational theory Keller first outlined in 1979, later codified as "ARCS."

15. Keller, "First Principles of Motivation to Learn, 176-178 .

16. Larry Fagin, *The List Poem: A Guide to Teaching & Writing Catalog Verse* (New York: Teachers & Writers Collaborative, 1991), 1.

17. Kenneth Koch, *Wishes, Lies, and Dreams: Teaching Children to Write Poetry* (New York: Chelsea House Publishers, 1970), 6.

18. Koch, "Wishes, Lies, and Dreams," 7.

19. Fagin, *The List Poem*, 14.

20. Travis Jonker, "The Fun of 'Found Poetry,'" *Children & Libraries: The Journal of the Association for Library Service to Children* 10, no. 3 (Winter 2012), 64.

21. Lisa Patrick, "Found Poetry: A Tool for Supporting Novice Poets and Fostering Transactional Relationships Between Prospective Teachers and Young Adult Literature" (PhD diss., Ohio State University, 2013), ii-iii.

22. "Framework for Information Literacy for Higher Education," Association of College & Research Libraries, adopted January 11, 2016, http://www.ala.org/acrl/standards/ilframework#authority.

23. "Framework for Information Literacy."

24. Sei Shōnagon, *The Pillow Book*, trans. Meredith McKinney (London: Penguin Books, 2006). This is a popular contemporary edition; however, any modern translation of *The Pillow Book* will work for the purposes of this exercise.

25. Joe Brainard, *I Remember* (New York: Granary Books, 2001). This is a contemporary compilation of Brainard's work from the 1970s, including material from *I Remember* (New York: Angel Hair, 1970), *I Remember More* (New York: Angel Hair, 1972), and *More I Remember More* (New York: Angel Hair, 1973).

26. At the time of publication, excerpts of both were readily available online in multiple locations as open access documents, found with a simple search.

27. Sei Shōnagon, *The Pillow Book*, 26–29.

28. Brainard, *I Remember*, 8.

29. Brainard, *I Remember*, 26.

30. Brainard, *I Remember*, 14.

31. Brainard, *I Remember*, 138.

32. Keller, "First Principles of Motivation to Learn and e³-Learning," 176-177.

33. Stefanou et al., "Supporting Autonomy in the Classroom," 101.

34. Stefanou, "Supporting Autonomy in the Classroom," 101-102.

35. Keller, "First Principles of Motivation to Learn and e³ Learning," 176-177.
36. Keller, "First Principles of Motivation to Learn and e³ Learning," 177.
37. Keller, "First Principles of Motivation to Learn and e³ Learning," 177-178.
38. Keller, "First Principles of Motivation to Learn and e³ Learning," 177.
39. Keller, "First Principles of Motivation to Learn and e³ Learning."
40. "Framework for Information Literacy for Higher Education."
41. "Framework for Information Literacy for Higher Education."
42. Keller, "First Principles of Motivation to Learn and e³-Learning," 176–77.
43. Avi Assor, Haya Kaplan, and Guy Roth, "Choice is good, but relevance is excellent: Autonomy-enhancing and suppressing teacher behaviours predicting students' engagement in schoolwork," *British Journal of Educational Psychology* 72, no. 2 (June 2002): 272–73. http://eds.a.ebscohost.com.ezproxy4.library.arizona.edu/ehost/detail/detail?vid=3&sid=b1de4059-84d0-46e0-b4a0-361babe-ab966%40sessionmgr4006&bdata=JnNpdGU9ZWhvc3Qtb-Gl2ZQ%3d%3d#AN=7167060&db=asn.
44. Stefanou et al., "Supporting Autonomy in the Classroom," 100–101.
45. Keller, "First Principles of Motivation to Learn and e³-Learning," 177.
46. Stefanou et al., "Supporting Autonomy in the Classroom," 101.
47. Edward L. Deci and Richard M. Ryan, "Education," in *Intrinsic Motivation and Self-Determination in Human Behavior* (New York: Plenum Press, 1985), 253–54.
48. Keller, "First Principles of Motivation to Learn and e³-Learning," 177.
49. Jacqueline Courtney Klentzin, "The borderland of value: examining student attitudes toward secondary research," *Reference Services Review* 38, no. 4 (2010): 568, doi:10.1108/00907321011090728.
50. Constance A. Mellon, "Library Anxiety: A Grounded Theory and Its Development," *College & Research Libraries* 47, no. 2 (1986): 162–63, https://doi.org/10.5860/crl_47_02_160.
51. Dale J. Vidmar, "Affective Change: Integrating Pre-Sessions in the Students' Classroom Prior to Library Instruction," *Reference Services Review* 26, nos. 3/4 (Fall/Winter 1998): 92, http://dx.doi.org/10.1108/00907329810307777.
52. Ellysa Stern Cahoy and Robert Schroeder, "Embedding Affective Learning Outcomes in Library Instruction," *Communications in Information Literacy* 6, no. 1 (2012): 75, http://eds.b.ebscohost.com.ezproxy4.library.arizona.edu/ehost/detail/detail?vid=4&sid=5578a8b0-dc40-4883-b2b9-01 23c6c34d9b%40sessionmgr102&hid=119&bdata=JnNpdGU9ZWhvc3Qtb-Gl2ZQ%3d%3d#AN=84110749&db=llf.
53. Mellon, "Library Anxiety," 163.
54. Ryan and Deci, "Intrinsic and Extrinsic Motivations," 54.
55. Ward, "Revisioning Information Literacy for Lifelong Meaning," 397.
56. Susan E. Cooperstein and Elizabeth Kocevar-Weidinger, "Beyond active learning: a constructivist approach to learning," *Reference Services Review* 32, no. 2 (2004): 142, http://dx.doi.org/10.1108/00907320410537658.
57. Andrew K. Shenton and Megan Fitzgibbons, "Making Information Literacy Relevant," *Library Review* 59, no. 3 (2010): 166, http://dx.doi.org/10.1108/00242531011031151.
58. Stefanou et al., "Supporting Autonomy in the Classroom," 101; Juan L. Núñez and Jaime León, "Autonomy Support in the Classroom: A Review from Self-Determina-

tion Theory," *European Psychologist* 20, no. 4 (January 2015): 276, doi:10.1027/1016-9040/a000234.
59. Keller, "First Principles of Motivation to Learn and e³-Learning," 176–78.
60. Keller, "First Principles of Motivation to Learn and e³-Learning," 176, 177.
61. Don Latham and Melissa Gross, "Instructional Preferences of First-Year College Students with Below-Proficient Information Literacy Skills: A Focus Group Study," *College & Research Libraries* 74, no. 5 (September 2013): 430, doi:10.5860/crl-343.
62. Keller, "First Principles of Motivation to Learn and e³-Learning," 177–78.
63. Trudi E. Jacobson and Lijuan Xu, *Motivating Students in Information Literacy Classes* (New York: Neal-Schuman Publishers, 2004), 12.
64. Barbara A. H. Harmes, "Intrinsic and Extrinsic Motivation: Mythic Aspects in the Tertiary Sector," in *Myths in Education, Teaching, and Learning*, ed. Marcus K. Harmes, Henk Huijser, and Patrick Alan Danaher (Houndmills, Basingstoke, Hampshire; New York: Palgrave Macmillan, 2015), 43, http://ebookcentral.proquest.com.ezproxy2.library.arizona.edu/lib/uaz/reader.action?docID=1953007&ppg=1.
65. Harmes, "Intrinsic and Extrinsic Motivation," 45.
66. Deci and Ryan, "Optimizing Students' Motivation in the Era of Testing and Pressure," 21.
67. Shelly Buchanan et al., "Inquiry Based Learning Models, Information Literacy, and Student Engagement: A Literature Review," *School Libraries Worldwide* 22, no. 2 (July 2016): 24, https://eprints.qut.edu.au/102823/13/102823.pdf.

Bibliography

Association of College & Research Libraries. "Framework for Information Literacy for Higher Education." Adopted January 11, 2016. http://www.ala.org/acrl/standards/ilframework#authority.

Assor, Avi, Haya Kaplan, and Guy Roth. "Choice is good, but relevance is excellent: Autonomy-enhancing and suppressing teacher behaviours predicting students' engagement in schoolwork." *British Journal of Educational Psychology* 72, no. 2 (June 2002): 261–78. http://eds.a.ebscohost.com.ezproxy4.library.arizona.edu/ehost/detail/detail?vid=3&sid=b1de4059-84d0-46e0-b4a0-361babe-ab966%40sessionmgr4006&bdata=JnNpdGU9ZWhvc3Qtb-Gl2ZQ%3d%3d#AN=7167060&db=asn.

Brainard, Joe. *I Remember.* New York: Granary Books, 2001.

Buchanan, Shelly, Mary Ann Harlan, Christine Bruce, and Sylvia Edwards. "Inquiry Based Learning Models, Information Literacy, and Student Engagement: A Literature Review." *School Libraries Worldwide* 22, no. 2 (July 2016): 23–39. https://eprints.qut.edu.au/102823/13/102823.pdf.

Cahoy, Ellysa Stern, and Robert Schroeder. "Embedding Affective Learning Outcomes in Library Instruction." *Communications in Information Literacy* 6, no. 1 (2012): 73–90. http://eds.b.ebscohost.com.ezproxy4.library.arizona.edu/ehost/detail/detail?vid=4&sid=5578a8b0-dc40-4883-b2b9-01-23c6c34d9b%40sessionmgr102&hid=119&bdata=JnNpdGU9ZWhvc3Qtb-Gl2ZQ%3d%3d#AN=84110749&db=llf.

Cooperstein, Susan E., and Elizabeth Kocevar-Weidinger. "Beyond active learning: a constructivist approach to learning." *Reference Services Review* 32, no. 2 (2004): 141–48. http://dx.doi.org/10.1108/00907320410537658.

Deci, Edward L., and Richard M. Ryan. "Conceptualizations of Intrinsic Motivation and Self-Determination." In *Intrinsic Motivation and Self-Determination in Human Behavior,* 11–40. New York, New York: Plenum Press, 1985.

———. "Education." In *Intrinsic Motivation and Self-Determination in Human Behavior,* 245–71. New York: Plenum Press, 1985.

———. "Optimizing Students' Motivation in the Era of Testing and Pressure: A Self-Determination Theory Perspective." In *Building Autonomous Learners: Perspectives from Research and Practice Using Self-Determination Theory,* edited by Woon Chia Liu, John Chee Keng Wang, and Richard M. Ryan, 9–29. Singapore: Springer Science+Business Media, 2016. doi:10.1007/978-981-287-630-0_2.

Fagin, Larry. *The List Poem: A Guide to Teaching & Writing Catalog Verse.* New York: Teachers & Writers Collaborative, 1991.

Harmes, Barbara A. H. "Intrinsic and Extrinsic Motivation: Mythic Aspects in the Tertiary Sector." In *Myths in Education, Teaching, and Learning,* edited by Marcus K. Harmes, Henk Huijser, and Patrick Alan Danaher, 40–58. Houndmills, Basingstoke, Hampshire; New York: Palgrave Macmillan, 2015. http://ebookcentral.proquest.com.ezproxy2.library.arizona.edu/lib/uaz/reader.action?docID=1953007&ppg=1

Jacobson, Trudi E., and Lijuan Xu. *Motivating Students in Information Literacy Classes.* New York: Neal-Schuman Publishers, Inc., 2004.

Jonker, Travis. "The Fun of 'Found Poetry.'" *Children & Libraries: The Journal of the Association for Library Service to Children* 10, no. 3 (Winter 2012): 64.

Keller, John M. "First Principles of Motivation to Learn and e³-Learning." *Distance Education* 29, no. 2 (July 2008): 175–85. doi:10.1080/01587910802154970.

Klentzin, Jacqueline Courtney. "The borderland of value: examining student attitudes toward secondary research." *Reference Services Review* 38, no. 4 (2010): 557–70. doi:10.1108/00907321011090728.

Koch, Kenneth. *Wishes, Lies, and Dreams: Teaching Children to Write Poetry.* New York: Chelsea House Publishers, 1970.

Latham, Don, and Melissa Gross. "Instructional Preferences of First-Year College Students with Below-Proficient Information Literacy Skills: A Focus Group Study." *College & Research Libraries* 74, no. 5 (September 2013): 430–49. doi:10.5860/crl-343.

Mellon, Constance A. "Library Anxiety: A Grounded Theory and Its Development." *College & Research Libraries* 47, no. 2 (1986): 160–65. doi:10.5860/crl_47_02_160.

Núñez, Juan L., and Jaime León. "Autonomy Support in the Classroom: A Review from Self-Determination Theory." *European Psychologist* 20, no. 4 (January 2015): 275–83. doi:10.1027/1016-9040/a000234.

Patrick, Lisa. "Found Poetry: A Tool for Supporting Novice Poets and Fostering Transactional Relationships Between Prospective Teachers and Young Adult Literature." PhD diss., Ohio State University, 2013.

Ryan, Richard M., and Edward L. Deci. "Intrinsic and Extrinsic Motivations: Classic Definitions and New Directions." *Contemporary Educational Psychology* 25, no. 1 (January 2000): 54–67. doi:10.1006/ceps.1999.1020.

———. "Self-Determination Theory and the Facilitation of Intrinsic Motivation, Social

Development, and Well-Being." *American Psychologist* 55, no. 1 (January 2000): 68–78. doi:10.1037/0003-066X.55.1.68.

Sei Shōnagon. *The Pillow Book*. Translated by Meredith McKinney. London: Penguin Books, 2006.

Shanbhag, Shilpa. "Alternative Models of Knowledge Production: A Step Forward in Information Literacy as a Liberal Art." *Library Philosophy and Practice* 8, no. 2 (Spring 2006). http://digitalcommons.unl.edu/libphilprac/.

Shapiro, Jeremy J., and Shelley K. Hughes. "Information Literacy as a Liberal Art." *Educom Review* 31, no. 2 (March 1996): 31–35.

Shenton, Andrew K., and Megan Fitzgibbons. "Making Information Literacy Relevant." *Library Review* 59, no. 3 (2010): 165–74. http://dx.doi.org/10.1108/00242531011031151.

Stefanou, Candice R., Kathleen C. Perencevich, Matthew DiCintio, and Julianne C. Turner. "Supporting Autonomy in the Classroom: Ways Teachers Encourage Student Decision Making and Ownership." *Educational Psychologist* 39, no. 2 (2004): 97–110. doi:10.1207/s15326985ep3902_2.

Vidmar, Dale J. "Affective Change: Integrating Pre-Sessions in the Students' Classroom Prior to Library Instruction." *Reference Services Review* 26, nos. 3/4 (Fall/Winter 1998): 75–95. http://dx.doi.org/10.1108/00907329810307777.

Ward, Dane. "Revisioning Information Literacy for Lifelong Meaning." *The Journal of Academic Librarianship* 32, no. 4 (July 2006): 396–402. http://dx.doi.org.ezproxy3.library.arizona.edu/10.1016/j.acalib.2006.03.006.

CHAPTER 14

Choose a Topic, Choose a Group, Choose a Focus

Maggie Murphy

Introduction

What do *American Horror Story*, the Second Amendment, Zora Neale Hurston, and climate change have in common? They're all topics my English composition and communication undergraduate students have recently selected for research projects. As a first-year instruction librarian in a university library, I often work with English composition and communication instructors who allow their students to choose topics for papers and speeches that range from literary analysis to current events to popular culture. The idea behind this strategy is that students can choose topics that interest them, so they are intrinsically motivated to engage in the iterative research and writing process. However, I often encounter difficulty in covering how to select and evaluate relevant information sources for different types of topics as well as demonstrate different database, catalog, and web-searching techniques—all in a single one-shot. Even worse, research indicates that students' natural curiosity and internal motivation to learn may decrease as they get older,[1] meaning that instruction librarians may have a difficult time keeping college students engaged in the research process even when they are working with a topic that interests them.

I designed this exercise around the concept that giving students choices during a one-shot library instruction session both promotes intrinsic moti-

235

vation and maximizes time for active learning instead of instructor demonstration. Instruction librarians can design lessons that inspire intrinsic motivation in students by creating "challenging learning situations that allow students to have some control over their learning and promote feelings of competence and mastery."[2] As Thompson and Beymer note, "Offering choice in the classroom is one way to increase student motivation by appealing to students' needs for autonomy and competence."[3] In fact, in a meta-analysis of research findings on the effects of choice on intrinsic motivation, Patall, Cooper, and Robinson found that "choice can have a positive overall effect on intrinsic motivation."[4] Building upon the choice they are given when asked to pick a topic, this exercise gives students control by allowing them to choose who to work with and what to focus on during the instruction session. The group-work prompt challenges students to immediately put into practice what they have learned.

Lesson Plan Overview

The exercise outlined in this chapter is best suited for English composition or public speaking courses in which students are able to choose their own topic of interest for a writing or speech assignment. Librarians may find this exercise is difficult to implement in fifty minutes if the class is comprised of more than twenty-five students. In order to make the most of the instruction period, students are asked to view two videos and fill out a form so that the librarian can become familiar with their chosen topics ahead of time. During the lesson, following a demonstration by the librarian, students are guided to form groups to explore and practice finding, selecting, and evaluating sources based on common or related topics, source types, or research techniques. I have provided some methods for integrating students who come to class unprepared in the Session Instructions below. The lesson aligns with several knowledge practices and dispositions within the Searching as Strategic Exploration frame of the ACRL Framework for Information Literacy, including matching information needs and search strategies to appropriate search tools, designing and refining needs and search strategies as necessary, based on results, and using different types of searching language appropriately.

Learning Outcomes

By the end of this session, students will be able to

- distinguish between information source types, such as scholarly journal articles, popular periodicals, books, reference sources, and websites;

- formulate appropriate keywords, synonyms, and related search terms on a chosen topic; and
- apply search techniques in a database, catalog, or internet search engine.

Materials

- Computer classroom with a computer for each student, an instructor computer, a projector, a screen, and a whiteboard
- Computer or web-based application for creating and presenting slideshows, such as Microsoft PowerPoint or Google Slides
- Web-based application for creating questionnaire forms and collecting form data, such as Google Forms and Google Sheets
- A few pairs of headphones for unprepared students

Session Instructions

Part 1: Pre-Lesson Preparation

Learning outcomes:

- Formulate appropriate keywords, synonyms, and related terms to search for information sources on a chosen topic.

Time to complete: 30 minutes to an hour

Setup: To prepare for the instruction session, create an online questionnaire that students will fill out ahead of the scheduled lesson. The form should have the following fields:

- student's name
- student's topic
- potential keywords, synonyms, or related phrases for searching
- reason(s) why the student has chosen the topic
- one thing they learned from each video

The form should indicate to the students that their names and topics will be shared with their classmates but their reasons for choosing a topic will be kept private.

The activity: Coordinate with the disciplinary instructor to assign two short tasks for students to complete at least two days ahead of the instruction session. If possible, ask the instructor to link a homework or extra-credit grade with these tasks. (You can provide the instructor with a list of the students who completed the work.) Associating a low-stakes grade with the pre-class work should minimize the number of students who come to class unprepared. The first pre-class task is to watch the *From Idea to Library, One Perfect Source?* and *Tips & Tricks: Phrase Searching* videos from the North Carolina State University Libraries' "Videos and Interactive Guides" site.[5] Each of these videos takes about three minutes or less to view and is licensed for reuse under a Creative Commons Attribution-NonCommercial-ShareAlike 3.0 United States license. The second task is to fill out the online questionnaire form. Once all students have filled out the form, create a slideshow with one slide per student. Each slide should have a student's name and chosen topic. Finally, review the topics and make notes about how students might organize themselves into groups based on similar topics, appropriate source types, or research techniques. These notes will be used to make suggestions for group formation in the instruction session.

Rationale: The videos give concise explanations of concepts related to academic research and help students become familiar with the concepts before the instruction session. Asking students to brainstorm keywords, synonyms, and related phrases challenges them to put their new knowledge into practice. The form data helps the librarian become familiar with the range of topics and students' motivation for choosing them ahead of time, which will facilitate group creation during class time.

Part 2: Introduction to Lesson
Learning outcomes:

- Distinguish between information source types, such as scholarly journal articles, popular periodicals, books, reference sources, and websites.

Setup: Open the slideshow on the instructor's computer

Time to complete: 15–20 minutes

The activity: Go through the slideshow so that the students become familiar with their classmate's chosen topics. Explain to students that they should pay attention to this activity because they will be forming groups based on topics shortly. Then, highlight distinguishing features of information source types that students may use in their research, such as articles, books, reference sources, and websites. Choose two topics as examples and demonstrate a search in a general academic database and a book catalog.

Rationale: Students receive reinforcement of the concepts introduced in the NCSU Libraries videos. The goal is not to give an exhaustive demonstration of all concepts related to academic research but to give students a starting point for their group work.

Part 3: Group Formation

Time to complete: 5–10 minutes

The activity: Ask students to form small groups of three to five students to practice searching for, selecting, and evaluating sources. Start by giving students suggestions on how they might form groups based on your lesson preparation and write these suggestions on the whiteboard for reference. For example, students may choose to form groups based on related topics (such as scripted television dramas or popular science topics), relevant information source types (such as students who want to practice finding statistics on government websites or look for arts and culture blogs that publish analysis and criticism of new films), or research techniques (such as students who want to practice developing keywords using Boolean operators or phrase-searching in academic databases). If students are having difficulty forming groups or choosing a focus, you may need to make recommendations based on their topics. Students who have not completed the pre-class activities can be given a different choice: either form a group together to watch the NCSU Libraries videos (wearing headphones), brainstorm topics and search terms, and complete the questionnaire for partial credit—or participate in the regular group formation activity with their classmates and receive no homework credit.

Rationale: Students feel a sense of autonomy in their own learning by choosing who to work with and what to focus on. Allowing students to make choices may inspire intrinsic rather than extrinsic motivation to engage in the activity.

Part 4: Group Work

Time to complete: 25 minutes

Learning outcomes:

- Formulate appropriate keywords, synonyms, and related search terms on a chosen topic.
- Apply search techniques in a database, catalog, or internet search engine.

The activity: Circulate from group to group, offering targeted instruction, demonstration, and advice while posing some discussion points based on the group's chosen focus. Encourage students to look for articles, books, or web sources that might be useful for writing on their topic, but explain that it is okay if they do not find them in this session so long as they start to form strategies for how they might find relevant sources on their own. The goal here is for students to explore relevant information resources, ask questions, and become more confident in source selection and search techniques rather than worry about finding specific sources by the end of the session. Manage your time carefully; spend no more than five to seven minutes with each group. Recommend additional research guides, interactive tutorials, or video resources from your library that students may view after the class session ends to become more familiar with searching for and selecting sources.

Rationale: Practicing a specific aspect of academic research related to their topic in depth allows students to develop competence and confidence—aspects of intrinsic motivation—in their new research skills. Connecting students with additional resources of learning and support through guides, tutorials, or videos allows students to continue to learn and practice after the session has ended.

Part 5: Closing Discussion

Time to complete: 10 minutes

The activity: Ask each group to briefly share an observation about the information sources or search strategies, a technique they tried, or a problem they encountered during their group exploration with the class. Reinforce that research is a process of trial and error and that more practice will lead to a better understanding of information sources and search techniques. Remind students that librarians are available to help them one-on-one should they encounter difficulty finding relevant information sources for their assignment as they engage in research after the session.

Rationale: The closing discussion gives students a space to reflect on what they have learned in the instruction session as well as share their successes and failures with the class.

Motivational Techniques

According to Small, Zakaria, and El-Figuigui, "Students with an intrinsic (or internal) orientation find satisfaction from simply participating in a learning experience that stimulates their curiosity and interest, promotes their feelings of competence or control, and/or is inherently pleasurable."[6] Yet, intrinsic motivation "tends to decline across grade levels,"[7] making it difficult to inspire intrinsic motivation in older students. Giving learners choices in the classroom is a motivational technique that can inspire intrinsic motivation in college students who are new to academic research. Specifically, Thompson and Beymer list giving students the choice of topics to research *and* allowing students to choose their own groups are instructional methods that increase intrinsic motivation in student learning situations.[8] This exercise incorporates both of those strategies to promote an intrinsic orientation for students in the instruction session.

Endnotes

1. Mark R. Lepper, Jennifer Hederlong Corpus, and Sheena S. Iyengar, "Intrinsic and Extrinsic Motivational Orientations in the Classroom: Age Differences and Academic Correlates," *Journal of Educational Psychology* 97, no. 2 (2005): 193.
2. Ruth V. Small, Nasriah Zakaria, and Houria El-Figuigui, "Motivational Aspects of Information Literacy Skills Instruction in Community College Libraries," *College and Research Libraries* 65, no. 2 (2004): 99.
3. Margareta Thompson and Patrick Beymer, "The Effects of Choice in the Classroom: Is There Too Little or Too Much Choice?," *Support for Learning* 30, no. 2 (2015): 105.
4. Erika A. Patall, Harris Cooper, and Jorgianne Civey Robinson, "The Effects of Choice on Intrinsic Motivation and Related Outcomes: A Meta-Analysis of Research Findings," *Psychological Bulletin* 134, no. 2 (2008): 294.
5. North Carolina State University Libraries, "Videos and Interactive Guides," *NCSU Libraries,* accessed March 10, 2017, https://www.lib.ncsu.edu/tutorials/.
6. Small, Zakaria, and El-Figuigui, "Motivational Aspects," 99.
7. Thompson and Beymer, "The Effects of Choice," 118.
8. Thompson and Beymer, 110.

Bibliography

Lepper, Mark R., Jennifer Henderlong Corpus, and Sheena S. Iyengar. "Intrinsic and Extrinsic Motivational Orientations in the Classroom: Age Differences and Academic Correlates." *Journal of Educational Psychology* 97, no. 2 (2005): 184–96.

North Carolina State University Libraries. "Videos and Interactive Guides." *NCSU Libraries.* Accessed March 10, 2017. https://www.lib.ncsu.edu/tutorials/.

Patall, Erika A., Harris Cooper, and Jorgianne Civey Robinson. "The Effects of Choice on Intrinsic Motivation and Related Outcomes: A Meta-Analysis of Research Findings." *Psychological Bulletin* 134, no. 2 (2008): 270–300.

Small, Ruth V., Nasriah Zakaria, and Houria El-Figuigui. "Motivational Aspects of Information Literacy Skills Instruction in Community College Libraries." *College and Research Libraries* 65, no. 2 (2004): 96–121.

Thompson, Margareta, and Patrick Beymer. "The Effects of Choice in the Classroom: Is There Too Little or Too Much Choice?." *Support for Learning* 30, no. 2 (2015): 105–20.

CHAPTER 15

Teaching Library Research and Critical Reflection Skills to Undergraduate Students Using the Techniques of Role Playing and Debate

Grace M. Jackson-Brown

Introduction

Successful engagement of undergraduates in information literacy instruction requires thoughtful alignment of many factors. Learners must be focused and feel confident in their abilities in an atmosphere of inquiry where problem-solving is key.[1] This chapter offers an instructional plan where librarians work with classroom faculty to design research-related literacy lessons that are both attention-getting and filled with just the right amount of challenge to inspire motivation. In the lesson, librarians and teachers collaborate to teach students to find information to support positions on various sides of a censorship challenge by using game-like debate techniques and role-playing. The lesson is adaptable to library research on any topic that has different or opposing viewpoints.

The ARCS model of motivation, developed by Keller,[2] underpins the lesson plan. In the ARCS Model, Keller synthesizes many concepts of human motivation into a systematic approach to instructional design. He identifies four variable constructs—attention, relevance, confidence, and satisfaction—that enhance motivation, and he devises sets of strategies that incorporate these into instruction.[3] He expounds upon these in his 2010 book, *Motivational Design for Learning and Performance*. Over the years, academic librarians have successfully integrated the ARCS model in information literacy instruction.[4] Several of Keller's instructional strategies, including inquiry, problem-solving, and role-playing, are highlighted in this exercise.

This instructional plan encourages critical thinking and tactical skills as students must seek and evaluate quotations and facts that support different positions. Through a short lecture, the librarian explains the information cycle and when and where in written and visual media different opinions, facts, and research-based evidence are likely to be presented. A major objective of the lesson is to teach students to investigate heterogeneous viewpoints and to evaluate information or evidence from the perspectives of different stakeholders in addition to the popular versus scholarly literature dichotomy. Cook and Klipfel argue that this sort of analysis builds "deep knowledge" for learners.

> ...deep knowledge is knowledge that focuses on the core meaning—or "deep structure"—of a practice. Deep structure is important because it is transferable to other contexts. It facilitates critical thinking by creating the right conditions for students to apply what they have learned to many situations.... What is the deeper meaning of the popular vs. scholarly dichotomy? The deeper meaning here is philosophical: Out of all the information available in the world, what should I believe? How do I know if it is reliable? The core knowledge that librarians can teach to is what makes a piece of information trustworthy *at its core*.[5]

Lesson Plan Design

This lesson plan works best when it is a collaborative effort between the librarian and the classroom instructor. The classroom instructor may prepare a debatable topic from course subject matter for her or his class to research in the library and, if feasible, may provide a pre-session reading assignment to help students understand the debate/research topic. Alternatively, the librarian may recommend a debatable topic to the classroom instructor to achieve the classroom instructor's desired research goal.

The librarian begins the instruction session by explaining the nature of scholarly literature and popular literature. The librarian may demonstrate how to locate and interpret information for the debate by searching a general database or a series of discipline-based databases. The goal of the instruction is to demonstrate how to find information that is representative of different stakeholders' positions on the debate topic. In addition, the librarian demonstrates how to provide attribution to sources of debate evidence as well as how to cite the information appropriately. (See Appendix 15A, Sample Search Results of Multi-Perspective Sources).

Students will be randomly assigned to roles/positions on the research topic on a card when they enter the library instruction room. Students conduct library database searches to find two or three pieces of evidence to support their assigned roles. In small peer groups, the students debate the topic with the evidence they find. Each group evaluates their small group's experience and decides upon a "winner position" from the debate based upon criteria that each group will determine.

The classroom instructor and librarian will actively circulate throughout the classroom to provide support as the students find information and engage in impromptu debate. The librarian and classroom instructor assist students in their searches and attribution or citation work. Providing support to students to achieve success in the information research exercise is an integral part of instilling confidence as part of the ARCS Model.

To conclude, a reporter from each small group provides a synopsis of their group's experience to the whole class. The librarian, then, answers any final questions.

Student Learning Outcomes (SLOs)

By the end of the session, students will be able to
1. use a database to find information on an issue or topic;
2. explain the importance of attributing credit to sources;
3. formulate a basic citation; and
4. engage in civil debate with peers to identify and differentiate opinions and facts in a debate with peers.

These outcomes reflect the information literacy frames or conceptual goals for post-secondary students and information literate adults adopted in 2016 by the ACRL Board of the American Library Association.[6] This lesson plan focuses on two of the six conceptual frames and selected associated knowledge practices.

Frames/Concepts
Frame: Authority is Constructed and Contextual

"Information resources reflect their creators' expertise and credibility, and are evaluated based on the information need and the context in which the information will be used. Authority is constructed in that various communities may recognize different types of authority. It is contextual in that the information need may help to determine the level of authority required."

Knowledge practices: Learners are developing their information literacy ability:

- "To define different types of authority, such as subject expertise (e.g., scholarship), societal position (e.g., public office or title), or special experience."
- "Recognize that authoritative content may be packaged formally or informally and may include sources of all media types."

Frame: Searching as Strategic Exploration

"Searching for information is often nonlinear and iterative, requiring the evaluation of a range of information sources and the mental flexibility to pursue alternative avenues as new understanding develops."

"The act of searching often begins with a question that directs the act of finding needed information. Encompassing inquiry, discovery, and serendipity, searching identifies both possible relevant sources as well as means to access those sources."

Knowledge practices: Learners who are developing their information literate abilities:

- "Determine the initiate scope of the task required to meet their information need."
- "Identify interested parties, such as scholars, organizations, governments, and industries, who might produce information about a topic and then determine how to access that information."
- "Utilize divergent (e.g., brainstorming) and convergent (e.g., selecting the best source) thinking when searching."

Example of a Debatable Topic for the Lesson Plan Design, Banned Books in America's Schools

Most attempts to ban books in America today occur in public and school libraries per reports compiled annually by the American Library Association (ALA) in the "Top Ten Most Challenged Book Lists."[7] The ALA opposes book banning as a restriction to the freedom to read, a right aligned with the First Amendment of the US Constitution.

An online article by Aliprandini and Sprague[8] provides a succinct overview of book banning. In the essay, the two authors contrast the challenge to access to books in closed and open societies:

> In totalitarian societies, books have been banned for challenging a government's ruling authority. Arguments for banning books claimed the need to promote political stability or maintain public morality. In more open societies, books that offend conventionality are often banned or challenged as well. If a book is deemed offensive, some persons may argue, that it is promoting ideas that can have a detrimental influence on individuals (often children) and on society as a whole.

The lesson plan design focuses, as an example, on the book title *The Absolute True Diary of a Part-Time Indian* by Sherman Alexie,[9] published in 2007. The main character in Alexie's book is Junior, a freshman student who transfers from a school in the Spokane Indian Reservation, where he lives with his family, to a predominantly white high school in a neighboring farming town. *The Absolute True Diary of a Part-Time Indian* was on ALA's "Top Ten Most Challenged Book Lists" because of objections to its use of profanity, sexual content, and racial slurs. Articles about the book and responses to its content can be found in scholarly journals, professional trade journals, newspapers, and in blogs.

Lesson Activities

When students enter the classroom, each will randomly draw a role label representing a stakeholder in the case of the book ban or challenge. For example, stakeholders might include a high school student opposed to the book ban, a principal in favor of the book ban, a parent in favor of the book ban, an English teacher opposed to book banning, a school board member in favor of the book ban, etc. Divide role assignments equally between those in favor of the book restriction and those against it.

Begin the library instruction session with an introduction to the students of the databases that they may use to find different types of resources (popular and scholarly journal articles, news articles, and social media sites) for debate. Instruct students about basic types of searches (particularly author, title, and keyword searches) and discuss combining search terms using Boolean connectors. A search demonstration may include a basic keyword search using the title of the book as a keyword phrase—"Absolutely True Diary of a Part-time Indian"—to generate useful articles to skim for the debate exercise. Another demonstration search may combine the author's last name and pertinent truncated keywords, i.e. "Alexie and (ban* or censor*)" that generate useful information source results for the debate topic. Give students a word of caution that sometimes the databases might generate "false" results that match inputted words; however, some "trial and error" searches are a normal part of the research process.

In addition, demonstrate how to locate information on the censorship topic *within* two or three articles and instruct how to provide attribution for the information in the debate exercise to follow. Attribution involves providing who is saying what and when. Underscore the need to include the names and title of persons, officers of organizations and elected or appointed government officials, as well as titles and authorship of articles/studies that are used. Emphasize the importance of giving each piece of evidence a source attribution during the extemporaneous debate exercise that will happen in the latter part of the class session.

In addition, inform students that the articles from which quotes and facts are pulled must be acknowledged or given credit by including a bibliographic citation in times of written reporting or in research papers. Demonstrate how to use the automatic citation tools that are often available in many databases. Mention that online bibliographic help tools are also available, such as *The Purdue OWL*.[10]

Allow a period of about ten minutes for students to individually find one or two pieces of information as evidence about the book challenge based on parameters of their randomly assigned roles. If students have access at their desks or work area, then they may cut and paste the quotes/facts into an electronic notepad along with the appropriate attributions or citations.

Allow a period of ten to twelve minutes for students to debate the book-banning case using pre-configured small groups. Each student will use the quotes/facts that they found in their individual research based on the role of the various actors that they have been assigned. Students from each group choose a student reporter from their group to summarize their group's experience and to announce the "winner" position based on small group consensus. You may want to encourage the students to select the winner based on the evidence presented rather than on their personal opinions.

Alternatively, the students from the whole class may divide in half based on pro/con sides of the book-banning topic after students have completed individual research. The instructor will call upon individuals from each side to share information in a pro and con exchange on the topic.

Allow a few minutes to answer any final questions and to address any concerns.

Suggested Schedule of Lesson Activities

18–20 minutes	Librarian instruction on how to use library databases to find debate topic information and how to provide appropriate attributions and citations.
10 minutes	Students individually search the databases to find 1–2 evidential bits of information on the debate topic and based on an assigned role and paste these into an electronic notepad along with appropriate attribution(s) and/or citation(s).
10–12 minutes	Students convene within small groups and share evidence with each other in an extemporaneous debate style.
8 minutes	A representative from each small group reports on their group's different evidence and most persuasive position(s). Alternatively, rather than small group debates the whole class may be divided in half, pro and con, and each side takes turns sharing information in a point/counterpoint debate style. Instructors may utilize as much of the last minutes of class as deemed necessary to summarize the debate exercise.

A Brief Overview of Motivation Theory and Rationale for Use of the ARCS Model for Instructional Design for the Information Literacy Lesson Plan

Students retain attention and interest throughout the lesson plan because it covers a real-life issue and problem-solving scenario. The lesson has further relevance to students because of student involvement in the activity of searching databases for information in a competitive context for debate. And students have opportunity for personal interactions in small groups. According to Keller, sustained attention of students in the learning process can be accomplished by "creating paradoxes, generating inquiries, and nurturing thinking challenges."[11]

In the lesson plan, students learn about the views of different stakeholders in the censorship challenge through research in the databases to locate information. By using various types of sources, students learn through personal experience about researching as strategic exploration. Students learn to approach an issue or topic from diverse perspectives by researching the literature and by dialogue with each other, which builds their critical-thinking skills. Students learn that by exploring the literature or various information resources that viewpoints from different stakeholders are sometimes based on social relationships. Thus, they learn that authority is constructed and contextual.

Students gain a deeper understanding of the viewpoints and the perspectives of others on important issues by exploring multiple perspectives through role-playing and debate.[12] Role-playing requires students to adopt positions that may be unfamiliar; they may "step outside of their own comfort zone" or personal viewpoint. The debate activity has an element of competitive fun while at the same time it opens a dialogue between students enabling them to learn from each other.[13] Some students may find this to be intimidating, while others may find the role-playing or acting element to be fun and exhilarating. This lesson, however, encourages and challenges students without requiring them to discuss personal opinions.

Through this lesson, students learn to engage in processes that reinforce and build information literacy skills, digital literacy skills, and critical thinking skills. The lesson activities, with support from the librarian and the classroom teacher, help to instill confidence and satisfaction in students.

How to Adapt This Model

This lesson plan can be adapted to many undergraduate courses, including communication, writing, and other humanities or social science courses. It is ideal for collaborating with the classroom instructor to conduct library research from many different disciplines. Rather than the librarian presenting a general session on how to do library research that might be confined to lecturing or demonstrating database searching, the classroom instructor can choose a topic from his or her course curriculum that has various sides and/or stakeholders to research using library resources. The librarian, together with the classroom instructor, facilitates and guides students through an interactive instructional session in how to find resources that cover different perspectives or positions on a topic or issue.

Appendix 15A. Sample Search Results of Multi-Perspective Sources

A college instructor (Donna Miller) at Aaniiih Nakoda College on the Fort Belknap Indian Reservation describes what some of her college students studying teacher education thought about the reading of *The Absolute True Diary of a Part-Time Indian* in schools:

> "By reading about negative experiences, students were im-pacted positively, calling literature 'the only hope left to some young adults.' Ultimately for many of them, Alexie provides inspiration. 'To deem this book as inappropriate only further shows the harsh and sometimes inappropriate criticism of life growing up on the reservation. It takes a great deal of courage to persevere when there are so many factors working against you,' responded one student."

Miller, Donna. "Honoring Identity with Young Adult Novels." *Tribal College Journal* 24, no. 4, Summer 2013, 28–29. Ebscohost.

A newspaper in Waterloo, Iowa, reported about a dispute caused by a parent complaint to the inclusion of the novel *The Absolute True Diary of a Part-Time* Indian in the cur-riculum at her son's middle school. The article quotes Kev-in Roberts, a literacy teacher at George Washington Carver Academy, a middle school in Waterloo. "Allowing one per-son to deem a book inappropriate and require all copies of that book to be returned is a breach of those guidelines," Roberts wrote about district policy, "More importantly, the choice to put this decision in the hands of one person re-flects poorly on our district's teacher professionals who de-serve a voice in this process."

Anderson, Mike. "Waterloo pulls book from classrooms, sparking Debate," *Waterloo-Cedar Falls Courier*, 08 April 2015. Ebscohost.

A newspaper in Wilmar, Minnesota reports on a public meeting about the reading of the book *The Absolute True Diary of a Part-Time Indian* by eighth graders in the New London-Spicer School District. One parent, "Jessica Collins said while several themes in the book have value, she and her husband, Dave, object to its inclusion in the school curriculum because it contains 'gratuitous and unnecessary' profanity and references to sexual acts." Collins said, "Parents have the right to teach their children regarding these topics and have assurance that a classroom teacher would teach those same values."

Lange, Carolyn. "Parents Request Removal of Books from NLS Curriculum." *West Central Tribune* (Wilmer, MN). May 11, 2017. Ebscohost.

An interview published in a trade journal with a library science assistant professor from the University of Illinois, Urbana-Champaign, Emily Knox, who speaks about her recently published a book titled *Book Banning in 21st-Century America* and cases of book banning challenges, including of *The Absolute True Diary of a Part-Time Indian*.

"As a professional who takes the kind of ethics of the American Library Association seriously, it is never my job to censor a book, of course. But I am willing to talk to people and really try to find a book that they would prefer to read. That's my job. And when I teach my classes, teaching people who are going to be librarians or information professionals, what I try to show them is that it's our job to protect all knowledge, even knowledge that we ourselves disagree with. But that doesn't mean that we can't have a conversation about what people find problematic."

Albanese, Andrew Richard. "Check It Out." *Publishers Weekly*, vol. 262, no. 5, 02 February 2015, 17–18. Ebscohost.

Endnotes

1. Dani Brecher Cook and Kevin Michael Klipfel, "How Do Students Learn? An Outline of a Cognitive Psychological Model for Information Literacy Instruction," *Reference & User Services Quarterly*, v. 55, n. 1 (2015): 34–41.
2. John M. Keller, "Motivational Design of Instruction," in *Instructional-Design Theories and Models: An Overview of Their Current Status*, ed. C. M. Reigeluth (Hillsdale, NJ: Lawrence-Erlbaum, 1983); John M. Keller, "Development and Use of the ARCS Model of Instructional Design," *Journal of Instructional Development*, 10 no. 3 (1987): 2–10.
3. Keller, "Development and Use of the ARCS Model," 3.

4. Robert Lindsay, "Research in the Real World: Improving Adult Learners Web Search and Evaluation Skills through Motivational Design and Problem-Based Learning," *College and Research Libraries*, 78 no. 4 (2017): 527–51; Meagan K. Christensen, "Designing One-Shot Sessions Around Threshold Concepts," *Internet Reference Services Quarterly*, 20 (2015): 97–104; Angela Weiler, "Information-Seeking Behavior in Generation Y Students: Motivation, Critical Thinking, and Learning Theory," *The Journal of Academic Librarianship*, 31 no. 1 (2005): 46–53; Ruth V. Small, Nasriah Zakaria, and Houria El-Figuigui, "Motivational Aspects of Information Literacy Skills Instruction in Community College Libraries," *College & Research Libraries*, 65 no. 2 (2004): 96–121.
5. Cook and Klipfel, "How Do Students Learn?," 38.
6. American Library Association, "Framework for Information Literacy in Higher Education," February 9, 2015, accessed December 23, 2017, http://www.ala.org/acrl/standards/ilframework, document ID: b910a6c4-6c8a-0d44-7dbc-a5dcbd509e3f.
7. American Library Association, "Top Ten Most Challenged Books Lists," March 26, 2013, accessed December 28, 2017, http:www.ala.org/advocacy/bbooks/frequently-challengedbooks/top10.
8. Michael Aliprandini and Carolyn Sprague, "Banned Books: An Overview," *Point of View. Banning Books* (March 2016), in *Point of View Reference Center*. EBSCOhost, accessed February 15, 2017.
9. Sherman Alexie, *The True Diary of a Part-Time Indian*, New York and Boston: Little Brown and Company, 2007.
10. *The Purdue OWL*, Purdue U Writing Lab, 2016, accessed December 28, 2017, http://owl.english.purdue.edu/owl.
11. John M. Keller, *Motivational Design for Learning and Performance* (New York: Springer, 2010), 92.
12. Li Wang, "Sociocultural Learning Theories, and Information Literacy Teaching Activities in Higher Education," *Reference & User Services Quarterly*, 47 no. 2 (2007):149–58.
13. Neda Zdravkovic, "Spicing Up Information Literacy Tutorials: Interactive Class Activities that Worked," *Public Services Quarterly*, 6 (2010): 49.

Bibliography

Alexie, Sherman. *The True Diary of a Part-Time Indian*. New York and Boston: Little Brown and Company, 2007.
Ambrose, Susan A., Michael W. Bridges, Michele DiPietro, Marsha C. Lovett, and Marie K. Norman. *How Learning Works: Seven Research-Based Principles for Smart Teaching*. San Francisco: Josey-Bass, 2010.
American Library Association. "Framework for Information Literacy in Higher Education." February 9, 2015. Accessed December 23, 2017. http://www.ala.org/acrl/standards/ilframework. Document ID: b910a6c4-6c8a-0d44-7dbc-a5dcbd509e3f.
———. "Top Ten Most Challenged Books Lists." March 26, 2013. Accessed December 28, 2017. http:www.ala.org/advocacy/bbooks/frequentlychallengedbooks/top10.
Aliprandini, Michael, and Carolyn Sprague. "Banned Books: An Overview." *Point of View. Banning Books* (March 2016) In *Point of View Reference Center*. EBSCOhost. Accessed February 15, 2017.

Barkley, Elizabeth, K. Patrick Cross, and Claire Howell Major. "Critical Debate." In *Collaborative Learning Techniques*, 128–31. San Francisco: Jossey-Bass. 2005.

———. "Role Playing." In *Collaborative Learning Techniques*, 150–55. San Francisco: Jossey-Bass. 2005.

Bean, John C. *Engaging Ideas: A Professor's Guide to Integrating Writing, Critical Thinking, and Active Learning in the Classroom*. San Francisco: Jossey-Bass, 1996, 6–7, 176–77.

Bizup, J. "BEAM: A Rhetorical Vocabulary for Teaching Research-Based Writing." *Rhetoric Review*, v. 27 no. 1 (2008): 72–86.

Christensen, Meagan K. "Designing One-Shot Sessions Around Threshold Concepts." *Internet Reference Services Quarterly*, 20 (2015): 97–104.

Cook, Dani Brecher, and Kevin Michael Klipfel. "How Do Students Learn? An Outline of a Cognitive Psychological Model for Information Literacy Instruction." *Reference & User Services Quarterly*, v. 55, n. 1 (2015): 34–41.

Foerstel, Herbert N. *Banned in the U.S.A.: A Reference Guide to Book Censorship in Schools and Public Libraries*. Westport: Greenwood, 1994.

Ford, Martin E. *Motivating Humans: Goals, Emotions, and Personal Agency Beliefs*. Newbury Park, California, 1992.

Keller, John M. *Motivational Design for Learning and Performance*. New York: Springer, 2010.

———. "Development and Use of the ARCS Model of Instructional Design." *Journal of Instructional Development*, 10 no. 3 (1987): 2–10.

———. "Motivational Design of Instruction." In *Instructional-Design Theories and Models: An Overview of Their Current Status*, edited by C. M. Reigeluth. Hillsdale, NJ: Lawrence-Erlbaum, 1983.

Kuehn, Scott A., and Andrew Lingwall. *The Basics of Media Writing: A Strategic Approach*. Thousand Oaks, CA: Sage Publications, CQ Press, 2018.

Lindsay, Robert. "Research in the Real World: Improving Adult Learners Web Search and Evaluation Skills through Motivational Design and Problem-Based Learning." *College and Research Libraries*, 78 no. 4 (2017): 527–51.

Nye, Valerie, and Kathy Barco, eds. *True Stories of Censorship Battles in America's Libraries*. Chicago: American Libraries Association, 2012.

The Purdue OWL. Purdue U Writing Lab, 2016. Accessed December 28, 2017. http://owl.english.purdue.edu/owl.

Small, Ruth V., Nasriah Zakaria, and Houria El-Figuigui. "Motivational Aspects of Information Literacy Skills Instruction in Community College Libraries." *College & Research Libraries*, 65 no. 2 (2004): 96–121.

Steers, Richard M., and Lyman W. Porter, eds. *Motivation and Work Behavior*. 4th ed. New York: McGraw-Hill, 1987: 3–6.

Wang, Li. "Sociocultural Learning Theories, and Information Literacy Teaching Activities in Higher Education." *Reference & User Services Quarterly*, 47 no. 2 (2007): 149–58.

Weiler, Angela. "Information-Seeking Behavior in Generation Y Students: Motivation, Critical Thinking, and Learning Theory," *The Journal of Academic Librarianship*, 31 no. 1 (2005): 46–53.

Wigfield, Allan, and Jacquelynne S. Eccles. "Expectancy-Value Theory of Achievement Motivation." *Contemporary Educational Psychology*, 25 no. 1 (2000): 68–81.

Zdravkovic, Neda. "Spicing Up Information Literacy Tutorials: Interactive Class Activities that Worked," *Public Services Quarterly*, 6, (2010): 48–64.

CHAPTER 16

Introducing the Research Process:
Lesson Plans for Undergraduate Instruction

Sarah Leeman and Amy Hall

Introduction

In 2015, National Louis University (NLU) responded to shifting trends in higher education with the launch of the Pathways program at its Chicago campus. The program offers an affordable, data-driven pathway to an undergraduate degree and is holistically designed to address common roadblocks to college completion, especially for historically underrepresented students. The program, which included a multi-session library component, presented unique challenges to NLU's library instruction team, especially with regard to student engagement and motivation. Not only were these traditionally aged undergraduates, a largely new population for National Louis, but many were also academically underprepared for college. The program's "off track" students, in particular, lacked family support, struggled with motivation, and frequently struggled to identify and engage as college students.

While teaching a three-week, nine-hour Introduction to the Research Process unit as part of the program's ten-week Student Success Seminar course, librarians observed many students who lacked engagement in the flipped coursework. Students seemed to need far more practice with fundamental skills, such as reading and understanding academic articles. Additionally, some activities and materials failed to resonate with the students' interests and experiences. Adding to the content-related challenges was the three-hour class period, which can be tiring for even the most motivated students. Many students lacked focus during periods of lecture and seemed to require near-constant stimulation to remain on task. Librarians took the opportunity to create a new, tailored approach focused on student engagement and motivation.

Revising the Curriculum

After the initial three-course sections of the Student Success Seminar (GEN 103) concluded, an additional section was offered the next term to accommodate five new students and to provide a retake opportunity for the fourteen students who had failed the course in the initial offering. This additional section provided a welcome opportunity to immediately apply lessons learned during the first run of the course.

Librarians worked with the new GEN 103 instructor to redesign the research process curriculum with a focus on enhancing motivation and engaging in active learning, all while fostering students' identity as college students and scholars. Developing a sense of scholarly identity is especially critical to the Pathways cohort, many of whom are low-income, first-generation college students who are juggling many competing responsibilities. This group often lacks strong familial/community support for their education as well as college-going models to emulate.[1] The development of a schema or "possible self"[2] as a college student can be highly influential on college motivation and achievement, especially for underserved populations.[3,4]

The Pathways program and student support philosophy are built heavily on Baxter Magolda's concept of self-authorship,[5] in which college students shift from relying on external authority to construct their sense of the world and develop an internal capacity for determining their own beliefs and identities. Nurturing this sense of agency works hand-in-hand with the ACRL Framework for Information Literacy,[6] which describes information literate learners as critical thinkers with mental flexibility and creativity who see themselves as contributors to scholarship and to the information marketplace rather than just consumers of it.

Librarians focused on building students' confidence and autonomy through the learning partnership model, wherein educational practices (1) validate students' capacity as knowers, (2) contextualize learning within students' own experiences, and (3) allow students and faculty to mutually construct meaning.[7] This approach has been shown to facilitate self-authoring behavior in both instructional and advising contexts.[8] Librarians designed classroom experiences that prioritized students' sharing of their understandings of scholarly work and validated their perspectives as worthy additions to the scholarly conversation.

The revised GEN 103 curriculum sought to help students practice fundamental academic skills that would build their confidence as students and scholars as they engaged in the process of finding, evaluating, and critiquing information. It included materials of particular interest to undergraduates: librarians selected news articles about Beyoncé and diet soda and presented scholarly research on snooping in relationships, oversharing on Facebook, and using cell phones in class. This approach follows Keller's ARCS Model of Motivational Design, which has proven effective in information literacy contexts.[9] According to Keller's model,[10] four categories (attention, relevance, confidence, and satisfaction) are all necessary components of a learning experience. By choosing topics that relate to students' personal interests, librarians sought not only to capture students' interest (attention) but to show that scholarly research can be directly related to content they encounter on a daily basis (relevance).

Students were engaged and eager to discuss the findings of the provided research articles. These observations are in keeping with research showing that connecting undergraduate classroom learning to real life and encouraging students to share their own opinions can increase student engagement.[11] This new approach and perspective were especially important in this new section when most of the students were taking the course for the second time.

Lesson Plans

During this three-week segment of the Student Success Seminar, students work toward writing an annotated bibliography on a research topic of their choice. In the first week, students develop a research question and initial research strategy and began initial searching on their topics. In the second week, students practice strategies for finding and reading different types of sources, including scholarly sources. They are asked to consider their own role in the scholarly conversation. In the third week, students discuss ethical use of information and are introduced to APA style. They also practice using evidence to support a statement.

With a flipped classroom model and three-hour sessions each week, librarians were able to develop tailored lesson plans for a variety of threshold concepts and learning outcomes. The following lesson plans are those which relate most directly to the scholarly conversation.

What's Your Research Process?

In this activity, students work together to develop a sample research question as well as a research strategy for their own projects.

Learning outcomes:
- Narrow a broad topic to a specific research question.
- Identify keywords and synonyms.
- Create an initial research strategy.

Time to complete: 45 minutes.

Setup:

Prepare materials:
- Load video: Libnscu. (2014). *Picking your topic IS research.* [Video file] Retrieved from https://www.youtube.com/watch?v=Q0B3Gj-lu-1o
- Print copies of "What's Your Research Strategy?" Worksheet (see Appendix 16A).

Introduce activity:
1. Show the video *Picking your topic IS research.*
2. Demonstrate a search for a broad topic and discuss the number and range of results returned. Explain that taking the time to develop a specific research question rather than a broad topic can save time and frustration and will make your final research product more effective and easy to understand. Share strategies for narrowing down a topic. Strategies for narrowing down a topic might include brainstorming related ideas or considering specific impacts, demographic groups, or geographic areas.
3. Transition to the activity and explain any parameters or requirements for student research topics.

Activity:
1. Write a broad topic on the board, such as "teen pregnancy." Students work in groups to brainstorm ways to narrow the topic down to something specific and manageable.
2. Students can write their examples on the board and discuss with the class. Work together to format one or two ideas as open-ended research questions.
3. Next, students can use the "What's Your Research Strategy" worksheet to develop their own topics and research questions. Students can begin by filling out questions 1–4.
4. Next, write an example question on the board. (Example: How does

pregnancy impact graduation rates among minority students?) Explain the benefits of developing keywords and synonyms when searching in library databases and online. Students work together to brainstorm keywords and synonyms for the sample topic. Students can then work independently or in pairs to finish filling out the first page of the "What's Your Research Strategy" worksheet. Explain that this worksheet can serve as a guide as they continue their research in the course.

5. In subsequent lessons, students will begin searching online and in library databases and can fill out the rest of the worksheet. Remind students that research is a process and they can always return to the first page if they need to modify their research questions at any point.

How to Read a Scholarly Article

In this activity, students practice strategies for interpreting scholarly articles and engage in discussion about an article's findings.

Learning outcomes:
- Identify the primary common elements of a scholarly article.
- Apply targeted reading strategies to interpret a scholarly article.
- Explain major purposes and conclusions of a research study.
- Discuss and articulate opinions on a research study's findings.

Time to complete: 45 minutes.

Setup:

Prepare materials:
- Load instructional video: Western University. (2012). *How to read a scholarly article* [Video file.] Retrieved from https://youtu.be/3SmO-q6gENPM.
- Load sample scholarly article: Hanson, T., Drumheller, K., Mallard, J., McKee, C., & Schlegel, P. (2011). Cell phones, text messaging, and Facebook: Competing time demands of today's college students. *College Teaching,* 59(1), 23–30. doi:10.1080/87567555.2010.489078
- Print articles and questions for group activity (see Appendix 16B for recommended materials)

Introduce activity:
1. Begin with a discussion about the specialized nature of scholarly articles, which are written for experts and can be difficult to interpret.
2. Play the *How to read a scholarly article* video, which breaks down

the major parts of a scholarly article. After it plays, open the sample scholarly article on video screen/projector. Highlight the major sections, including abstract, introduction/literature review, methods, results, discussion, and conclusion.

3. As outlined in the video, discuss strategies for reading scholarly literature. This may include reading out of order, such as starting with the abstract and then moving straight to the conclusion. Share your own reading strategies and invite students to share their own.

Activity:

Break the class into small groups. Each group is provided a different scholarly article (make enough copies for each student to have their own) and answers a set of questions that requires them to identify and understand major purposes and findings of the study. Groups share their findings with the class. Articles should be selected to appeal to the specific student population, so the findings may be of interest to their peers. Encourage students to discuss their perspectives on the studies' designs and conclusions.

Using Evidence to Support an Argument

In this activity, students practice selecting and citing specific evidence to answer a research question.

Learning outcomes
- Discuss the role evidence plays in constructing an argument.
- Select appropriate evidence to answer a research question.
- Cite evidence using APA style.

Time to complete: 30–40 minutes.

Setup:

Prepare materials:
- Load the article to open class discussion: Williamson, A. M., & Feyer, A.M. (2000). Moderate sleep deprivation produces impairments in cognitive and motor performance equivalent to legally prescribed levels of alcohol intoxication. *Occupational and Environmental Medicine,* 57(10), 649–655. http://www.ncbi.nlm.nih.gov/pmc/articles/PMC1739867/
- Print the article for group activity: Monto, M. A., & Carey, A. G. (2014). A new standard of sexual behavior? Are claims associated with the "hookup culture" supported by General Social Survey data? *Journal of Sex Research,* 51(6), 605–615. doi:10.1080/00224499.2014.906031

Introduce activity:
1. Begin by presenting two example sentences:
    a. It's important for college students to get enough sleep.
    b. It's important for college students to get enough sleep because sleep deprivation produces effects similar to being drunk.
2. Ask students which statement is more convincing and why. Ask them to share their own personal examples of using evidence to support an argument. What do they do to convince someone they are right or wrong? Discuss how citing specific evidence in their academic work adds weight to their argument.
3. To finish, show students the study this information came from and then create the in-text APA style citation on the board: (Williamson & Feyer, 2000).

Activity:

Break up the class into small groups. Each group receives the same article. Each group must select two pieces of evidence—a quote and a paraphrase—to support a provided research question. The group writes these statements, with in-text citations included, on their whiteboards. Students then share findings with the group and discuss how well each piece of selected evidence answers the research question. Why might one piece of evidence be more convincing or appropriate than another? Suggested question: How have the sexual attitudes of college students changed in the past three decades?

Adaptations

Though the materials and instructional approach described here were developed specifically for the Pathways student population, they may easily be adapted for multiple audiences. For example:

*   Scholarly articles may be selected from a specific discipline. Activities focused on how to read such literature may feature classic, influential, or controversial articles from the field.
*   Articles may be selected for various reading levels.
*   The difficulty level of the assessments may be revised. The "How to Read a Scholarly Article" (see Appendix 16A) activity asks students to answer a series of questions about the article they read. Undergraduates may be asked to simply identify hypotheses or conclusions, while graduates may be asked questions that require additional synthesis and analysis.
*   Instruction models can be adapted for larger programs. This adaptation soon proved necessary at National Louis University as fall

2016 welcomed 292 new students who were distributed across nine sections of GEN 103. NLU librarians found that co-teaching the research process was no longer an option. Instead, prior to the start of the unit, librarians met with all GEN 103 instructors to review the curriculum together in detail and support instructors in teaching the content themselves. Once the unit began, librarians sent weekly emails with reminders and tips for each module and provided in-class support on an as-needed basis.

Conclusion

Though a variety of factors impact student success, program faculty did see an increase in the number of students who passed the course the second time after participating in these revised activities. Librarians also observed an increase in student participation and engagement in the classroom. Student feedback for the course varies, with some students finding the work difficult, and others noting that some aspects of the course are a review of material they learned in high school. Librarians continue working with faculty to improve these aspects of the course.

As program development continues, librarians serve on committees with program faculty, engage in research and planning for new initiatives, and participate in orientations and programming for students. These endeavors help build relationships and keep lines of communication open among librarians, faculty, administration, and instructional designers. Librarians and faculty continue to identify opportunities to include information literacy instruction in other courses. For example, librarians have assisted faculty in teaching information literacy skills for political science courses and, most recently, have been approached for assistance with the students' sophomore capstone class, which includes a research component.

While we plan to maintain our presence in the Student Success Seminar, these additional opportunities will help us scaffold content in a meaningful way throughout the entirety of the Pathways program and assist students in preparation for their junior and senior years at National Louis University.

Appendix 16A
What's Your Research Strategy?

Part One: Research Questions & Key Words

1. **What is your broad topic?** Remember, your topic should relate to barriers to student success.

   | **Example:**
   | *Tutoring*

2. **How can you make this topic more specific? List at least three related ideas.**

   | *Impact on students, academic achievement, undergrads*

3. **What is your new, specific topic?**

   | *Impact of tutoring on undergraduate academic achievement*

4. **Formulate your topic into a research question. This should be a full sentence.**

   | *How does participation in tutoring impact the academic achievement of undergraduate students?*

5. **What are your keywords?** These are the main ideas from your research question.

   | *Tutoring, academic achievement, undergraduates*

6. **What are some synonyms for your keywords?** These are words that are related to or mean the same thing as your keywords.

   | *Tutoring=student support, learning support*
   | *Academic achievement=student success*
   | *Undergraduates=college students, higher education*

What's Your Research Strategy?

Part Two: Finding Sources and Next Steps

7. **In which library database will I search?**

   | *Example:*
   | *Academic Search Complete, EBSCOHost Education Databases*

8. **Use your keywords and synonyms to find two sources that will help you answer your research question. Record them here.**

   Source One:
       Author:
       Title of Article:
       Name of Journal:

   | *Example:*
   | *Author: S. Smith*
   | *Title of Article: Impact of a writing center on student success.*
   | *Journal: Student Support Monthly*
   | *Publication Year: 2015*
   | *Volume: 16*
   | *Issue: 10*
   | *Page Numbers: 22–35*

Publication Year:
Volume Number:
Issue Number:
Page Numbers:

Source Two:
Author:
Title of Article:
Name of Journal:
Publication Year:
Volume Number:
Issue Number:
Page Numbers:

Make sure you'll be able to find these articles again. It's a good idea to save them to your computer or copy their permalinks so you can access them later.

9. **What are your next steps? Select at least one, even if you've already found your two sources. You'll need to find more next week!**

- I will try these keywords in my next search:

- I will look for a source about:

- I will meet with a librarian for help developing my research strategy or finding sources.

- *Set up an appointment with the librarian in your class!*
  - O   Appointment date: _____ Time: _____
  - O   Questions I will ask at my appointment:

Appendix 16B

Suggested articles for the How to Read a Scholarly Article activity.

Derby, K., Knox, D., & Easterling, B. (2012). Snooping in romantic relationships. *College Student Journal*, 46 (2), 333–43.

1. What were the researchers trying to determine?
2. What methods were used in the study?
3. What were the two biggest reasons that college students snooped on their partners?
4. What were the two most frequent ways that undergraduates snooped?
5. How many students reported that they snooped on their partners?
6. What do you think about the study and its findings?

Hanson, T., Drumheller, K., Mallard, J., McKee, C., & Schlegel, P. (2011). Cell phones, text messaging, and Facebook: Competing time demands of today's college students. *College Teaching*, 59 (1), 23–30. doi:10.1080/87567555.2010.4 89078.

1. What was the study trying to determine?
2. What were the three instruments used to complete the study?
3. What activity do students spend the most time doing? The least?
4. What are the researchers' recommendations?
5. What do you think about the study and its findings?

Monto, M. A., & Carey, A. G. (2014). A new standard of sexual behavior? Are claims associated with the "hookup culture" supported by General Social Survey data?. *Journal of Sex Research*, 51(6), 605-615. doi:10.1080/00224499. 2014.906031.

1. What was the researchers' first hypothesis (H1)?
2. What is one example of a question that participants were asked?
3. What were the two date ranges studied?
4. What were the overall findings of the study?
5. What do you think about the study and its findings?

Riddle, K., & De Simone, J. J. (2013). A Snooki effect? An exploration of the surveillance subgenre of reality TV and viewers' beliefs about the "real" real world. *Psychology of Popular Media Culture*, 2(4), 237–250. doi:10.1037/ ppm0000005.

1. What is the researchers' primary hypothesis (H1)?
2. How were students recruited to participate in the study?
3. What were some of the findings of the study?
4. What is a possible limitation of the study?

5.   What do you think about the study and its findings?

Roche, T. M., Jenkins, D. D., Aguerrevere, L. E., Kietlinski, R. L., & Prichard, E. A. (2015). College students' perceptions of inappropriate and appropriate Facebook disclosures. *Psi Chi Journal of Psychological Research, 20*(2), 86–96.

1.   What did the researchers ask participants to do?
2.   What was the age range of the participants?
3.   What type of Facebook post was rated as the most inappropriate by participants?
4.   What were some possible limitations of the study?
5.   What do you think about the study and its findings?

Endnotes

1.   Patrick T. Terenzini, Alberto F. Cabrera, and Elena M. Bernal, *Swimming Against the Tide: The Poor in American Higher Education* (New York: The College Entrance Examination Board, 2001), 19.
2.   Susan E. Cross and Hazel Rose Markus, "Self-Schemas, Possible Selves, and Competent Performance," *Journal of Educational Psychology* 86 (1994): 424.
3.   Jane E. Pizzolato, "Achieving College Student Possible Selves: Navigating the Space between Commitment and Achievement of Long-term Identity Goals," *Cultural Diversity and Ethnic Minority Psychology* 12, no. 1 (2006): 66, doi:10.1037/1099-9809.12.1.57.
4.   Suzanne M. Bouffard and Mandy Savitz-Romer, "Ready, Willing, and Able," *Educational Leadership* 69, no. 7 (2012): 41–42.
5.   Marcia B. Baxter Magolda, "Self-Authorship," *New Directions for Higher Education* 2014, no. 166 (2014): 26, doi:10.1002/he.20092.
6.   American Library Association, "Framework for Information Literacy for Higher Education," 2015, http://www.ala.org/acrl/standards/ilframework.
7.   Marcia B. Baxter Magolda and Patricia M. King, *Learning Partnerships: Theory and Models of Practice to Educate for Self-authorship* (Sterling, VA: Stylus, 2004), 37–62.
8.   Nancy J. Evans, *Student Development in College: Theory, Research, and Practice* (San Francisco, CA: Jossey-Bass, 2010), 190–92; Jane E. Pizzolato, "Complex Partnerships: Self-Authorship and Provocative Academic-Advising Practices," *NACADA Journal* 26, no. 1 (2006): 41–44.
9.   Trudi Jacobson and Lijuan Xu, "Motivating Students in Credit-based Information Literacy Courses: Theories and Practice," *portal: Libraries and The Academy* 2, no. 3 (2002): 436–38.
10. John M. Keller, "Development and Use of the ARCS Model of Motivational Design," *Journal of Instructional Development* 10, no. 3 (1987): 3.
11. Twila Lukowiak and Jana Hunzicker, "Understanding How and Why College Students Engage in Learning," *Journal of Effective Teaching* 13, no. 1 (2013): 57.

Bibliography

American Library Association. "Framework for Information Literacy for Higher Education." 2015. http://www.ala.org/acrl/standards/ilframework.

Baxter Magolda, Marcia B. "Self-Authorship." *New Directions for Higher Education* 2014, no. 166 (2014): 25–33. doi:10.1002/he.20092.

Baxter Magolda, Marcia B., and Patricia M. King. *Learning Partnerships: Theory and Models of Practice to Educate for Self-Authorship.* Sterling, VA: Stylus, 2004.

Bouffard, Suzanne M., and Mandy Savitz-Romer. "Ready, Willing, and Able." *Educational Leadership* 69, no. 7 (2012): 40–43.

Cross, Susan E., and Hazel Rose Markus. "Self-Schemas, Possible Selves, and Competent Performance." *Journal of Educational Psychology* 86 (1994): 343–48.

Evans, Nancy J. *Student Development in College: Theory, Research, and Practice.* San Francisco, CA: Jossey-Bass, 2010.

Jacobson, Trudi, and Lijuan Xu. "Motivating Students in Credit-based Information Literacy Courses: Theories and Practice." *Portal: Libraries and The Academy* 2, no. 3 (2002): 423-41.

Keller, John M. "Development and Use of the ARCS Model of Motivational Design." *Journal of Instructional Development* 10, no. 3 (1987): 2–10.

Lukowiak, Twila, and Jana Hunzicker. "Understanding How and Why College Students Engage in Learning. *Journal of Effective Teaching* 13, no. 1 (2013): 44–63.

Pizzolato, Jane E. "Achieving College Student Possible Selves: Navigating the Space Between Commitment and Achievement of Long-Term Identity Goals." *Cultural Diversity and Ethnic Minority Psychology* 12, no. 1 (2006): 57–69. doi:10.1037/1099-9809.12.1.57.

———. "Complex Partnerships: Self-Authorship and Provocative Academic-Advising Practices." *NACADA Journal* 26, no. 1 (2006): 32–45.

Terenzini, Patrick T., Alberto F. Cabrera, and Elena M. Bernal. *Swimming Against the Tide: The Poor in American Higher Education.* New York, NY: The College Entrance Examination Board, 2001.

CHAPTER 17

Piecing It Together:
Encouraging Student Learning through Self-Assessment and Active Learning

Heather Johnson and Ashley Duguay

Introduction

To librarians, an hour may seem like a paltry amount of time to cover everything they believe students should know. But to an unengaged student, an hour may seem endless. To mitigate potential student boredom and to overcome their expectations about the one-shot instruction session, librarians must create lesson plans that motivate students to engage with the content presented. With only an hour, librarians may default to didactic lectures where they point to every resource the library has to offer, but with careful planning, librarians can forego giving traditional lectures and design instructional sessions that create fun and meaningful learning experiences that whet students' appetite for more. One strategy for creating these learning experiences is to use active learning methods that allow students to engage with content and create their own assessments. This chapter provides an easily reproducible lesson plan that can be adapted to a variety of teaching and learning needs.

The Lesson Plan
Overview

In this lesson, students engage in a series of active learning exercises designed to increase their understanding of library resources. Students engage with content via the Jigsaw Classroom and participate in a student-created formative assessment activity. During the formative assessment activity, librarians evaluate students' comprehension, assess their learning needs, and gain an understanding of their progress toward meeting the learning objectives.

This assessment strategy is supported by the following ACRL frames (Association of College & Research Libraries):[1]

1. **Authority Is Constructed and Contextual:** Students think about the authority of sources and recognize that sources may be presented in a variety of formats depending on the intended audience. Students identify ways to interpret information from scholarly sources to levels that are more understandable to general audiences.

2. **Searching as Strategic Exploration:** Students think critically about what information they need, parse through the resources they know about, and then choose the appropriate source. Students understand that some resources may serve as pathfinders to other sources of information.

Learning Outcomes

At the end of this lesson, students should be able to do the following:

1. Extract the most meaningful information pertaining to each of the six resources (Wikipedia, MedlinePlus, UpToDate, PubMed Health, Google, and Google Scholar) in order to create trivia questions.
2. Compare each of the six resources in order to determine when each would be useful.
3. Explain the characteristics of a reliable source in order to differentiate reputable sources from non-reputable sources.

Lesson Preparation

1. Learning outcomes: Meet with the faculty member who requested the instructional session. If there is an assignment associated with the session, determine what students should be able to do in order to successfully complete it. In either case, develop learning outcomes for the session.
2. Resources: Identify several resources (internet, databases, etc.) that will help students to meet the learning objectives.
3. Resource handouts: Prepare handouts about each resource. Each handout contains information about the resource and a few "Questions for Consideration" to prompt students to think critically about their resource. Print multiple copies of each resource handout.

Distribute one handout per pair of students.

4. Index cards: Create sets of four index cards. The number of sets depends on the number of resources. Write the group number on each of the four cards in each set. Highlight the group numbers in different colors for convenience in sorting.

5. Graphic organizer: A graphic organizer is a blank table with the resources listed in separate rows and ample space next to the name of that resource. Print one graphic organizer per student. See the example below. Note that spacing has been intentionally reduced in this example.

6. Classroom arrangement: If possible, arrange classroom furniture in a way that is conducive to group work. See Lesson Plan and Possible Adaptations below for information on group size.

NOTES	
UpToDate	
Google	
Google Scholar	
MedlinePlus	
PubMed Health	
Wikipedia	
Questions? Contact Your Librarian!	

Lesson Plan

The lesson plan below is based on the introduction of six resources to about thirty students. Each group contains five students.

Part I: Required Activity

Length: 2 minutes.

Librarian activity: The librarian shares the learning objectives with the students.

Evidence-based rationale: Students participating in student-driven assessment activities are likely to focus on achieving learning objectives and therefore must be aware of the objectives if they are expected to focus on and achieve them.[2]

Part II: Required Activity

Length: 12 minutes.

Librarian activity: Divide students into six small groups and assign one resource per group. Distribute several handouts containing information about the assigned resource to each group.

Student activity: As a group, students discuss the assigned resource and use their graphic organizer to record notes.

Librarian activity: Once groups begin discussing their assigned resource, the librarian circulates and prompts students to answer the Questions for Consideration. The librarian also asks students to think about why that resource a reputable one and when using that resource is appropriate.

Evidence-based rationale: This is the first leg of a modified version of the Jigsaw Classroom, a cooperative learning method that may enhance student motivation, foster deeper learning, and create gratifying learning experiences.[3,4] Students participating in active learning activities may benefit from deeper learning for the fact that they discuss their interpretation of the content with their classmates and engage in discussion-based learning with the instructor.[5]

Part III: Optional Activity (when limited to less than one hour)

Length: 10 minutes.

Librarian activity: The librarian distributes one set of index cards to each group.

Student activity: As a group, students create four trivia questions/answers written on index cards.

Librarian activity: The librarian circulates and assists students with creating questions, prompting them to create questions that relate to the learning outcomes.

Evidence-based rationale: Think-pair-share activities allow students to discuss their interpretation of the resources and consider information from an alternative vantage point.[6] This think-pair-share activity involves a student-centered assessment that gives students ownership of their learning and the opportunity to discuss the aspects of the resource they believe to be most important.[7]

Part IV: Required Activity

Length: 12 minutes.

Librarian activity: Divide students into new small groups. Each new group contains a representative from each of the original groups.

Student activity: Each student shares information about their assigned resource and uses the graphic organizer to record notes about the other resources. By the end of this phase, students' graphic organizers contain information about each resource.

Librarian activity: The librarian circulates among groups and prompts students to raise questions about the utility and application of the resource.

Evidence-based rationale: Students engaged in cooperative learning activities are likely to experience a sense of self-efficacy since they are responsible for imparting their own knowledge on others.[8]

Part V: Optional Activity (When limited to 30 minutes)

Length: 20 minutes.

Librarian activity step 1: Put students back in their original groups. While students rearrange themselves, sort the trivia cards into four rounds. Each round contains one question about each resource.

Librarian activity step 2: The librarian asks trivia questions and announces the original group that created each question.

Student activity: Students answer trivia questions created by their classmates. Students cannot answer questions created by their original group.

Librarian activity step 3: The librarian provides immediate feedback.

Evidence-based rationale: Students may be increasingly motivated to participate in game-based assessments for their competitive design and for the opportunity to receive positive reinforcement.[9]

Why It Motivates Students

In the context of education, motivation is described in two ways: as a force that propels students to learn and as an outcome of educational experiences, whether positive or negative.[10] Many factors affect student motivation: assessment, student interest, goal orientation, locus of control, self-esteem, self-efficacy, and self-regulation. This lesson touches all factors, but most heavily on interest, goal orientation, and self-efficacy.

Student interest relies on two factors: personal interest and situational interest.[11] Some students may be intrigued by a particular activity because they possess an existing interest in the content, while others may need an extra push. When a lecture may be insufficient for creating that extra push, the instructor may incorporate active learning, a teaching method proven effective at motivating and generating interest among students.[12] Under this teaching method, instructors forego giving traditional lectures and instead facilitate student learning by providing more opportunities to engage with instructional content than would otherwise be given during a traditional lecture. Students who engage in active learning activities may experience a deeper sense of ownership of the content and responsibility for their learning.

Goal orientation is a core component of student motivation and happens when students perform based on the learning objectives.[13] When students understand the goals or learning outcomes of the lesson, they may be more inclined to focus on the learning outcomes and think about how to apply information to real-world scenarios.[14]

Self-efficacy is a core component of student motivation.[15] When instructors grant students autonomy in their learning and allow them to create their own learning artifacts, students may feel a greater sense of self-efficacy while providing valuable feedback about their learning.[16] This feedback has a multi-fold benefit: instructors may identify inconsistencies or areas of confusion in their teaching materials and then have the opportunity to make adjustments to the lesson and provide descriptive feedback. Giving descriptive feedback allows instructors to elucidate misconceptions, reinforce important concepts, and give suggestions for bringing their learning to the next level.

Active learning encompasses a variety of pedagogical methods, including cooperative learning, where students work together in small groups to achieve a common goal.[17] In the right context, cooperative learning has shown to improve the attitudes, behaviors, and work ethic of students, who may also show greater interest in learning compared to other learning techniques that aren't considered to be active.[18] This chapter deploys two cooperative learning techniques: A modified version of the Jigsaw Classroom and a think-pair-share activity.

The Jigsaw Classroom is a cooperative learning technique that provides a structured environment for students to work interdependently to share with and receive new information from one another.[19] In this method, instructors act as facilitators of learning and students serve as purveyors of information who take ownership of their learning. This technique promotes motivation among students and encourages them to listen, engage, and become empathetic learning partners.[20] This chapter uses a modified version of the Jigsaw Classroom, in that all original group members are responsible for the same content and are later redistributed to share their newly acquired information with their classmates.

Think-pair-share is another cooperative learning technique.[21] During think-pair-share activities, students think individually about an assigned resource, coordinate with a partner or small group to discuss that resource, and together share their learning with the rest of the class. One example of a think-pair-share activity is convening students to create assessments for their classmates. Students who create their own assessments reap two benefits: students share their collective knowledge and manage their own learning by identifying the components of the lesson they consider to be most relevant.[22] The lesson plan explained in this chapter allows students to generate their own formative assessments.

Formative assessment is an instructional technique used to evaluate the students' comprehension, learning needs, and progress during the lesson, while summative assessment uniformly administers assessments that are used to measure student success at the completion of a project or instructional unit.[23] When instructors use formative assessments, they acquire the information needed to help students to progress in their learning. As such, formative assessment is sometimes referred to as assessment for learning. When formative assessment takes place, students participate in ungraded, real-time assessment activities that allow instructors to identify gaps in learning and provide feedback as necessary. Formative assessment may take place informally as casual questioning or as a structured activity such as a game developed to check for students' understanding.

Game-based formative assessment enhances students' motivation, attention, confidence, and satisfaction by activating their competitive nature.[24] Students participating in this assessment technique have the opportunity to answer questions and receive positive or constructive feedback. Game-based instruction may create a safe, informal environment that fosters student learning and participation. Gamified learning allows instructors to reinforce concepts, provide students with immediate feedback, and evaluate if they have met the learning outcomes.

Assessment

This activity ultimately involves the creation of a formative assessment, which in this case is a trivia game. When instructors use trivia questions as instructional tools, they have the opportunity to reinforce concepts, offer additional information on a topic, and clarify information or elucidate misconceptions. For example, some questions and answers may be accurate and provide opportunities for instructors to reinforce that information. Other questions and answers may be incomplete, giving instructors the opportunity to fill in gaps, while other questions and answers may be entirely inaccurate. The latter is perhaps the most important area for instructors to focus their attention; since trivia questions will have been written prior to the reformation of groups, students may have potentially spread misinformation.

Possible Adaptations

The original lesson plan serves as a guide, rather than as an authority on creating a lesson plan designed to introduce students to a variety of resources. Lesson plans can and should be adapted to satisfy the needs of students and the goals of the librarian and course director. Librarians should consider the class size, number of resources, and length of time. The following considerations may provide assistance with adapting the lesson plan.

1. **Large class size.** If the class comprises many students, instructors may wish to create several small groups not based on the number of resources. They may also wish to enlist another librarian to allow adequate time for each group to connect with an instructor.

2. **Limited number of resources/several small groups.** If there are several small groups and/or a limited number of resources, assign multiple groups to cover the same resource. In doing this, the librarian may discover duplicate trivia questions. While they are redundant, they provide an additional opportunity to discuss important content with students.

3. **Limited time.** If the instruction session is limited to less than hour, eliminate the trivia component, leaving only the modified Jigsaw Classroom activity. The Jigsaw Classroom may be sufficient for motivating students to take ownership of their learning even if time does not allow for the additional gamified reinforcement of information.

Concluding Thoughts

Librarians may have a tendency to view one-shot instructional sessions as insufficient for teaching students what they need to know. Librarians often want to introduce students to multiple resources but may not have enough time to do more than an ineffective point-and-click demonstration. To motivate students, librarians may use active learning instructional techniques instead giving point-and-click demonstrations or delivering a didactic lecture.

Librarians may also assume there is not enough time to include elements of active learning in their teaching and that active learning may equate to introducing less content. While active learning activities may reduce the number of resources introduced, the information retained about the resources may be improved over traditional content delivery. In this chapter, we described a one-shot lesson plan where students engaged in a series of active learning activities designed to help them engage with resources carefully selected to help them meet the learning outcomes. In this session, students learned about an assigned resource and taught their classmates about their resource for a shared learning experience. They then laid the groundwork for an active formative assessment activity. During the formative assessment activity, librarians evaluated students' comprehension, assessed their learning needs, and gained an understanding of the progress made toward meeting their learning objectives.

By creating an engaging lesson plan that uses active learning techniques, librarians may give students the freedom to construct their own learning while creating an interactive, engaging environment. Using this lesson plan as a guide, librarians can create lesson plans that use active learning and self-assessment to motivate students to take ownership of content and experience deeper learning.

Endnotes

1. Association of College & Research Libraries, "Framework for Information Literacy for Higher Education," accessed September 6, 2016, http://www.ala.org/acrl/standards/ilframework.
2. Val Klenowski, "Student Self-Evaluation Processes in Student-Centred Teaching and Learning Contexts of Australia and England," *Assessment in Education: Principles, Policy & Practice* 2, no. 2 (August 1, 1995): 145–63, doi:10.1080/0969594950020203; Susan Pedersen and Doug Williams, "A Comparison of Assessment Practices and Their Effects on Learning and Motivation in a Student-Centered Learning Environment," *Journal of Educational Multimedia and Hypermedia* 13, no. 3 (July 2004): 283–306.
3. J. S. Mari and Sani Abdullahi Gumel, "Effects of Jigsaw Model of Cooperative Learning on Self-Efficacy and Achievement in Chemistry among Concrete and Formal Reasoners in Colleges of Education in Nigeria," *International Journal of Information and Education Technology* 5, no. 3 (2015): 196–99; Social Psychology Network, "The Jigsaw Classroom," accessed January 9, 2017, https://www.jigsaw.org.
4. Social Psychology Network, "The Jigsaw Classroom."
5. Heather A. Johnson and Laura C. Barrett, "Your Teaching Strategy Matters: How Engagement Impacts Application in Health Information Literacy Instruction," *Journal of the Medical Library Association* 105, no. January (2017): 44–48, doi:10.5195/jmla.2017.8.
6. Mahmoud Kaddoura, "Think Pair Share: A Teaching Learning Strategy to Enhance Students' Critical Thinking," *Educational Research Quarterly* 36, no. 4 (June 2013): 3–24.
7. Pedersen and Williams, "A Comparison of Assessment Practices," 283–306; Lorrie A. Shepard and Carribeth L. Bliem, "Research News and Comment: Parents' Thinking about Standardized Tests and Performance Assessments," *Educational Researcher* 24, no. 8 (1995): 25–32, doi:10.3102/0013189X024008025.
8. Klenowski, "Student Self-Evaluation Processes," 145–63.
9. Pedersen and Williams, "A Comparison of Assessment Practices," 283–306; Shep-

ard and Bliem, "Research News and Comment," 25–32.

10. Wynn Harlen, "The Role of Assessment in Developing Motivation for Learning," Chap. Part 2; Theory, in *Assessment and Learning*, 61: London: Sage: Publications, 2006.
11. Harlen, 61.
12. Johnson and Barrett, "Your Teaching Strategy Matters," 44–48.
13. Harlen, "The Role of Assessment," 61.
14. Klenowski, "Student Self-Evaluation Processes," 145–63; Pedersen and Williams, "A Comparison of Assessment Practices," 283–306.
15. Harlen, "The Role of Assessment," 61.
16. Pedersen and Williams, "A Comparison of Assessment Practices," 283–306; Shepard and Bliem, "Research News and Comment," 25–32; Harlen, "The Role of Assessment," 61.
17. Johnson and Barrett, "Your Teaching Strategy Matters," 44–48.
18. Lynda Carroll and Susan Leander, "Improving Student Motivation through the Use of Active Learning Strategies," Master of Arts Action Research Project, Saint Xavier University and SkyLight Field-Based Masters Program, 2001, 75; David W. Johnson, *Cooperative Learning: Increasing College Faculty Instructional Productivity*, ASHE-ERIC Higher Education Report (New York: Jossey-Bass, 1991).
19. Social Psychology Network, "The Jigsaw Classroom."
20. Johnson and Barrett, "Your Teaching Strategy Matters," 44–48; David V. Perkins and Renee N. Saris, "A 'Jigsaw Classroom' Technique for Undergraduate Statistics Courses," *Teaching of Psychology* 28, no. 2 (May 1, 2001): 111–13, doi:10.1207/S15328023TOP2802_09; Céline Darnon, Céline Buchs, and Delphine Desbar, "The Jigsaw Technique and Self-Efficacy of Vocational Training Students: A Practice Report," *European Journal of Psychology of Education* 27, no. 3 (2012): 439–49, doi:10.1007/s10212-011-0091-4; Mari and Gumel, "Effects of Jigsaw Model," 196–99; Jennifer Phillips and Julie Fusco, "Using the Jigsaw Technique to Teach Clinical Controversy in a Clinical Skills Course," *American Journal of Pharmaceutical Education* 79, no. 6 (2015): 1–7.
21. Kaddoura, "Think Pair Share," 3–24.
22. Pedersen and Williams, "A Comparison of Assessment Practices," 283–306; Shepard and Bliem, "Research News and Comment," 25–32.
23. Black and Wiliam, "Assessment for Learning in the Classroom," Chap. Part 1; Practice, in *Assessment and Learning* (London: SAGE Publications, 2006), 9; Margaret Heritage, "Formative Assessment: What Do Teachers Need to Know and Do?" *Phi Delta Kappan* 89, no. 2 (2007): 140; Rick Stiggins and Jan Chappuis, "Enhancing Student Learning," *District Administration* (2008): 42, https://www.districtadministration.com/article/enhancing-student-learning.
24. Guy J. Leach and Tammy S. Sugarman, "Play to Win! Using Games in Library Instruction to Enhance Student Learning," *Research Strategies* 20 (3) (2005): 191–203; James D. Klein and Eric Freitag, "Enhancing Motivation Using an Instructional Game," *Journal of Instructional Psychology* 18, no. 2 (1991): 111.

Bibliography

Association of College & Research Libraries. "Framework for Information Literacy for Higher Education." Accessed September 6, 2016. http://www.ala.org/acrl/standards/ilframework.

Black, Paul, and Dylan Wiliam. "Assessment for Learning in the Classroom." Chap. Part 1; Practice. In *Assessment and Learning*, 9: London: SAGE Publications, 2006.

Carroll, Lynda, and Susan Leander. "Improving Student Motivation through the Use of Active Learning Strategies." Master of Arts Action Research Project, Saint Xavier University and SkyLight Field-Based Masters Program, 2001.

Darnon, Céline, Céline Buchs, and Delphine Desbar. "The Jigsaw Technique and Self-Efficacy of Vocational Training Students: A Practice Report." *European Journal of Psychology of Education* 27, no. 3 (2012): 439–49. doi:10.1007/s10212-011-0091-4.

Harlen, Wynn. "The Role of Assessment in Developing Motivation for Learning." Chap. Part 2; Theory. In *Assessment and Learning*, 61. London: SAGE Publications, 2006.

Heritage, Margaret. "Formative Assessment: What Do Teachers Need to Know and Do?" *Phi Delta Kappan* 89, no. 2 (2007): 140–45.

Johnson, David W. *Cooperative Learning: Increasing College Faculty Instructional Productivity*. ASHE-ERIC Higher Education Report. New York: Jossey-Bass, 1991.

Johnson, Heather A., and Laura C. Barrett. "Your Teaching Strategy Matters: How Engagement Impacts Application in Health Information Literacy Instruction." *Journal of the Medical Library Association* 105, no. January (2017): 44–48. doi:10.5195/jmla.2017.8.

Kaddoura, Mahmoud. "Think Pair Share: A Teaching Learning Strategy to Enhance Students' Critical Thinking." *Educational Research Quarterly* 36, no. 4 (June 2013): 3–24.

Klein, James D., and Eric Freitag. "Enhancing Motivation Using an Instructional Game." *Journal of Instructional Psychology* 18, no. 2 (1991): 111.

Klenowski, Val. "Student Self-Evaluation Processes in Student-Centred Teaching and Learning Contexts of Australia and England." *Assessment in Education: Principles, Policy & Practice* 2, no. 2 (August 1, 1995): 145–63. doi:10.1080/0969594950020203.

Leach, Guy J., and Tammy S. Sugarman. "Play to Win! Using Games in Library Instruction to Enhance Student Learning." *Research Strategies* 20 (3) (2005): 191–203.

Mari, J. S., and Sani Abdullahi Gumel. "Effects of Jigsaw Model of Cooperative Learning on Self-Efficacy and Achievement in Chemistry among Concrete and Formal Reasoners in Colleges of Education in Nigeria." *International Journal of Information and Education Technology* 5, no. 3 (2015): 196–99.

Niemi, Hannele. "Active Learning a Cultural Change Needed in Teacher Education and Schools." *Teaching and Teacher Education* 18, no. 7 (2002): 763–80. doi:10.1016/S0742-051X(02)00042-2.

Pedersen, Susan, and Doug Williams. "A Comparison of Assessment Practices and their Effects on Learning and Motivation in a Student-Centered Learning Environment." *Journal of Educational Multimedia and Hypermedia* 13, no. 3 (July 2004): 283–306.

Perkins, David V., and Renee N. Saris. "A 'Jigsaw Classroom' Technique for Undergraduate Statistics Courses." *Teaching of Psychology* 28, no. 2 (May 1, 2001): 111–13. doi:10.1207/S15328023TOP2802_09.

Phillips, Jennifer, and Julie Fusco. "Using the Jigsaw Technique to Teach Clinical Controversy in a Clinical Skills Course." *American Journal of Pharmaceutical Educa-

tion 79, no. 6 (2015): 1–7.

Shepard, Lorrie A., and Carribeth L. Bliem. "Research News and Comment: Parents' Thinking about Standardized Tests and Performance Assessments." *Educational Researcher* 24, no. 8 (1995): 25–32. doi:10.3102/0013189X024008025.

Stiggins, Rick, and Jan Chappuis. "Enhancing Student Learning." *District Administration* (2008): 42. https://www.districtadministration.com/article/enhancing-student-learning.

Social Psychology Network. "The Jigsaw Classroom." Accessed January 9, 2017. https://www.jigsaw.org.

CHAPTER 18

Can I Have Your Attention, Please:
Using Motivational Design and Feminist Pedagogy to Create Group Activities

Samantha Becker

The work of motivating students to achieve higher levels of active learning, engagement, and retention can be an uncertain element of library instruction. So much of how the students view the library session is dependent on the framing of the instructor of record, and often the librarian takes on the role of the guest lecturer. The librarian is an expert in a field where content may be broadly relevant to a student's course of study but is largely focused on skills that students believe themselves to be already proficient in.[1] A result of this misconception is that engaging pedagogy and attention to design are even more critical to the library instructor. Among the tools available, an often overlooked one is the ability to leverage the pre-existing social bonds of students through group work. Viewed through the lens of feminist pedagogies, group work can also fit well into larger conversations around motivational design. In this chapter, I will introduce activities that use feminist pedagogy to inspire motivation in students as understood through the Attention, Relevance, Confidence, and Satisfaction Model (ARCS).

Motivational Design

At its core, the study of motivation asks us to consider *why*. This question can be daunting for instructors to tackle when it comes to student behaviors and attitudes. Various models of motivational design emphasize different aspects of motivational study. One such example is the ARCS model, developed by John Keller, which focuses on attention, relevance, confidence, and satisfaction.[2]

Before considering motivational tactics, the ARCS model asks us to perform an audience analysis. This step forms the basis of the design process. It is comprised of five categories of information, much of which is likely already collected in preparation for a library session. The table below adapts Keller's audience analysis with guiding questions.[3]

Keller's ARCS Guiding Questions

	Guiding questions
Course information	What is the course description? What is the rationale behind the sequence of assignments? Is there a pattern to classroom activities already?
Audience information	What year are the students? Are there pre-requisites? If so, what are the skills or information students are covered? What has the instructor of record noticed about their research skills? Is there a more advanced course this will feed into?
Audience motivations	Does the instructor have a sense of why the students are taking the course? Is it required?
Existing motivational conditions	What motivational strategies are currently in place?
Objectives	What is this library session meant to accomplish? Is another topic or assignment being set up?

Once an audience analysis has been completed, motivational tactics to best address lesson goals and audience motivation can be generated. The *Attention* aspect of ARCS focuses on managing, directing, and sustaining the attention of learners;[4] librarians can win student attention through activities and standard attention-getting strategies like variety, surprise, novelty, and humor. Though important to establish, attention-getting strategies are not enough to inspire motivation over longer periods of time, making the other aspects of ARCS crucial. *Relevance* asks how a learning experience can be made personally valuable to students.[5] It is useful if content can be related back to students' interests and life goals in addition to the class assignments that tend to structure our lessons. *Confidence* refers to students' belief in their ability to succeed and control their success.[6] Belief in the ability to succeed can greatly impact motivation to participate in learning, and ARCS asks us to be mindful of how to build confidence into the learning experience. *Satisfaction*, the last element of the ARCS model, plays a critical role in a student's long-term desire to learn. It asks us to consider ways that we can help students to feel good about their learning experience and desire to continue learning.[7]

Feminist Pedagogy

The ARCS model provides a process through which an instructor can develop motivational tactics; however, these tactics must still be embedded within a pedagogical framework. One of the basic assumptions of ARCS is that motivational design is not about finding a prescriptive set of steps, but rather problem-solving.[8] Flexibility is cooked into this model and feminist pedagogy is particularly well-suited to fold in as several of its principles echo the guiding ARCS questions.

At its broadest level, feminist pedagogy is "theory about the teaching/learning process that guides our choice of classroom practice by providing criteria to evaluate specific education strategies and techniques in terms of the desired course goals or outcomes."[9] It is a lens through which we can interpret the classroom space, create instructional strategies, and generate learning outcomes for students. Though there are many ways to consider and define feminist pedagogy, this chapter will look most closely at the student-teacher relationship and notions of community through principles of empowerment, personal experience, and challenging traditional views.

Student-Teacher Relationship and Community

The library instructor's frequent position as guest lecturer fits well into one of the fundamental principles of feminist pedagogy: the emphasis on reforming the relationship between student and teacher. It seeks to challenge the traditional role of the educator as the sole source of knowledge in a teacher-centered classroom.[10] Often, library instruction happens as a one- or two-shot workshop in the classroom of another instructor. There may be a deep, long-standing relationship between the instructor of record and the library instructor or this may be the only time they will meet. In either situation, the library instructor is, by design, not the only source of knowledge in the classroom. In some cases, particularly where the instructor of record is not present, the students may be in a position of knowledgeable authority in terms of course context or previous scaffolding. Students become, in feminist pedagogy, more responsible for teaching and instructors become more responsible for learning.[11] As guests in the classroom, the library instructor may need to learn in the moment about course content, pre-established classroom dynamic, and assignment expectations. Acknowledging our need to learn can help establish the role of the library instructor in the classroom community.

Group work is particularly well-suited to feminist pedagogy due to its emphasis on the development of community within the classroom. In reforming the role of the instructor and recognizing the knowledge of the student, students are encouraged to integrate the ability to think critically with "a respect for and ability to work with others."[12] Once the student has been recognized as a source of knowledge, they become responsible not only for their own learning but for the learning of others. Students are expected to pool their understanding and teach each other in order to create a participatory environment in which students "learning actively and work cooperatively."[13] One means of resisting instructional tactics that reduce students to passivity is to lean on their knowledge and encourage them to work together in order to solve problems and complete tasks. Collaborating in group work can also help create a sense of community.[14] Librarians may benefit from employing tactics that encourage students to work with the sense of community a class has already established. Particularly later in the semester, the library instructor's role as a guest presents an opportunity to leverage familiarity into participation.

Lesson Plans

In the following sections, a few of the elements of feminist pedagogy are introduced and followed by activities that represent what that element could look like in a library classroom. Many of the lessons embody more than one principle but are grouped together based on a primary element. In addition to the prompts, motivational rationale is described with the corresponding aspect of ARCS. Finally, each lesson includes a prompt for an exit essay as a means of assessing student learning and achieving student satisfaction. Between each part, expect two or three minutes of moving and re-focusing time before students are able to fully engage with the next section. An example audience analysis is included to frame the motivational tactics of each lesson.

Example Audience Analysis Using Keller's ACRS Guiding Questions

	Guiding questions
Course information	• First-year seminar class with writing assignments spaced throughout the semester to move from reflection to academic writing • Learning objectives in writing, information literacy, and critical thinking Class is themed around feminism and popular culture
Audience information	• 20 first-year students with no pre-requisites • Students will work in 5 groups of 4 for all lessons • Stand-alone class in the first semester that does not feel into more advanced writing class
Audience motivations	• Students required to take seminar • Varying levels of interest in content theme
Existing motivational conditions	Relate back to current events where possible
Objectives	• No research assignment embedded in this course • Objective is to set up general research skills applicable to a variety of majors

Empowerment

Empowering students is one aspect of feminist pedagogy that relates deeply to the concept of reforming the student-teacher relationship. Empowerment becomes linked to notions of democracy and participation.[15] In the feminist classroom, students are encouraged to be active and contribute to constructing and contextualizing new information into their pre-existing knowledge. They are asked to take power and control over their own knowledge.[16] Just as the ARCS model asks us to consider how to allow students to control their learning experience in order to build confidence, feminist pedagogy similarly focuses on shifting some of the power and control in the classroom to the student.

The lesson plans in this section seek to uphold the principle of empowerment through encouraging students to construct their own meaning and knowledge from the classroom activity. In the first activity, they construct their own understanding of audience and purpose in order to examine the services and articles used. In the second lesson, students outline their own understanding of academic writing. They teach each other academic formatting as well as what information we can easily skim for.

Evaluating Audience and Purpose

Total time	32 minutes
Outcomes	Students will be able to identify the impact of the intended audience, platform, and purpose in different types of websites in order to construct an understanding of how audience and purpose impact product.
Materials	• Requires computers for all students • The name of one online dating service per group • When selecting dating sites, choose a variety in terms of the target population (HER vs. grindr), platform (exclusively mobile vs. web and mobile), dominate age groups (match.com vs. tinder), special interest (Christian mingle vs. J date). You can also think of this in terms of purpose like casual encounter (tinder), women messaging first (bumble), economic arrangement (seekingarrangement.com), bonding over dislike (Hater).
Motivational strategies	• Attention (A): The topic of online-dating services is meant to be humorous and novel enough to capture attention. • Relevance (R): Online dating services are often on the periphery of student life, even if the student in question is not using them. • Confidence (C): Questions of audience and purpose are generally quite visible since dating services seek to be unique and distinguish themselves in an increasingly saturated market. Students practice the same skill twice but in different environments. By seeing the differences in audience and dating service, students are better prepared for the more difficult task of identifying audiences beyond "people who read magazines?"
Part 1 10 minutes	Content prompt: In your groups, do some background web research on your dating service in order to answer the following questions: • What is your dating service? When was it created? • Who is the primary audience for your service? • Is there a specific purpose it was created for? Does it focus on creating long-term relationships, casual interactions, or something else entirely? What makes it different from other services?
Part 2 15 minutes	Content prompt: In your groups, locate a website or video on how to use your dating service and read it. Be prepared to teach the class about your dating service using the following questions as guides: • How does your service function? • How has the service tried to appeal to its target audience or its intended purpose? What are the specific characteristics you look at to determine that? • What makes it different from other services (or other services at the time of its creation) and why do you think it was created that way?

Part 3 5 minutes	Content prompt: Consider the articles your group selected in order to complete this assignment thus far. Select one article and be prepared to introduce the class to it using the following questions as guides: • Which part of the assignment did you use this to complete? In other words, what was its purpose? • What made you select this article as a believable resource? • Who is the intended audience? How can you tell?
Exit essay prompt 2 minutes	How is the purpose and/or audience of the academic sources you read for class different than the purpose of the materials we found today and how can you tell?

Anatomy of a Peer-Review Article

Time	
Outcomes	Students will be able to identify the different pieces of a peer-review article communicating original research and articulate their purpose in order to construct their own understanding of academic formatting and reading strategies.
Materials	Peer-reviewed articles that include elements like: • Abstract, keywords, intro/background, conclusion, methods/ methodology, results/discussion • One article per group This can also be done more quickly using detailed records and citation styles.
Motivational strategies	• A: The more ridiculous the articles, the easier attention-getting is for this activity. • R: Most students will need to work with academic writing at some point in their career. Relevance for this activity is often found in the last part—reading strategies. Acknowledge that an outcome is meant to be understanding more while doing less reading in any class that uses academic writing. • C: Reading for purpose rather than content can be a difficult skill. If students become frustrated, continually ground this in academic reading they may have already seen or the experience of trying to skim an article right before class starts. Where do you look when you are short on time and you need just enough to get by in class that day? Why do you look there?
Part 1 10 minutes	Skim through your article and label the parts of it. Do not focus on what the article is about or what is being researched. Focus on labeling or naming elements you've seen before or you suspect are common to all articles of this type. To get you started, one element of all of the articles in the room is a title. The title concisely communicates the specifics of what is being researched and communicated.

Part 2 5 minutes	Compare articles with your groupmates, discuss your results, and locate the pieces of a peer-review article that everyone has labeled.
Part 3 3-5 minutes	On a blank sheet of paper, collect your pieces together in order to answer the following: • What are the pieces of a peer-reviewed article? • What kind of information can you skim for?
Exit essay prompt 2 minutes	Explain which sections of a peer-review article you should read more closely and which you can skim and why.

Personal Experience

Personal experience is a body of knowledge heavily emphasized by feminist pedagogy and often overlooked in library instruction. When grounded in personal experience, critical thinking becomes about the process of reflection and inquiry rather than an abstract concept.[17] It is easy to turn critical thinking into something removed from the lives of students. By linking critical thinking to personal experience, it becomes more about reflecting on and questioning one's everyday life rather than meeting the expectations of an instructor. Through the lens of feminist pedagogy, understanding and knowledge are rooted in personal experience and factors related to identity.[18] Bringing personal experience more explicitly into the classroom can serve as a means of acknowledging the identity of students. In doing so, instructors attempt to privilege the student voice over that of the teacher.[19] This act of privileging student voice can be particularly useful in building the kind of relevance the ARCS model focuses on. Skills related to research and academia can first be practiced in situations common to the students' everyday lives in order to make learning experiences personally relevant.

The lesson plan in this section seeks to uphold this principle by asking students to connect their everyday experiences back to the process of academic research. Students do many kinds of searches every day without paying attention to the processes they use. Those processes can often be made relevant to academic research.

Identifying information needs

Time	
Outcomes	Students will be able to identify information needs for different scenarios and compare how information needs change in order to identify appropriate source types.

Materials	Scenarios like the ones below
Motivational strategies	• A: One of the goals while writing the scenarios is to make them somewhat relatable to students to inspire interest through familiarity. • R: The scenarios are all meant to be familiar while emphasizing the transferability of searching habits they likely already have and connecting it back to their coursework. • C: Understanding information needs or gaps can be challenging in academic writing, so this lesson is designed to ask students to practice the skill first in a more accessible environment.
Part 1 5 minutes	Content prompt: Read through the scenario carefully. Talk through it to ensure we all have a common understanding of the task at hand. As a group, generate at least 4 questions or pieces of information we would need to make a decision. To do so, consider the following: • Who are the people or information sources that will be most helpful in this scenario? Why? • What do we need to consider or gather more information about in order to make a choice? • What will impact how confident we feel in our decision? • When we have a list, generate a few sources we might consult in order to locate the information you identified.
Part 2 5 minutes	Content prompt: Rotate to another scenario and read through it. Add to the previous group's list. • What is missing? • Is there additional information we may need? • Is there something we particularly agree with? • Do we have questions about what the previous group did? If so, add them around the edges Return to your own scenario and review what has been added or changed
Part 3 10 minutes	Content prompt: Introduce your scenario to the class using the following as guides: • What was the information, identified by you or the group that visited your scenario, that you needed to make a decision? • What were your information sources? • How was this information different or unique from the one you visited?

Scenarios	Scenario 1: An election is quickly approaching and you're undecided about who to vote for. You know that the candidates all seem well-qualified. You don't strongly identify with any particular party because to some degree you can see sides with different platforms for each party. You know you need to collect some more information about each of the candidates in order to make the most informed choice. Scenario 2: You've been saving up your money for as long as you can remember, and it's finally paid off! You now have enough money to buy a new car for the first time. You asked around, but no one has been very helpful. Since you know you're going to have this car for a long time, you know you need more information in order to make sure you're making a good investment. Scenario 3: You and your friends are looking to try a new restaurant, but no one seems to have anything specific in mind. You know that you don't want to go to the same old place, but at the same time no one wants to spend money on a bad place. If only because you're tired of talking about it, you decide you all need to collect more information in order to make a choice. Scenario 4: You finally have a day off at the same time as a few of your friends! You want to go see a movie together, but no one seems to really know what they want to go see. One of your friends won't spend the money unless it's to go see an award-winning movie. You're not really sure what falls into that category right now so you decide to collect a little more information before you pitch a title to the group.
Exit essay prompt 2 minutes	How does this activity compare to how you start researching for a class?

Challenging Traditional Views

Feminist pedagogy challenges traditional views of information by emphasizing the connection between ideas and the social conditions of those who contribute to their creation and continuation.[20] Education can reproduce specific ways of knowing which, when left unexamined, can undermine the goals of empowerment and community. As students become more aware of the social construction of societal values, they are also more likely to become more open to questioning and changing those social values.[21] One of the goals of feminist pedagogy is to equip students with the ability to transform the world around them.[22] In order to transform the world, they must first understand and question it.

The lesson plans in this section seek to uphold the principle of challenging traditional views from two angles. In the first, students are asked to deconstruct an argument for claims, supporting reasons, and evidence. In doing so, students are prompted to question how robust the evidence in support of the central claim is. In the second, students are asked to consider constructions of authority and come up with different ways a figure can be considered authoritative.

Understanding Arguments

Time	
Outcomes	Students will be able to identify central claims, reasons, and evidence in order to think critically about the argument presented.
Materials	One magazine article per group and a short presentation like the one below. Ideally, the magazine article will be no more than a page in length.
Motivational Strategies	• A: Claiming the fifth Harry Potter book is the best is usually contentious enough to grab attention. • R: Many classes ask students to identify claims and evaluate them without using this language. • C: Discussing the presentation helps students build confidence in understanding what is being asked of them before they practice it on their own
Part 1 3–5 minutes (continues on next page)	Content prompt: Short lecture by library instructor: Argument: a central claim, backed by reasons and supported by evidence. Ex.: Argument: Harry Potter and the Order of the Phoenix is the best Harry Potter book because it is the first time Harry asserts himself as an independent leader." Argumentation: a process of call and response in which two people make arguments and respond. It is not a process in which two people say the same thing to each other. Claim: a potentially arguable statement; must be something others can dispute Ex.: Not a claim: "I like Harry Potter and the Order of the Phoenix." Claim: "Harry Potter and the Order of the Phoenix is the best."

Part 1 3–5 minutes (continued from previous page)	Reason: statement in support of the claim. Without reasons, a claim is not an argument but a simple declarative statement. Reasons are the answer to the hypothetical question, "What makes you say that?" and are often linked with words like "because." Ex.: "…because it is the first time Harry asserts himself as an independent leader." Evidence: specific examples offered in support of the reasons. Can be qualitative or quantitative but is meant to convince the audience of the reasons and thus the claim. Evidence is distinct from but related to the reasons. Ex.: • Harry becomes the leader of Dumbledore's Army in the book. • Interviews with readers or moviegoers who are emotionally moved by Harry's decision to step up and form Dumbledore's Army • J. K. Rowling commenting on Harry's leadership ability and growth • A leadership studies professor's article on the theory behind Harry as a leader
Part 2 8–10 minutes	Content prompt: Individually read through the magazine article assigned to your group and identify the following: • What is the claim being made by this article? • What are the reasons you've been given in support of the claim? • What is the evidence presented to convince you of the reasons? In your groups, once you've identified the claim, reasons, and evidence, work backward to determine if you are convinced. • Do you believe the evidence? • Does the evidence fully support the reasons? • Do the reasons fully support the claim?
Part 2 5 minutes	Content prompt: Present your article to the class using the following questions as guides: • What is the central argument? • Are you convinced of it? • Why or why not? Is anything missing? Any reasons left unsubstantiated?

Part 4: (Bonus round: counter-arguments) 10 minutes	Content prompt: Counter-argument: an argument put forth in opposition to another argument. A challenge to an argument but not necessarily in direct or complete opposition to the original argument. May challenge individual reasons or evidence. In your groups, generate as many counter-arguments as you can to: • *"Harry Potter and the Order of the Phoenix* is the best Harry Potter book because it is the first time Harry asserts himself as an independent leader." • What kind of support evidence do you have or would you need for your counter argument?
Exit essay prompt	How would you apply what we did today to reading an academic article?

Evaluating Authority

Time	
Outcomes	Students will be able to identify their own areas of authority and generate a list of criteria in order to evaluate authority.
Materials	Paper and writing utensil
Motivational Strategies	• A: Students have an opportunity to talk about their interests, which also sets the stage for more participation. • R: Relates their own interests to types of authority used in their classes • C: Starts students out with talking about types of authority they actually use and interact with in order to work toward the academic concept of credibility.
Part 1 5–8 minutes	Content prompt: Take 2–3 minutes and free write about what you're an authority in. What do you feel like you can speak about knowledgeably? Come up with three areas of knowledge in which you're an authority and explain why you're authoritative. Briefly share with your group. Using the areas of authority identified, compile a list of different categories of authority (i.e., academic, experiential, societal, etc.).

| Part 2 5 minutes | Content prompt: Come up with at least 3 criteria for determining authority in each category. What do we look at to determine if a person can speak credibly and knowledgeably in a topic? What did you look at for yourself? Be ready to share what kind of authority your group has and how you know. We will compile a list of authority criteria which you can add to or ask questions about. |
| Exit essay prompt 2 minutes | How does evaluating and understanding authority in our everyday lives compare to how we would use this in our academic ones? |

Assessment and Satisfaction

Each of the lessons above includes an exit essay prompt. The purpose of these prompts is two-fold since they seek to make student learning visible, but they also seek to provide the satisfaction the ARCS model asks us to close with. In these exit essays, students explain what they have learned and connect it to something larger. They are similar to the one-minute essay Maria Accardi discusses in her book *Feminist Pedagogy for Library Instruction*.[23] Unlike the more traditional survey, these essays are intended to fall under the Writing Across the Curriculum (WAC) umbrella of writing-to-learn activities or informal, thinking-on-paper kinds of writing.[24] Unlike more formal writing assignments that focus students on the rhetoric and mechanics of writing, writing-to-learn activities focus on thinking. They ask students to share the development of thought rather than at the point that "thinking turning into declaring."[25] Writing-to-learn renders visible and slows down the process of arriving at a declarative statement. It allows for students to reflect and process a question in order to transform knowledge rather than simply tell or repeat it.[26]

As a writing-to-learn activity, it is particularly important that students write for the entirety of the time provided. To that end, making it clear to students that finishing their free-write early will not result in them leaving can encourage students to continue writing for the full time. When opening this activity, I will generally tell students they have a minute free-write after while I have a few more things to tell them and class will conclude. After the free-write, I will do a standardized conclusion that includes how to contact a librarian in the future. Free-write activities can be helpful for opening conversations with faculty about follow-up sessions or activities. They can also generate space for additional conversations with campus writing centers or tutoring services, which may be headed by faculty already advocating for WAC in disciplines other than writing programs.

Endnotes

1. Melissa Gross and Don Latham, "Undergraduate Perceptions of Information Literacy: Defining, Attaining, and Self-Assessing Skills," *College & Research Libraries* 70, no. 4 (2009): 336.
2. John Keller, *The ARCS Model of Motivational Design* (Boston, MA: Springer US, 2010), 45.
3. Keller, 59.
4. Keller, 45.
5. Keller, 45.
6. Keller, 45.
7. Keller, 45.
8. Keller, 55.
9. Carolyn Shrewsbury, "What Is Feminist Pedagogy?" *Women's Studies Quarterly* 25, no. 1/2 (1997): 166.
10. Sharon Ladenson, "Paradigm Shift: Utilizing Critical Feminist Pedagogy in Library Instruction," in *Critical Library Instruction*, ed. Maria Accardi, Maria T. Drabinski, Emily Kumbier, Emily Drabinski, and Alana Kumbier (Duluth, MN: Litwin Books, LLC, 2010), 106.
11. Lynne Webb, Myria Allen, and Kandi Walker, "Feminist Pedagogy: Identifying Basic Principles," *Academic Exchange Quarterly* 6, no. 1 (2002): 68.
12. Shrewsbury, "What Is Feminist Pedagogy?," 167.
13. Ladenson, "Paradigm Shift: Utilizing Critical Feminist Pedagogy," 106.
14. Shirley Parry, "Feminist Pedagogy and Techniques for the Changing Classroom," *Women's Studies Quarterly* 24, no. 3/4 (1996): 46.
15. Shrewsbury, "What Is Feminist Pedagogy?," 167.
16. Parry, "Feminist Pedagogy and Techniques," 46.
17. Shrewsbury, "What Is Feminist Pedagogy?," 167.
18. Parry, "Feminist Pedagogy and Techniques," 46.
19. Maria Accardi, *Feminist Pedagogy for Library Instruction* (Sacramento: Library Juice Press, 2013), 67.
20. Webb, Allen, and Walker, "Feminist Pedagogy: Identifying Basic Principles," 71.
21. Webb, 71.
22. Accardi, *Feminist Pedagogy for Library Instruction*, 36.
23. Accardi, 84.
24. Nancy Lester et al, "Writing Across the Curriculum: A College Snapshot," *Urban Education* 38, no. 1 (2003): 7.
25. Lester, 7.
26. Susan McLeod, "Writing Across the Curriculum: An Introduction," in *Writing Across the Curriculum: A Guide to Developing Programs*, eds. Susan McLeod and Margot Soven (Newbury Park, CA: Sage Publications, 1992), 3.

Bibliography

Accardi, Maria T. *Feminist Pedagogy for Library Instruction*. Sacramento: Library Juice Press, 2013.

Gross, Melissa, and Don Latham, "Undergraduate Perceptions of Information Literacy: Defining, Attaining, and Self-Assessing Skills." *College & Research Libraries* 70, no. 4 (2009): 336–50.

Keller, John. *The ARCS Model of Motivational Design*. Boston, MA: Springer US, 2010.

Ladenson, Sharon, "Paradigm Shift: Utilizing Critical Feminist Pedagogy in Library Instruction." In *Critical Library Instruction*, edited by Maria Accardi, Maria T. Drabinski, Emily Kumbier, Emily Drabinski, and Alana Kumbier. Duluth, MN: Litwin Books, LLC, 2010.

Lester, Nancy, Corrine Bertram, Gregory Erickson, Ernie Lee, Abraham Tchako, Kacy Wiggins, and James Wilson. "Writing Across the Curriculum: A College Snapshot." *Urban Education* 38, no. 1 (2003): 5–34.

McLeod, Susan. "Writing Across the Curriculum: An Introduction." In *Writing Across the Curriculum: A Guide to Developing Programs*, edited by Susan McLeod and Margot Soven. Newbury Park, CA: Sage Publications, 1992.

Parry, Shirley. "Feminist Pedagogy and Techniques for the Changing Classroom." *Women's Studies Quarterly* 24, no. 3/4 (1996): 45–54.

Shrewsbury, Carolyn. "What Is Feminist Pedagogy?" *Women's Studies Quarterly* 25, no. 1/2 (1997): 166–73.

Webb, Lynne, Myria Allen, and Kandi Walker. "Feminist Pedagogy: Identifying Basic Principles." *Academic Exchange Quarterly* 6, no. 1 (2002): 67–72.

———. "Feminist Pedagogy: Identifying Basic Principles," *Academic Exchange Quarterly* 6, no. 1 (2002): 67–72.

CHAPTER 19

Practicing in Public:
A Social Constructivist Approach to Research Skills Work in Online Discussion Boards

Katherine Luce

Introduction

Imagine a dance class. The instructor asks the students to execute a combination of steps and they do so, each working at the appropriate level, listening to feedback, observing each other, and trying different approaches to find what works best for each of them. Ideally, the atmosphere is serious, yet positive, relaxed, and playful, so students feel able to experiment in front of each other. The students are at different levels of proficiency, but each of them attempts every exercise. Failure is accepted as part of the learning process, which takes place in an atmosphere of mutual respect. The instructor's feedback and the design of the class help students learn, but they acquire and reinforce their skills mainly through individual practice, shared in a community of other learners. This scenario may not seem to have much to do with information literacy instruction, but I propose that the conscious practice, in a community of peers that encourages experimentation and even failure, is well adapted to motivate students to improve their research skills.

I was inspired to develop the exercise described in this chapter by my dance background, which taught me that practical skills are best acquired through intentional, shared practice; my observations as an online student that effectively designed online discussions offer an opportunity for shared learning that can surpass in-person interactions; and my awareness that stu-

297

dents need significant hands-on experience with online searching to move beyond their existing search habits. By incorporating elements of communities of practice and positive assessment, the exercise uses a social constructivist approach to motivate students to engage with the material and obtain a robust amount of practice.

The exercise asks students to practice their acquisition of research skills in plain view of each other by using the online discussion boards provided in my institution's learning management system (LMS). The exercise gives students a structured assignment, asking them to perform specific tasks in a search interface such as a web search engine, a library database, or a discovery service, and it requires them to report back to each other on their actions, their search results, and their overall experience. It also asks for documentation of their search, so the instructor can give individualized feedback in private. Students' discussion board posts must include specific details, such as the keywords and database expanders or limiters they used, and I encourage them to report on their difficulties as well as their successes. They benefit from the clarity about their searches they gain from describing them to their peers and from experiencing each other's searches vicariously. If we return to our imaginary dance class, this is parallel to learning a difficult skill, such as pirouettes in ballet, where practice is needed to cement learning; some failure is likely before success can be reached, and learning happens in view of the rest of the class.

While the nature of the tasks students complete in this exercise is not unusual, sharing their search experience with the full class is less common. The exercise contemplates a shift in the learning environment to one that values engagement over results, welcomes experimentation and failure, and promotes peer-to-peer learning. Students engage not only with the material but with each other, preparing them for the communities of practice they will participate in. This approach gives students more power over their success and reduces the gap between student and faculty authority, allowing students to develop the self-motivation required for the twenty-first-century learning environment and workplace.[1] This chapter provides a brief overview of the exercise, then full details of the exercise itself, and will end with a discussion of how this approach can motivate students and a look at the relevant literature.

The Lesson Plan
Overview

This exercise asks students to use a search interface with specified search parameters and report back about their experience to their classmates using an online discussion board. The example I give below uses EBSCO Discovery

Service, but any search interface will do. It is relevant to the frame "Searching as Strategic Exploration" from the ACRL Framework for Information Literacy and is particularly helpful in developing the following knowledge practices:

- design and refine needs and search strategies as necessary, based on search results;
- understand how information systems (i.e., collections of recorded information) are organized in order to access relevant information;
- use different types of searching language (e.g., controlled vocabulary, keywords, natural language) appropriately; and
- manage searching processes and results effectively.

The exercise is also connected to the framework's view that information literacy is part of a social landscape and moves students toward participating in a community of practice (Authority is Constructed and Contextual).

Learning Outcomes

Learning outcome 1: By the end of the exercise, students will be able to apply specified search techniques to retrieve topically relevant information sources in a specified search interface.

Learning outcome 2: By the end of the exercise, students will be able to clearly and specifically describe the success and failure they encountered while searching to an audience of their peers.

Learning outcome 3: By the end of the exercise, students will be able to assess peers' search strategies for strengths and weaknesses and offer substantive, courteous feedback.

Lesson Preparation

This exercise takes place online. You will need to prepare the exercise in your institution's Learning Management System (LMS). I have most recently used Canvas, though the exercise should work well in any LMS.

Lesson Plan

Setup: Before the exercise begins, you will need to provide students with information on the search interface chosen for the exercise and its features, using any format that suits your situation, such as tutorials, lectures, or visual aids. Students then complete a search using specified parameters, submit a screenshot documenting their search, write a discussion post describing their search and reflecting on the experience, and, finally, write a reply to at least one other student post.

Discussion board prompt and search documentation: The discussion prompt you prepare for this exercise must be specific and detailed, yet as brief as possible. Bullet points, bold fonts, and other formatting tools can make the directions easier to read. Students should use a topic that is both college-level and meaningful, such as a topic connected to coursework or one they choose, probably with some restrictions to ensure their topics work well for the assignment. In the discussion board prompt, ask students to use a specific search interface, such as a web search engine, an OPAC, any database, or a discovery system, to search for resources connected to their topic. Give instructions that ensure they use the interface's search features, encourage them to play, and give them a measurable goal, such as reducing their results below a given number or finding an article with specified characteristics. Require them to reply to at least one other post, so that they read each other's work, and include a clear statement of expectations about online etiquette. Reminding students to be kind to each other and to be courteous when they disagree sets a tone of mutual respect in the discussion boards and encourages participation.

Requiring documentation of the search in addition to the discussion board post is necessary to ensure that students actually do the search; many students can do a reasonable job of describing a search they didn't do. The documentation can take one of several forms, such as a printed or submitted article, a link, or a screenshot. Asking students to submit screenshots of their search screens allows the librarian to see their actual searches and facilitates private, personalized feedback on their search choices; it is also a useful technological skill for students to master.

Once the exercise is underway, your role is to be available for questions, either in person, via email, or via your participation in the discussion. Keep your role encouraging more than corrective. Your general comments to the whole class can encourage them or steer them away from common mistakes, but students' main focus should be on interacting with each other, not with the librarian. Your substantial feedback can go to individual students, privately.

Time to complete: Allow one to two hours for the students to complete the assignment, in addition to the time they spend becoming familiar with the search interface.

Example exercise: The following example explanation and discussion prompt are closely based on an exercise I give my students using EBSCO Discovery Service, called OneSearch, at my institution. I have made minor revisions to make it more easily adaptable.

The Exercise, Part 1: Search Instructions and Documentation

In this exercise, you will explore the library's single search box, OneSearch. You have read about it; now, you will use it!

- Go to the library home page (URL) and explore OneSearch. It's kind of like Google, and just like with Google, you need to focus your search carefully to get good results. How to explore:
- Look for information on your topic. You are searching most of the library's resources, millions of articles, books, and more. You need to be specific to find the good stuff, so use at least three to five keywords to search. Just use the nouns instead of typing in a question. For example, "nutrition" would be too general; you need a specific issue connected to nutrition, such as "protein" and "vegetarians" and "adolescents." BUT just use the nouns instead of typing in a question such as. "Can vegetarian teens get enough protein?"
- Then, use at least two of OneSearch's features to limit your search. Full text is already the default. Try limiting by format, subject, time period, database, or any other feature that strikes your fancy. You can also use quotes around an exact phrase.
- Try to limit your options to the point where you have fewer than 500 results, either by adding more specific keywords or by using the features on the left. Play with it! Take a screenshot of your final search screen. Example below.
- Choose an interesting-looking article that looks like it could add something to your topic and click on it. You will be taken to that article in its database and will be asked for your user name and password if you're off campus. Take a second screenshot of the actual article.

For this assignment, you need to turn in two screenshots: (1) your search screen in OneSearch, and (2) your article.

The Exercise, Part 2: Discussion Prompt

For this discussion, report on your searching with OneSearch. In your post, tell us

- which words you used at first in OneSearch
- which OneSearch features you used
- how your numbers of results changed
- why you were interested in the article you chose, and
- what you think of the experience compared to other searches you have done. Could you easily find results that looked useful? Did the changes you made have the effect you wanted?
- Remember to reply to another post! Also remember that I love specific details!

Remember the rules of online communication:

- Be positive, courteous, respectful, and supportive of each other.

- Feel free to disagree. Really. Just be respectful about it.
- Remember that sarcasm and humor don't read well online.
- Emoticons (happy faces, etc.) are fine; bad language, even in abbreviated form, is not.
- You don't need to be very formal in your posts, though you should be polite. Think of it as an in-class discussion and write the way you would talk.
- The best way to make sure you have interesting posts to reply to is to post something interesting yourself early in the week.

Use the Reply button below to write your post. Don't be scared—the discussions are graded on EFFORT and DETAIL, not being right. There are no wrong answers! As long as you follow the instructions and do the whole thing, on time, you'll get 100%. You get 70 points for each main post and 30 points for your reply.

Feedback and Assessment

The assessment for this exercise focuses on engagement rather than success. Instructor feedback can be given in private to individual students, and a good grade should be within reach for all students. As long as students attempt the entire exercise, describe their efforts, and reply courteously and specifically to another post, they should receive full points, even if they struggle with the search or get poor results. Correcting writing mechanics or style is outside the scope of this exercise and can have a chilling effect, especially for students outside the majority culture. Fear of making mistakes can inhibit their participation; we learn at least as much from failure as from success. While assessing student work for their engagement with practice instead of their results may seem amorphous or subjective, I have found it to be surprisingly straightforward in practice. Similarly, courtesy may seem difficult to assess but its absence is so rare that it is not an issue. An example rubric is below.

Figure 19.1 Example Rubric

Main Post			Reply to another post		
Inadequate	Needs Improvement	Meets Expectations	Inadequate	Needs Improvement	Meets Expectations
Absent or responds to less than 50% of prompt	Responds to more than 50% but less than all of prompt; vague or too brief	Responds fully to all parts of prompt with specific details	Missing, very brief, or generic; does not contribute to conversation with courtesy	Present but brief or vague; limited contribution to conversation; may be courteous	Responds fully to post with specific details; advances the conversation with courtesy

Evidence-Based Rationale

The design of this exercise focuses on requiring the class to practice searching in a structured way and asking the students to observe each other searching, so they will improve their understanding of the features offered by different search interfaces. While assessing their work, I look for their completion of the requested tasks, their consciousness of the choices they make while searching, and their ability to articulate their search experiences to each other. In other words, the assessment focuses on whether the students can complete and then describe the assigned search, not the success of the search or the quality of the results. The exercise focuses on search skills, the "apply" level of Bloom's Taxonomy, as revised, although "higher" levels of "analyze" and "evaluate" come into play, especially in connection with their reactions to each other's work.

I assign this exercise as part of a semester-long graded information competency course, which is a co-requisite to a college composition course taught in the English department. The same students are enrolled in both classes, with a few exceptions of students who have passed one but not both courses in a previous semester. The classes have different instructors, a librarian, and an English faculty member, and receive separate grades.

In fall semester 2016, I taught three sections of the information literacy course. Of eighty-nine students, forty-nine consented to have their discussion board contributions analyzed, as long as their personal information wasn't used. This sample may not accurately represent the entire course since it doesn't include those students who were absent from the paired in-person English class when the forms were distributed. These students are more likely to have low grades in the class. Six students who did not pass the class gave their consent, so some struggling students are represented in the sample.

Of the forty discussion board posts submitted, only four were vague or incomplete. The remainder described the authors' use of the search interface's features to limit their search with specificity. None violated the etiquette of the discussion board. Very few students have shown any disrespect toward other students over the seven years I have taught this course, on average less than one per year, even though I teach an average of close to 100 students each semester. If there is a disrespectful communication in the discussion board, I communicate with both students, and, if the communication is clearly hurtful, remove it from the board. (Discursive footnote: In these interactions, I assume that the students do not intend to be hurtful and phrase my comments in terms of how their posts could be misunderstood. Something that seems clearly and intentionally disrespectful to me may well be inadvert or may not bother the student I'm concerned is the target. While it's important for the discussions to be free from disrespectful speech, it's also important to allow for the perspective of the students, which may differ from mine. If a student is adopting a corrective tone towards other students, I will ask privately for corrections to be reframed as questions. If students disagree with each other but remain respectful, even if disagreeing is uncomfortable for them (and me!), I congratulate them on disagreeing with courtesy.) The screenshots confirmed that students were engaging with the discovery service's features. Most made positive statements about OneSearch's benefits, such as ease of use, access to relevant, reliable, and full-text materials, and convenient limiters for focusing their search. Students would be unlikely to focus on these issues without this structured exercise. Of the three students who stated a preference for Google, one cited the difficulty of using keywords in other search environments and two cited familiarity. The prompt does not ask students to choose a preferred search interface, but most of them do. Overall, the students whose posts were detailed and specific show an understanding of how to use OneSearch's features to engage with their topics instead of adjusting their topics in response to their search results. Their posts show a sense of agency and an understanding of the way their choices can affect their search results. While assessing "courtesy" may seem difficult, in practice I have had very few entries that were in any way problematic; there were none in this sample. I do not assess students' writing mechanics or style, since welcoming their differences is an important component of this exercise.

A few selected posts follow:

> So I searched up "Plastic Bag Ban" and TONS of search results came up, more specifically Thousands of searches. I chose that topic because not only am I doing a paper on this, but because a new law just passed that plastic bags in grocery stores are now coming to a ban. Lowering my search results to 500 was a little tricky, but I finally narrowed it down to Academic Journals in the past year. I figured since the new law was passing, that articles in the past year would be more relevant. Being that there was thousands of results to begin with, when I narrowed down the search to 2015 to present, it help out my searches a lot.

> [Reply to another student:] I experienced the same thing with the search results. I thought that this unit was very helpful, because it helped me to learn new ways in looking up topics. I also found it very cool that "One Search" is like a google for databases.

At first I used time management as the main search and the "and's" I used the words activity and health. I did not get a lot of result and none that appealed to me. I redid my search with stress management and the "and" as activities and I got much better results. I used the filters like crazy. I chose to filter my search to full text, published within the past year, academic journals, research, and adjustment. My numbers went from over 6,000 to under 400. I was interested in this topic because in college we all have jobs and are going to school so life can be pretty stressful sometimes and I wanted to find some tips to help relieve stress. I personally would choose to do a google search over this any day of the week because it searches a little bit of everything and thats good enough for me. But I will admit I do like the quality of results I get from using the OneSearch or like EBSCO.

The one search features I used were the the date in which I made sure the year was more current so that the research wasn't outdated. I also made sure to only limit the formats to academic journal no books and no magazines and such. Also chose the to apply the social linguistics subject. At the first the results were around 400,00 then with each feature I narrowed it to under a hundred which is something I found useful to find the exact article.... I decided to try out new ways of researching by using this class and using my interest in sociology. Compared to google and such I would use this to find well written articles that I could actually read. I wouldn't necessarily use google to look for an available article. I also think that the expanders were very helpful and something not a lot of search engines have.

The first words I used were, "impact of media violence on children." Then, I got around 730,000 results and changed my words to just nouns and put, "media violence children." I was a little confused when I still had so many results and I did not know how else to limit my search. There were still about 1,000 results so I tried check marking a whole bunch of options and found the column where it said, "limit by subject," and check marked children and aggression. After checking those my results lowered to 400 and fewer which made it easier for me to look for an article that seemed interesting to me…. At first, using OneSearch was confusing because I had difficulties limiting my search to less than 500 but clicking the options on the left side it became easier. I actually did like how there were a lot of articles to choose from that were specific whereas other databases are vague.

Motivational Techniques in Play

This exercise uses the social constructivist concept of communities of practice and a design (and approach to assessment) that reduces the role of the instructor and encourages learners to interact with each other. In promoting peer conversation, the exercise provides them with an opportunity to acquire real-world skills in a community that is accepting and positive.

Why Is Motivation Necessary?

Students perform research in their personal lives on a daily basis, often using web search engines. Why, then, do they need motivation to engage with research in an academic context? It may seem like a disingenuous question, but there are some specific reasons behind students' discomfort with research. A large body of extant research indicates that many students experience anxiety or discomfort when faced with using academic library resources. The sources of these feelings vary among students but can include insufficient preparation, deficiencies in libraries available to students before entering college, and uncertainty about how to begin research or use library resources; the result is often less engagement with the library and its resources.[2] An ethnographic study of Illinois Wesleyan University (IWU) undergraduate and graduate students found that many students were unfamiliar with the best databases for their topics, used simple searches suitable for web search engines in other search environments, were easily discouraged by too few or too many search results, let minor barriers prevent them from obtaining a desired source, and would change their topic quickly if they couldn't find the information they immediately wanted instead of making a serious effort to answer their initial question.[3] The study found that "many students described experiences of anxiety and confusion when looking for resources."[4] Library anxiety is a recognized phenomenon, first articulated by Constance Mellon in 1986 and developed since then; anxiety about using library resources is a recognized component of it.[5]

Carol Kuhlthau's work on the Information Search Process (ISP) emphasizes the insight that some parts of the research process necessarily produce feelings of uncertainty, and that this uncertainty, while uncomfortable, is productive over the course of a research project.[6] Information retrieval systems can overwhelm searchers with large numbers of undifferentiated results all at once, making it difficult for searchers to go through a research process that embraces complexity.[7] Personalized results in web search engines, social media sites, and many other open web resources lead students to expect lightning-quick results with a minimum of effort and encourage them to be passive, unreflective searchers. They tend to rely on familiar yet ineffective search techniques, such as typing a few words in a search box and selecting from among the results without seriously evaluating the usefulness of their sources.[8] In a 2008 reassessment of the continuing usefulness of the ISP, Kuhlthau, Jannica Heinström and Ross J. Todd found that because searchers expect the process to be easy, they have become even more likely to avoid uncertainty.[9] Students' initial negative feelings about research are connected to "lack of knowledge and insecurity as to how to proceed."[10] Kuhlthau, Heinström, and Todd advocate for librarian or teacher interventions at points in the research process where students might try to avoid uncertainty by staying at a more superficial level.

Overall, many students demonstrate discomfort with academic research, often because of unfamiliarity or lack of skills in using academic resources, and find it difficult to engage with them. This exercise was developed for community college students, who are especially likely to experience these barriers to engagement with the library; many are the first in their family to attend college, they are often underprepared by their education to date, and they also face the competing demands of work and family.[11] In California, community college students' barriers to perseverance and success include family responsibilities, excessive hours spent at work, administrative difficulties, and the cost of books, transportation, housing, and food.[12] The success rates for the course I teach vary between 61 and 70 percent, largely due to these factors.

Communities of Practice and Information Literacy

The concept of communities of practice has received increasing attention in educational literature generally, and the conversation on information literacy specifically, as a model to encourage students' authentic engagement with acquiring information skills. It originated in describing workplace learning in which workers build the knowledge they need by collaboration, instead of turning to outside authorities such as instruction manuals.[13] Andrew Cox, in a 2005 review of four major articulations of communities of practice, noted that the four approaches give "community of practice" a variety of interpretations, some of which share few features, but that they all consider meaning to be created through social interaction, and that participants' identity is "central to learning."[14] Some "communities of practice" in the corporate world exist to serve the interests of management, while offering limited, coercive self-determination for the participants.[15] Cox ascribes the imprecision of the phrase to ambiguities in the meaning of both "community" and "practice," and notes that the word "community" has uniformly positive yet ill-defined associations and can refer to anything from a tightly knit group of people in the same physical space to a loose online group.[16]

The community of practice model holds that knowledge isn't acquired in isolation but is inherently social. In "What Is a Community of Practice and How Can We Support It?," Christopher Hoadley ties theories of communities of practice to educational goals and proposes that knowledge is created by "practice in authentic contexts by communities."[17] Anne[maree] Lloyd specifically applies Lev Vygotsky's social constructivism to information literacy instruction, and proposes that changing perspectives to see information literacy as a social activity causes it to assume a "different shape."[18] Michael Olsson and Annemaree Lloyd distinguish between two different ways of understanding how people acquire information: "*information behaviour,* [is] constructed as a problem-focussed, individual, purposive and cognitive process" while "the *information practices* literature acknowledges how people engage with and are shaped by existing and ever evolving discourses through social practices."[19] They hold that knowledge is created through active practice in a social environment. As such, they look at the role that the physical body, including the use of senses such as sight, smell, and touch, plays in information acquisition.[20] In the introduction to a volume devoted to communities of practice and information literacy, Dora Sales and Maria Pinto link the concept of communities of practice to sociocultural learning theories and critical information literacy.[21] Barber, King, and Buchanan also point to the role that collaborative activities can play in motivation, knowledge formation, and students' adaptability to new situations.[22]

In 2008, Benjamin R. Harris critiqued the Association of College and Research Libraries' (ACRL) 2000 Information Literacy Competency Standards for Higher Education because they, in contrast to earlier iterations of similar standards, omitted to recognize the vital role that social interaction plays in information literacy acquisition.[23] ACRL's Framework for Information Literacy for Higher Education ("framework"), adopted in 2016, instead includes "communities of learning" in its definition of information literacy. Several parts of the framework refer to the role of community, and "participating in communities of practice" is part of the knowledge practices associated with the first frame, Authority is Constructed and Contextual.[24] Lloyd had earlier questioned standards-based information literacy instruction, pointing out that it omits to prepare students for the different, more socially constructed information landscape of their future communities and workplaces, and recommending that librarians engage with workplaces, consider the practice of affordance through which more experienced practitioners bring novices into a community of practice, and adopt an integrated approach instead of relying on one-shot instruction.[25] She recommends the development of "more collaborative approaches to information skills development through the use of assessment tasks that focus on group information seeking and use."[26]

Alfred P. Rovai, Michael K. Ponton, and Jason D. Baker make a distinction between cooperative learning (which involves active learner participation in groups with a strong instructor presence, assigning roles, monitoring, and intervening) and collaborative learning (which is based on the social constructivist perspective and recognizes that a hierarchy with the teacher at the top can inhibit peer-to-peer learning).[27] In collaborative work, there is no one correct answer. They delineate several relationships learners can experience: learner-content, learner-instructor, learner-learner, learner-interface, and self-talking, in which learners silently deliberate.[28] Online discussion boards offer unique opportunities for collaborative learning, providing "all students with an opportunity not only to interact but also to observe and learn from the comments of their peers and instructor."[29] Online discussion boards can foster intrinsic motivation by reducing student isolation, providing an opportunity for both individual and class-wide feedback, and allowing hesitant students to participate in an asynchronous environment which may be less intimidating than the classroom setting.[30] In face-to-face classes, discussions may be dominated by more confident or extroverted students, and it is more difficult for instructors to reduce their presence so students can focus on interacting with each other. Even students who share personal information easily through social media may feel hesitant to do academic work in front of their peers. This exercise takes place in the context of a closed class open only to students, not to the general public. This smaller stage "will help to build trust within the community of inquiry and promote open interactions and a sense of community."[31]

Reducing the size of the instructor's role in order to foster peer-to-peer learning and student motivation has implications for feedback and assessment. Trudy Jacobson and Lijuan Xo point out that extrinsic motivation, such as a grade, can motivate students to complete requirements but often works against true engagement with the material and can reduce the quality of their learning.[32] Grading runs the risk of focusing students' engagement on the instructor instead of each other. Intrinsic motivation, by contrast, takes place within the students. The feeling of accomplishment from gaining a new skill or performing successfully in front of one's peers is an example of an intrinsic motivator.[33]

Praising students to foster their intrinsic motivation seems like a natural approach. In examining why some students persevere in the face of adversity while others give up, Claudia M. Mueller and Carol Dweck (well known for her work on the growth mindset) found that praising students for their intelligence could, counter-intuitively, damage their self-efficacy by making them unwilling to take risks for fear of losing their "intelligent" status.[34] Meanwhile, praising students for effort, which is in the students' control, made them more able to tackle challenging tasks.[35] Dweck's work was specifically in my mind when I developed this exercise, though I use it loosely. Instead of verbal praise, I use written feedback in the LMS and am careful to praise students' specific actions instead of their overall success. Their grade for each discussion depends on how thoroughly the students complete each search exercise, not on whether their searches are correct or effective. I want each student, no matter how "good" at searching or comfortable with technology they are, to be able to move through these exercises with as little fear of failure as possible so that they will be more able to weather any feelings of uncertainty that arise. By ceding control over their success to the students, I avoid falling into the trap of coercion and increase their motivation.[36] Giving students more control also demonstrates my respect for them and the different backgrounds and experiences they bring to the class.

In a recent interview, Dweck commented on "false growth mindset," in which students can be misled into continuing ineffective behaviors by praise for efforts that aren't successful.[37] In order to avoid this trap, I give students individual comments and suggestions based on their screenshots, so they won't continue using ineffective search techniques. Approaches to assessing collaborative work are less developed than those relating to standards-based assignments.[38] Alfred P. Rovai suggests using positive assessments to raise the status and increase the motivation of students who aren't part of the majority culture and may therefore face additional barriers to motivation.[39] Rovai, Ponton, and Baker point out the dangers of assessments that perpetuate a Eurocentric perspective and advocate designing assessments, and by extension entire assignments, with students' background in mind.[40] In this case, focusing on students' effort allows for a multiplicity of student voices to be correct. Students are successful at the exercise I describe in this chapter if they stay with it long enough to gain confidence and satisfaction by improving their search skills and to gain mastery of new search environments. In themselves, these are motivating factors.[41] This exercise does not use peer assessment. A discourse analysis conducted by Geoff Walton and Jamie Cleland, for example, found that students' assessment of each other tended to reinforce received ideas of good information literacy practices and did not encourage critical thinking.[42] I assess students individually and give individual feedback privately, along with a summary of issues and insights to the entire group. Making mistakes in public can be stressful, and my goal is to encourage students to take these risks. Overall, thinking in terms of students' effort instead of the correctness of their response involves a shift of perspective similar to that Anne[maree] Lloyd noted in moving toward a view of learning as socially constructed. In this context, assessing students based on the extent of their engagement with the act of practicing is both meaningful and quantifiable.

Using structured exercises in a supportive environment to give students hands-on experience with different search interfaces can act as the equivalent of exposure therapy. This scenario gives students time with library resources in a low-risk setting so they will be less likely to let fear determine their choices when faced with an actual research assignment. Situating information literacy skills acquisition in a social context improves students' success with research while also giving them a more realistic view of how others search for and find information.

Adapting This Exercise

The exercise described above using EBSCO's EDS discovery service (One-Search) is one of many possible similar exercises, limited only by your imagination and the resources available to your students. I use similar structured discussion boards when I ask students to

- explore potential topics using reference databases;
- use Google Advanced Search;
- search in both the library catalog and an ebook database;
- report on their search experience using one of two general academic databases (Academic Search Complete and Proquest Research Library); and
- use a subject-specific database, such as PsycArticles or JSTOR.

The general structure of a detailed search assignment, with documentation and a discussion, can be adapted for a free-standing online information literacy module or in conjunction with an in-person instruction session. Using a flipped classroom model, librarians could ask students to complete the exercise before an in-person session, so students arrive with focused search experience. As colleges and universities offer more fully online courses, libraries need to develop fully online methods for delivering the equivalent of a one-shot instruction session. One-shot instruction is an extremely limiting format, especially when promoting the development of a community among the students but may be the only format available to librarians. In order to foster collaborative learning within the limited structures sometimes available, I recommend focusing on two things: (1) the principles of facilitating peer-to-peer learning in a large group context, and (2) positive assessment that focuses on effort, not accomplishment, and welcomes multiple experiences and perspectives. This approach also helps bridge the gap between traditional information literacy instruction and the socially constructed information environments students are likely to find outside formal instruction.

Endnotes

1. Wendy Barber, Sherry King, and Sylvia Buchanan, "Problem-Based Learning and Authentic Assessment in Digital Pedagogy: Embracing the Role of Collaborative Communities," *Electronic Journal of E-Learning* 13, no. 2 (2015): 60, http://files.eric.ed.gov/fulltext/EJ1060176.pdf; Wendy Barber and Sherry King, "Invisible Pedagogy: Developing Learners' Self-Responsibility in Digital Environments through Problem-Based Learning," *Proceedings of the International Conference on E-Learning* (January 2016): 29, Education Research Complete, EBSCOhost (117804578).
2. Marisa McPherson, "Library Anxiety among University Students: A Survey," *IFLA Journal* 41, no. 4 (2015): 317–20, http://dx.doi.org/10.1177/0340035215603993.
3. Andrew D. Asher and Lynda M. Duke, "Searching for Answers: Student Research Behavior at Illinois Wesleyan University," in *College Libraries and Student Culture: What We Now Know*, ed. Lynda M. Duke and Andrew D. Asher (Chicago: ALA Editions, 2011), 71–85, PDF ebook.
4. Asher and Duke, 76.
5. McPherson, "Library Anxiety," 317–25.
6. Carol C. Kuhlthau, Jannica Heinström, and Ross J. Todd, "The 'Information Search Process' Revisited: Is the Model Still Useful?," *Information Research* 13, no. 4 (2008), http://InformationR.net/ir/13-4/paper355.html; Carol C. Kuhlthau, "Accommodating the User's Information Search Process: Challenges for Information Retrieval Designers," *Bulletin of the American Society for Information Science*, 25, no.3 (1999): 12–16.
7. Kuhlthau, "Accommodating the User's Information Search Process."
8. Asher and Duke, "Searching for Answers," 76.
9. Kuhlthau, Heinström, and Todd, "The 'Information Search Process' Revisited."
10. Kuhlthau, Heinström, and Todd.
11. Ann Roselle, "Community College Students," in *Information Literacy Instruction that Works: A Guide to Teaching by Discipline and Student Population*, ed. Patrick Ragains, 2nd ed. (New York: American Library Association, 2013), 47.
12. Debbie Cochrane and Laura Szabo-Kubitz, *On the Verge: Costs and Tradeoffs Facing Community College Students* (Oakland, Institute for College Access & Success, 2016), ERIC, http://files.eric.ed.gov/fulltext/ED571624.pdf.
13. Christopher Hoadley, "What Is a Community of Practice and How Can We Support It?," in *Theoretical Foundations of Learning Environments*, ed. David H. Jonassen and Susan M. Land (New York: Routledge, 2012): 286–300; Anne Lloyd, "No Man (or Woman) Is an Island: Information Literacy, Affordances and Communities of Practice," *The Australian Library Journal* 54, no. 3 (2005): 230–37, http://www.tandfonline.com/doi/pdf/10.1080/00049670.2005.10721760.
14. Andrew M. Cox, "What Are Communities of Practice? A Comparative Review of Four Seminal Works," *Journal of Information Science* 31, no. 6 (2005): 530, http://dx.doi.org/10.1177/0165551505057016.
15. Cox, 534.

16. Cox, 530.
17. Hoadley, "What Is a Community of Practice," 289.
18. Lloyd, "No Man (or Woman) Is an Island," 231.
19. Michael Olsson and Annemaree Lloyd, "Being in Place: Embodied Information Practices," *Information Research* 22, no. 1 (2017): 1–11, http://www.informationr. net/ir/22-1/colis/colis1601.html.
20. Olsson and Lloyd.
21. Dora Sales and Maria Pinto, "Introduction," in *Pathways into Information Literacy and Communities of Practice: Teaching Approaches and Case Studies,* eds. Dora Sales and Maria Pinto (Amsterdam: Chandos Publishing, 2016): xxiv-xxv, PDF ebook.
22. Barber, King, and Buchanan, "Problem-Based Learning," 61–62.
23. Benjamin R. Harris, "Communities as Necessity in Information Literacy Development: Challenging the Standards," *The Journal of Academic Librarianship* 34, no. 3 (2008): 248–55.
24. Association of College & Research Libraries, "Framework for Information Literacy for Higher Education," http://www.ala.org/acrl/standards/ilframework.
25. Lloyd, "No Man (or Woman) Is an Island," 234–35.
26. Lloyd, 235.
27. Alfred P. Rovai, Michael K. Ponton, and Jason D. Baker, *Distance Learning in Higher Education: A Programmatic Approach to Planning, Design, Instruction, Evaluation, and Accreditation* (New York: Teachers College Press, 2008), 87.
28. Rovai, Ponton, and Baker, *Distance Learning*, 93.
29. Ponton and Baker, 84.
30. Jacobson and Xu, *Motivating Students*, 134–35.
31. Rovai, Ponton, and Baker, *Distance Learning*, 96.
32. Jacobson and Xu, *Motivating Students*, 4–6.
33. For a more detailed discussion of extrinsic versus intrinsic motivation, see Trudi E. Jacobson and Lijuan Xu, *Motivating Students in Information Literacy Classes* (New York: Neal-Schuman, 2004), 4–7.
34. Claudia M. Mueller and Carol S. Dweck, "Praise for Intelligence Can Undermine Children's Motivation and Performance," *Journal of Personality and Social Psychology* 75, no. 1 (1998): 33–52, http://dx.doi.org/10.1037/0022-3514.75.1.33.
35. Mueller and Dweck.
36. Jacobson and Xu, *Motivating Students*, 60.
37. Christine Gross-Loh, "How Praise Became a Consolation Prize," *The Atlantic,* December 16, 2016, https://www.theatlantic.com/education/archive/2016/12/how-praise-became-a-consolation-prize/510845/.
38. Rovai, Ponton, and Baker, *Distance Learning*, 81.
39. Alfred P. Rovai, "Facilitating Online Discussions Effectively," *Internet and Higher Education* 10, no. 1 (2007): 83–86, https://doi.org/10.1016/j.iheduc.2006.10.001.
40. Rovai, Ponton, and Baker, *Distance Learning*, 80.
41. Jacobson and Xu, *Motivating Students*, 105–06.
42. Geoff Walton and Jamie Cleland, "Information Literacy in Higher Education—Empowerment or Reproduction? A Discourse Analysis Approach," *Information Research* 19, no. 1 (December 2014): 229–31, http://www.informationr.net/ir/19-4/isic/isicsp3.html#.WdFV162ZPVo.

Bibliography

Anderson, A., and B. Johnston. "Toward a Community of Practice: A Case Study of Adult Returners to Higher Education." In *Pathways into Information Literacy and Communities of Practice: Teaching Approaches and Case Studies,* edited by Dora Sales and Maria Pinto, 205–27. Amsterdam: Chandos Publishing, 2016. PDF ebook.

Asher, Andrew D., and Lynda M. Duke. "Searching for Answers: Student Research Behavior at Illinois Wesleyan University." In *College Libraries and Student Culture: What We Now Know,* edited by Lynda M. Duke and Andrew D. Asher, 71–85. Chicago: ALA Editions, 2011. PDF ebook.

Barber, Wendy, and Sherry King. "Invisible Pedagogy: Developing Learners' Self-Responsibility in Digital Environments Through Problem-Based Learning." *Proceedings of the International Conference on E-Learning* (January 2016): 26–31. Education Research Complete, EBSCOhost (117804578).

Barber, Wendy, Sherry King, and Sylvia Buchanan. "Problem-Based Learning and Authentic Assessment in Digital Pedagogy: Embracing the Role of Collaborative Communities." *Electronic Journal of E-Learning* 13, no. 2 (2015): 59–67. http://files.eric.ed.gov/fulltext/EJ1060176.pdf.

Cochrane, Debbie, and Laura Szabo-Kubitz. *On the Verge: Costs and Tradeoffs Facing Community College Students.* Oakland: Institute for College Access & Success, 2016. ERIC. http://files.eric.ed.gov/fulltext/ED571624.pdf.

Cox, Andrew M. "What Are Communities of Practice? A Comparative Review of Four Seminal Works." *Journal of Information Science* 31, no. 6 (2005): 527–40. http://dx.doi.org/10.1177/0165551505057016.

Gross-Loh, Christine. "How Praise Became a Consolation Prize." *The Atlantic,* December 16, 2016. https://www.theatlantic.com/education/archive/2016/12/how-praise-became-a-consolation-prize/510845/.

Harris, Benjamin R. "Communities as Necessity in Information Literacy Development: Challenging the Standards." *The Journal of Academic Librarianship* 34, no. 3 (2008): 248–55.

Hoadley, Christopher. "What Is a Community of Practice and How Can We Support It?" In *Theoretical Foundations of Learning Environments,* edited by David H. Jonassen and Susan M. Land, 286–300. New York: Routledge, 2012.

Jacobson, Trudi E., and Lijuan Xu. *Motivating Students in Information Literacy Classes.* New York: Neal-Schuman, 2004.

Kuhlthau, Carol C. "Accommodating the User's Information Search Process: Challenges for Information Retrieval Designers." *Bulletin of the American Society for Information Science.* 25, no. 3 (1999): 12–16. http://dx.doi.org/10.1002/bult.115.

Kuhlthau, Carol C., Jannica Heinström, and Ross J. Todd. "The 'Information Search Process' Revisited: Is the Model Still Useful?" *Information Research* 13, no. 4 (2008). http://InformationR.net/ir/13-4/paper355.html.

Lloyd, Anne, "No Man (or Woman) Is an Island: Information Literacy, Affordances and Communities of Practice." *The Australian Library Journal* 54, no. 3 (2005): 230–37. http://www.tandfonline.com/doi/pdf/10.1080/00049670.2005.10721760.

McPherson, Marisa. "Library Anxiety among University Students: A Survey." *IFLA Journal.* 41, no. 4 (2015): 317–25. http://dx.doi.org/10.1177/0340035215603993.

Mueller, Claudia M., and Carol S. Dweck. "Praise for Intelligence Can Undermine Children's Motivation and Performance." *Journal of Personality and Social Psychology*

75, no. 1 (1998): 33–52. http://dx.doi.org/10.1037/0022-3514.75.1.33.

Olsson, Michael, and Annemaree Lloyd. "Being in Place: Embodied Information Practices." *Information Research* 22, no. 1 (2017): 1–11. http://www.informationr.net/ir/22-1/colis/colis1601.html.

Rovai, Alfred P. "Facilitating Online Discussions Effectively." *Internet and Higher Education* 10, no. 1 (2007): 77–88. https://doi.org/10.1016/j.iheduc.2006.10.001.

Rovai, Alfred P., Michael K. Ponton, and Jason D. Baker. *Distance Learning in Higher Education: A Programmatic Approach to Planning, Design, Instruction, Evaluation, and Accreditation.* New York: Teachers College Press, 2008.

Roselle, Ann. "Community College Students." In *Information Literacy Instruction that Works: A Guide to Teaching by Discipline and Student Population*, edited by Patrick Ragains, 47–63. 2nd ed. New York: American Library Association, 2013.

Sales, Dora, and Maria Pinto. "Introduction." In *Pathways into Information Literacy and Communities of Practice: Teaching Approaches and Case Studies,* edited by Dora Sales and Maria Pinto, xxi–xxxiii. Amsterdam: Chandos Publishing, 2016. PDF.

Walton, Geoff, and Jamie Cleland, "Information Literacy in Higher Education—Empowerment or Reproduction? A Discourse Analysis Approach." *Information Research* 19, no. 1 (December 2014): 229–31. http://www.informationr.net/ir/19-4/isic/isicsp3.html#.WdFV162ZPVo.

Woods, Kathryn, and Kadi Bliss. "Facilitating Successful Online Discussions." *The Journal of Effective Teaching* 16, no. 2 (2016): 76–92.

Author Biographies

Tarida Anantachai is an outreach librarian at the Syracuse University Libraries. She received her MS in library and information science from the University of Illinois at Urbana-Champaign and her BA in English and American literature from Brandeis University. Her research interests include diversity and inclusion, early career development and mentoring, and outreach programming. Prior to her stint in librarianship, Tarida also worked for several years in the academic publishing industry.

Samantha Becker is a campus engagement librarian. She and her dog, Naomi, currently work at Drake University. They received their degree from University of Wisconsin Madison and emphasize equity and inclusion work as well as instruction and campus collaboration. They have presented on credit-bearing classes and pedagogy. Though it is generally Sam who does the talking, it is really Naomi who is responsible for all of the behind-the-scenes support.

Alan Carbery is the head of academic technology and communication at University College Cork, Ireland. He earned his MLS from University College Dublin, as well as an MA in teaching & learning in higher education. Prior to his current role, he led Champlain College's programs of embedded information literacy instruction for both on-campus and online students. He publishes and presents on information literacy instruction, teacher development, and learning outcomes assessment. He was the chair of ACRL's Value of Academic Libraries Committee for 2017-2018.

Camille Chesley is a reference librarian and subject librarian for journalism at the University at Albany Libraries. She received her MS in library and information science from the University of Illinois at Urbana-Champaign and her BA in East Asian studies from Oberlin College. Her research interests include gaming and gamification in library instruction, information literacy assessment, critical librarianship, and diversity and inclusion in LIS.

Rebecca Ciota is the discovery and integrated systems librarian at Grinnell College. She received her degree from the University of Illinois of Illinois Urbana-Champaign. She has worked in special collections, acquisitions, electronic-resources, online reference, and systems. Outside of her librarian duties, she trains her horse in dressage.

Chapel Cowden is health and science librarian and UC Foundation assistant professor at the University of Tennessee at Chattanooga. She is passionate about applying mechanisms to promote critical thinking and the construction of authentic learning environments into her classroom, with the belief that we should strive to prepare students not only for "what's now" but for "what's next." Her current projects explore culturally relevant pedagogy, citation analysis, and information literacy scaffolding.

Wendy Doucette is an assistant professor and the graduate research and instruction librarian at East Tennessee State University. She is the lead instructor and developer of the Sherrod Library Graduate-Level Academic Workshop series and an embedded librarian for the Graduate School's Thesis and Dissertation Boot Camp. She holds an MS in library and information science from Florida State University and a PhD from Stanford University. Her research interests center on 360-degree literacy, visual literacy, copyright, and serving first-generation and international graduate students. She has been a practitioner and teacher of applied Japanese philosophy for over two decades.

Ashley Duguay is a medical librarian for Maine Medical Center where she is out-based at Pen Bay Medical Center in Rockport, Maine. She provides expert searching and reference services, manages collection development, and provides research and educational support and instruction. She earned her MLIS degree from Simmons College and has several years of experience in public, academic, school, and medical libraries.

Kevin Engel is the science librarian at Grinnell College. He has been at Grinnell since 1986 and is also involved with collection development/acquisitions. In that role, he works on shared purchasing with three groups—the Iowa Academic Library Alliance, Iowa Private Academic Libraries, and the Central Iowa Collaborative Collections Initiative.

Nick Faulk is the digital learning librarian at Champlain College in Burlington, Vermont. At Champlain College, he designs online information literacy learning objects for both traditional and online students. He has a BA in English from Northern Arizona University and an MA in information resources and library science from the University of Arizona.

Amy Hall is a teaching and learning librarian and assistant professor for library and learning support at National Louis University in Chicago, where she helps a diverse community of students and faculty grapple with issues in digital information literacy. She received a bachelor's degree in journalism from Northwestern University and a master's degree in library and information science from Florida State University, and she has a real weakness for gummy bears.

Jenny Holcombe is assistant professor of nursing and education at the University of Tennessee at Chattanooga. She has a PhD in evaluation, statistics, and measurement from the University of Tennessee. Her passion is teaching, research design, statistics, and evaluation regardless of the topic. She is currently involved in research related to undergraduate diversity perspectives, problem-based learning, and end-of-life decision-making.

Grace M. Jackson-Brown is a research and instruction librarian with Missouri State University in Springfield. She teaches information literacy one-session instruction and for-credit courses. She holds a PhD in communication from Indiana University, School of Journalism and an MLS from Emporia State University, School of Library and Information Management. She enjoys planning educational multicultural programs for communities, especially K-16 youth in collaborative partnerships between libraries.

Trudi E. Jacobson is the head of the Information Literacy Department at the University at Albany and holds the rank of distinguished librarian. She earned her degree from the University at Albany and has worked in information literacy, reference, and, in the far past, interlibrary loan. She publishes and speaks regularly on metaliteracy, the new ACRL Framework, and innovative teaching techniques. She is the co-author or co-editor of twelve books, with another in progress, and numerous articles. She was the 2009 winner of the ACRL Instruction Section Miriam Dudley Instruction Librarian Award.

Heather Johnson is a research and education librarian at the Biomedical Libraries at Dartmouth College. She earned her degree from University of Rhode Island and has worked in reference, curriculum development, and project development and management. She publishes and speaks on research support services, innovations in curriculum design, and interdepartmental collaborations. She chairs two NAHSL committees. She enjoys cooking, spending time with her golden retriever, and exercising at the barre.

Sarah Kortemeier is the instruction and outreach librarian at The University of Arizona Poetry Center. She holds an MA in library and information science and an MFA in poetry, both from The University of Arizona. Her scholarship focuses on intersections between arts education and library outreach. As a graduate student, she received the Miriam Braverman Memorial Prize from the Progressive Librarians Guild and the Rovelstad Scholarship in International Librarianship from the Council on Library and Information Resources.

Anna Kozlowskais a liaison librarian and assistant professor in Research Services and Resources department in the Richard J. Daley Library at University of Illinois at Chicago. She has diverse experience working in academic libraries—both in liberal arts and public education settings. In addition to her library degree, she also received a M.A. degree in Political Science with a primary focus on international relations and comparative politics. She feels invigorated working with traditional, first generation, and international student populations.

Sarah Leeman is a teaching and learning librarian and assistant professor at National Louis University in Chicago, IL. She earned her degree from the University of Wisconsin Madison, and has worked in e-resources management, reference, and instruction in special and academic libraries. She enjoys online teaching, curriculum development, and working closely with students and faculty.

Kristen Lemay is a digital services librarian at the Richmond Public Library (British Columbia). She earned her MLIS from the University of Western Ontario and has worked in government, academic, and public libraries. Kristen enjoys developing new ways of engaging young people by combining instruction with popular culture.

Katherine (Kitty) Luce is the librarian for user engagement at Solano Community College. She has been teaching research to community college students since 2010—because they're awesome! She has also worked with collections, curriculum, and library planning. She received her MLIS from Jan Jose State University and also holds a master's degree in English from Mills College and a BA in Renaissance studies from Yale.

Tim Miller is the digital media and learning librarian at the Humboldt State University Library, where he focuses on teaching digital and information literacy using interest-driven methods in which students have the freedom and confidence to design their learning experience, explore new ideas, learn new skills, and engage with peers to innovate, create, and learn.

Maggie Murphy is a first-year instruction and humanities librarian at the University of North Carolina at Greensboro. She received her MLIS from

Rutgers University and has previously worked in instruction and reference at academic libraries in New York and Georgia. She currently serves on the ACRL IS Information Literacy in the Disciplines Committee, and co-authored *Teaching First-Year College Students: A Practical Guide for Librarians* (Rowman & Littlefield, 2019).

Sarah Fay Philips is passionate about connecting people to ideas, resources, information, and experts that will challenge, surprise, and inspire them. She is the librarian at Oregon State University Cascades in Bend, Oregon. From 2012-2018 she was the coordinator of instruction and reference at the Humboldt State University Library. She strives to transform higher education with a focus on collaborative and deep learning for students, faculty, and staff.

Rebecca H. Price PhD, MEd, MLIS is a research and editorial consultant. She works with libraries, museums, and publishers to incorporate research instruction into out-of-classroom settings. Formerly research and instruction librarian at Duquesne University and Community College of Allegheny County, her articles have been published in *RUSQ, College Teaching, Journal of Heritage Tourism* and elsewhere.

Krista Reynolds is head of reference and instruction and liaison to the science and nursing departments at Concordia University in Portland, OR. She earned her MLIS from the University of Washington, her MEd from Concordia, and has a BS in biology from Willamette University. In addition to her interest in designing motivational instruction, she keeps up-to-date on intellectual freedom issues as a member of the Oregon Library Association's Intellectual Freedom Committee.

Miriam Rigby is a social sciences librarian and serves as the collection manager for the social sciences at the University of Oregon Libraries. She earned her MLIS from University of Washington and a MA in cultural anthropology from the University of Chicago. Miriam's research interests currently are focused on instruction and open access publishing.

Lindsay Roberts is assistant professor and education librarian at University of Colorado Boulder. She holds an MLIS from University of Denver. Her research interests include motivational design, transfer of learning, and meta-cognition/metaliteracy, particularly as they relate to adult learners.

Elizabeth Rodrigues is humanities and digital scholarship librarian at Grinnell College. She earned her MLIS from the University of South Florida and her PhD in English from the University of Michigan. Her research interests include critical data studies, digital humanities, and US multi-ethnic literatures. She co-organizes the professional development subgroup of the Digital Library Federation's Digital Library Pedagogy working group (#DLFteach).

Josefine Smith is the instruction & assessment librarian at Shippensburg University. She earned her degree from University of Pittsburgh and a masters from Penn State, Harrisburg in American Studies. She has worked in research support, instruction, and government documents. Her research interests are exploring ways that information literacy instruction can enhance student success and student empowerment and how libraries can better communicate their value. She loves working with students to help them connect with their passions.

Sarah Steiner is the head of Research & Instruction Services at Western Carolina University in Cullowhee, North Carolina. Sarah earned her master of library science degree from the University of South Florida and a master of arts degree in English literature at Georgia State University. Her current areas of research focus are instruction, library administration, and gender performance.

Ngoc-Yen Tran is the research impact and sciences librarian at San José State University with academic liaison responsibilities for biological sciences, chemistry, physics and astronomy, geology, and meteorology and climate science. She received her MLIS from University of Washington and her BA in English and BA in art history from Willamette University. Previously, Yen worked as the coordinator for undergraduate instruction at University of Oregon, manager of collection development and science librarian at California Lutheran University, and as a reference librarian at University of California Santa Barbara. Yen's research interests are mostly focused on libraries and high-impact educational practices. When not at work, you can find her running, hiking, or being outdoors.